# FIFTY YEARS OF ANTHROPOLOGY AND EDUCATION
## 1950 – 2000

## A Spindler Anthology

# FIFTY YEARS OF ANTHROPOLOGY
# AND EDUCATION
# 1950 – 2000

## A Spindler Anthology

**George and Louise Spindler**
*Stanford University*

Edited by
**George Spindler**

LAWRENCE ERLBAUM ASSOCIATES, PUBLISHERS

2000    Mahwah, New Jersey                                London

Lawrence Erlbaum Associates, Inc., Publishers
10 Industrial Avenue
Mahwah, NJ  07430

Cover design by Kathryn Houghtaling Lacey

**Library of Congress Cataloging-in-Publication Data**

Spindler, George Dearborn.
    Fifty years of anthropology and education, 1950-2000: a Spindler anthology / George
    and Louise Spindler; edited by George Spindler.
         p.   cm.
    Includes bibliographical references and index.
    ISBN 0-8058-3495-8 (cloth: alk. paper)
      1.   Educational anthropology.  2. Educational sociology.  I. Title. Spindler anthology.  II.
Title:  50 years of anthropology and education 1950-2000.  III.  Spindler, Louise S.  IV. Title.

  LB45 .S66   2000
    306.43--dc21                                                    99-086789

**Acknowledgments/Sources**

**Chapter 1.** Anthropology and Education:  An Overview. From *Education and Anthropology*.
G. Spindler, ed. 1955. Stanford University Press. pp. 5-25.

**Chapter 2.** The Transmission of American Culture. Adapted with abridgement and revision from
*The Transmission of America Culture*. Third Burton Lecture in Elementary Education. G. Spindler.
Copyright 1959 by the President and Fellows of Harvard College and reprinted by permission of the
publisher, Harvard Graduate School of Education.

**Chapter 3.** Education in a Transforming American Culture. Reprinted, with revisions from
*The Harvard Educational Review,* xxv, 1955, 3 (Summer). pp. 145-156. Copyright © 1955 by
the President and Fellows of Harvard College. All rights reserved.

*(continued at back of book on page 421 which constitutes an extension of the copyright page)*

# Contents

# Foreword

*Henry T. Trueba*

I have followed the work of George and Louise Spindler since I first met them at Stanford in 1964, although at the time I did not have the privilege of working with them. In the mid-1980s when George and Louise came as visiting professors to the University of California in Santa Barbara, I had the opportunity of spending more time with them and finally began to understand the significance of their work. Our personal rediscovery in Santa Barbara was followed by a genuine epiphany that suddenly gave my academic life direction and permitted me to articulate my work for several decades. Much of what I learned in the 1980s was in their writings but I had not internalized it and it was not self-evident. Their unique concept of culture dynamically changing in the process of transmission, their requirements for genuine ethnographic research (as the study of culture *in vivo* via diachronic and systematic methods), the intimate nature of the relationship between the psychological and the sociocultural, and the undeniable comparability of human behavior across languages and cultures, were all powerful incentives for many of us who were attempting to follow in the steps of George and Louise.

The Spindlers' research on culture and personality among the Blood Indians, on acculturation and adaptation among the Menomini, and their work in Germany were all clearly related to their serious concern for the evolving self: the enduring self, the situated self, and the endangered self. Their research in California in schools was also related to the adaptation of children to school and the cultural expectations of teachers. What was unique to the Spindlers, however, was their extraordinary knowledge of world ethnography and their rare skills in making well-grounded inferences on human behavior from observations of day-to-day interaction. Indeed, their observations of lifestyle within the American society offered intriguing contrasts and insights that appear consistently in their written work until the last few years. For example, their concern for educational processes, equity and support for low-income and underrepresented students, was perfectly congruent with their notions on race, ethnicity, power, ethnocentrism, and actual academic production.

In the rich intellectual climate of the simple but intensive academic life of George and Louise, they established a unique personal independent and interdependent relationship as thinkers and doers (teachers, researchers, and active healers in academia, via cultural therapy), as well as innovators and creators of the new field of educational anthropology. This field was clearly and profoundly cemented in a close and loving relationship with students, colleagues, publishers, and other academicians that permitted them to work in synchrony and harmony for over 50 years. George would provide new scenarios and projects, new ideas and theoretical interpretations, while Louise would offer genuine counter-proposals with other ideas and contributions she alone could make. At times, she honestly and bravely stated objections, complementary positions, and other dimensions of an issue not discovered by George. The result was an overall balanced and substantially improved joint set of ideas that would lead to new articles, books, lectures, classes, presentations in conferences, and often in serious reflection over long-term trends in the discipline, and the need for an appropriate course of action. George and Louise, in my opinion, somehow knew the enormous intellectual power they held jointly over thousands of readers, students, and colleagues through their writings, their lectures, editorial comments, and personal suggestions; but, they never abused this power and often patiently waited until an individual was ready to listen and to act before they gave advice or direction. They took seriously their responsibility as leaders in the field, but not so seriously that they would become righteous or isolated, arrogant or manipulative. Probably no other quality was ever more evident that their intellectual honesty; this alone earned them universal trust; what was more peculiar of Louise, however, was her nurturing nature that consistently pursued the welfare of the students with love and patience; her intuition of what was appropriate and helpful tempered George's impartiality and tough intellectual stances. Somehow, together, they managed to lead to success minority students who were hurt and often psychologically unprepared to deal with academia. Both earned the respect of an international research community that has remained loyal to their work until today.

The present volume is a very good selection of the best work done by George and Louise Spindler. The significance of these pieces and their interrelationships can be appreciated if we provide some historical contextualization. In the early 1950s, when George convoked the first Educational Anthropology conference at Stanford with the participation of salient figures who today occupy important positions in the history of the social sciences, anthropologists were not aware of the role of their discipline (both in terms of cultural studies and ethnographic research methods) in the field of education. Extraordinary intellectual giants such as John and Beatrice Whiting, George DeVos, Gregory Bateson, Jules Henry, Margaret Mead, Melford Spiro, and others had something in common. As many other contemporary anthropologists in the midst of the 20th century, some shared a profound commitment to what we call today *psychological anthropology*, seen as the study of human psychology in specific cultural settings. Many of them were deeply rooted in psychoanalysis, and their empirical research was clearly guided by the psychology of the time: dream analysis, the study of myth and folklore, cross-cultural and comparative studies of culture and personality, social organization, learning, and adaptation. George Spindler's own account of the anthropological literature that affected teachers and teaching suggests that Hewett wrote in 1904 the first piece on education published in the American Anthropologist, and that education was not listed as an area of application for anthropology in the encyclopedic inventory written by Kroeber in 1953. Anthropologists described the results of education, but not the process. George Spindler categorically states in his introductory chapter to the 1955 publication of the 1954 famous Stanford Conference on Education and Anthropology that:

> Anthropology can help shed light on human behavior in educational situations just as it has on behavior in factories, hospitals, peasant communities, air force installations, Indian Reservations, New England towns, and various primitive societies. ... Directly relevant are the concepts and data of specialized and relatively new fields in anthropology, such as personality and culture ("psychological anthropology"), and cultural dynamics (culture change and acculturation) (1955:58).

What is extraordinary in the Spindlers' work is the consistency of themes and research activities. Their original concerns for disadvantaged students in 1960s, and their original approach to working with teachers (*cultural therapy*) continues over 45 years and culminates with articles and a special volume (*Pathways to Cultural Awareness: Cultural Therapy with Teachers and*

*Students,* 1994, Corwin Press). So, Part I that includes chapters 1–6, entitled "Character Definition" captures the central themes that the Spindlers developed over their entire life: the scope of educational anthropology, cultural transmission, education in American culture, cultural therapy and teachers misperceptions of children's behavior, and students disadvantaged by their own schools. Part II, entitled "Comparisons" encompasses chapters 7–10 and pursues further the disadvantaged students with an insightful inquiry on dropouts from a cross-cultural perspective. The impact of these thoughts is seen in the work of the Spindlers' students (the work by Ray McDermott, for example), the genre differences in behavior across four different cultures, the misperception teachers exhibit of their own instructional behavior (the classic "Roger Harker" and the cultural dialogue in a cross-cultural context). There is obvious continuity from the early discussions of the 1950s, and 1960s with that of the 80s and 90s. Although there is plenty of theoretical continuation and return to the central topics via cross-cultural comparison, what does not come clear until the following part is the reason why the first two parts are closely knit: Both share on the same ethnographic research methodology that is clearly spelled out in several volumes edited by the Spindlers, but especially in *Education and Cultural Process: Anthropological Approaches* (in its three different editions), and *Interpretive Ethnography of Education: At Home and Abroad.*

Thus, Part III, chapters 11–13 entitled "Ethnography in Action," brings together method and theory with a masterful description of rigorous methodology in ethnographic research. Although the first three parts provided a good sample of the classic pieces that made George and Louise Spindler internationally known as the founders of educational anthropology and most cited scholars, the last three parts (IV, V, and VI) are examples of the more recent, provocative, and bold statements about schools and society. Part IV, "American Culture" includes three chapters on American society, both regarding the apparent contradictions we live as Americans, and the most recent maladjustment of the mainstream "White ethni-class" in the mid-90s. These bold statements present George's position that is most sensitive to the younger and more liberal generations confronting American traditions and contradictions: religious radical right, militias, anti-government secret organizations; anti-immigrant, anti-Black, anti-semitic and anti-Latino groups; the rationale for our contemporary phobias and racial/ethnic hatred.

Part V, "Cultural Therapy" includes one chapter very appropriately discussing the nature of cultural therapy as a partial solution to the modern problems confronting American society. It is this part that has attracted the most attention in the last 5 years. Many of the young scholars who had read Paulo Freire's *Pedagogy of the Oppressed,* and who were exposed to "critical theory" and the reactions against "hegemonic" structures in educational institutions, view racism, hostility and ethnophobias as the reason for perpetuating the neglect of students of color (in G. Spindler's terms disadvantaged students). Thus, the comparison between Freire and Spindler continues to be a topic of interest among doctoral students. Freire's concept of "conscientization" comes across as parallel to the Spindler's notion of reflectivity or reflective analysis via ethnographic knowledge of who we are. There are also profound differences in philosophy between Freire and George Spindler. Freire views education as inherently, necessarily political and part of the power structure. In other words, for Paulo Freire, literacy ("reading the word and reading the world") is the key instrument to understand oppression and the way out of oppression (via conscientization and the construction of "utopias"). Furthermore, Freire views "culture" in its context of class, power and oppressive international relations of countries such as the United States with developing countries (some Latin American, Asian and African societies, for example). George Spindler does view education as socialization into a given group; that is, the acquisition of the necessary cultural and social knowledge in order to function effectively in that group. Thus, education is not necessarily political, but a mechanism within each society to prepare members for life in their community.

There are things we did not know about George and Louise that we learn in this volume. George and Louise engage in a dialogue with Ray McDermott and, separately, with Fred Erickson to share candidly their view of anthropology. Some of the most important insights triggered by the questions asked, offer a deeper understanding of the relationships between culture, the concept of the self and the culture of therapy. George coins another term *heritage culture*. This is how he explains it:

> In Louise's and my movement for the past few years, there has been a shift from regarding each culture as a bounded entity to a concept of culture, or at least one kind of culture, as a heritage, a predetermined influence on behavior, that is present in some form in most social interactions and behaviors, but that is in process, being modified and then added to by cultures people constantly manufacture to fit the circumstance of their lives ... We have come lately to relate the manufactured cultural products to the individual in the notion of "situated selves," and regard the more stable aspects of the cultural heritage as related to the individual via the "enduring self" (Excerpted from a Life with Ethnography, interviews with George and Louise Spindler by Ray McDermott and Fred Erickson).

These concepts of the self and the adaptive mechanisms used by individuals was the lifelong preoccupation of George and Louise since they began to work with the Menominee, but it continued as they moved to urban schools and classrooms. Indeed, the relationship of the concept of the self, as survival via adaptive strategies in the face of change is studied by the Spindlers across ethnic, linguistic, and cultural groups. What the Spindlers begin to rediscover in their later years is the profound relationship between their interests in cultural therapy and their interests in effective classroom teaching, equity, and cultural democracy within the schools. Their work in the two classic pieces "Roger Harker" and "Beth Anne" would seem at first unrelated to these theoretical contributions and interests. But, to the contrary. Here is George's testimony:

> I worked with Roger Harker before I worked with Beth Anne. Roger, as you know, is the case I have often said I wouldn't have had a career in the anthropology of education if it had not been for him ... Roger, as they all said (and he agreed) was doing a great job of teaching—about forty percent of the kids in his class. He was totally secure in his position. ... The other sixty percent he was never hostile to, abusive in any way, or sarcastic. He simply ignored them. He couldn't believe that he had done the things I said he did, or not done the things that he was doing with the forty percent who were like him culturally" (Excerpted from a Life with Ethnography, interviews with George and Louise Spindler by Ray McDermott and Fred Erickson).

What is going to impact the work by the Spindlers was the tacit inclination they had for equity issues in education that became gradually a central preoccupation with the need for understanding culturally different children and of working effectively with them. This passion for equity was cast not in political terms of action to restructure the political balance in schools and do away with cultural hegemonic centers but in terms of cultural therapy. In fact, what links both the work with Roger Harker and that with Beth Anne is this same concern. The study of Beth Anne was "an attempt to study success, and grew up out of my concerns about massive failure," as George confesses. The results of the study of Beth Anne was a total surprise:

> It turned out that she had an abdominal tic, that she spent sleepless nights worrying about her school work, that she was tense and worried most of the time, that she was not liked by her classmates. Yet the teachers, without exception, voted for her as the "best adjusted" child in the school (Ibid.)

The outcome of this surprising finding for the Spindlers was to pursue relentless cultural therapy in order to broaden the cultural perspectives of school personnel and to understand better the emotional consequences of inappropriate cultural expectations on children. Yet, the Spindlers remain committed to ethnographic studies, not to any action that may seem logically following the studies, and they make important discoveries about cultures in America; about their heterogeneity, coexistence and permeability. Ray McDermott pushes the dilemma:

Thirty years ago it was important to get culture into educational discourse, it was important to get something other than experimental methods and rating scales into educational research. Now that they are there we have to deliver something else. Increasingly we can no longer simply say, "I have described something," we must say, "I have changed something." This creates enormous pressures on the ethnographer.

George and Louise agree and insist (during the dialogue with McDermott) that their attention to cultural therapy is precisely a response to the need to change something. George is committed to start educational anthropology programs with cultural therapy and to end with cultural therapy.

These statements are as of themselves extremely powerful and reveal a great deal of what is behind the work of the Spindlers and how such work presents a cohesive nucleus with a very forceful intent to change anthropological inquiry into action for a better understanding of cultural expectations in school contexts. The question is, how did George and Louise became the champions of cultural therapy in an anthropological world that was inherently colonialist, oppressive, and insensitive. What peculiar events in their 50 years of anthropological research and publications led them from the beginning to pursue cultural understanding for the sake of equity. Although we knew part of the answer, this volume provides the most eloquent and powerful statements, and the most touching candid revelations about their family life that explain why the Spindlers accomplished so much in their search for equity.

There is no question that both George and Louise will be seen by history as giants in the development of modern anthropology, a science that transitions from colonial approaches, somewhat mentalistic and detached from the social reality of communities, to the anthropology that finally comes to grips with the social responsibilities of the scientists, and the consequences of conducting research. George and Louise were socialized into rigorous academic disciplines and intensive scholarship; yet, both shared the love for nature, the liberal acceptance of other individuals from different ethnic, racial, and linguistic backgrounds, and their profound commitment to intellectual growth and a total dedication to scholarly work. In their own ways each pursued a distinct and distinguished career in college teaching, and later in graduate work that culminated in joint, systematic cross-cultural research, and that yielded an encyclopedic knowledge about cultures of the world. Their massive effort in publishing hundreds of ethnographies, their intensive field-based research, their teaching to thousands of students and multiple generations, and their publishing original research as well as classic selections of authors around the world, are accomplishments that have no parallel. This incredible output of original and extraordinary intellectual work enhanced their understanding of cultures and behavior, and their commitment to equity. No one ever doubted at Stanford that George and Louise were not only fair and tough academicians, but also compassionate human beings willing to accommodate even the most demanding and difficult minority students, writers, colleagues and contributors to journals.

The Spindlers' work with the Menominee, the Blood, and the Cree, was not less important than their work in Schoenhausen, Germany, California, and Roseville, Wisconsin. Being truly committed to comparative cross-cultural approaches, and capable of drawing parallels and contrasts from their incredible ethnographic repertoire, they were able to create the magic of their undergraduate anthropological courses that attracted hundreds of students year after year for decades. This vast knowledge of cultures around the world is still today the most capturing feature of any, albeit brief, conversation with George Spindler. Although he wants to insist humbly that he is just like any other scholar, his impressive knowledge and profound insights immediately set him apart from any other anthropologists in the world. He still is the most knowledgeable ethnographer of the world, without any doubt. Yet, some anthropologists wonder why he has made no special efforts to theoretize more and expand his insights, to create new theories and play with discourse along the lines of postmodern anthropologists and other social scientists. George, as did Louise, while she was alive, never did anything to impress anybody; they were happy and content with being themselves, and they gave their candid opinions to anybody asking. It is this simplicity and candor that may mislead the new generations who do not really know what anthropology has gone through in the last half-century. George (as did Louise until her death) still represents the very best of scholarship in a science that is now searching for new truths, and searching for a place in a world that is less and less understandable; a world of high-tech communication, military power and confrontation, a world facing contradiction and challenges never expected. In this context, perhaps the most important contribution of the Spindlers in Educational Anthropology was to alert us to conflicts and contradictions of doing research and teaching in the social sciences, and to stress the need for equity and fairness. Their most important message has been to urge us to continue the pursuit of comparative, cross-cultural research around the globe in the hope of reaching a deeper understanding of human behavior and the unity of the human species as an undivided and cohesive entity that binds us all together.

This volume is concluded by Susan Parman's chapter 18, summarizing and interpreting the Spindlers' work beyond the anthropology of education, thus providing a broad context for their publications in this particular area.

# Preface

This book samples the work of George and Louise Spindler in Anthropology and Education, or "Educational Anthropology." It is an attempt to see where we have been and where we are going. The rationale for this effort is that we appear to be widely regarded as significant founders of the field. If this is the case, one can learn something about anthropology and education by reading our works and commentary. We have selected articles and foci that highlight the major developments in our careers as educational anthropologists. We have another career, too, in psychological anthropology and the psychology of culture change. To us, all of these orientations are not separated by more than convention.

There is an inevitable overlap between publications within this volume because all of the articles are taken from our published works and we have chosen to keep the articles in their original form, rather than editing them to fit contemporary usage or incorporating them in a comprehensive essay. As Louise was involved in all of the work since the "transmission of culture (1963)" this book is to be regarded as authored by George and Louise Spindler, and edited by George Spindler. "I" is used only when the work referred to was done by George alone, though in truth Louise was always involved as an informal consultant. Louise died on January 23, 1997, just after we taught our seminar in ethnographic methods at Stanford University. She was active not only in the creation of the articles included in this volume but also in their selection.

We make an attempt to present what we think are our most representative works in a series of publications that began in the 1950s and continued to the present. We have resisted recommendations that we combine these works into essays, written with the wisdom of hindsight. This would be difficult, as one of us is no longer here to participate and undesirable, from our point of view, because doing this would make it impossible for the reader to understand how the separate works related to each other and to an unfolding perspective on educational anthropology. We proceeded without a lot of regard for what others were doing, not because we were arrogant or did not value collegial efforts but because we always had a purpose in mind that grew out of our own experience. We wanted to find out about relationships that seemed interesting to us, not necessarily to others. We often pursued these interests without outside funding, as we had little patience for explaining what we were up to and why in academic language for people who were not necessarily sympathetic to our purposes or style. Nor did we enter into arguments with our peers about concepts, theory, or methods, as we regarded such arguments as a waste of time and energy. Consequently, we are an anomaly—apparently highly regarded as contributors to a developing field of inquiry and analysis but outside the mainstream of discussion. This position has both positive and negative consequences, as well one might imagine. In any event, it makes this volume more significant, for in it we explain ourselves, though the reader is made to work to gain insight. The original articles must be read and pondered.

We wish you well in your journey through this book.

—*George Spindler*

## Acknowledgments

Every author incurs countless debts for information, insights, friendship, encouragement, and tolerance. We have incurred the usual ones, and more. During the 50 years of our active collaboration we were given a helping hand by mentors, colleagues, publishers, students, and a legion of people native to the places we were researching. There is no way of thanking them all. We can only acknowledge that without their help none of the articles contained in this book would have been written.

# About the Authors

George and Louise Spindler began as a research team in anthropology in 1948 when they started fieldwork with the Menominee Indians in Wisconsin. For seven summers, from mid-June until mid-September, we camped near the Menominee community and worked nearly every day on the reservation. Our research was aimed at the psychological and cultural adaptation of individuals to radical culture change, but we investigated every aspect of Menominee life as context for these adaptations. From this experience came George's dissertation (1952) and first monograph (1995) and Louise's dissertation (1956) and first monograph (1962) and a number of other articles and books.

George began education-related research in 1950 when he joined a team headed by Professor Robert Bush that had started doing case studies of teachers and other educational personnel in three communities near Stanford University. He wanted an anthropologist to join the team and do observations and conduct case studies, though he was not entirely sure why.

No one at that time knew what an anthropologist might be able to do in a study of schooling. The effect of this appointment on my career was profound. The study of "Roger Harker," one of my first cases as a member of the research team, is represented in some way in nearly everything that we did in applying anthropological concepts and methods in the analysis of educational problems and processes.

George, however, published his first article on anthropology and education in 1946, well before the experience with Roger Harker, evidence that his interest in educational applications started early (and stayed late).

George and Louise's collaboration on anthropology and education began explicitly with the research in Germany, though Louise was in on everything George did long before that. Our first experience in Germany was in the fall of 1959; we went as instructors in the Stanford in Germany program and found 70 eager potential ethnographers whom we could release on the Remstal, a wine-producing valley in Germany stretching southeast from Stuttgart. We continued research in Germany; every time we went as instructors in the Stanford in Germany program, which was often. We continued with our research after the center closed in 1976, with field trips in 1977, 1981, and 1985.

We have accumulated various honors, including most notably the Dinkelspiel Award for Outstanding Contributions to Undergraduate Education at Stanford University, the American Education Research Association award for outstanding career contributions to the status of minority groups, the George and Louise Spindler Award for Outstanding Contributions to Anthropology and Education, awarded by the Council for Anthropology and Education each year at the national meetings of the American Anthropological Association, the Distinguished Scholar Award of the Southwestern Anthropological Association, and election to the National Academy of Education at its meetings in Stockholm, Sweden.

George continues part-time teaching appointments at Stanford, the University of California at Davis, the University of Wisconsin at Madison, at the University of California at Sacramento, and at Harvard University, as well as an active writing career. He lives with his partner and colleague, Lorie Hammond, in Davis, California. Lorie is assistant professor of Teacher Education at the California State University at Sacramento.

—G. D. S.

# A Life With Anthropology and Education

## Interviews With George and Louise Spindler
### (1995)

*Ray McDermott*
Stanford University

*Frederick Erickson*
University of California at Los Angeles

These interviews range broadly over the whole of educational anthropology in an informal and informative manner. Reading them will provide a provocative introduction to the writings following in Parts I through V. The interviews raise questions, some of which are answered in the text and some of which are left as stimuli for work to be done. These interviews are valuable also because they are informal and spontaneous. Some things are better said in interviews than in a formal text.

Another view of the Spindler oeuvre is provided by Susan Parman in chapter 18 "Making the Familiar Strange: The Anthropological Dialogue of George and Louise Spindler." Some readers will benefit from reading this chapter first.

RAY McDERMOTT INTERVIEWS
GEORGE AND LOUISE SPINDLER

Ray:    In your work, what do you feel to be essential?

George:  I get excited when there are two or more cultures involved. For me there has to be an "other" as the Menominee, Blood, and Cree were for us, or German culture, as we have experienced it for the past 30 years or so (first visit to Germany was 1959). We can pick

1

up observations in German classrooms, and in our interpretation they seem to us to show the influence of the heritage culture of Germany. Then, we compare them to like observations from American classrooms. If we can do this, our understanding of both situations is enormously enhanced. In Louise's and my movement for the past few years, there has been a shift from regarding each culture as a bounded entity to a concept of culture, or at least one kind of culture, as a heritage, a predetermined influence on behavior, that is present in some form in most social interactions and behaviors, but that is in process, being modified and then added to by cultures people constantly manufacture to fit the circumstances of their lives. Some aspects of the heritage culture remain relatively stable, at least in memory, for most persons, and provide an enduring continuity to the sense of self. We have come lately to relate the manufactured cultural products to the individual in the notion of "situated selves," and regard the more stable aspects of the cultural heritage as related to the individual via the "enduring self." But for us it all becomes more clear with comparisons.

Louise:    For me, the necessity of comparison is equally present, but I have made my essential comparisons between the adaptations of men and women to culture change. In all of our fieldwork, as you know, George, I have insisted on an equal sample of women in psychological testing, interviews, and observations. I think my work has conclusively demonstrated that men and women adapt differently to culture change, though I didn't think of this as an established fact until we subjected our data to rigorous statistical testing. But the point is, in my work and thinking there was the comparison between men and women as well as the comparisons between the various cultures we worked in.

George:    Yes, what you say is certainly true but you never confined yourself to just the study of women. You were always the complete anthropologist in our fieldwork, whether in a Blood Indian household or a German or American classroom. You saw things I did not, and I thank you for that. It certainly turned around my observations and interpretations in our German fieldwork. The boys always related well to me on hikes and picnics as well as in the classroom, but the girls kept their distance. In contrast, when you started working in the school, the girls rushed to be near you. I'll never forget how they crammed into our Volkswagen when we came to the Schoenhausen elementary school each day and you and they would sing songs and tell jokes and riddles.

Louise:    It was all great fun!

George:  It sure was! Twenty-eight field trips in all and every one was an adventure. We never took vacations. Fieldwork and the fun on the side we always had at the places we did fieldwork was all the vacation we needed.

Ray:  I don't think everyone feels like that about their fieldwork.

George:  It is worth mentioning that our work with the Menominee got us started on the comparative line. We were actually comparing five groups, almost communities, within the Menominee Reservation, such as native-oriented, Peyote, transitional, and two groups of "acculturated." This was the heart of our research and our first major research project.

Ray:  George, would you enlarge a bit on the *enduring* and *situated* selves concepts, before we forget?

George:  Well, this is relatively new terminology for us, though we have used the concept of *self* before. We tend to work within a cultural frame of reference, but keep finding a need for psychological or social psychological concepts. We think of the enduring self as giving the person a sense of continuity, something everyone finds necessary but harder and harder to find in modern society. It is laid down in early experience, and is decisively influenced by one's heritage culture. But in any case, the self is not static, not even the enduring self. People adapt to changing circumstances. They also create circumstances. They create selves that work effectively in those circumstances. We are lucky if the selves thus created do not conflict with the enduring self so much as to produce what we have called the "endangered" self (Spindler & Spindler, 1992). We see this as being a potential problem for any minority child who comes to school with an enduring self based on a heritage culture that is not mainstream. Most schools require that the child adapt to the mainstream culture. These required adaptations may be in some degree of greater or lesser conflict with those required by the child's heritage culture and with the child's enduring self. Further, we think that the situated selves one invents as adaptations in school (or elsewhere) feed into the enduring self, altering it to some extent, as one reacts to the reactions of others to one's behavior, and then in turn to one's own reactions—you know, the George Herbert Mead self and other interactions. However, the enduring self may resist these inputs. Then, we have a conflicted self—an endangered self. It is all quite complex and there are layers of selves, some readily voiced, and some quite unvoiced.

Louise:  I think I can claim some originality in my use of the *self* in my early work with Menominee women (L. Spindler, 1962). I drew directly from Mead (George Herbert), drawing examples of self other relationships and relating them in turn to observations of behavior indicating relative degree of acculturation and to Rorschachs that I had collected from the sample of women.

George: Yes, your early work was certainly influential in our recent use of these concepts. I suppose that's why Tom Schram titled his review in the *Anthropology and Education Quarterly* "The Self that Never Left" (Schram, 1994). Perhaps this is where your and our interests part company Ray—where the psychological concerns become apparent. Are you interested in the psychological side of the relationships you observe?

Ray: Yes, of course, and of course not. For 20 years I have been trying not to get involved in it, but I always am involved in it. Twenty years ago the concerns *which* your new language called the *enduring self* were something I was trying to resist, both in my own life and in the work being done in the late 60s and 70s we didn't need enduring selves—we thought. Tomorrow, everything was going to be different. I wanted to understand being alive, and the moment-to-moment nature of it all. Now it seems, looking back, that I have lived fundamentally the same life; it is very related back to what it was when I was a little boy. I used to go to your office when I was a graduate student and hear about the enduring self, even though you didn't call it that then. The situated selves that develop are very important, but somehow it seems that life has a certain continuity over periods of what seem to be gross change. So, I have to be interested in both. It would be wonderful if a lot of people in education could be interested in both. But I don't think we are thinking about either one. We seem to be mostly thinking about the aggregated self.

George: I'm so fascinated by what you are saying that I can scarcely think of what I want to say! But is what we are talking about ethnography? Or is it even anthropology? Or do we give a damn?

Ray: The center of anthropology is emptying out so fast, and we are so diffused, that I want to be careful what I say about ethnography. It was OK to throw rocks at the center when there was a center, but now . . .

George: The history of ethnographic work in education is interesting. As you know, Louise and I convened a conference on the relations between anthropology and education in 1954 and invited people in anthropology who had said things about education, people like John Gillin, Margaret Mead, Bernard Siegel, Sol Kimball, even Alfred Kroeber whom anybody (except our new graduate students) would recognize, and a number of educators, most from

Stanford University, who were interested in the subject. We presented papers and talked for four whole days. The conference is reported in *Anthropology and Education*, 1955, Stanford University Press. What is interesting to me is that the word *ethnography* is not present in the discussions or in the papers presented that we discussed. It is not in the index to the book. On the one hand, it was taken for granted as the base method of anthropology. On the other, it was not a method that anyone thought of as particularly apt for education. It was not until just recently that ethnography became the self-conscious, definitive, relevant method of study for virtually anyone interested in the influence of culture on school-related behavior. Many people use the term ethnography to describe any qualitative research, whether culture is involved or not. Ethnography became the contribution of anthropology to education. That's not where it started, and I don't think it is where the emphasis should be now. I think where the emphasis should be now is on the problems, the truly crisis problems, in education. Anyone who reads, even *Time* and *Newsweek*, knows that the demographics of America are changing very rapidly, and that in states like California the majority of persons will soon not be White mainstream. The scale will tip toward ethnic minorities, rather than to White, and certainly not to WASP groups. I'm saying things that are banal, since everyone should know them. But the schools are constructed out of the demographics and culture of the past, and are predicated along White mainstream lines. Schools have always been constructed as major interventions in the lives of children so that the children will grow up to be like the parent generation. We have wanted our children to grow up to be culturally like the population that has furnished most of the Senators and Congressmen, doctors and lawyers, most of the members of corporate boards, Presidents of Universities and most of the school teachers in America ... White, middle-class, and more often Protestant than Catholic. This is true in every society as we go cross-culturally in our studies of education. Schools are created in every society to ensure the continuance of the status quo. It will require a massive reorganization of our educational facilities to accommodate the new population, the new majority in the United States. Experiments are going on all over the country. We just visited a multicultural school in the middle west that has representatives from 27 ethnic minorities and a small minority of middle-class White children. The teachers are all White and young, and have aides who are representative of the minorities in the school. What is most interesting about this school is that cultural diversity is celebrated in many dramatic ways. There is no overt prejudice, or covert as far as I know, against any minority group. The classes are run much as good classrooms are run elsewhere, but there is special emphasis on learning English and concepts of logic and the rationale for the way the world works. The point is, that the children are being taught the mainstream culture, but in ways that do not damage their concepts of themselves. The children are eager to learn, work hard at it, and seem to be succeeding. If this is the model that prevails, the mainstream in America will simply be enlarged to include a wide variety of ethnic groups, and of course the cultural content of the mainstream will be likewise broadened, but it will still be recognizable as an American mainstream. In any event, if we do not solve the problems created by our demographics, we will cease to exist as a recognizable society, and our republic will crash. No society can long survive where the majority of students are alienated by their school experience. I am pessimistic that the latest wave of "reform," the back-to-standards movement, will wipe out gains made to accommodate cultural diversity.

Ray:      Spin, you've said a number of provocative things. We are in a colossal crisis, and we can use all the help we can get from any source, including anthropology, but the help cannot be simply in the form of ethnography. Let's go back to the central crisis. You published a paper titled "Beth Anne" based on work you did in the early 1950s. The excitement in reading about Beth Anne is that George Spindler goes out in one of the most rapidly developing areas of America (California) during the early 1950s and finds a wonderfully accomplished child picked by her teachers as the "best adjusted" child in the school, but finds a child suffering from carrying the burdens of our achievement-oriented culture. Can we get you to talk about that a bit?

Louise:   I remember so well when you were working with Beth Anne. You would come home and talk about how this child was doing everything right, but that she was so nervous, so tense!

Ray:      I think the Beth Anne case tells us that the crisis we are now in didn't come from nowhere and that you were trying to tell us that more than 40 years ago.

George:   This whole business is a three-sided coin, if you can conceive of such an anomaly. The first side is a bit of a digression. I worked with Roger Harker before I worked with Beth Anne. Roger, as you know, is the case I have often said I wouldn't have had a career in the anthropology of education if it had not been for him. He, too, was highly touted by his administrators, fellow teachers, and by those who entered his classroom occasionally, such as the school psychologist, as an excellent person, as a highly qualified young teacher who would become an administrator soon. Roger was, as they all said (and he agreed) doing a great job of teaching—about 40% of the kids in his class. He was totally secure in his position. The evaluators all thought he was doing a great job, he thought he was doing a great job, and he knew the evaluators thought he was doing a great job. He was doing everything he could to support and reinforce, to push this 40% on to achievement. The other 60% he was never hostile to, abusive in any way, or sarcastic. He simply ignored them. He didn't engage them in the learning process. They were the Mexicans and the lower-status Portuguese who had only recently come to the school as the district was redrawn. He had no vocabulary, no range of understandings that would have enabled him to work effectively with them. He did try to make them like the other 40%, but it didn't work. But they liked him well enough so that they were not obstreperous. They were just silent. He didn't know that this was happening and he never would have known it if I just didn't happen to come along to do a case study of his classroom and his behavior as a teacher. Part of my contract was to inform him about what I found out. When I started to do this, after about 6 months of work in his classroom, he blew up. He couldn't believe that he had done the things I said he did, or not done the things that he was doing with the 40% who were like him culturally. But he stayed with the process, and that is where the idea of cultural therapy was born. Working with Roger got me started to thinking about kids like Beth Anne, though when I started work with her I did not start with the assumption that the teachers were wrong and that actually she was a screwed-up child just because she did conform to their expectations so well.

However, there was something else that happened about then that I have never written up. I got curious about the 60% who weren't getting educated in Roger's class. I concentrated on the Mexican-Americans, and working through school records was able to reconstruct their academic histories. It is complicated but my major finding was that the longer a Mexican child stayed in school, the lower his or her academic performance, and that even his or her IQ test performance (California Mental Maturity) performance tended to suffer. In short, schooling wasn't working for most children of Mexican descent. So, the problem was not confined to Roger Harker's classroom. It was district-wide, at least.

You have to remember that this was in the 1950s. We hadn't begun thinking the way most of us think now. Beth Anne was an attempt to study success, and grew up out of my concerns about massive failure. We wanted to find out what made for a successful school experience. What we found out about her came as a total surprise. It turned out that she had an abdominal tic, that she spent sleepless nights worrying about her school work, that she was tense and worried most of the time, that she was not liked by her classmates. Yet, the teachers, without exception, voted for her as the "best adjusted" child in the school. Our interpretation was that for them Beth Anne represented what they wanted to be, and that they wanted their children, both their own and their students, to be. It seemed a clear case of the projection of cultural values. The whole weight of achievement orientation, of expectations for high performance from a child that dressed so well and looked so good and came from such a "nice family," fell on the shoulders of this 10-year-old girl. We (the Stanford Consultation Service) worked with the teachers and the parents to get them to loosen up a little bit, to let her know it was alright to get an occasional "B" grade, to not make her bed perfectly if she was running late and that she did not have to come to school every day looking like Shirley Temple. The situation eased and Beth Anne, when we visited her briefly a year later, seemed in better emotional shape. The system does certain things to the people it doesn't approve of, and other things to the people it does approve of, both to the detriment of the child. I felt that we needed to broaden the cultural perspective of school personnel, and better their understanding of the emotional consequences of inappropriate cultural expectations. I wanted them to look at the situation of each child and work from there through the cultural mazeway with them.

Ray:     I find it exciting that you discovered cultural therapy when working with Roger, and I presume, Beth Anne, because it means that cultural therapy as you conceive of it does not have to be directed solely at the 60% who are not doing well in school, but just as much at the 40% who are presumably doing well. It will take a reorganization of the whole culture to resolve the problems of these two groups.

Louise:  I remember Harry Wolcott saying that an Australian student in his class reacted quite violently to the notion of cultural therapy, as he understood it. He thought that the whole effort was directed at bringing ethnic minorities in line with mainstream expectations! This, or course, was never our intention. In fact, I think you,

George, were always most interested in doing cultural therapy with teachers.

George: Yes, but some of our students such as Patricia Phelan and Ann Davidson, Christine Finnan, Juan Garcia, Frank Logan, and others, were more interested in working with children; and in both Schoenhausen and Roseville we worked with children as well as teachers. Anyone can use a little cultural therapy!

Louise: As you have often said, George, actually cultural therapy has been an undeclared goal for most of the things we do, particularly in teaching. Anthropology 001 was our favorite course. It was certainly aimed at cultural therapy. We wanted to enlarge cultural horizons, shake up students, particularly the sons and daughters of very mainstream people, make them realize the world was more diverse than their relatively narrow cultural perspectives would lead them to believe.

George: Yes, you're right! There always has been a strong do-good orientation to our professional operations. I do think that some form of cultural therapy was a part of our motivation for most of the things we did as anthropologists, particularly as anthropologists of education.

Ray: Interesting! Now back to ethnography as the gift of anthropology to education. If you asked any 500 people at the AERA meetings what anthropology is or does, I bet that the most frequent response would be "the study of minorities." Probably many educational anthropologists would say the same. But this is not what you have stressed. You have stressed the need to understand the whole process of culture(s) in this country, or elsewhere for that matter.

George: Yes, Louise and I have always worked holistically, even though we reported on discrete aspects of our studies. But our fundamental problem is one of complexity. Twentieth century America is just too complicated to study all at once! We don't have the vocabulary for doing so, and we try to connect A to B in a linear fashion when things are not connected that way. They are connected in a configuration, or a matrix, where A rarely connects to B, unless it goes through X P W first.

Ray: The great danger is that ethnographers may reify what they study. They find Chicano culture, Italian culture, White culture, African-American culture, and then try to relate these presumed characteristics of students to teachers. But cultures are not that homogeneous in America. They are all in the process of change and their boundaries are permeable.

George: You are absolutely right! There is no point in ascribing characteristics to any ethnic group as though they were a homogeneous entity. The day of the bounded ethnic culture in America is past. I
think this is one way in which the postmodern influence and the
critical theorists have done some good. We are less prone to think
in terms of homogeneous ethnic groups than we once were. They
loosened up the concept of ethnicity and of identity.

Ray: I thought you were critical of postmodernism and critical theory!

George: Well, I am. They make me mad sometimes. Nevertheless, despite
my negative reactions to some of their writing, I feel that we all
need to do some real self-examination. Postmodernism and critical theorists have called our attention to some persistent tendencies in our thinking that are like Roger Harker's blindness to his
failures with children who were culturally different than himself
(see McLaren, 1997, & Scheurich and Young, 1997). Louise and I
have tried to take post modernism into our style of working and
writing. We always gave voice to our informants. Much of our
Book, *Dreamers With Power; The Menominee Indians,* 1984 (original 1971) consists of verbatim statements by informants, and our
recent work comparing Schoenhausen and Roseville in the framework of the cross-cultural comparative interview (1993) gives
voice to children, teachers and administrators but also pays attention to positionality and its influence on cultural perspectives.
And we have been working hard to get the authors of case studies
we publish to be reflexive in their reporting. Actually we started
trying to be reflexive, and to get others to be, in our book, *Being an
Anthropologist: Fieldwork in Eleven Cultures* (1970). We didn't
quite know how to be reflexive, but it was a step in the right direction. Ethnography is in a crisis like the rest of anthropology. Many
of use have lost our nerve, and feel uncertain as to what we are doing or why. I personally don't feel too uncertain and think that our
work through the years stands as valid. But I do want to keep an
open mind!

Ray: Is there any particular thing you and Louise have written that you
think represents well the things we have been talking about?

Louise: Don't you think that our edited book on cultural therapy (1994)
represents it quite well?

George: Yes, if you are thinking about this particular area, cultural therapy,
and of course cultural therapy covers a lot of territory and is complex enough. However, I do think that our *American Cultural Dialogue and Its Transmission* (1990) represents better our attempt to
deal with the complexity of American culture, ethnic minorities,

and the problems of education in this complex whole. At least it is an attempt to deal with the complexity. It is a little half-baked here and there, but that is to be expected. As the reviewer for the American Anthropologist said (paraphrased) "This is an interesting book, a peculiar book, a sophisticated book."

Louise:  Yes, I think you are right. I remember the discussions we had as the book was being written at Santa Barbara. They were certainly complex enough. You did a good job of boiling them down to become more understandable, but it was always your point of view that prevailed.

George:  Well, you should have fought harder for yours, if it was different! I don't remember any big disagreements in interpretation.

Louise:  Oh, they weren't really big!

George:  Part of our problem as ethnographers is that we don't quite know how to talk about what we find out. There has been a lot of talk about microethnography versus macroethnography. I have always thought we were doing macroethnography, trying to describe wholes, and glossing over some details of relationships. And I always thought, Ray, that you were doing microethnograpy, exhaustively going over a limited set of interactions, as in your famous reading group, to find out exactly what people were doing and how they were communicating with each other. I know you used to drive us nuts with your (what seemed to us to be) an obsession with the tiniest details: a lift of a shoulder, a cant of the head, a change in bodily posture—you called it "carpentering" if I remember correctly. But now, for us, I think that the distinction has gotten blurred. The problem is that the smallest part of the whole seems to reflect the whole. Every classroom in America is a microcosm of the whole of America, if we know how to read it. Every teacher/student interaction is a microcosm of authority of relationships in every other situation where there is presumed authority interacting with someone subordinate, if we know how to read it. So, the distinction between microcosm and macrocosm is of a different order than we once thought.

Ray:  A holographic model demonstrates that every piece of the holography contains information about all the other pieces. But it's hard to detail enough information about the pieces so we know how they are related. Beth Ann's abdominal tic might have contained enough information to predict the next 30 years, if we knew enough about her tic, and about American culture.

George:  If her life had played out in line with her abdominal tic, it would have been recognizable in terms of middle-class neurosis and growing pressures for achievement in middle-class American Culture. Hopefully, it didn't. But millions of people have neuroses and are subject to great pressures from the achievement orientation of American culture. But even that isn't the whole picture. There are counterbalancing forces at work in American culture, such as pleasure seeking, escapism, sex—it isn't all grim! It may be we are looking for explanations that are too complex. You know, in all of the natural sciences the ultimate explanations have a beautiful simplicity about them. They explain more with less. But I don't have the imagination to think coherently about what form those explanations might take. I suppose the best we can do is to keep on trying to understand whatever situation we are working in but keep in mind that we are working in a colossal crisis situation and that if we can't help we had just better keep out of the way. Thirty years ago I couldn't have said that.

Ray:      Thirty years ago it was important to get culture into educational discourse, it was important to get something other than experimental methods and rating scales into educational research. Now that they are there we have to deliver something else. Increasingly we can no longer simply say, "I have described something," we must say, "I have changed something." This creates enormous pressures on the ethnographer.

Louise:   I think that is why we have recently focused explicit attention on cultural therapy. We want to do some good as well as find out something

George:   No doubt about it. All of our most recent writing has taken this turn; even when it is not labeled *cultural therapy.*

Ray:      (looking at watch) We should try to sum up. The tape will run out soon.

George:   Since we are processual, somewhat postmodernist, perhaps we shouldn't try to sum up. That would give an appearance of solidity and stability that would be misleading and possibly counterproductive.

Ray:      That's why we're always in trouble! The world rewards the sum-ups. Let me ask one more question. You have been extraordinarily generous to students who want to try this, that, or other thing. They jump around, almost drown, get dirty, and you brush them off and set them to work. You're famous for that. If you were going to develop a program of study for the next 20 years in education and anthropology what would it look like? Would you tackle that?

George: I wish I had a ready answer. I couldn't say, for instance, "take more anthropology courses!" It wouldn't work. Some courses are relevant, many are not. Experience is a good teacher. Anthropologists learn to be anthropologists by going out into the field and doing anthropology. But for courses, training in the university, I guess I would start with cultural therapy and end with cultural therapy. This would include everything I would do to challenge the preconceptions with which everyone enters every situation, to create a state of mind that would enable the trainees to look at any phenomenon without prejudging it, and yet to have some tools that would enable them to move freely, past their own identities and come out with data that they would be able to analyze with high-tech devices as well as their own freed-up minds and produce something that would be enlightening, that could be shared widely and that would change people's thinking. Whatever it would take to do this is what I would make the program.

## FREDERICK ERICKSON INTERVIEWS GEORGE SPINDLER

Fred: George, I was thinking about northern Wisconsin and Stevens Point. We're both from northern Wisconsin. It's a long trip from northern Wisconsin to northern California. How did you get into academic work and particularly into anthropology and education? Did your father talk much about education, about teaching? I know he was a professor in a teachers college in Stevens Point.

George: You're thinking of education with a capital E—professional education, not education in the broad sense of the cultivation of human possibilities?

Fred: Right.

George: I didn't hear much teacher-talk at home. It was just a part of the background. My mother had been a teacher for a while, my grandfather was a teacher before he became a judge, my favorite aunt was a teacher, and one of my uncles was a superintendent of schools. I had decided that I wanted to become a professor when I was about 5-years-old, maybe because I wanted to be like my Dad. I had two dolls, Chris and George. They were rag dolls, the kind you make out of socks; my mother made them. They became my class. I taught them on the stairs that went up to our second story. I would be sitting on the third step and they would be sitting on the first step, to keep the proper student–teacher relationship as I conceived of it. I taught them all sorts of subjects. But my father ranged so broadly—logic, aesthetics, ethics, psychology, and education. I didn't think of him as an *educator* with a capital E, but as an *intellectual* with a capital I. He started putting things into my hands to read at a very early age, hoping that I would read them. I remember one morning I came down to breakfast and said to my Father. "Boy, that was a good book!" I was probably about 10. He said, "What are you reading?" I told him it was a book by William James. His face lit up, "Really?" "Yeah, it was a darn good book." "Well, what was it?" He probably thought I had gotten hold of *Varieties of Religious Experience* or something like that. "It was *Smoky the Cowhorse*," I replied. His face fell but he wasn't one to stay down long, and he said, somewhat ruefully I feel in retrospect, "I'm glad you enjoyed it." Later on, I did read *Varieties of Religious Experience*, and other books by James from my father's library. William James was his major professor at Harvard.

These readings and hearing my father talk about virtually everything took me far beyond Stevens Point. He was so broadly educated, at Oberlin and Harvard. He gave me an unusual background. He read Greek, Latin; he had read all the great philosophers like George Santayana, King, and of course James, who was more of a philosopher in some ways than he was a psychologist. My mother, too, was broadly educated, but in a different way. She had been a court reporter, and a management secretary for the observatory at the University of Wisconsin, Madison, as well as the Registrar for the college my father taught in. I learned about somewhat more "practical" things from her, but she wrote so well, too. I remember that she rewrote a paper I had written about Shakespeare in high school, to show me how to do it. I submitted the paper as she wrote it, and Miss Glennon, a wonderful English teacher, gave it back to me with a note. "Your Mother gets an A+, and you get zero." It took only one of those to convince me that you can only be judged by what you do yourself. But my mother served as a model, and a good one.

So, that is the environment I grew up in. I thought it was perfectly normal. In fact, it didn't occur to me until I was a little older that anyone lived any differently. It is no wonder that I became an academic. Oh, I thought of becoming a cowboy. I thought a lot about it but it didn't really seem feasible, given my background.

And then there was nature. It wasn't too far away from where I lived as a boy. A walk of a mile took you out to the woods and streams, and I spent a lot of my time out there, through all seasons, with my pal George Lawrence. Somehow nature and the intellectual life my parents gave me blended in together and this blend has stayed with me all of my life. When I graduated from Central State

Teachers College in 1940, at the age of 20, I taught for 1 year in the local high school, but then was looking for a job for the next year. I wouldn't take a job anywhere the fishing and hunting weren't good, and in fact that is how I happened to meet Louise and fall in love with her. She was teaching in Park Falls, a small but complete town in northern Wisconsin, where there was good deer hunting less than 5 miles from town, and where it would be hard to go in a straight line for any distance without encountering a body of water with fish in it. Louise and I rambled around in the woods with a .22 pistol for target shooting, and went boating and fishing, even ice fishing. It was an important part of our courtship. And of course, there were Friday nights with a jukebox and Musky Jack's Tavern. Musky had a neat trick of serving a drink with a live minnow in it. It was always a surprise to encounter a live fish in your drink! We had a wonderful time together for the 9 months of the school year.

We knew by Christmas that we would marry, and the instant school let out for the year in June, we went to Bessemer, Michigan, where you could get a license to marry with no delays. We got our license but felt the need to be married in a church, so we found a little Presbyterian Church and the pastor was kind enough to conduct a marriage ceremony on short notice, and he even dug up an organist to play the wedding march. I had turned 22 by then and I am so glad that we married while we were young, for the army loomed ahead, and life was going to take us along for a fast ride. Actually, we had a small wedding party with my best friend and best man, George Lawrence, my mother (Louise's could not come much to our regret), Louise's two best friends from Portage, Wisconsin, and Park Falls. It was a very sweet event. I have always felt sorry for people that have to stage big weddings, with all the tension and worry that goes into them. For us, the way we did it was perfect.

Fred:     Was Louise's background like yours? You seemed so compatible, right from the start.

George:  We were indeed. From the moment I met her in September 1941, I felt perfectly comfortable in her company, and apparently she felt so in mine. We spent every moment we could together right from the start. She had the same love of nature that I had. When she was little, her father invested in gold mines that had already been worked in the Sierras near Tehachapi, California. Summers, the family would go up to the mine when he supervised attempts to discover more veins of gold. She loved the mountains, the streams, the gold mines, and the people she met there. Her friends were Asians and Mexicans. She never tired of telling us all about those times. They made a deep impression on her. So, there was something parallel in our experience with nature. Her family was not an academic family but both her mother and father were broadly educated. Her father, who was in his 60s when she was born, was a kind of self-made lawyer and politician. He was always active in politics, supporting this or that candidate, but he never ran for office himself. He invested in real estate among other things. Her mother, long after Louise's father died, saw to it that she had a good advanced education at Carroll College in Waukesha, Wisconsin. Louise brought some scholarships with her because she was an outstanding high school student, but her mother had to make up the difference at a time when her own funds were quite low. Louise was active in literature, drama, stage production, and writing and editing (we were both editors of our respective yearbooks in college). Then she went on to graduate work in English and German literature between stints of teaching in a 1-room country school and a small town high school for 2 years until she went to Park Falls. She started taking anthropology courses after we went to graduate school when the war was over in 1945, at the University of Wisconsin at Madison, and she found her intellectual home there, in anthropology, as I did. Our professional collaboration really began in graduate school and lasted for more than half a century. We were partners in every sense of the word.

But tell me Fred, how did you get into education and anthropology?

Fred:     You know, I had this rather esoteric kind of academic career. I was in music. I was a composition major, and interested in early music, so I was very different than anyone working in the ghetto, but my professional fraternity started giving free music lessons in the ghetto, and I got more and more interested in what was going on there. And, I also got into musicology and my interest in early music gave me an understanding that what people thought was interesting, important, or beautiful varied greatly from place to place and from time to time. For instance, 12th century music sounded beautiful to people of that era, as we know from comments they made then, but it sounds pretty strange to us. This, combined with my ghetto experience, made me more and more interested in the social and cultural lives of people and less interested in my master's thesis on early music. I worked there for a while and when I went back, I enrolled in anthropology and education and soon met the 1955 book that you edited on the conference, and that cinched it. It was the first thing I ever read in the field.

George:  That was a pretty good book. I was reading it the other day and felt that it anticipated many of our concerns today. But it is noteworthy that nowhere in that book is the word *ethnography* mentioned.

Fred:  I guess it was pretty much taken for granted.

George:  Yes. An anthropologist simply did whatever needed doing in order to understand what was going on in the field site, and that actually includes a lot of activities that are not strictly speaking, ethnography. And now we seem to have gone too far in the other direction; we're all method, and mostly ethnography. Sometimes people seem to forget what it is they are studying, but they work hard at the method. And incidentally, where would you place yourself in terms of methods?

Fred:  umm, well … I don't really think of myself as an ethnographer. I am the convener of the ethnographic forum but not an ethnographer.

George:  That is strange. We cite you as an ethnographer, and most of us think of you as one. Why do you avoid this label?

Fred:  Well, I think that what I am thinking of is that I never wrote a full length ethnographic monograph in the classic genre. I am certainly interested in the issues that ethnography raises, and I don't simply look at isolated scenes. I try to put a lot of layers together in thick descriptions but they don't come out like the classic ethnography.

George:  Have you thought of yourself as a participant–observer?

Fred:  Yes. I have been accused of not being a participant–observer hiding behind the camera, but I was always there with the camera. I put the camera down very often to talk to people. I do the rest of the fieldwork, too. The audiovisual material is usually in the foreground. I suppose that is because of my background in musicology. Musicologists collect a lot of audiovisual material. I assume that if you were doing a serious study of what people do, you would record it while you were studying it.

George:  I think that you use video somewhat differently than Louise and I have. You saw some of the worst examples in Alaska when we were all up there together in 1981. (Actually, we did super 8 mm filming, not video.) I showed some of the first films we had taken, where I was essentially taking snapshots of the action in classrooms. I would zap this group, then that group, for about 2 seconds each. The films had a certain hebephrenic quality to them. I don't know to this day what you thought of them. You asked to see some repeats of them at the time. "That technique is really fascinating. Would you mind going over that again?"

Fred: (Laughing) Maybe I thought it was some brilliant new way of getting group action, because I had been told to turn the camera on and leave it. Actually, I think that what you were doing was ethnography in the classic sense. Fieldwork is not passive; it is prehensile, active.

George: That's a kind interpretation but it is true that in ethnographic field work one tries to keep as many pseudopodia out as possible. I sometimes think of myself as a reaper. I go into a classroom (or into a medicine dance) and turn on a tape recorder, use 35 mm cameras, take notes, do videos, collect term papers and art products, or artifacts. Louise and I were always so busy in classrooms, running equipment and trying to keep track of what was going on that we sometimes got pretty frustrated and would start swearing at each other *sotto voce*. We always went home with a bunch of stuff, some of which got digested and some not.

But the video, or films, played two different roles for us. One was as a record of the activity, whatever it was, that could be examined at a later date, sometimes with purposes that were not there when we did the filming itself. The other, which developed somewhat later, in fact we're still in it, was to use the films as evocative stimuli, to evoke reactions and discussions, to get teachers to reflect on their own classes, but in the light of what they saw in other classrooms that we had filmed that were much like the teacher's own class but in a different cultural context. We found that usage to be tremendously valuable, and it has become a significant part of what we call cultural therapy.

Fred: It is a bit like your earlier work with still pictures, in the Instrumental Activities Inventory, only now there is a dynamic quality to the stimulus.

George: The most valuable part for us is that this technique uncovers basic assumptions that teachers bring into classrooms with them. They are always there but remain unvoiced unless there is some unusual procedure or stimulus to bring them out, to make them voiced. You can't get at this by direct interviewing. People don't even realize that they have these basic assumptions about what is right or wrong in human relations, or about behaviors that students and teachers habitually engage in. They know it because they behave it, but they don't verbalize it.

For instance, we would show films of classrooms when the teacher was not there in both Roseville and Schoenhausen. In Schoenhausen, the kids would act up when the teacher was gone, run around the room, wrestle with each other, jump off of desks. In Roseville, the kids would mostly stay on task. We asked the teachers what they do when the kids act up when they are gone. Their responses are in chapter 13 and I won't repeat them here. It was clear that the Roseville teachers were interested in instilling guilt mechanisms in the children ... that they had violated a trust with the teacher when they got rowdy when the teacher was absent. The Schoenhausen teachers took the attitude that children will be children, and expected them to let off steam when the teacher was absent. Neither one would have said it that way without the evocative stimuli provided by the films.

This may be one reason why we are so threatened by aggressive or violent behavior on the part of children. We think they should have internalized rules against it, and when they act as though they had not it is threatening. We found it difficult to keep our composure in the Schoenhausen School—it was so noisy! Louise and I were both schoolteachers and keeping control of the class, keeping an orderly and essentially quiet class was deeply ingrained in us.

Fred:  I think there is a whole thing going on about violence. We expect to keep the lid on. We really demonize people who show inclinations toward aggressive or violent behavior.

George:  I'll never forget, when I got the job at Park Falls (in 1941), the Superintendent sat me down and talked at me about his expectations. Basically his message was that he didn't give a damn what I taught them but that I had better keep control of my classroom. Every time a youth (this was high school) was sent to the principal or to him for disciplinary reasons it was a black mark against the teacher and it was not difficult to accumulate enough black marks so that your contract would not be renewed for the next year. The next hour, after I talked with him, I had to take charge of a study hall with about 150 kids in it. Some of the boys were bigger than I was, and had been working in the woods or the lumber mill. And I was supposed to keep order.' I was never so scared in my life. But it worked out after a while. The thing Louise and I had going for us was that we enjoyed some of the same things they did about the country—deer hunting for instance (at least I did, Louise didn't hunt deer). In any case, we were understandable to them. They were on her side before they were on mine and I think it helped me that I was going with her.

Control seems to be on top of the list. Without control in the American classroom there is nothing. In the German classroom, a teacher would walk in, kids would be screaming and chasing each other around. He, or she, would pick up a workbook and start explaining the lesson in a normal tone of voice and the kids would stop screaming and running around and start to work. There are all sorts of cultural issues imbedded in this. Unpacking them would get us into the core of American versus German heritage culture.

Fred:      If we don't get some show of contrition, some indication of respect, we get very upset. It is all tied up with our culture of authority.

George:  Yes, that's anthropological thinking. In contrast, a psychologist would talk about the personalities of the children and the personality of the teacher. Well, that's stretching it a bit, but psychologists would be unlikely to employ a cultural explanation.

We (anthropologists) would go into the cultural antecedents to the behavior in whatever situation we were trying to analyze, and determine what of these antecedents the principals involved were using to maintain some stability and a feeling of self-respect. So, there would be a psychological element in our analysis but it would not be the main thing.

Fred:      Changing the subject a bit ... how did you get from teaching high school into teaching at the University, and Stanford to boot? And how did you get into anthropology?

George:  Well, I was really always in anthropology. When I was a little kid, I made a complete set of tools for my parents and myself because we were going to live in a cave in some remote wilderness. I made spears out of broomsticks I sawed off (I remember my mother was a little upset because I sawed off the stick of her best broom) and made points by wrapping the tops of tin cans around the end and nailing them down. When lunchtime came I brought in all of my tools. My parents were quite surprised! I told them we would use all of these when we went to live in the cave. I don't know how old I was, perhaps 6 or 7, perhaps a bit older. But before then and afterwards my fantasy life took me to another world, not that my world was such a bad one, in fact it was pretty good, but one where people lived by hunting and fishing and gathering fruits and roots, lived in caves, and hung around fires at night talking about interesting things. When I went to college, there was a guy there named Robert Morrison. He had traveled widely and done some archeological work in Turkey. He described the countryside, the people, and told of having tea with the Emir. Somehow this reinforced something that was already there ... something far off and exotic. When I got in the army I took along a couple of books. I remember one of them was *The Science of Man in the World Crisis*, edited by Ralph Linton, but they were both broadly anthropological in their approach. I read and reread them to keep my mind on what I had decided would be my vocation once I got out of the army. And when the war ended, I was discharged at Fort Sheridan, Illinois, and Louise and I drove up to Madison, Wisconsin. I walked into the Department of Sociology and Anthropology, and said, "Here I am!"—as though they had been waiting for me for the last 4 years. It was sort of like that. They hadn't had many whole, live bodies around and I was a welcome sight. By the time I had walked down to the end of the hall, I had two offers of teaching assistantships: one from Bill Howells in physical anthropology, which I took, because I thought I was going to be a physical anthropologist. He was a great teacher and a great person to work with. He wrote books like *The Heathens*, and *Mankind So Far*, as well as many innovative scholarly articles on evolution and genetics as the knowledge of them existed at the time. In fact, I just heard from him the other day. He had seen something I had said about him in the *Anthropology Newsletter*. He sounded much like himself. But what I don't understand is why anybody who has any interest in the world beyond their immediate concerns doesn't become an anthropologist. When Louise and I got into it, anthropology was different than it is now. It covered the whole world, it was mainly concerned with diversity—the different lifeways that humans had created to solve the problems of life on this planet—it dealt with the exotic and esoteric. Now, emphasizing the exotic quality of life in a culture is considered immoral; in fact, the whole enterprise of ethnography is seriously questioned in some quarters as a remnant of colonialism and hegemonic authoritarianism. For both of us, the magnet was experience in a way of life that was remote to our own, not necessarily geographically but philosophically. What I wanted was to have the kind of experience I had when we first started working with the Menominee in 1948. There was a medicine lodge erected by the side of Highway 57 as it goes through the reservation. I wanted desperately to get into it. I tried to find someone who could give me permission to enter, but to no avail. I finally took the bull by the horns and forced my way through a place where two pieces of canvas didn't quite meet. I stumbled and fell into the elliptical path around which members of the lodge dance. It was a critical time ... they were shooting each other with their medicine bags. If you were an initiated member, you were immune to the shooting. A large Winnebago woman glared at me and then swung her bag around at me and uttered the shooting cry. I had surely been hit by the "magical" megise (a small mollusk's shell) in the bag. Napone Perrote, a medicine man whom I had already met, motioned for me to sit next to him. He looked worried. After leaving the lodge some hours later, I began to feel feverish, and actually ended up in a hospital with a fever of undiagnosed origin. After leaving the hospital I went to see Napone and asked him for some protection against future events of this kind. He was surprised that the bag and megise worked on a white man, but said to come back in four days and he would have something for me. I did, and he did, and I carried it all the time we worked with the traditional Menominee. I am happy to report that I suffered no more ill effects from sorcery. This was the kind of experience I wanted. Such motivations are now considered inappropriate, at least. But if anthropology is all work, and particularly all academic work, it would not be interesting to me, nor I suspect to many of my colleagues.

When I went to work for Robert Bush in the Stanford Consultation Service and ended up in Roger Harker's classroom, I spent weeks wondering what in hell I was doing there. It was all too familiar, but then suddenly his classroom became an exotic place for me, where there was one person standing up front, facing 35 10–12 year old kids, telling them about things they had no reason to think were important or relevant in any direct way to their lives, and where about half of them seemed left out of the process and the other half engaged in it quite seriously. Once it became exotic to me, I could study it with almost the same enthusiasm as for the Menominee Medicine Lodge, Chiefs Dance, and Peyotism. It was proper anthropological sustenance! All the things we study in schools we now see in this way. Every act is ritualized. Everything depends on a rationale of delayed gratification, and many other assumptions and beliefs that are quite exotic in themselves, seen cross-culturally. The school is really a strange place!

Fred:     Yes, and you can't see it from Highway 47. I once went down Highway 47, knowing that is where you did field work. You can go through that whole reservation on the highway without realizing that there is anything there that is different than in the countryside outside. You can walk through a school without realizing that there is a culture in that school, and that there is something there of interest to the anthropologist.

George:   That is a really good point! Actually, we did travel up and down Highway 47 in our first weeks on the reservation. We would stop

and talk to people, and they would say things about the reservation, but it was all so prosaic. How do we get started, we wondered? And then a break came. There was a woman walking along
the highway. We stopped and asked her if she wanted a ride. She
did. So we stopped at a tavern and had a few beers together, then
resumed our ride. Suddenly she blurted out, "Say, would you guys
like to meet my uncle? He's a medicine man. Turn right here (on a
little dirt road winding off into the woods)." After a mile or two of
this road, we came to a clearing in the middle of which there was a
neat tarpaper shack, and an old man chopping wood out front. We
were introduced. I had the wit to give him some tobacco, and we
were off to seven seasons of great fieldwork with the Menominee.
The traditional and peyote groups remained our favorites, though
we worked through the whole gamut of adaptations people were
making to culture change. But the acculturated were too much
like us to be really interesting. Anthropological fieldwork has that
character. It is fortuitous; the unexpected always happens. That is
one of the things we found particularly exciting about it.

Fred:      We have talked quite a bit about the Menominee. Do you see your
           work with them, and for that matter, with the Blood and the Cree,
           as related to your work in education?

George:    To us, all of our research is interrelated. This is particularly clear in
           the case of the Menominee, where we drew the major foci of cul-
           tural therapy from analogies to their situation. For us there were
           problems—the psychological adaptation of people to radical cul-
           ture change, or rapid urbanization, or rapid modernization—the
           ways in which culture is transmitted or acquired from one genera-
           tion to the next—the way authority is exercised and order is
           kept—the way culture conflicts are resolved—the symbolic
           meaning of repetitive behavior, as in rituals—it doesn't matter
           where we study those problems, though some places are more fun
           than others. Perhaps in our next book, on our work in anthropol-
           ogy that does not fall under the heading educational anthropol-
           ogy, we will be able to make this more clear. But perhaps our next
           book will be *Two Anthropologists Loose in North America and the
           Roads in Between*—the story of our fieldwork from the bottom up,
           so to speak. It all depends—

Fred:      On what?

George:    How we feel!

# REFERENCES

James, William. 1929. *Varieties of Religious Experience: A Study in American Nature.* New York: Modern Library.

McLaren, Peter. 1997. Unthinking Whiteness: Rethinking Democracy: Or Farewell to the Blond Beast: Towards a Revolutionary Multiculturalism. *Educational Foundations,* Spring, 1–35.

Scheurich, James Joseph and Michelle D. Young. 1997. Coloring Epistemologies: Are Our Research Epistemologies Radically Biased? *Educational Researcher,* 26(4), 4–16.

Schram, Tom. 1994. Sense Making across Disciplines. The Spindlers' Adaptations and the Self that Never Left. *Anthropology and Education Quarterly,* 23(4), 463–472.

Spindler, George, ed. 1955. *Education and Anthropology.* Stanford: Stanford University Press.

Spindler, George. 1964. Beth Anne—A Case Study of Culturally Defined Adjustment and Teacher Perceptions. In G. Spindler, Ed., *Education and Cultural Process: Toward an Anthropology of Education.* New York: Holt, Rinehart & Winston.

Spindler, George, ed. 1970. *Being an Anthropologist: Fieldwork in Eleven Cultures.* New York: Holt, Rinehart & Winston. Reprinted by Waveland Press, 1986, with a new foreword.

Spindler, George and Louise. 1971. *Dreamers Without Power: The Menominee.* New York: Holt, Rinehart & Winston. New Edition by Waveland Press, 1984, *Dreamers with Power.*

Spindler, George and Louise. 1992. The Enduring, Situated, and Endangered Self in Fieldwork: A Personal Account. In B. Boyer and R. Boyer, Eds., *The Psychoanalytic Study of Society, Vol. 17, Essays in Honor of George and Louise Spindler.* Hillsdale, NJ: Lawrence Erlbaum Associates.

Spindler, George and Louise, eds. 1994. *Pathways to Cultural Awareness: Cultural Therapy with Teachers and Students.* Thousand Oaks, CA: Corwin.

Spindler, Louise. 1962. Menominee Women and Culture Change. *American Anthropological Association,* Memoir 91.

Spindler, George and Louise, with Henry Trueba and Melvin Williams. 1990. *The American Cultural Dialogue and its Transmission.* Hampshire, England, and Bristol, PA: Falmer Press.

# Previews

*Rather than parcel out the preview discussions to accompany the various parts of this volume, we have grouped them all together. Reading all of the previews at once gives the reader, we think, a grasp of the whole to which the parts contribute.*

## PART I
## CHARACTER DEFINITION

The 1950s and early 1960s were a seminal period for the development of anthropology and education. The conference on education and anthropology sponsored by the Carnegie Foundation with the blessings of the Department of Anthropology at Stanford University and held in 1956 is often hailed as the beginning of it all. This is far from true. One may check this out by reading two history-oriented chapters by Elizabeth Eddy and Rosalie Ford in *Education and Cultural Process: Anthropological Approaches*, Third Edition, 1997, edited by G. Spindler. These authors make it clear. This subdiscipline has roots in the 19th century just as the rest of anthropology has. Its genealogy is just as long as any other field of anthropology. However, it is true that the 1954 conference consolidated, focused, and dealt systematically with issues that had been raised but hardly pursued in the previous era. In that sense, the conference is the beginning of the formal period of an *educational anthropology.*

The conference was held at a guest ranch in Carmel Valley, California. We spent 4 whole days together. Papers were presented by James Quillen, George Spindler, Bernard Siegel, John Gillin, Solon Kimball, Cora DuBois, C. W. M. Hart, Dorothy Lee, Jules Henry, and Theodore Brameld. Anthropologists participating but who did not present formal papers included Margaret Mead, Alfred Kroeber, Louise Spindler, and Roland and Marianne Force. Educators participating included James Quillen, William Cowley, Lawrence Thomas, Arthur Coladarci, Fannie Shaftel, Lawrence Frank, Hilda Taba, Robert Bush, and psychologist William Martin. Rose Hauer Wax recorded, transcribed, and did preliminary editing of the entire conference. A volume containing all of the original papers and substantial parts of the discussions ensuing, *Education And Anthropology,* edited by G. Spindler with Louise Spindler's assistance, was published in 1955 by Stanford University Press.

The first chapter in Part I, "An Overview," gives the flavor of the conference in the language of the times, but the conference itself goes far beyond the overview. Taking the conference as a whole, there appear to be four concerns that were thematic throughout all of the discussions and papers.

1. the search for a philosophical as well as a theoretical articulation of education and anthropology.
2. the necessity for sociocultural contextualization of the educative process and its analysis.
3. the relation of education to "culturally phrased" phases of the life cycle.
4. the nature of intercultural understanding and learning.

I am not sure that we have made significant progress on all four of these concerns. Certainly we are not much ahead on the search for a philosophical as well as theoretical articulation of our field. Theory seems to go every which way in all of anthropology, and educational anthropology is certainly no exception, and as for a philosophical articulation we seem there to have lost ground, if anything. Critical theory and postmodernism seem to confront works already accomplished without much suggestion as to how they might be considered useful and "Political Correctness" seems to have been substituted for a philosophy of educational anthropology.

The necessity for sociocultural contextualization of the educative process and its analysis seems to have fared better. Modern approaches to the analysis of educative process are heavily weighted by sociocultural considerations including some imported from abroad in the works of scholars such as Vygotsky, Bourdieu, and Foucalt.

The relation of education to "culturally phrased" phases of the life cycle has not disappeared as an interest in educational anthropology, but surely it is less emphasized now than it was at the time of the conference. Perhaps this is due to the strong emphasis on minority relations and the problems of the mainstream as it attempts to make adaptations to the needs of minority students with various cultural backgrounds. The conference was much concerned with the Supreme Court decision on segregation made on May 17, 1954. Consequences of desegregation and the influence of traditional prejudices in the South, but elsewhere as well, were the focus. Massive increase in diversity due to immigration was not foreseen, and certainly no one every guessed that many public schools in urban areas would have a dominant majority of persons of other than European ancestry 42 years later.

The conference may have missed the boat with respect to this change in the demographics of the population of the United States and its corresponding effect on schools, but it anticipated, in one form or another, many of the current concerns of a present-day educational anthropology. Sometimes these concerns have to be translated into modern vernacular to make them understandable, but they are there in the conversations recorded and transcribed by Rose Hauer Wax. The report of the conference is worth careful study and should be a part of the preparation of every person making educational anthropology a major concern.

The next chapter in Part I, "The Transmission of American Culture," was given as the Third Burton lecture in elementary education at Harvard University in 1957 (published in 1959 by the Graduate School of Education). The focus is on the unintended consequences of cultural transmission in schools in our society that are at variance with the intended goals of transmission. I draw from the work of Jules Henry and Dorothy Lee, both of whom provided papers for the conference on discrepancies of note, and went quickly to my own data after a bit of talk about the acculturation of the school teacher. This discussion still has value. The teacher is seen as a cultural agent, which was a critical step at that time, but one subject to cultural influences that are beyond the range of conscious attention. It is these hidden processes that are of the greatest importance in understanding what schooling is about and what role the teacher plays in it. They are still the least understood aspect of teaching and learning and one that is refractive to observation and recording.

It is in the report of the case study of a fifth-grade teacher in "The Transmission of American Culture" where I began a train of thought that has lasted about a half a century. My case was a young man of 25 who was extremely well thought of in the school system. He had volunteered for the case study treatment hoping to improve his professional competence. Professed aims in teaching, beyond the management of instruction so that his students would acquire the requisite knowledge, were to bring out the creativity of each child to the maximum capability of that child, to help children express themselves clearly, and learn how to get along with each other. He believed that he gave every student in his class a chance to participate, and was particularly fair and just with all the children. He claims that every child got a fair break in his classroom. He tries to understand the problems of his students and believes that he has a better than average understanding of their problems. His aims were clear and his concept of himself was just as clear. He thought that he had attained his aims and he further thought that all of the school personnel that judged him felt that he fulfilled his aims as well. I collected data from him that showed very clearly that he attained his aims very well indeed for the 40% of the students in his class who were culturally like himself—Anglo Saxon middle- to upper-middle class and Protestant. The others he failed badly. It was my job to convince him that he needed to pay more attention to students who were not culturally like himself and that he was not as fair and just and understanding as he thought.

The upshot of all of this was that the notion of cultural therapy suddenly came into focus for me. In feeding back the data that I had collected over a period of some 6 months to my case, I was doing *cultural therapy*, though I did not make much of it. (The first use of the term, however, was in that third Burton Lecture.) The truth was hard for him to take. He resisted it at first quite vigorously, but as time went on he began to accept more and more of it. As a consequence, his perspective and understanding of what he was doing were broadened significantly and he was able to interact more effectively with the broad cultural range represented by his students. The district had just been enlarged to include Mexican-American, Japanese, and lower-status Portuguese.

We find that most of our education-related work is somehow connected with the notion of cultural therapy—trying to bring to a level of awareness the cultural assumptions and prejudices that all teachers, in fact all of us, carry around as a part of our cultural baggage. They are part of the hidden agenda that we carry into the classroom. This agenda is not amenable to direct remedial treatment, nor is it discoverable by direct overt, research. This makes much educational research worthless, and prevents us from researching and treating the crucial communications in the relations between teachers and students. More of this later in Part V of this volume, devoted to cultural therapy.

In the next chapter, "Education in a Transforming American Culture," published about the same time as the conference, I identified certain conflicts that appeared to me to be endemic in American culture and constructed a traditional versus emergent values dichotomy. Puritan morality, work–success ethic, individualism, achievement, and future time-orientation constituted the promontories in the traditional values, whereas sociability, relativistic moral attitude, consideration for others, hedonistic present time-orientation, and conformity to the group constituted the promontories for the emergent values. I then placed various groups and actors on the educational scene on a continuum from traditional to emergent. School boards appear at the traditional end and younger teachers appear at the emergent end and administrators, students, and general public fall in various places in between. The purpose of the article was to explain the increasingly bitter and strident attacks on educators coming from the public and particularly from what appeared to be its conservative elements. The article does have a certain decisiveness about it that made it quite popular at the time. It is the most frequently reprinted article that I have ever written. The problem with it as I see it in retrospect is that I tended to place whole individuals in one or another category, whereas actually it appears that the same individual may hold quite contradictory value allegiances for emergent and traditional values as posited.

For example, one respondent may regard the individual as "sacred" or "supreme," but believe that the individual exists only in the context of the group. However, the article does furnish a focus on conflict that began with the first attempts to make sense out of the dynamics of education and culture. This bud blooms to its full extent in a later book by George and Louise Spindler, *The American Cultural Dialogue* (G. & L. Spindler, 1990). We present pivotal American values and analyze the structural oppositions arranged around them as dialogue. In that book, we supply the Values Projective Technique, and suggest that its administration make a good parlor game. This lighthearted approach horrifies some scholars who regard research procedures and data as sacred. We have used it in classes, with individuals in a clinical setting, and as a parlor game. The discussions engendered in the latter usage can be particularly revealing of cultural processes affecting everyday communication.

In "Beth Anne—A Case Study of Culturally-Defined Adjustment in Teacher Perceptions," the fourth chapter in Part I, attention to conflict and discrepancies is deepened further. Our research team asked the teachers of one small elementary school to pick the best adjusted child in their school. They did, and we studied her. The results of a rather intensive study, utilizing psychological as well as cultural techniques, showed her to be far from well-adjusted and in fact suffering from the unrelenting standards of performance placed on her by teachers and parents. The question then became "Why was she selected as best adjusted?" The teachers picked as best adjusted what they would like to think of themselves as being. So again there is the projection of values into arenas of action and judgment and a discrepancy between perceived and real.

Reality is what one makes it, a truism in the communication arts, is never truer than in teaching and learning. The teacher, if successful, creates an environment for learning. This environment is a constructed reality. Her values, understandings, latent wishes, and undeclared assumptions, are all reflected in that reality. Beth Anne could not be perceived as other than "best-adjusted" even though some teachers had picked up cues that suggested that not all was well in her adjustment, given the construction of the reality within which her adjustment was evaluated.

"Why Have Minority Groups in North America Been Disadvantaged by their Schools?" the next chapter meets head-on what has come to be regarded as the central problem for the American democracy. The problem is that minority students are being coopted into a cultural framework that is alien or hostile to their identity. This fact and the way this co-optation is performed create serious conflicts that are damaging to them. But if there is no common cultural framework in America there is no America, no United States, and no Republic. We must learn to bring children of diverse backgrounds into the cultural mainstream without destroying or eroding their sense of personal cultural identity. To do this, the mainstream itself must change. It can no longer be predicated on Anglo-Saxon terms alone. How to overcome the defense of identity common to all school personnel (and everyone) is the problem now in America and it was the problem then, at the time the article was written (1963). Our efforts toward cultural therapy are directed by these purposes, at overcoming defenses by bringing unconscious motivations, assumptions, orientations to conscious awareness, then dealing with them in modern terms.

Peoples like the Hutterites and the old-order Amish managed to take their schools out of the arena of the state and local administration and build walls around them so that there could be continuity between the community and the school. By doing this, separate identities are created. To the outsider, this seems to be too great a cost to pay for independence and continuity. The issues are far from resolved.

The last chapter in Part I, "The Transmission of Culture," shows how child training and cultural transmitting techniques vary from one culture to another. The analysis shows clearly how the training of youth in intact cultures provides a continuity of experience, even though there may be culturally patterned techniques used at adolescence, as in rites of passage, that appear to create discontinuity. In fact, such within-system discontinuity may be seen as necessary for learning as adults acting as mentors absorb the subject generated by the discontinuity. The concerns of this article remain valuable because it is necessary to keep in mind the cultural variations that mark education in every society in relationship to every other. It is a universal human tendency to regard the situation in one's own society as normal. This chapter puts education in its cultural context and into a framework of relativism. This is exactly where many anthropologists would like to see the case rest, but in contemporary society relativism rarely works. Educational programs advanced by professional educators and by school boards, parents, and various interest groups are rarely marked by relativistic attitudes. And the efforts of change-oriented professionals, among them many ethnographers, are not relativistic.

A focus on the transmission of culture has been prominent in our writings and thoughts about educational anthropology. Early on, we thought that it was desirable for the emerging field to have a focus, and as learning fell more or less in the province of the psychologists and social structure in the province of the sociologists and social anthropologists, we felt that cultural transmission would be a natural for anthropological applications to education. This orientation has been challenged of late, particularly by the writings of Harry Wolcott. He points out that most of culture is not really transmitted but is, rather, acquired. Our point of view has been that what we are most interested in as cultural anthropologists are the intentional interferences with learning that take place in situations designated in a society as learning situations. All "schools" teach children what is believed to be normative, and they try to dissuade children from learning things that are not taught. The school defines what is to be known and, as well, what is not to be known. However, as every schoolteacher knows, children learn the "not to be learned" readily. This seems to be a powerful argument for making cultural acquisition the focus rather than cultural transmission. However, we should note that in our studies we have consistently paid attention to the discrepancies and hidden agendas occurring in cultural transmission. This emphasis anticipates the acquisition process because it is in children learning what is not intended to be taught that reinforces the discrepancies and conflicts and generates new ones. This guarantees that there will be no mechanistic repetition of what is transmitted. The culture acquired is never exactly the culture to be transmitted. We have no particular argument with an emphasis on cultural acquisition, excepting that we hope that an emphasis on the individual learner can be avoided, and that is difficult. The individual learner is a natural subject for psychologists, and we may find ourselves turning over our field to them.

The problem may be more semantic than real in that children acquire culture in a variety of ways, only some of which we understand at present. A singular focus on either transmission or on acquisition seems inappropriate at this point.

Part I serves as an orientation for this whole book. The transmission of culture is the focusing orientation, but we are not confining ourselves to the simplistic notion that culture is transmitted directly and purposively. Indeed, culture is transmitted purposefully, intentionally, but these intentions never survive the transmission process intact not even in presumably stable, presumably timeless societies. The act of transmission defeats the intent of the transmission, as hidden discrepancies, conflicts, and undeclared assumptions play out their functions in communication and the ordering of the educational reality. Our effort was directed from the beginning at trying to find out what it is we are doing when we educate. We assume that we do not know what we are doing. The rest of this volume explores ways in which we went about on this mission of discovery.

## PART II
## COMPARISONS

In the first paper in this section, "There Are No Dropouts Among the Hutterites or the Arunta," we try to communicate the idea that there are many cultures in which the educational system is designed to ensure success and not designed as a way of evaluating learners and ensuring that some significant portion fails. Our system of schooling, and in fact schooling in Western culture in general, seems to be centered on the idea of evaluation. This focus combined with the strong emphasis on competition and on achievement guarantees that a significant number of learners will experience discouragement and rejection by the school system. It is not entirely clear why this should be so. Various theorists point to the need of an industrial economy for low-grade and lowly paid workers. This makes some sense, but workers with inadequate education prove to be a liability rather than an asset in the long run. It would seem that cultural values and motivations are at the heart of the dynamics of this process. As Ray McDermott wrote (he was the discussant for this paper in the conference that resulted in the book, *What Do Anthropologists Know about Dropouts?*, H. Trueba and G. and L. Spindler, 1989):

> In American culture it has become shockingly clear that we do not send our children to school to learn to read and write, but to read and write better than their neighbors. We know this from looking closely at how our children measure themselves against each other at appointed times in every classroom in the country. We know this from looking at parents reading their children's report cards and figuring out where they stand relative to each other. We know this from looking at the success of the testing industry. The only solution to anyone's education problem in America is to have that person do better than

someone else, preferably better than half of the someone else's, and for a maximum of mobility better than all of the someone-else's. School success comes hard in America. The very tools we have for making some people successful drive other people down. When anthropologists notice that school failure is a culturally constructed problem, they notice as well that culturally it is a problem that we are not well tooled to solve. (McDermott, 1989, p. 18).

Any culturally constructed problem is very difficult to resolve. The very measures that are designed to solve the problem are also culturally constructed. McDermott goes on to say,

We have a system that is well designed to make dropouts. This is a political problem and it will not give way until we struggle to disconnect schooling from the distribution of resources throughout the country. Few cultures can afford to let their members know what their problems are; the rest prefer to keep everyone busy chasing shadows. The problem is such a shadow until we use it to confront the more pressing problem, namely, the increasing divide between those who have and those who do not. (Ibid. p. 23).

A "political problem" is in part a politically phrased way of stating a "cultural problem." The cultural basis of inequality, as well as the economic bases in our society must be examined along with the ways in which it is guaranteed through schooling that this inequality will persist. This sentence points to a good example of a culturally based orientation that is institutionally imbedded and linked to cultural assumptions that enact inequality, and yet is denied at every level from the President of the United States on down. The dimensions of culture involved permeate every aspect of human relations in our society, yet they are believed not to exist. This is a massive example of the way in which hidden agendas affect our behavior, in and out of schools.

The next chapter, Das Remstal (the Remstal is a valley stretching southeastward from Stuttgart, Germany) is a bit of a maverick in the context of this book in that it is not primarily education-centered. We include the last half of a chapter on male and female in four changing cultures because it underlines the significance of gender in all of our work and because much of the data on Schoenhausen was derived from the school populations that we studied there, particularly in 1968 and 1977. The most single significant generalization, and the most stable on the basis of our data, is that gender is more powerful than any other variable that was entered into our data matrix. Our data matrix included socioeconomic variables such as occupation, income, two-income versus one-income families, cultural variables such as education, region of origin in Germany, dialect and control of Hoch Deutsch, religion (Catholic or Protestant or other), and other like variables. It looked as though we had one other significant generalization, and that was that females tended to elect instrumental activities that were connected with the outside world, whatever that outside world might be. This was true for the Blood Indians and the Cree community in Quebec that we worked in, and the Menominee of Wisconsin, for whom we did not have an instrumental activities sample, but whose choices can be inferred from our extensive case data.

The early data from the Remstal indicated that the generalization held true for that sample as well. In the Remstal, our first (1968) sample showed that elementary school girls preferred city life more often than did boys. And the life of the factory worker was better than that of the Weingartner, the modern house was preferable to the traditional Fachwerk house, white collar work was being preferred to Weingartner, the factory to the independent small shop, the new over the old (traditional) church, and the party outside the home over the quiet party inside the home. Girls also rejected living in a Baumhaus more frequently than boys did, and they were more often neutral-to-negative about the time-honored Weinlese (grape harvest). So, the early Remstal sample extended our generalization that females preferred instrumental activities in the outside world more often than males. But after 10 years of reform implemented by the federal government, we were surprised to find that girls now chose more frequently the traditional instrumental activities, which is just the opposite to what one would expect to find as a result of the reform programs of the Bundesrepublik, which were all aimed at modernization and the elimination of traditional images and allegiances. The differences between boys and girls were still there, but their direction was reversed. The article included here tries to make sense of this change.

The role of the school is less emphasized in this article than in others we wrote about the Schoenhausen research, but our underlying interest was in how the school functioned in a culture change situation. It became clear in this research that the school was a weighty factor in maintaining traditional identities. This, despite the fact that the reforms reached deep into the school. Textbooks were changed, older teachers were retired, and the entire curriculum was reformed. But teachers found new names for old procedures and subjects and the textbooks repeated themes from the prereform era but in quite different settings. The school gave the illusion of great change, but no transformative change occurred. Rather, substitute changes were made that gave the appearance of change. The refractiveness of the school to mandated change was abundantly clear. The role of the school in preparing children for sweeping developments in the direction of urbanization and modernization can therefore be considered as predominantly conservative.

Of particular interest to us in the present discussion is the instrument we used, together with continuing ethnography—the Instrumental Activities

Inventory (I.A.I.). This technique was developed by us for use with the Blood Indians, in a study of personal adaptation to culture change (1965). We had tired of the cultural ambiguities of the Rorschach projective technique, though it penetrates to a level of psychodynamics deeper than the I.A.I. The Instrumental Activities Inventory proved to be an indispensable instrument in our continuing research. The technique is true to a time-honored anthropological principle that any instruments used should be generated out of the ethnography. The pictures from which the line drawings are made that constitute the Instrumental Activities Inventory are actual pictures of Remstal structures, possessions, and activities, just as they were of Blood Indian structures, possessions, and activities. This paper represents as well another, more problematic, principle and that is that quantitative and qualitative methods may be combined to good effect. The drawings used in the Instrumental Activities Inventory (I.A.I.) are based on variables defined by the ethnography and are used to determine the broad distribution of instrumental choices in the subject population. These and other quantitative methods can be used to test the distribution of variables that have been defined by careful ethnography. This paper also documents Louise's focus on male–female differences in adaptations to rapid and disjunctive culture change, and extends it to the educational arena.

The next chapter, "Roger Harker and Schoenhausen: From Familiar to Strange and Back Again," is an analysis of two of our major research studies, one of them of a single individual and his classroom that you have already heard about, the other of the Schoenhausen school. The chapter is about the need to make the behavioral data from Roger Harker's fifth-grade classroom strange enough so that he could see it. But first it had to be strange enough for us, the field workers, to see it, and that didn't come easily. I had been working with the Menominee during the summer, before I started working on the research team with Dr. Robert Bush where I worked with Roger Harker. I had been witched in a medicine lodge ceremony, come down with a high and undiagnosed fever the day after the witching, and had solicited an amulet for protection from future sorcery from Napone Perote, a shaman. This was one among many other experiences.

My assignment with Dr. Bush's team, to do an ethnographic study of Roger Harker's classroom did not seem extraordinary, but it proved to be most difficult. With the Menominee, and particularly when something really interesting was going on such as a medicine dance, there was no doubt about what I as an ethnographer was supposed to be doing. But in Roger Harker's classroom, everything was far too familiar for me to be taking notes on, and all of the actions that he and the students engaged in seemed very prosaic to me. It was not until I began to see a pattern of favoritism of which he was not aware that things started getting interesting. This pattern became obvious to me in a short time, relatively speaking—6 weeks. But it did take me 6 weeks to see it and to communicate it to Roger was even more difficult. He was so embedded in the school and its system of rewards that he couldn't "believe" he was doing the things that I said he was doing. Working in Schoenhausen was different. At first the German school seemed quite exotic. Not exotic like the native-oriented Menominee were, but exotic enough to be interesting. But as time went on it became all too familiar. We lost our sense of strangeness. Schoenhausen became ordinary, prosaic. It wasn't until we started working in the Roseville Elementary School in Wisconsin that Germany began to look different again. In many ways this is the central problem of the field anthropologist—to make the exotic and different familiar enough to be perceived and communicated and yet not to lose that flavor that differentness gives to behavior. In some circles it is regarded as bad form to see the "other" as different or exotic or strange. This orientation of strangeness can certainly be carried too far, to the detriment of good ethnographic reporting, but a sense of it is essential and ethnographic reports dry up without it.

Again, we are reminded that cultural therapy had its beginnings through the work with Roger Harker. We did not explicitly make much of it until later on in our careers, but it is dear that we were always in some way concerned with it. Roger's denial of what became quite obvious to me in the course of my study of him and his classroom was my first introduction to the notion of discrepancies between intention and actuality and called my attention to the undeclared, mostly unconscious patterning of the teacher's culture.

The next article, "Cultural Dialogue and Schooling in Schoenhausen and Roseville: A Comparative Analysis," is included because it introduced several different developments that bore fruit in other contexts that you will encounter later in this book. One is the notion of comparison itself. We felt then and we feel now that the comparative stance is essential to an anthropological position. We have lost sight of this in recent times and most articles published as educational anthropology are published as though we were dealing with only one culture. The second idea is that of dialogue. We hold, for example, that American culture is a culture because we are in continual dialogue about freedom and constraint, equality and difference, cooperation and competition, independence and conformity, and so forth.

We see both the German school and the American school as representing the German and the American dialogue, respectively. We do not claim that they are "typical" schools in either country, but that they participate in the national dialogue seems undeniable and is what makes them German or American. Dealing with dialogue rather than whole cultures both enables a holistic view, strangely enough, but permits one to escape the strictures of an exhaustive cultural analysis of the whole cultural system. The article also introduces the use of film in reflective cross-cultural interviewing.

As often happens in ethnographic fieldwork, this innovative development was quite accidental. We initially filmed because we wanted to have a permanent record of the actual behavior of teachers and students in classrooms. The film in this regard does have its uses, but more importantly we found it to be an especially evocative stimulus for interviews. Teachers found themselves making culturally meaningful statements without self-consciousness. It isn't that they were self-consciously talking about either German culture or American culture, but rather about the things they did and the reasons they did them that were American or German. The kinds of talk that we wanted to hear flowed spontaneously and with great involvement on the part of our informants. Later, we expanded this into a procedure that not only produces valuable research data but also results in cultural therapy as the object of cultural therapy is to raise to a level of consciousness hidden cultural assumptions and prejudices. It is apparent that this method brings forth such materials and that we have only to bring the native informants (teachers, administrators, and children) to a realization and understanding of what they have themselves said. There are profound implications that many workers in the Elysian Fields of education seem to miss. It does no good to ask informants questions about hidden assumptions unless some diversionary and evocative tactic is utilized. Films, videos, pictures, even stories and like materials can be used. The assumptions we want to get at are not only well-defended but often so hidden to the informant that s/he could not talk about them directly even if they were labeled for him or her in the question, in an interview context.

## PART III
## ETHNOGRAPHY IN ACTION

We have selected three articles that raise issues current in the ethnography of education and represent our most recent work in this area. The first chapter has the dual purpose of communicating what ethnography does, and to teach how to do it. Because we believe that the only way that ethnography can be learned is by experience, our classroom is heavily experiental. We contrive interview situations and observations in which the student participates. Every hour has some experience of this kind organized. This requires a significant amount of roleplaying both on the part of students and of us. One day I may be a naked old man in the Central Desert of Australia and Louise may be an equally naked young woman from the same place (we keep our clothes on—role playing can be carried only so far). We have very different points of view, very different experiences, and yet we are both called Arunta. Students interview us (they have already seen film strips of the Arunta) and we respond and act in ways indicated in the excellent and detailed ethnographies of these people. This is the first lesson the student learns. No culture is made up of a single point of view. Ted Schwartz has referred to this individuality as idioverse (Schwartz, 1978). That is, every person's interpretation of his or her culture is idiosyncratic and cultural knowledge varies from person to person, depending on age, sex, status, and individual experience. Of course, there are common areas that everyone does share, and part of the exercise is ultimately to arrive at a point that we understand both commonality and difference as aspects of culture.

In teaching and learning how to do the ethnography of schooling, we lay out explicitly what we have done in our training seminar in the ethnography of schooling, as we taught it together at Stanford for many years, at the University of Wisconsin at Madison, the University of California at Santa Barbara and Davis, and now (1999) at Harvard University (but I teach it alone now, with some valuable help from Lorie Hammond.) We have emphasized the interactions of the ethnographer and the informants, and the problems of translation and construction from field notes, audiotapes, and visual tapes. Our presentation of these has grown more sophisticated as time has gone on. The interaction of ethnographer and informants is frequently referred to as *reflexive*. This process is more subtle and complex than meets the eye. It is more than the personal interaction of the ethnographer with native informants. It is the perception and reporting of behaviors affected by deep-seated cultural assumptions and organized cultural knowledge.

We start each seminar with an intensive exposure to one's own cultural persuasions and the way they affect what is observed in the "other's" behavior. The *Transcultural Sensitization Technique* is applied (see next chapter). This technique makes it possible to talk about the influences of the observer's cultural knowledge on perceptions of others' behavior. It is a chastening experience to realize that the absence of a category of cultural knowledge for a manure pile in front of a house in a German village makes one miss the basic cue to a correct interpretation of a large Bauernhaus (a large structure housing both humans and farm animals) or that the assumption that "stoneage" people would have no use for money or accounting techniques makes one miss the entire significance of the Kapauku (New Guinea highlands) slide depicting lineage payoffs, when an accounting grid is perfectly visible on the ground in front of the principle actors, and shell money (often interpreted as a snake skin) is about to be deposited on it. (This picture, courtesy Leopold Pospisil, is not included in the chapter.)

The same purpose is implemented by exposure to film strips on male and female behavior among the Arunta, the Australian central desert aboriginal people referred to previously. The assumptions brought into the interpretations are patently ludicrous. Students learn that caution is advisable in interpreting or generalizing. In fact, that it is desirable to make no interpretations at all until one knows the culture well but merely to report the behavior observed as accurately as possible. These exercises are both designed to show how personal culture affects observation and interpretation of behavior.

There is also the reflective element in the ethnographer's interaction in the field to consider. We pursue this topic with personal anecdotes from our own field experience and readings of selected pages from the now-extensive literature on the subject. Though this emphasis is useful, we find that the techniques that we use to sensitize students to the effect of personal cultural knowledge on perception of behavior are more productive than the rather haphazard and highly personalized discussions by colleagues about their field experiences, however insightful they may be. We have recently (we taught the seminar together for the last time in the winter of 1997) made some other innovations in the course. We play audiotapes of interviews that we have taken in the field, distribute our field notes on the matters for examination, and then read the published ethnographic report on certain behavioral episodes. This makes possible a fresh and open discussion of construction and translation from raw data to published piece.

The sensitization technique has proven to be useful in other classes than the ethnographic methods course. When we have taught the course titled "Cultural Transmission: Cross-Cultural Perspectives on Education," we have found that when we use the technique, students quickly become oriented to the problems of perception, construction, and translation that are heuristic to a case-study approach.

The last of the three chapters in this section, "Crosscultural, Comparative, Reflective Interviewing in Schoenhausen and Roseville," applies many of the principles we have discussed so far, and adds a few. It all began when we showed films we had taken of classrooms in Schoenhausen to the teachers. We first screened them before all nine of the Schoenhausen teachers. Their reactions were quite unexpected. They talked all at once in excited exclamations. "I didn't know I looked like that." "I think I have been doing the same things for the past 20 years." The teachers not only reacted to their own images, but also to the classrooms and behaviors of their colleagues. During the discussion afterwards, over wine and Kuchen, teachers exclaimed enthusiastically over the experience and asked us if we could take comparable films of classrooms in Roseville, and bring them back with us when we returned to Germany. That we did, and in 1985 the CCCRI was born as we collected interviews stimulated by the evocative stimuli of seeing and responding to both the films of one's own classroom and comparable classrooms in Roseville, Wisconsin.

The interviews are culturally much richer than any others we have collected using any other means. They are culturally phrased and are stated with knowledge of the counterpart culture in the light of one's own. The procedure also revealed the influence of position (administrator, teacher, and student) on perception. There was common ground, representing shared culture, but there were also divergences, reflecting the differences in the positions of the three groups of viewers. We regard both the common ground and the divergences as part of the cultural system of the school. The task of the researcher–analyst is to bring out aspects of these relationships that are not known, or if known are rationalized out of existence, by the "Natives" (anyone in the field of action).

We made further use of this type of interview in doing cultural therapy, but more of this later.

It is apparent that what we started learning about behavior in schools early on continued to hold good as our careers proceeded. Discrepancies, conflicts, unconscious patterning, denial are all processes in which all teachers in some degree and all students, are caught up in. Our methods of teaching and learning how to do ethnography, the use of transcultural sensitization procedures, and our cross-cultural, reflective interviewing are all based on this conception of the relation of culture to teaching and learning. This makes our research and its results at times murky, ambiguous, and tenuous. It also makes securing funds for research difficult, for foundations seem to send applications for funds out for review to people who view reality as linear, and all research procedures as designed to elicit wholly conscious, predetermined responses. To us, most of the research procedures advocated in education and hard social science seem naive because they treat only with what to us is a superficial level.

## PART IV
## AMERICAN CULTURE

In this section, "American Culture," we have selected three articles that develop central ideas about American culture, show how the substance of American culture is transmitted (or not transmitted) in schools, and analyze some current radical right action as representing a reaffirmative movement. In the first chapter, "Consensus and Continuity in American Culture," we selected from the whole article that was published in the Biennial Review of Anthropology that part most germane to our interests in this book. This chapter describes a consensus among anthropologists who have written about American culture. This consensus served as the foci around which our *Values Projective Technique* was developed, already described in chapter 4, "Education in a Transforming American Culture." We termed the result an American *ideology* in the 1983 article. As the processes of opposition and conflict became more and more evident, we generated the term *dialogue* to replace the term ideology. Lists of cultural values are relatively static. Dialogue is more active and shifts analytic focus to a process, rather than a static structure of values. The final result of this shift is apparent in our book *The American Cultural Dialogue* (1990), where the theoretical position is developed much more. This chapter concludes with a discussion of "the problem of women," and thus ties into the chapter "Das Remstal."

In "Schooling in the American Cultural Dialogue," we discuss two cultural transmitters—one an Italian immigrant woman of 65 who had been a counselor in the middle school for more than 30 years. The dialogue between her and the students she is counseling about choices of courses for the first years of high school they are about to enter shows clear positive bias towards college entrance and clear negative bias towards everything else. She leaves youth that are not college-bound very little that is positive. They are in her eyes, clearly discards. And the majority of the discards are Mexican-American. The sorting process is evident. The school is a "factory for failure" as well as for success. The other culture transmitter is a young man who appeared in chapter 2, "The Transmission of American Culture," and chapter 9, "Roger Harker and Schoenhausen, from the Familiar to the Strange and Back Again." He is the case about which I (George) have often remarked, that I would not have had a career in educational anthropology if it hadn't been for Roger Harker (a pseudonym, of course). He is the perfect case because he illustrates so well many different dimensions of the roles of cultural transmitter and mediator in a culturally diverse American society. Readers will have now encountered Roger three times. In each analysis of his case, different concepts and purposes have been applied. This is the nature of useful case material. The problem with Roger is that he was not a problem. No one thought he was, including his superiors, colleagues, and least of all, himself. Only a few children timidly asserted some problem areas. The chapter details the relationship between Roger and the cultural diversity of his classroom. It is now a familiar story, but one never to be forgotten, for it is at the heart of American educational problems today.

It is in this context that the conception of cultural therapy occurred, as we have said previously. It was clear, by the end of my time with Roger, that I was trying to change his personal culture. I was trying to enlarge it, to make it possible for him to interact more effectively with a broader range of ethnic and cultural diversity in his classroom. What I did was a form of critical anthropology, though I resist the term. I did not start my case study of Roger with any clear persuasions of what he was or what he was not doing. Nor did I think of myself as trying to criticize his operation as a teacher. I thought of myself as studying him—trying to find out how he operated and why. There is a difference.

The last of these three chapters is "Cultural Politics in the White Ethni-classes in the Mid-90s," Is quite different from anything else in the volume. It starts with a clear bias: to show how recent radical right activities constitute a reaffirmation movement, not unlike one we participated in among the Menominee Indians of Wisconsin. We perceived some common attributes in the behaviors of figures such as William Bennett, Newt Gingrich, Pete Wilson, the NRA, the bombers, the angry militias, the patriots, and western activists. To some, perhaps many readers, this is going too far, and yet, the logic of the analysis makes this categorization inevitable. It is not that William Bennett, Newt Gingrich, or Ted Kaczynski (the Unabomber) are the same kinds of people. They are separated by a great distance in character, personality, position, and values, but they share some key characteristics that make them participants in a reaffirmation movement. The implications of the movements for the chances that cultural therapy will be effective in schools is discussed, perhaps too pessimistically, but it is the way it seemed to us at the time we wrote the article.

To many of our readers, the foregoing discussion of American culture will seem fruitless. American culture is too variegated, too complex, too dynamic, to permit analysis. Our view is that there is coherence despite this complexity and dynamism, and that this coherence is present in all of the situations that together constitute American society, including the school especially, because the school is a normative institution charged with transmitting values. We attempt to describe this coherence and the main forms of deviation from it, in our writings on American culture. It is therefore important, if one wants to understand what we did in our research on schooling in America to understand our attempt at analysis of the American culture and its variations. We recommend *The American Cultural Dialogue And Its Transmission* (1990) for a more full exposition of this effort and the difficulties encountered. The principles of conflict and hidden agenda permeate the analysis of educational situations in this book. But we fall short of a truly systematic exposition of these principles, in all of our writing. Perhaps, if I, George, still have a decade of work left in me I will be able to provide this more full analysis of these critical processes, but I will be lacking the keen insights that my long-term partner always had into them.

## PART V
### CULTURAL THERAPY

We discuss cultural therapy in relation to a number of ideas that originated mostly in our fieldwork with native Americans—the Menominee, Blood, and Mistassini Cree. We stress the origin of these ideas partly to demonstrate their possible universality and partly because they seemed to provide a dynamic orientation for the analysis. Probably this puts off some readers who have not met these ideas before and may even irritate some who see them as esoteric and irrelevant.

The concepts (ideas become concepts) are: education as a calculated interference with learning; the cross-cultural comparative reflective interview, the enduring, situated, and endangered self; the Remstal and the enduring and situated self; the self and instrumental competence; and personal adaptations to culture conflict. Treating with each of these ideas in relationship to cultural therapy creates a complex whole that will not be appreciated by everyone. We consider them to be conceptual promontories around which the processes of cultural therapy can be organized.

This chapter integrates concepts that are ordinarily left separate. Surveying each relationship briefly, we can say that education as calculated interference produces a need for delayed gratification on the part of the student, for much is always taught that is irrelevant to the problems of everyday life. Students who already have the mechanisms for delayed gratification built in when they enter school, and whose home environment reinforces the validity of delayed gratification, manage well. Those who do not, do not.

The CCCRI has already been discussed, so there is little that needs to be said here. It occurs when an informant is presented with pictures (in video form) of her or his own classroom and self in juxtaposition with pictures of another teacher and classroom that are significantly different. Our experience has been that it works best when the cultural context of the two classrooms is quite different.

The interview stimulates the teachers to voice concerns that otherwise lie dormant and to express basic assumptions that ordinarily remain unvoiced. Once things of this kind are said, it is possible to bring them to a level of consciousness that permits reflective interpretation to occur—a major objective of cultural therapy.

The enduring, situated, and endangered self concepts may be difficult for some readers to relate to cultural therapy. We use our experience as field workers with the Menominee and Blood to raise questions about the adaptations of students, particularly those with strong, divergent enduring selves with a need to operate with situated selves in school situations that are not congruent with the enduring self, thus creating danger for his or her sense of self continuity. We suggest that the features of the enduring self and the situational adaptations necessary in the school could be deemotionalized and put in the context of instrumental competencies. It would be possible for students and teachers under these circumstances to face the problem with more equanimity.

We cite the situation in the Rems Valley (Remstal) of southern Germany as an example of how an enduring and situated self can be at odds without endangering the self. This relates closely to the idea just presented—that instrumental adaptations if deemotionalized, are possible for culturally diverse populations of students in American mainstream schools. But the American mainstream has a long way to go before this state can be achieved. The self in relation to instrumental competence builds on the ideas presented so far. Instrumental competence and a sense of self-efficacy can be acquired, we suggest, by critical examination of what the instrumental competencies are, and to what extent they are embedded in a cultural matrix that gives them unnecessary and destructive emotional loading.

The idea of adaptations, drawn from our Menominee research, is an attempt to generalize responses to cultural conflict. The responses are reaffirmation, withdrawal, constructive marginality, biculturalism, and assimilation. It seems to us that all of these adaptive modes are possible for students for whom adaptation to school requirements and criteria of performance are in conflict with the enduring self and one's ethnic culture. Cultural therapy can, through open discussions and self-critical examination, bring these conflicts and the adaptations to them into the light of day so that they can be perceived in less threatening ways than when they remain unclassified but powerful determinants of potentially self-destructive behavior.

We have been criticized for using the term "cultural therapy" for the processes of reflection and self-examination constituting the heart of the remedial process we are working with. *Therapy* suggests illness. Indeed, having a culture may be regarded as an illness in today's diversified global culture. *Cultural reflection*, or *clinical anthropology* has been suggested. As we see it, cultural reflection only partially suggests the totality of what we want to do, and clinical anthropology is more encompassing. Cultural therapy is a form of clinical anthropology, to be sure, and displaces a psychological model of therapy with a cultural model, which is our intention. Of course, the cultural model is situated in a context of feelings and perceptions, which can be regarded as essentially psychological. Perhaps the term *psychocultural model* is appropriate terminology, but still does not communicate any specific approach to the problem. In any event, arguments about terminology are essentially unproductive.

Behind all of this, there is the assumption that cultural therapy depends on bringing culture that is hidden or at least not at an operational conscious level to a level where it can be dealt with consciously and purposely. This assumes in turn that culture comes in patterns and categories. We draw from ethnoscience in that we organize culture into kinds of cultural knowledge—that knowledge necessary to make the situations that our society provides for us workable. One has cultural knowledge about a myriad of things—place settings at a dinner table, how to behave in an elevator, how to handle an irate spouse, how to get out of work, and into it. The most mundane tasks require cultural knowledge to make them work—putting on one's pants, for example, or how to get into a car. Much of this knowledge is relegated to a preconscious level. We do not have to think about it, it is just there when we need it. But much cultural knowledge works at an unconscious level. We may, for example, have deep prejudices against people of color but conceivably, be a tireless worker on their behalf in an unfair society. It is this deeper level of cultural knowledge that it is most difficult to bring to a level where it can be worked on, with the help of a good cultural therapist. It is always well-defended, and we depend on it for psychic energy. It is intimately linked with our personal identity, either as we compensate for it, as in our previous example, or play it out in social interaction directly, as the skinheads do.

As we see it, there are three major types of cultural knowledge that are involved in cultural therapy: the mundane; self–other reflexive; and hidden assumptions (Spindler, 1999). All three must be brought to a level of consciousness that permits one to see them and their relation to one's behavior. In the feedback of data to Roger Harker, he learned about all three. The teachers in Schoenhausen and Roseville learned about hidden assumptions and less about mundane and self–other cultural knowledge.

Mundane cultural knowledge can be represented by the manure pile in front of the Bauernhaus. It is a perfectly everyday piece of cultural knowledge (that the manure pile indicates a Bauernhaus) that every native in the Remstal knows and makes use of when s/he sees such a manure pile and immediately forms an image of a Bauernhause in which both humans and animals are housed. Newcomers to the village such as tourists and others who "do not know" need to be informed if they are to move about in village space appropriately or if they are to report matters to others accurately.

Self–other knowledge is best represented by Roger Harker's understanding of his favored standing with colleagues and the administrators but also his failure to understand that his favoritism damaged the identities of students who were not in the chosen group. He lacked the requisite cultural knowledge that would have enabled him to make a more professional and fair adaptation to the presence of diverse minorities in his classroom.

Hidden assumptions are best illustrated by statements of purpose by Roseville and Schoenhausen teachers such as those concerning the individual. In one case, the teachers believed that their major purpose was to bring the children up to group standards (Schoenhausen). In the other case, the teachers believed their major purpose was to bring the child up to a full realization of his or her potential (Roseville). These assumptions penetrated all aspects of their teaching. They were aware of their assumptions but not of their ramifications nor were they aware that these were not universal assumptions that all teachers made. American advisors overseas go burdened with a myriad of such assumptions.

They were not aware of their assumptions in the sense that they did not see them as different from all teachers' assumptions about the importance of the individual, and did not see them as imbedded in a Germanic and an American value orientation.

The purpose of cultural therapy in these terms is to make these three types of cultural knowledge available to the person or persons receiving the cultural therapy, thus acquiring an objective view of their own behavior in situations where this knowledge plays a significant role in determining their perceptions of others and in their behavior in interactions with them.

## PART VI
## ORIENTATION

"Making the Familiar Strange: The Anthropological Dialogue of George and Louise Spindler," 1999, by Susan Parman, provides an overview of the Spindlers' *oeuvre*, referring to their works in other sectors of anthropology beyond the anthropology of education.

## REFERENCES

Eddy, Elizabeth. 1997. Theory, Research and Application in Educational Anthropology. In G. Spindler, Ed., *Education and Cultural Process: Anthropological Approaches*. 3rd ed. Prospect Heights: Waveland Press. (First published in 1974).

Ford, Rosalie. 1997. The History of Educational Anthropology. In G. Spindler, Ed., ibid.

Parman, Susan D. 1992. George and Louise Spindler and the Issue of Homogeneity and Heterogeneity in American Cultural Anthropology. In L. Boyer and R. Boyer, Eds., *Essays in Honor of George And Louise Spindler*. Special Issue of *The Psychoanalytic Study of Society*. Vol. 17, pp. 29–44. Hillsdale, NJ: The Analytic Press.

Schwartz, Theodore. 1978. Where is the Culture? Personality as the Distributive Locus of Culture. In G. Spindler, Ed., *The Making of Psychological Anthropology*, pp. 417–441. Berkeley: University of California Press.

Spindler, George. 1955. Education in a Transforming American Culture. *Harvard Educational Review*, XXV, 145–156.

Spindler, George D., ed. 1955. *Education and Anthropology*. Stanford: Stanford University Press.

Spindler, George. 1959. *The Transmission of American Culture*. Cambridge: Harvard University Press.

Spindler, George and Louise. 1965. The Instrumental Activities Inventory: A Technique for the Study of the Psychology of Acculturation. *Southwestern Journal of Anthropology,* 21(1).

Spindler, George and Louise Spindler. 1990. *The American Cultural Dialogue and its Transmission.* London and Bristol, PA: Falmer Press.

Spindler, George D., ed. (with H. Trueba & L. Spindler). 1989. *What Do Anthropologists Have to Say about Dropouts?* London, England, and Bristol, PA: Falmer Press.

Spindler, George D. 1999. Three Kinds of Cultural Knowledge Useful in Cultural Therapy. *Anthropology and Education Quarterly.* December.

Trueba, Henry T. 1992. The Spindlers as Ethnographers: The Impact of their Lives and Work on American Anthropology. In L. Boyer and R. Boyer, Eds., *The Psychoanalytic Study of Society,* Vol. 17, 73–94. Hillsdale, NJ: The Analytic Press.

Wolcott, Harry. 1997. The Anthropology of Learning. In G. Spindler, Ed., *Education and Cultural Process; Anthropological Approaches.* 3rd ed. Prospect Heights: Waveland Press (First published in 1982).

# Part I

# CHARACTER DEFINITION

# Part
# I

# CHARACTER DEFINITION

In Part I, many of the major themes of this volume are first encountered. The 1954 conference of anthropologists and educators is overviewed. Much of what we have all been up to since that time is anticipated but much was unanticipated, such as the vast demographic changes in the population of the United States in favor of nonEuropean-Americans, and the role of ethnography as anthropology's major gift to education. The Third Burton Lecture, chapter 2, is included, in which I engage for the first but not last time with Roger Harker, the fifth-grade male teacher who has served as the vehicle for so many of my discussions of how schools in the United States function. The theme of cultural conflicts and discrepancies is established as a major orientation for much that follows. The conflict theme is pursued in the next chapter on education in a transforming American culture. In the chapter on Beth Anne, the ways in which values held by teachers influence perception, in this instance, in the selection of the "best adjusted" child in the school, are analyzed.

In other articles in Part I, cultural therapy first appears as a result of work with "Roger Harker," George Spindler's first major case study, and conflicts in culture as they affect schools becomes a theme. The way in which schools fail minority groups is brought into focus in chapter 5. Part I ends with defining the teacher as a cultural agent and education as a process of cultural transmission. This part sets the stage for much that follows.

# Anthropology
# and Education:
# An Overview
## (1955)

*George D. Spindler*

Although no "educational anthropology" exists at present, and this conference is not aimed at its creation, the purpose of this overview is to survey the articulation of these two fields. Education is not listed in *Anthropology Today* (Kroeber, 1953) as a field of application for anthropology. There are only rare instances of self-conscious attention to the mutual relevance of these two fields in the various interdisciplinary symposia. Few professional anthropologists are required by the institutional definition of their positions to interact with professional educationists, and only a handful of joint appointments in education and anthropology exists in American colleges and universities.

Despite this, some educational philosophers cite the concept of culture as most important in their systematic thinking, modern texts used in the training of teachers abound with references to anthropological literature, elementary school teachers include projects on "Peoples in Other Lands" and "Our Indian Friends," and a growing number of departments of anthropology are offering courses with the specific needs of teachers-in-training in mind. But most surprising is the fact that the relations between these two fields have a history in this country extending back to at least 1904, when Hewett wrote his first pieces on education for the *American Anthropologist* (1904, 1905).

These introductory statements suggest that a whole symposium of papers could be devoted to the systematic explication of these sometimes obscure and unacknowledged relationships. Only this overview paper will serve this interest directly. Its purpose is to outline the parts of both anthropology and education as they articulate into one mutually relevant framework of interests, trace briefly the history of such articulations, indicate what anthropologists have written about education and what educators have used of what anthropologists have written, and describe certain potentials and problems that exist in the relationships. It follows on the introductory statement by Dean Quillen of the problems in education for which anthropological help is sought.

The purpose of this overview is thus sharply different from that of the rest of the papers in this symposium. It *is about* the relations of education and anthropology. The other papers are designed to put into motion some applications of mutual relevance to both fields. They are experimental and question-raising, therefore, since no articulated education anthropology structure exists from which they could draw. Most of them move well out toward the margins, away from traditional anthropological interests. This is not necessarily good, but it is assuredly inevitable.

## RELEVANT FIELDS AND INTERESTS IN ANTHROPOLOGY

Some of anthropology articulates, or can articulate, with education, and some of it does not. Anthropology as the "study of man," with its traditional interests in cultural variability, culture history—both ethnological and archeological—language, race, and human evolution, is admittedly a prime potential contributor to a good general education. While no claim is made here that anthropology should necessarily become the skeleton or the core of a complete "liberal arts" education at the secondary school or college level, it seems clear that no other existing discipline provides an integration, however loose, of so much that is important concerning man and his manifold behaviors. The study of man thus broadly conceived makes it possible to bridge the gap between the human animal and the human being, to conceive of both the relativity and universality of human behavior and propositions about it, to project human affairs upon a time plane that stretches far into the past and future, and turns the focus on the basic round of life and man's relation to nature.

It is not even necessary, as is often done, to argue that the vicarious crosscultural experience afforded by an anthropological Cook's tour leads to a better understanding of our own culture. It does or can lead to a more universalistic understanding of human life, and this is more important. Anything else is a byproduct.

The implication is clear that anthropology should be used as a contribution to general education more widely than it is. It should not be taught as it is to young anthropologists-in-training or as it usually is at the college level—as an introduction to a discipline—but rather as an introduction to a new perspective on human life. It should also be taught at the secondary school level, possibly under some more conventional and already existing rubric (Spindler, 1946). It is being taught at the elementary school level when teachers develop lesson units or activities centering on American Indian tribes—but sometimes badly because the teachers have had little or no exposure to anthropology as such and consequently contravene the primary goals of this kind of curriculum design. Anthropologists have been aware of these possible contributions of their field to general education and have written about it (Ehrich, 1947; Howells, 1952) but they have only rarely done anything about it, because they conceive of themselves primarily as producers of data and contributors to science and secondarily as teachers or curriculum designers.

In the sense outlined above, all of anthropology is relevant to education. From this point on, the relationships real and potential are more selective. But these selections need not be made only from the sociocultural side of the discipline. Indeed, the contribution of physical anthropology to education had an early and significant beginning in Montessori's fascinating applications in a "pedagogical anthropology" (Montessori, 1913). To be sure, Maria Montessori, though armed with millimetric tape measures and anthropometers, called for recognition of educable man as a "speaking animal" and a "social animal," and in her practiced philosophy of education anticipated Goldenweiser's arguments for an anthropologically sound and progressive "education for social participation" (Goldenweiser, 1939). But more of Montessori later.

Aside from Montessori the most important contribution of physical anthropology to education has been on the subject of race, and the relationships —rather the lack of them—between race, culture, and intelligence. Anthropological perspectives on the meaning of race and the myth of racial superiority have been popularized by Ethel Alpenfels in her capacity as staff anthropologist for the Bureau for Intercultural Education, and have become familiar to every well-grounded social studies teacher through this and other agencies. Otto Klineberg has given us the classic treatment on relationships between race, culture, and I.Q. (1935), that has wide circulation in an encapsulated form in a UNESCO pamphlet (1951) and a symposium edited by Linton (1947).

What has not been used sufficiently in education from physical anthropology are the techniques, concepts, and methodology concerning growth patterns, maturational sequences, sexual differences, and glandular processes that could add needed dimensions to the psychosomatic data of educational psychology. Nor have the school plant planners—a new specialization in education—yet consulted the physical anthropologists for ideas, methods, or facts on the anthropometry of the classroom. If anthropologists can design better bucket seats for flying boxcars, they can also design better desks for school children and contribute heretofore unconsidered applications to playground equipment, audiovisual devices, space-to-person ratios, and lavatories.

Directly relevant to the interests of this seminar–conference are the concepts and data of specialized and relatively new fields in anthropology, such as personality in culture and cultural dynamics. In fact, when anthropology–education relations are considered, this is usually where people in both disciplines begin to look first.

For some, interests in crosscultural education are identical with interests in crosscultural socialization. This creates confusion. Socialization of the child to human, group-accepted status is a total process of growth and adaptation. The center of the process is the child—adapting to an environment structured by culture, as well as by group size, climate, terrain, ecology, and the peculiar personalities of his always-unique parents or parental surrogates. Education is not this whole process. It is what is done to a child, by whom, under what conditions, and to what purpose. It is the process of transmitting culture—if we can think of culture as including skills, knowledge, attitudes, and values, as well as discrete elements of behavior. It is the culture of the human being—where culture is used as a verb.

There are many books, monographs, and articles by anthropologists reporting research on socialization of the child in environments structured by various cultural sets. The most recent significant comparative research is Whiting and Child's *Child Training and Personality* (1953). There are relatively few studies on education. British anthropologists, with their functional predilections, have provided many of the most useful descriptive analyses of education as cultural transmission in particular cultural settings. One of the better studies by an American anthropologist in terms of application to the who, what, when, where questions has been produced by Pettit, as he summarizes and analyzes education in North American Indian cultures (Pettit, 1946). This work illustrates the kind of thing that needs to be done with more comparative crosscultural data.

This suggests the relevance of another field of anthropology—traditional ethnography—the factual core of cultural anthropology. Pettit drew his data from ethnographies written by others. The fact that he could do so is a tribute to the inclusiveness of good ethnography. But he had to search for the relevant facts and too often couldn't find them, or could find only indirect allusions to a who, what, when, and how process in cultural transmission. The success of his search indicates that an ethnographic corpus lies waiting to be cannibalized by researchers interested in crosscultural education, but that more definitive and inclusive categories of observation need to be devised if future reports are to be of maximum use. Ethnography has produced the raw materials for more treatment than has been committed—and it also furnishes the sources for the vicarious culture shock that is an essential step in the education of a public school teacher.

That amorphous and loosely defined problem area in anthropology called cultural dynamics is the source of many relevances—most of them potential. If this field is seen as that concerned primarily with processes of culture change and stability, its relation to educationist interests is immediately clear. Change and stability must be mediated by what is transmitted from parent to child in the educative process. This transmission process is not seen as a causative variable—excepting within a limited interaction cycle. But unless this variable intervening between changes in conditions of life and the adaptations of people is understood, the "dynamic" part of cultural dynamics is left unilluminated. And the educative process can be understood better by viewing it as such an intervening variable, for then it is seen as an instrumentality that is sensitive to the cultural and extracultural exigencies under which it operates. Anthropologists have done little systematizing here. Herskovits has supplied one of the few explicit statements in his "Education and Cultural Dynamics" (1943).

One field of interest in anthropology that has realized relatively more of its potential in relation to educational problems is that of social structure. If the interests here are conceived as broadly relating to group alignments, prestige ranking, status and role interrelationships, and social control in the community context, all of the very useful work of the Warner group and other closely related efforts may be regarded as a contribution from this area. The contributors include, besides Warner, such workers as Allison Davis, Gardner, Dollard, Loeb, Withers, Useem, and many nonanthropologists who have been strongly influenced therein such as Havighurst, Taba, Hollingshead, the Lynds, et al. The relevance of this field to education, particularly with respect to a concept of social class that has been regularized by Warner and his associates, is indicated by two recent special issues of the Harvard Educational Review (1953) on the subject. No claim is made that this is exclusively an anthropological domain or contribution, but one of the mainsprings driving the interest and its application is fastened to an anthropological pivot.

In this instance the situation as it exists otherwise in the various potential or emergent articulations with education is reversed. More is known about how the educative process is affected by social class and community structure in Jonesville and Elmtown than in the nonliterate societies that are the accustomed habitat of the anthropologists. To be sure, nonliterate societies rarely have social classes in the same sense that Jonesville has, but some do, and all have groups structured into a social organization. Whether this structure is formalized by a widely ramifying kinship system, or by rank, or by a complex political–social system, or is atomistic and individuated—the who, what, when, and why of education will reflect this structure at every turn. For the sake of a clearer concept of education as a sociocultural process something more should be known about these functional interrelationships between educative system, educative process, and social structure in non-Western and particularly smaller, simpler societies.

## RELEVANT FIELDS AND INTERESTS IN EDUCATION

When the sights are turned on education, it becomes clear that there are more relevant problems and interests than anthropologists could begin to bear appropriate gifts to—even if they were so motivated. Some of the particularly significant problems have been succinctly described by James Quillen. Others have been listed by Fannie Shaftel in a memorandum circulated to the participants in this conference. The discussion below will approach some of these same problems from a different perspective and describe certain interests and fields in education in which these problems occur.

One of the areas within education that most obviously calls for an anthropological contribution is that of the "foundation" fields. These are designated by various names in teachers' colleges and schools of education about the country. The general rubrics are social, psychological, philosophical, historical and comparative, and biological. They represent what is drawn into education as a science, and into education as a professional field, from the behavioral and social sciences, the humanities, and natural sciences, as their data and concepts are used in empirical and logico-deductive analyses of the educative process, and in the training of teachers.

Anthropology has only recently begun to make a significant contribution to these fields, largely because of its newness as an academic discipline. Within the social–behavioral foundations, educational psychology has clearly dominated the scene, partly because of a historical accident that institutionally wedded psychology and education rather early—at least in

America—and partly because the problems of educational tests and measurements, principles of learning, and personality development have been naturals for psychological applications. In many teacher-training institutions psychology is still the only behavioral science explicitly recognized in the organization of professional education courses.

Of the various social sciences, education as a professional field has drawn from political science, economics, and jurisprudence, but particularly from sociology. Educational sociology has its own house organ, numerous texts bearing its name, and an impressive pile of research to its credit. Most foundation courses in professional education in the social area are called *educational sociology*. In a few places where teachers are trained in America—particularly at Teachers College at Columbia under the leadership of Lyman Bryson and now Solon T. Kimball, at New York University under Ethel Alpenfels, and at Chicago, Harvard, Yale, and Stanford—an explicit anthropological contribution is integrated with those of other social sciences in the foundation program. Hunter College, in New York City, may soon be the site of an unusually wide-ranging curriculum of "foundational" education and anthropology (Rosenstiel, 1954), and New York University's School of Education has a longstanding development of this sort. Courses in anthropology are required of teachers-in-training at some universities and colleges where there is no formalized integration of anthropological contributions with the foundation fields in education.

At Stanford, as an illustration of the ways in which anthropology can contribute to the foundation fields in teacher training, relevant materials are presented in three courses: "Social Foundations in Education"; "Cultural Transmission"; and "Social Anthropology in Education." These courses are given under the aegis of a joint appointment in the School of Education and the Department of Sociology and Anthropology, and credit is given in both fields.

"Social Foundations in Education" is required of all upper division education students and all candidates for the Master of Arts degree in education as well as for the various professional credentials. It combines selected materials from sociology, anthropology, and social psychology. The anthropological contribution lies mainly in a systematic analysis of American cultural patterns and values as they bear directly upon the role and functions of the teacher and public school system. Crosscultural data are used here for illustrative purposes. Other topical areas covered include social class and education, problems in student-teacher communication, group stereotypes and prejudice in schools, the community context of the school, and the school as a social system.

"Cultural Transmission" is offered as a course for doctoral candidates, and is presented within the advanced social foundations sequence in education. Its coverage includes the construction of a frame of reference for viewing transmission and enculturation processes. This frame of reference is then used in the analysis of these processes in two nonliterate societies, one European society, and American society. The course ends with analysis of case studies of selected types of teachers and their classrooms, and schools, in our society. Sociometric, autobiographic, socioeconomic, observational, and community "social base" data are included in the case study materials.

"Social Anthropology in Education" is a seminar constituted of a majority of advanced graduate students in education and a sprinkling of degree candidates in anthropology and psychology. It has been devoted so far to an analysis of the educative process in nonliterate societies, using standard ethnographic references. A simple outline of educative process is used, with major headings like "teaching personnel," "content taught," "time and sequence of impact," "techniques used," and "formal and informal contexts."

These courses accomplish different things in different ways. An important point in relation to the problem of education-anthropology articulation is that only in the seminar is the greater part of the frame of reference supplied by anthropology; in the other courses it seems essential to provide an integration of selected aspects of sociology and psychology. This is not simply because the titles of the courses are self-determinative. When the educative process is the focus and particularly in our own society, the anthropological frame of reference is not sufficient alone. But it is essential. The core of the contribution is in the attention to culture as a behavioral compulsive, as a perception-directing set of patterns, and in the attention to the variable forms these patterns take. Cultural awareness is one vital aim of each course, but not merely generalized cultural awareness; the aim is to create in the teacher an awareness of how culture influences specifically what he does as a teacher, and how to think about, observe, and analyze this influence. Courses in conventional institutionalized anthropology do not serve this same purpose, though they are quite necessary as a first phase of the experiences of the student in training as a professional educator.

This role of anthropology in the foundation fields of education may be regarded as a contribution to teacher training. The conclusion to be drawn is that it does not suffice to throw some standard anthropology courses at the teacher-in-training. By the time he is preparing to be a professional educator, or is improving his already established proficiency, he should have had an introduction to the materials of at least cultural anthropology as a part of his general education. The anthropology he gets in his *professional* education should be integrated with the other foundational offerings and used to solve problems in analysis of educative process. Otherwise we are asking him to provide this integration and this application; and most students—in education or otherwise—simply cannot.

There are other parts of the structure of professional education that need, or at least can use, some anthropological help: curriculum construction, for instance, once largely psychology-based, is now beginning to be socioculturally based as well. Elementary school curricula are being reorganized with direct attention to culture content, universal human activities, cultural values, and sequences of culturally patterned experience (Hanna, 1954). The emphasis on intergroup relations and utilization of community resources in the development of social education curricula in elementary schools likewise indicates this shift (Taba, 1950; Willcockson, 1950).

Other relevant interests in education are represented in the problems of educational administration, and the training of professional educational administrators. Cultural awareness is perhaps even more important for the administrator, since he manipulates the setting in which the teacher interacts with students and parents. He must not only have cultural awareness but must also understand the mechanics of culture change, the cultural expectations affecting the leader's role, the concrete as well as idealistic meaning of cultural values, and the social system of the school in the setting of the encompassing community and national social structure. Anthropology has a clear potential utility on the first three scores. In the latter instance sociology supplies more materials perhaps, but does so through community study approaches that are at least claimed to be partly an anthropological invention.

Up to this point, the discussion of fields and interests in education relevant to the problem of education–anthropology articulation has centered mainly on the training and manipulative side of professional education. But education as a professional field is not only concerned with teacher training, teaching, curriculum design, and administration of schools; it has a research base. Probably no social or behavioral science has as great a backlog of research nor encompasses such a high degree of variability of quality of research. The reason for the first is obvious. The reason for the second is partly that education crosscuts every phase of human activity and it is impossible to do good research without a high degree of specialization in the science or discipline treating with selected dimensions within this range. This is very difficult when so much has to be done all at once.

Be that as it may, there are many phases of research within the framework of education that call for anthropological attention. There has been an incorporation of anthropologically based concepts and methods in the studies of social class influences on learning (Davis, 1952), social class and community structures in relation to the social organization of the school and educational opportunities (Warner, Havighurst, Loeb, et al., 1944), and problems of adolescence (Havighurst & Taba, 1949), in the extensive study of the relationships between intelligence and cultural differences by the Chicago group (Eells et al., 1951), and in the studies of social class differences in socialization with their implications for education (Davis & Havighurst, 1947). This interest in social class and learning, and social class and school organization, has been the main stream of influence on research directly relevant to education and stemming from anything that can be regarded as an anthropological source. The main contribution of anthropology, other than in the form of some of the personnel involved, has been in the notion of cultural relativity, and in a functional total-community approach. As for methodology, it is doubtful that many clear claims to contributions can be made by anthropology, other than in a devotion to informants and informal participant observation.

Thus, a definite and extensive contribution to research on educational problems, in American society at least, has yet to be made. This is a reflection of the fact that anthropologists have not been very interested in our own society until quite recently. Their proper object of study has been the nonliterate peoples, in their pure or reconstructed form, or as they have struggled for existence under the impact of the industrial-based civilizations.

Anthropologists have been interested and involved with the problem of education in dependent, trust, and colonial territories, and Indian reservations, where nonliterate indigenes have been exposed to a Western-mediated education. But the involvement has been largely in terms of an applied anthropology, in various administrative and consultative capacities, and actual research reports on the processes involved are quite scarce. Felix Keesing has described some of the interesting problems that arise in these contexts in a summary of the content of a seminar conference including educators, anthropologists, sociologists, and government officials on the problems of education in Pacific countries (Keesing, 1937). Margaret Mead has provided a provocative analysis of the feasible educational objectives and the major factors to be taken into account in the 20th-century education of dependent peoples (1946).

There are many areas of potential application of anthropologically based concepts and methods in educational research in our own society to which attention may some day be given. The roles of teacher and school administrator in American society call for treatment from a cultural point of view that will call attention to some of the excruciating paradoxes projected in the role expectations. The effect of culturally based values on teacher perceptions of behavior and personal qualities of students needs to be explicated in a way that the positionally oriented social class studies have not yet developed. The informal transmission of value orientations and covert culture by teachers and in peer groups has received only preliminary attention. New approaches to the study of the school as a social system need to be devised—perhaps in the manner of the factory system studies that were in part anthropologically inspired. American culture as a specific context of the goals, expectations, and functions of education needs exploration—possibly in the vein of national character approaches. The conceptual categories and symbolic referents of speech in communication between teacher and child call for a meta-linguistic, language-in-culture application.

Particularly appropriate to traditional anthropological interests is the need for crosscultural research in education that illuminates the process in our own society indirectly but powerfully. This must be distinguished, as indicated, from primarily psychologically oriented interests in socialization. The educative process—the who, what, when, where, and how of common-human and culturally variable cultural transmission—furnishes understanding of not only basic processes of education but also cultural dynamics, for education thus broadly conceived is culture in motion. Culture is idealized in the educative process. Every teacher, whether mother's brother or Miss Humboldt of Peavey Falls, reenacts and defends the cultural drama as experienced. As the culture is passed on from one generation to the next in the hands of the teacher, it assumes a patent and rationalized shape. The whole world view is somehow encapsulated in each gesture, admonition, indoctrination, or explanation. And this seems equally true whether physics or sacred dreamtime truths are being taught.

Some of these possibilities are elaborated in various ways in the papers of this conference. Many of them will stay in the state of possibility only. But other approaches and avenues not seen as yet will be opened, perhaps as a result of this conference.

## THE ROUTES OF DIFFUSION

*Anthropological Routes.*   Some of the routes of diffusion of concepts and knowledge between education and anthropology have been described. The community structure–educational system stream of influence has been most important. Montessori's influence is another, and of longer standing (1913). Her principal assumptions have been integrated into the framework of modern progressive education. She saw clearly the need for stressing the "organic" relation of the whole child to the environment, emphasized the developmental process so that the child was not seen as a "diminutive adult," anticipated the problem of the differential meaning of school experience to children from various social classes and ethnic groups in her concept of a "regional ethnology" and study of local conditions, called for respect for individual differences in growth and function, demanded that a "scientific pedagogy" concern itself with normal individuals primarily, and developed a "biographical chart" that took the place of the report card and included "antecedents"—vocation of parents, their aesthetic culture, their morality and sentiments and care of children—as well as reports of physical and psychological examinations and ongoing observations in the form of diaries.

Education may contest the characterization of this as an anthropological influence, since Montessori is so clearly a part of the educationist's heritage, but she called her approach a "Pedagogical Anthropology," and used what were regarded, in Italy at least, as anthropological concepts, methods, techniques, and data. Though her cultural anthropology is guilty of what today would be regarded as certain racist errors, and her physical anthropology is now outmoded, her farsighted anticipation of much of the best of the contemporary art and science of education is impressive. Whether this is true because she had genius or because she had an anthropological orientation cannot be divined. She had both.

A history of anthropology-to-education diffusion cannot omit the early contributions of Edgar L. Hewett (1904, 1905). His articles "Anthropology and Education" (1904) and "Ethnic Factors in Education" (1905) in the *American Anthropologist* were the first and almost the last contributions of their kind in that journal. He argued for an "enrichment of the course of study of every public school in the land" through the incorporation of ethnological materials, particularly on culture history not confined to the Western world; called for joint meetings of the national education and anthropology societies to discuss mutual problems; scored culture historians for misuse and lack of use of ethnological data; claimed the clear relevance of an "ethnic psychology" that would contribute to the teacher's understanding of the fact that " ... Italian and Bohemian, Celt and Hebrew, Anglo-Saxon and African, look on questions of honor, morality, and decency out of separate ethnic minds ... "; asked educators to realize that "a civilization imposed from without is usually harmful, often destructive, always undesirable," because the "development of a race must be from within"; and suggested that for all these reasons "normal schools and other institutions for the training of teachers should give a prominent place to the anthropological sciences." The fact that none of his calls was implemented reflects partly an ethnocentrism of American culture, partly the peculiar conservatism of American public education/ and particularly the fact that American anthropologists did not have time for much of anything but, ethnographic and culture history salvage until the 1930s.

Franz Boas, the dean of American anthropology, clearly saw the relevance of anthropological and educational interests. In his *Anthropology and Modern Life* (1928), he devotes one whole chapter to these interests. He points out that "anthropological research offers, therefore, a means of determining what may be expected of children of different ages, and this knowledge is of considerable value for regulating educational methods." He talks of "normative data for development," sex differences, ethnic differences, and differences in environmental conditions that should be taken into account. He treats of some of the problems of cultural transmission, and points out that "our public schools are hardly conscious of the conflict" between democratic ideas of freedom and flexibility, and coercion; "they instill automatic reactions to symbols by means of patriotic ceremonial, in many cases by indirect religious appeal, and too often through the automatic reactions to the behavior of the teacher that is imitated." He suggests that tradition-based transmission of values and ethics is particularly strong among intellectuals and that the "masses" respond "more quickly and energetically to the demands of the hour than the educated classes ... "

The writings of Montessori, Hewett, and Boas on anthropology and education have been discussed in some detail because an examination of what anthropologists have written since then reveals that, with some notable exceptions, not much more has been said, and a critical examination of the implementation of their suggestions indicates that no more than a beginning has actually been accomplished.

Articles by anthropologists on this subject have turned up persistently in educational journals and elsewhere for the past 25 years. The place of anthropology in a college education, the contributions of anthropology to the training of teachers, the place of primitive education in the history of education are the favorite themes. The articles add to what their forerunners spelled out, but few of them produce clear innovations. Exceptions to this general rule include Mead's suggestive article on education in the perspective of primitive cultures (1943) and her Inglis Lectures, under the title, *The School in American Culture* (1950); Kluckhohn's comments in *Mirror for Man* (1949); Opler's "Cultural Alternatives and Educational Theory" (1947); Goldenweiser's "Culture and Education" (1939); and Herskovits' stimulating discussion in his text, *Man and His Works* (1948). The whole issue of the *American Journal of Sociology* (1943) devoted to "Education and Cultural Dynamics," including articles by Johnson, Redfield, Malinowski, Mekeel, Benedict, Herskovits, Powdermaker, and Embree is an especially outstanding contribution.

It seems clear, on examination of what has been done, that anthropologists have not been able to say much more than was said 50 years ago by Hewett when they talk about the general relevance of anthropology to general education. This is primarily because there is not much else to say. When the anthropologists have either analyzed their own intimately understood cross-cultural data in the perspective of education in modern society, or vice versa, or have moved over into a direct analysis of the educative process in our society with few methodological or conceptual binders, they have made a definite contribution. But the capital available in these activities has just begun to be utilized.

*Educational Routes.*    Irrespective of the worthy attentions by anthropologists to education, the educators have gone ahead on their own to search out and utilize what seemed relevant to them of the anthropological products. An examination of representative and substantial texts in the psychological, sociocultural, philosophical, and comparative–historical foundations of education used in professional teacher-training institutions about the country reveals a clear shift toward appropriation of social and cultural concepts and data produced by anthropologists.

In educational psychology, for example, the text by Pressey and Robinson (1944) mentions no anthropological references, and uses no cross-cultural data for illustrative purposes. The text edited by Skinner, revised twice, shows an increase of anthropological citations in the last revision (1950). Cole and Bruce, in their 1950 edition, take a strong culture-oriented position, using section headings like "Life Styles as the Product of Cultures ... Diverse Cultures with Their Contrasting Life Styles ...; The Culture as Definer of Perceptions, Beliefs, and Behaviors"; "The Teacher An Agent of Culture"; use Samoa, Zuni, Kwakiutl data as culture case-study materials; and cite extensively literature by Benedict, Davis, Dennis, Kardiner and Linton, Linton alone, Mead, Redfield, Whiting, and Kluckhohn. Cronbach, in his sparkling new 1954 model for educational psychology texts, draws upon Mead, Davis, Warner, Benedict, and Kluckhohn, among others, and makes considerable reference to cultural pressures, different cultural settings influencing personality development and learning, and formation of social attitudes and values. Martin and Stendler's new text, *Child Development* (1953), intended for use by educators and noneducators both, and already used widely in elementary education and other professional education courses, places a very heavy emphasis on culture–personality relationships. Culture case data are cited for the Alorese, Balinese, Comanche, Japanese, Kwoma, Mentowie, Navaho, Samoans, Sioux, Tanala, Tepoztecans, Yurok, Zuni, and others. Cultural relativism has found its way into the heart of this book.

In educational sociology—a field that is rapidly being expanded into a sociocultural foundation of education—a like trend is occurring: The Cook and Cook book (1950, revised edition), a text of long standing and wide use in educational sociology and social foundations, cites crosscultural materials infrequently but draws much from the anthropologically influenced community studies on Middletown, St. Denis, Yankee City, and Plainsville. Robbins' *Educational Sociology* (1953) uses many of the same references and refers to writings by Mead, Benedict, Murdock, and Linton for the notion of cultural relativity. Brown's 1954 edition of *Educational Sociology* uses extensive reference to cultural data on the Navaho, Australian tribes, Zuni, and the Acoma Pueblo, and cites anthropological pieces—by Gillin, Kluckhohn, Wagley, Herskovits, Goldfrank, Redfield, Tylor, Stirling, Warner, Rivers, Linton, Hewett, Mead, Powdermaker, Benedict, and Montague—approximately twice as often as in the 1947 edition.

The trend is not as noticeable in the philosophical and comparative foundations of education—the limits of the sample of texts forbid generalizations. The tendency in these fields has apparently been to utilize highly generalized and Western-limited concepts of culture as an important part of the frame of reference, but to draw relatively little from any of the work by anthropologists in crosscultural contexts. Brameld has made one of the strongest arguments for a culture base for educational philosophy (1950), but even he cites only a few anthropological works—namely, some by Davis, Kluckhohn, Benedict, Warner, and Herskovits. He is currently engaged in an appraisal of the implications of anthropological concepts and works for educational theory—an activity reflected directly in his paper for this conference.

An overall summation of the anthropological concepts and data utilized in the contemporary texts in the foundations of education reveals certain general trends. Quite clear is the fact that educators interested in childhood education, elementary curriculum, school–community interrelations, and all of the social and behavioral foundations of education have arrived at the point where an anthropological point of view and, particularly, cross-cultural materials have a positive value for them. They indicate an awareness of culture concepts and cultural data produced by anthropologists by fairly extensive documentations with appropriate literature. They include anthropological references in their recommended reading lists. They consider it desirable to qualify generalizations about learning, cultural transmission, human nature, the functions of education, child growth and development, by invoking the notion of cultural relativity. Some of them incorporate a cultural perspective into their thinking—beyond using cultural relativity as a valued checkative.

The number of concepts relating to culture and culture process is impressive. Anthropologists have no copyright but certainly some possessory rights over them. Values, acculturation, cultural normalcy, cultural diffusion, cultural change, cultural transmission, subcultures, peer culture, folk culture, and even that rather new term—*enculturation*—ring with authentic familiarity to the anthropologist as they are used by the educationist authors.

But it is also clear that the range of materials being diffused via educationist channels from anthropological sources is in actuality quite limited.

The same names and same references keep turning up constantly. A frequency-of-citation chart for the literature examined reveals that Kluckhohn, Mead, Benedict, Davis, West (Carl Withers), and Warner are cited in great disproportion to all others. This suggests that the purveyance of anthropological thinking to education has at most two main disciplinary vehicles—personality and culture, and community studies—and that the mediation of data and concepts is inevitably given an indelible impress by these particular workers. Particularly significant is the fact that it is the relatively most popularized works of these contributors that are cited most frequently. These two tendencies indicate that however useful the contributions and however able the contributors, the educators are not getting a fair and substantial diet of anthropological materials. This will only change when the educators take the next step and get their hands dirty with some of the dust-laden monographs back in the stacks, and when anthropologists exhume their portfolios of esoteria and put them into more publicly usable form. The educators and anthropologists who have respectively done these things already are due some applause.

## THE ROLES OF THE ANTHROPOLOGIST
## IN THE EDUCATIONAL CONTEXT

One clear implication in this overview has been that if anthropology is actually going to contribute to education, the anthropologists will have to act at least more than occasionally within the setting of professional education. This is no argument that all anthropologists should. The discipline has many dimensions and interests, and nothing should be permitted to happen in relations with other fields that draws many anthropologists away from the central obligation to do basic research. But anthropologists have always been marked with a certain versatility. If there is a job to do in education some anthropologists will, for one reason or another, be bound to do it, Therefore an explication of some of the roles possible in the context of professional education is in order.

The anthropologist may act as a consultant. Ideally, he should be able to contribute ideas to every division of educational specialization—elementary, secondary, higher education, health, guidance, administration. He contributes, ideally, a widened perspective on human behavior. He sees the educative process as a cultural process, and thus not bounded by formalized, or ritualized lines of specialization or conceptual compartmentalization. He devotes some of his attention to breaking down ethnocentric biases.. He is, ideally, not time-bound. He provides objectification of cultural values and, if he is successful, brings educational objectives into appropriate congruence with them. He contributes some useful analytic–descriptive categories, the foremost of which is culture, followed by a train of constructs like cultural transmission, enculturation, role and status, and social organization. To do these things he has to act as a participating member of the groups for which he acts as a consultant, for it is necessary for him to grasp the point of view and problems of those with whom he is consulting. He has already had experience in doing this within a somewhat different setting in his field research.

The anthropologist may do research in education or act as a consulting member of a team that is doing research. He does so with the same perspectives and capabilities that have been outlined above, and in attacks upon problems that fall into areas described previously in this paper. His major contribution lies in the molar approach that characterizes anthropological method. His greatest problem is one of relevance. His problems, definitions, and research values cannot remain exactly the same as they would if he were doing anthropological field research in a nonliterate, or even an acculturating community. He must understand what it is that educators need to know in order both to build a better educational theory and to solve problems of immediate applied relevance. In the research team developed at Stanford under the direction of Robert Bush and known as the Stanford Consultation Service, it was found that a good *modus operandi* was achieved when the educator, psychiatrist, and anthropologist exchanged roles for a time so that each could achieve insight into the other's problems. In this project also, a unique combination of ameliorative case consultation goals and pure research goals has been achieved, so that neither endpoint of the value pendulum in educational research is lost. There are frustrations inherent in this procedure, to be sure.

The anthropologist need not necessarily work strictly within the framework of immediate education interests in his cross-disciplinary research. He may elect to confine himself to his own cross-cultural field, chasing down questions on educative process in non-Western societies. Possibly the most significant contributions of anthropology to education via research channels actually lie here.

The anthropologist may act as a teacher in the setting of professional education. Certain propositions concerning this role have already been explicated. His obligation lies mainly in making explicit the cultural assumptions and values that are a substratum of every move in educational action or theorizing. His contribution is particularly critical because education is a sensitive part of the total cultural process, and because in its very nature as an art and science of human cultivation it is loaded with a heavy burden of values. To achieve this contribution he goes to cross-cultural variability first, then turns to our own cultural modes as they bear directly on the educative process—from the viewpoint of both the learner and the teacher. His aim is to create cultural awareness, which is perhaps even more important than self-awareness in the teacher's sphere of activity and which is pedagogically much more attainable.

## LIMITATIONS AND RESERVATIONS

The list of particulars for the roles the anthropologist may assume in the context of professional education is stated in ideal terms. No one anthropologist could do all of these things equally well. Choices have to be made on the basis of personal inclination and necessity.

But other limitations on his functions call for statement. One danger is that the "study of man" can sometimes seem so total that it becomes *the* study of man. One ethnocentrism is substituted for another. The anthropologist's comments seem to glitter like gold—to him at least—because for a time they are new and fresh. He becomes a kind of cultural oracle. But when his stock of illuminating asides on the Upper Pukapuka on the Lower Zambesi runs low he will be forced to take another stance. Then he may be reduced to making broad, conjectural statements that he may confuse as final judgments or substantial generalizations rather than a potential source of hypotheses. He may fool some of the educators some of the time, but he can't fool them all.

Further, the anthropologist's experience with small and relatively integrated societies sometimes gives him an extraordinary naivete about the complex relations in our own society—a society that he himself may have escaped from—into anthropology. He fails to see complications and looks for integrating features, consistencies, and values where there are none. And as a consequence he may make outlandish pronouncements as to what educators should or should not do.

Beyond this, the anthropologist is not always particularly sophisticated intellectually. He is often not sufficiently familiar with the social and intellectual histories of the great civilizations, including his own. He may have become an anthropologist in order to become an explorer (subconsciously, of course), or buried himself so thoroughly in ethnographies that he has no room in his head for other thoughts. If so, his suggestions to educators would fall short of the mark when he talks about cultural transmission, as he would not know the culture to be transmitted.

And there are limitations inherent in the culture concept. Although the utility of this construct cannot be denied, it is not a theory in itself. It is not sufficiently dynamic, or field-oriented, but tends to contain itself around patterning phenomena that provide form but not function as variables for analysis. This may in fact be part of the reason for the anthropologist's descriptive bias—a limitation that American anthropology is just now getting over. He will usually find in the educational context that he has to turn to other disciplines for concepts and methods in order to do adequate research on or even adequate talking about any single dynamic problem in education in our society. Then perhaps he ceases being an anthropologist and becomes a social scientist with a crosscultural perspective, and a molar approach to problems.

## CONCLUSION

This overview has been an attempt to present some of the actual and potential articulations between education and anthropology, and is designed to set the stage for the papers and discussions that follow. No attempt can be made to anticipate the many issues and rich content of the conference as a whole. The overview should serve to alert both educators and anthropologists to some of the problems in communication that will prevail. The anthropologists have been asked to do a very difficult thing: to address themselves to problems in a relatively unfamiliar context, using whatever tools and materials they find appropriate. The anthropological identity may be lost in the attempt, or the understandings intended may be lost because the identity is kept. In any event, the anthropologists must use certain criteria of relevance that presumably stem from within anthropology—yet be aware of the perceptual field of the educator audience. The educators must accept the necessity for internal relevance of anthropological material—and yet apply their own criteria for selection and modification of what is offered. This means that both anthropologists and educators must exercise a species of "double awareness" that is always necessary in interdisciplinary efforts but which is rarely exercised sufficiently. The conference is an experiment in this possibility.

## REFERENCES

Boas, Franz. 1928. *Anthropology and Modern Life*. New York: W. W. Norton.
Brameld, Theodore. 1950. *Patterns of Educational Philosophy*. New York: World Book.
Brown, Francis J. 1954. *Educational Sociology*, 2nd ed. New York: Prentice-Hall.
Bryson, Lyman. 1939. Anthropology and Education. In D. D. Brand, Fred Harvey (Eds.), *So live the works of men*. Albuquerque, pp. 107–15.
Cole, Lawrence E., and William F. Bruce. 1950. *Educational Psychology*. New York: World Book.
Cook, Lloyd A., and Elaine F. Cook. 1950. *A Sociological Approach to Education*. New York: McGraw-Hill.
Cronbach, Lee J. 1954. *Educational Psychology*. New York: Harcourt Brace.
Davis, Allison. 1952. *Social Class Influences on Learning*. Cambridge: Harvard University Press.

Davis, Allison, and Robert J. Havighurst. 1947. *Father of the Man.* Boston: Houghton Mifflin.

Eells, Kenneth, Allison Davis, Robert J. Havighurst, Virgil E. Herrick, and Ralph W. Tyler. 1951. *Intelligence and Cultural Differences.* Chicago: University of Chicago Press.

Ehrich, Robert W. 1947. The Place of Anthropology in a College Education. *Harvard Educational Review,* XVII, 57–61.

Goldenweiser, Alexander. 1939. Culture and Education. *Stanford Education Conference.* New York: Social Education.

Hanna, Paul. 1954. "Needed Changes in Elementary Curriculum." Paper presented at the AASA meeting, Atlantic City.

*Harvard Educational Review.* 1953. Social Class Structure and American Education. Parts I and II: XXIII, 149–338.

Havighurst, Robert J., and Hilda Taba. 1949. *Adolescent Character and Personality.* New York: Wiley.

Herskovits, Melville J. 1943. Education and Cultural Dynamics. *American Journal of Sociology,* XLVIII, 109–121.

_____. 1948. *Man and His Works.* New York: Knopf.

Hewett, Edgar L. 1904. Anthropology and Education. *American Anthropologist,* VI, 574–575.

_____. 1905. Ethnic Factors in Education. *American Anthropologist,* VII, 1–16.

Howells, W. W. 1952. The Study of Anthropology. *American Anthropologist,* LIV, 1–7.

Johnson, Charles S. (ed.). 1943. Education and the Cultural Process. *American Journal of Sociology,* XLVIII, 11–36.

Keesing, Felix M. 1937. *Education in Pacific Countries.* Shanghai: Kelly and Walsh.

Klineberg, Otto. 1935. *Racial Differences.* New York: Harper.

_____. 1947. "Racial Psychology," in Ralph Linton (Ed.), *The Science of Man in the World Crisis.* New York: Columbia University Press.

_____. 1951. *Race and Psychology.* UNESCO.

Kluckhohn, Clyde. 1949. *Mirror for Man.* New York: McGraw-Hill.

Kroeber, A. L. (Ed.). 1953. *Anthropology Today.* Chicago: University of Chicago Press.

Martin, William E, and Celia Stendler. 1953. *Child Development.* New York: Harcourt Brace.

Mead, Margaret. 1943. "Our Educational Emphasis in Primitive Perspective." *American Journal of Sociology,* XLVIII, 633–639.

_____. 1946. "Professional Problems of Education in Dependent Countries." *The Journal of Negro Education,* XV, 346–357.

_____. 1950. *The School in American Culture.* Cambridge: Harvard University Press.

Montessori, Maria. 1913. *Pedagogical Anthropology.* New York: Frederick Stokes.

Opler, Morris. 1947. Cultural Alternatives and Educational Theory. *Harvard Educational Review,* XVII, 28–44.

Pettit, George A. 1946. Primitive Education in North America. *University of California Publications in American Archeology and Ethnology,* XLIII, 11–82.

Pressey, Sidney, and Francis Robinson. 1944. *Psychology and the New Education.* New York: Harper.

Robbins, Florence G. 1953. *Educational Sociology.* New York: Henry Holt and Company.

Rosenstiel, Annette. 1954. Educational Anthropology: A New Approach to Cultural Analysis. *Harvard Educational Review, XXIV,* 28–36.

Skinner, Charles E. (Ed.). 1950. *Elementary Educational Psychology.* New York: Prentice-Hall.

Spindler, G. D. 1946. Anthropology May Be an Answer. *Journal of Education, CXXIX,* 130–131.

Taba, Hilda, and staff. 1950. *Elementary Curriculum in Intergroup Relations.* Washington, DC: American Council on Education.

Warner, W. Lloyd et al. 1949. *Democracy in Jonesville.* New York: Harper.

Warner, W. Lloyd, Robert J. Havighurst, and Martin B. Loeb. 1944. *Who Shall Be Educated?* New York: Harper.

Whiting, John, and Irvin L. Child. 1953. *Child Training and Personality.* New Haven: Yale University Press.

Willcockson, Mary (Ed.). 1950. *Social Education of Young Children.* Washington, DC: National Council for the Social Studies, NEA.

# The Transmission
# of American Culture*

## (1959)

*George D. Spindler*

The transmission of American culture and the teacher as a cultural transmitter are the subjects of this chapter. Within this framework the analysis will center on the unintended, unanticipated consequences of cultural transmission in schools in our society that are at variance with the intended goals of transmission.

This is one of the less well illuminated areas of educational practice and conceptualization. Discrepancies between intended educational goals and what is actually transmitted are present in curriculum design, in the literature of textbooks and teaching aids, and in classroom procedure. They permeate all phases of the student–teacher relationship, the professional education of teachers, and the very subculture of education.

*Adapted with revisions and abridgment from *The Transmission of American Culture*, copyright 1959 by the President and Fellows of Harvard College, and reprinted by permission of the publisher, the Harvard Graduate School of Education. Revised for publication in *Education and Cultural Process*, 1974, G. Spindler, ed. New York: Holt, Rinehart and Winston.

The treatment of processes within this focus must be exploratory and incomplete, for there is so much that is unknown. But the problem is important. With more knowledge of the ways in which the goals of education can be defeated in the very process of education, we may achieve better control over the results of education.

## THE TRANSMISSION OF CONFLICTS
## IN AMERICAN CULTURE

The discrepancies and conflicts between intent and outcome, between ideal and real that the teacher transmits to children in any classroom must originate in the culture. As Theodore Brameld has demonstrated so well in his book, *The Cultural Foundations of Education*, the educator must look beyond the schools and the people in them to the cultural context of education, in order to understand the problems and aspirations of education.

The American culture is dynamic and is composed of many once-separate streams of cultural influence. It is adapting to radical changes in the human environment. It is now, and for some time has been, a culture notable for the conflicts woven into the very fabric of its value system. We place a traditional value upon thrift, but we appear to believe even more strongly in the value of keeping up good appearances that depend upon mortgages and installment payments, which make thrift impossible as we play the game according to the rules of the American Dream. We believe in deferring satisfactions to the future but want the benefits of deferment now. We believe that success is to be won by hard work, but emphasize "personality" and social contacts as means to getting ahead. We laud honesty as a virtue but acknowledge the primacy of pragmatic expediency in real life. We are egalitarian in ideal and in much of our practice, but indulge in wide-ranging and destructive expressions of invidious prejudice. We deny sexuality but titillate ourselves with sex in our mass media, dress, and imagery. Our culture is patterned in conflicts that in part mirror the struggle between the puritan ethic and the demands and opportunities of an industrializing society of abundance. And we are undergoing the confused transformation from traditional to emergent values that I have already described and will apply further in this analysis.

When I discuss the transmission of conflicts and discrepancies in our classrooms I am not, therefore, simply blaming the teacher. If the teacher is a cultural transmitter and if teachers have experienced and, in some degree, internalized the conflicts in values described, it is probable they will transmit them to children. But it is equally important to avoid the error of assuming that because these conflicts and discrepancies are present in our culture they *should* be transmitted. If we accept this proposition, we accept the defeat and contradiction of many of our declared goals.

To illustrate concretely what is meant, permit me to describe certain educational situations in which discrepancies are transmitted. In doing so I will borrow from examples afforded by two of my anthropological colleagues as well as from my own research. I have reinterpreted what my colleagues have written to fit the format of my analysis, and they can be held responsible only for the observations that provide the data.

The first example is provided by Jules Henry's "Attitude Organization in Elementary School Classrooms," (Henry, 1963). He points out that one of the most striking characteristics of American culture is the phenomenon of intragroup aggression, which finds its most pure expression in "witch hunts." This "witch's brew," he declares, consists of destructive criticism of others, docility, feelings of vulnerability, fear of internal (intragroup) hostility, confession of evil deeds, and boredom.

He describes a number of specific situations in elementary school classrooms where elements of this pattern are inadvertently transmitted by teachers. He does not find the full-blown pattern in the majority of classrooms in which he conducted research observations. But he found it in a few and was able to identify elements and tendencies in this direction in more.

For example, he describes one classroom situation where the teacher organized a Vigilance Club. The purpose of this club was to teach children to be better citizens. The club functioned as a means by which the "good deeds" and "bad deeds" of the children could be recorded in a booklet kept by the teacher for each child. Every child was required to report the wrongs and rights of his own conduct during the week, and the class was asked to contribute information about his behavior. Miscreants were placed in an "isolation ward" in the back of the room until their record was favorably balanced. In the recorded observations of this procedure it becomes abundantly clear that intragroup aggression, docility in conforming to external pressure of the group and to teacher authority, feelings of vulnerability and fear of detection, and the value of spying and confession were activated and encouraged and, therefore, transmitted. These must be regarded as unintended consequences of the teacher's purposeful action, since the intended purpose was to encourage good citizenship. These unintended consequences did not appear out of a vacuum. The pattern was already available in the culture, was present in varying degrees of latency in the children, but was activated in the behavioral setting created by the teacher.

This is admittedly an extreme example, and is cited as almost a caricature of what normally happens in many classrooms. Let me extract another less extreme illustration from those provided by his work. In one fifth grade classroom the period was devoted to short reports and stories by the children. The class was requested by the teacher to criticize each report. Children responded by pointing out that the sentences were too short, there was too much detail, there was too little expression, and so on. No positive criticisms emerged, nor did the teacher seek out any. Probably many teachers would do so, since they would realize that criticism by one's peers, particularly at that age level, is more likely to be destructive than constructive. But the net effect of this procedure was to support children in their tendency to be carpingly critical of their fellows and, therefore, to contribute to the development of patterns of intragroup aggression that were already internalized in some degree by the children from their culture. The experience was organized by the teacher, however, for the purpose of increasing skill in writing and reporting, and also, I infer, to contribute to learning to "take criticism"—one of the frequently cited criteria for good adjustment. The contradiction of ends and means is apparent.

Another documentation of the processes involved in transmitting cultural discrepancies in educational situations is provided by Dorothy Lee (Lee, 1963). She has attempted to answer this question: "What covert attitudes and concepts are communicated through the home economics program in public schools?" She makes it explicit that the study is concerned with what is communicated implicitly, unintentionally, and contrary to the intention of the program. Her work has been particularly influential in the development of my own thinking on the matter.

Professor Lee used state and city manuals for teachers of home economics, representing different regions, and one textbook in common use as sources of data. Admittedly, teachers deviate from manuals in actual instruction. This study therefore provides illustration of the fact that cultural discrepancies are found in the design of classroom procedures and not only in their implementation.

These programs, it is stated in the manuals, are designed to help the student develop a healthy personality through participation in human relations in the home, and to help students mature into adults who will establish democratic, happy, cooperative homes, as well as to pass on the skills necessary for homemaking.

She cites a number of instances where the design of the manuals can be interpreted as introducing contradictions to this purpose. For example, in one manual, presumably not atypical, the lesson on family relationships states other objectives: to realize the purpose of restrictions, to realize one's contributions to family conflict, and to help the student to learn ways of reducing conflict. The student is to relate herself to a family life that is full of conflict and restriction. "Why do parents always say 'no'?" "What can a boy or girl do about a 'pesky' sister or brother?"—These are some of the questions posed for the student.

Other examples drawn from those she provides include the contradiction between the declared goal of learning to share meaningful experiences in the home and an implementation of this goal in curriculum design that provides great detail on selecting recipes, nutritional needs, finishing seams and doing laundry, but nothing on who shares these activities or who is being helped. Another dualism is conveyed by the declared emphasis on creative enjoyment of the home and of family living but an implementation in design that characterizes housekeeping as work that needs to be done efficiently so that one can have more leisure time away from it all. Only escape has value. Ordinary home life seems to provide little emotional nourishment. And, lastly, another declared goal is to develop mature personalities (that development, presumably, requires some sustenance for the inner self), but it is solely the external characteristics of good grooming, pleasant manners, being popular and making friends, and being efficient about one's expenditure of time that are stressed.

It is only fair to point out that Dorothy Lee felt that her interpretation might have been biased by certain personal values that she holds because she was a Greek before she was an American. Apparently a happy life, sharing family activities, enjoying the ordinary routine of family living, and developing a self-actualized personality are valued in Greek culture. But I have always thought they were valued in American culture as well. What is important for our purposes here is that the design of the manuals for homemaking includes these values as goals but also includes designs for implementation that are in varying degrees of contradiction to them. In one sense this design is therefore an accurate projection of American culture. This makes it all the more important that the contradictions be analyzed and perhaps in some instances reduced or eliminated.

For a last example of direct transmission of obvious but culturally patterned contradictions, I would like to use one of my own case studies of teachers and their classrooms.

The cultural transmitter in this case was a highly respected teacher in a large elementary school, who had certain duties as a counselor. He originated from a respectable immigrant family and had improved his social status during his lifetime by becoming a schoolteacher. The particular situation from which I have extracted certain verbatim records to follow was one of the "rites of passage" that occur now and then throughout the educational life cycle of children. The students in the eighth grade were being prepared for the choice of programs in high school and were making out proposed study lists under his guidance. The class group consisted of thirty-five children, twenty-four of whom were Mexican-Americans. The range of scores on the California Mental Maturity test was 80 to 120, with a median of 102. There was a broadly corresponding variety of reading and academic achievement represented in the group. I will present a few items from the verbal interaction of the teacher-counselor and the students.

T:      You must be a good citizen, or they won't accept you. Now, what do you need to get into Orthodox State College? (*Children raise hands, repeat answers previously learned.*) What do you need to get into Junior College?" (*Students respond likewise.*)

T:      In arranging your programs for next year, there are certain things that everyone must take, so we'll just put them down. You will all take P.E., English, and Social Studies. (*Teacher writes these down on the board opposite numbers 1, 2, and 3*). Now you have to decide whether you want to take Algebra or not. You have to take math all the way through high school if you want to be an engineer. Now, if you've gotten B's and C's all the way through eighth grade, what are your chances of doing well in ninth grade Algebra? (*Students murmur various things.*) That's right! Not so good! So what can you do?

S:      Try to raise your grade.

T:      Yes.

S:      Work harder.

T:      That's one thing. But what else? ... Do like I did when I wanted to be a singer but found I couldn't sing. What did I do? Yes. ... that's right; I changed my plans.... With respect to language, how many here speak Spanish? (*Six of the Mexican-Americans raised their hands, but all speak some Spanish.*) It will help you if you do. But you have to realize that there is some work to homework! It is good to take Spanish if you want to go on to college and need a language. But you can't take Spanish and General Business. They come at the same period. Now, one of the things you have to do is to be neat and orderly. If you aren't good at that it might be hard for you until you learn to do it better.

T:      Now here we have Mechanical Drawing. This is exclusively a boy's class. I don't know why some girls couldn't take it if they wanted to. But only boys take it. Now Home-making is for girls, so you can take that.

T:      Now when you come to see me, if I tell you to take General Business instead of Spanish, it should be understood that you don't have to take it. You can do as you wish. But it means that I think you will do better in General Business. (*Several more subject choices are covered.*)

T:      And here is typing. It looks interesting when you pass the typing room, doesn't it? But do you know there aren't any letters on those keyboards? You have to watch a chart at the front of the room, and if you look at the keyboard, you fail!

Of course a great deal more went on during this hour of counseling. I have purposefully selected those verbal items that constitute the most clear indications of bias in cultural transmission. And this is always unfair to the cultural transmitter. But I believe the extracted items accurately reveal persistent trends in his counseling of the mixed Mexican-American and Anglo groups in the eighth grade.

After this particular class session, the teacher-counselor said, "This is a passive group. There is no spark in there. The better groups get quite excited about this. Of course, most of the better groups are college-preparatory and perhaps only three or four of these students will go to college." Previous to the session, in his statement of educational philosophy, he had commented, "I believe that our job is to make the most of the potential of each child. Of course there is a wide range of ability among our students. A good many of them will never go on to college. And we have to do the best we can to help them on to a satisfactory adjustment."

He was defeating his own aims in the way he handled this crucial rite of passage, this point of compression in the relation of the child and his culture where choices made affect future development decisively. He opened the gates to valued channels of development and then shut them in the children's faces. And he did not open the gates to any alternative channels. What he transmitted, it seems to me, was that the only worthwhile goal was to go to college so that one could become an engineer or something equivalent, that if the child did not have the necessary qualifications there was no other dignified and worthy choice, and that most of the members of this class group did not have the necessary qualifications.

If this person were a small, mean individual with explicit prejudices, and if he were not concerned with making the most of the potential of each child, I would be less concerned. But he is not small and mean. He is a generous, well-intended person, and believes in democratic opportunity. In his counseling he projects his own struggle to improve his status, mirrors the discrepancy in our culture between ideal and real in the definition of opportunity, and inadvertently defeats his own professed aims.

## THE ACCULTURATION OF THE SCHOOL TEACHER

What has been established so far is that our culture is one in which conflicts in values, and between goals and the means to them, are present and patterned. And that teachers, as cultural transmitters, convey these patterned conflicts to children in their classrooms, with the consequence that many professed goals are defeated, or at least obscured. It should also be clear that I have not been castigating teachers. They are the agents of their culture.

A further step must be taken if we are to see the full meaning and scope of the problem. Teachers are a special group. They are not selected at random as official culture transmitters; they are trained and accredited to that status and role. They must take courses in educational psychology, the social foundations of education, curriculum design, philosophy and history of education and the methods of education, and must do supervised practice teaching. In short, they must attend teacher-training institutions and graduate with the stamp of approval from the established professional cadre. But professional educational instruction and training consist not only of courses and training in techniques. Every institution with a history and internal organization and a specialized personnel has a culture or, more properly, a subculture. Certain values, symbols, beliefs, and certain basic premises are patterned into the structure and process of the institution. The institutions of professional education—the teacher-training schools and the literature of education—are no exception.

At this point it is necessary to refer back to the traditional and emergent value patterns. The traditional pattern includes emphasis on thrift, self-denial, faith in the future, a strong emphasis on success and a belief that hard work was the means to it, absolute moral norms, and a strong value placed upon the individual. The emergent pattern includes value placed upon sociability, sensitivity to the feelings of others, a relativistic attitude, a present-time orientation, and high value placed upon the group.

The dynamic process of greatest relevance to us at the moment is the relationship between the culture that the schoolteacher brings to the professional teacher-training institution subculture and the patterning of that subculture, the adaptation that the teacher-in-training makes to this patterning and the consequences in selective culture transmission in the classroom.

This is a complex relationship with many subtle ramifications. I have outlined it in the preceding chapter. Because an understanding of it is essential to the logic of the analysis to follow, I will restate and expand the argument. It is well established that the majority of public school teachers originate from a middle and lower-middle social class culture. The value pattern that I have termed "traditional" is probably found in this cultural context in its most pure form. To the extent this is so, it means that whatever selective processes are operating tend to bring many people of traditionalistic value orientation into teacher-training.

The question that the anthropologist raises is—what are the characteristics of the subculture of the teacher-training institution to which these students bring their traditionalist orientations? Analysis of a sample of some of the influential literature of curriculum design for elementary education reveals that there is present a strong values bias that fits in general terms the "emergent" pattern. The literature of child development and educational psychology reveals some of the same trends. Interpretations of the social behavior of boys and girls, intended for educational consumption, provide both implicit and explicit value judgments in the same pattern. The popularity of sociometric techniques is diagnostic of this orientation. The topical content of many of our teacher-training courses suggests it as well.

The basic premise underlying the specific emergent values is that what is most important is the social adjustment of the child. His place in the group, the responses of his peers to him, his ability to get along well, to work and play with others are penultimate concerns. This is not all bad by any means. The emphasis on social adjustment is the educator's attempt to meet the demands of a new kind of society, where this kind of adjustment is of vital importance. When balanced by a concern for individual differences, by support for the deviating child, the creative student, intellectual development, and the acquisition of cognitive skills, and when it does not become a form of "groupism," this emphasis on social adjustment is a possible compensatory process for some of the more harshly competitive anxiety-arousing patterns of our culture.

But the point is that however understandable and useful the emphasis may be, this pattern of values incorporated in the ethos of professional education is frequently at variance with what the new teacher-in-training brings into the situation. The neophyte in training must reorient his value system wherever the conflict in values is encountered.

When neophyte teachers in training or people in any other acculturating group adapt to sharply disjunctive value systems, their adaptations assume predictable forms. The individual meets the new value system and feels threatened because it challenges his established, familiar, and comfortable values. He does not, of course, necessarily interpret the experience in these terms. He is more likely to see it as a personal conflict, which heightens the intensity of the threat. After some exploration in the new dimensions of feeling and belief offered to him by the opposing system, his feeling of threat overcomes him and he seeks refuge in the comforting shelter of his established values. But something has changed. He has been driven back to his "native state" by threat. Therefore he overcompensates, and rigidifies the original system in what may be psychologically termed a reaction formation, or culturally termed a "nativistic reaffirmation." I will term him a "reaffirmative traditionalist" in the framework of this analysis. The teacher of this type will tend to be rigid in his uncompromising projection of traditional values in his classroom behavior.

An alternative adaptive response is represented by the person who encounters the new value system which is sharply disjunctive with his own, likewise feels threatened by the conflict in personal terms, but adapts by overcompensating in the direction of the new system. Perhaps he is more threatened by the possibility of being out of step than he is by the demand to change. He uncritically appropriates the new values in their entirety and frequently becomes a strident proselytizer for them. This kind of teacher I term a "compensatory emergentist." His channels of communication with children, and his criteria for their behavior, become narrowed to individual-in-harmony-with-the-group. "Groupism" reigns in his classroom. Individualistic differences and deviations become smothered by group conformity.

A third alternative adaptive response is exhibited by the person who encounters the conflict of value systems and superficially internalizes segments of both but does not rework them into any coherent synthesis. He is a mixed type but quite different from a type that I shall describe shortly. He is usually not particularly thoughtful about the conflicts he encounters and leaves them unresolved, but still a part of his acquired culture. This person as a teacher is likely to vacillate between different modes of group leadership and different modes of interaction with individual children. Obvious discontinuities in his classroom management cause trouble for both him and his students. We can call him the "vacillator."

The fourth alternative is a happier one than any of the others. This person comes into the acculturative situation with a capacity for adjustment to differences in values and conflicts between them. Usually he is thoughtful or philosophic-minded and has the ability to combine useful features from more than one system of belief on a rational basis. He does not need to overcompensate as a defense against conflict because he is not threatened by it. He is a mixed type but does not internalize the mixture segmentally. He recombines the aspects from both systems into a creatively coherent synthesis. I have labeled this an "adjusted" type.

As a matter of fact I believe that increasing numbers of teachers are of this latter type. They exhibit workable combinations of what seem to be the best of both the emergent and traditional values. For instance, they accept the need of the individual to be a member of the group but believe that the individual should also be self-possessed and self-actualized. They believe that hard work is necessary for success but that there is no point in being unpleasantly puritanic about it. They take a relativistic, tolerant view of differences between individuals and between groups, but they have a personal moral code that governs their own behaviors within broad but definite limits. Whether they represent a shift in the kind of training they receive or whether they represent a change in the culture of generations, or both, is not clear. In any event, I am happy to see them and hope their numbers increase, for I am convinced that large numbers of teachers, at least new ones, are reaffirmative traditionalists, compensatory emergentists, or vacillators.

A value judgment is made here because it seems clear that teachers fitting into the first two adaptive categories tend to exhibit highly selective biases as culture transmitters. They transmit in narrow channels with few alternatives due to their rigidity. Without intending to do so, they open some doors to self-cultivating developments for some children but close them for many others. And the vacillator, though he is not rigid and transmits along many channels, issues only weak signals and produces little but static as a result.

## A CASE STUDY ILLUSTRATION

To illustrate further what is meant, another case study that is representative of others we have made of elementary school teachers and their classrooms will be presented.[1] The salient features of this case classify him as a re-affirmative traditionalist. This type may be encountered more frequently in other parts of the country than it is on the West Coast where my observations were made, and the analysis should, therefore, have wide applicability.

This fifth-grade teacher is a young man of twenty-five. He originates from a clearly traditionalistic middle-class family. His father is an executive of middle rank in a wholesale business organization and belongs to the usual service and fraternal organizations. His mother is college educated and active in the League of Women Voters. His father is not college educated and achieved his position by hard work. Both parents like to play bridge. They belong to the country club and own a summer cottage where the subject spent many happy hours as a boy. Twice during the subject's lifetime the family moved to more expensive homes in better neighborhoods.

The subject likes to play golf, drinks socially but moderately, attends the Methodist church, and reads the local newspaper, *Reader's Digest*, and the *Saturday Evening Post*. He aspires to be a school administrator and regards his teaching experience as preparation for that role. He is a pleasant, good-looking young man who appears somewhat constrained but not visibly anxious. He is well liked by his colleagues and is rated as one of the outstanding young teachers in the school system.

His professed aims in teaching, beyond the management of instruction so that his students acquire the requisite knowledge, are to bring out creativity to the maximum ability of each child, help children to express themselves clearly and help children to learn how to get along with each other. He states that he tries to give every student in his class a chance to participate. He prides himself particularly on being fair and just with all the children. He says explicitly that every student gets a "fair break" in his classroom. He feels that he is very concerned about the problems of his students and always tries

---

[1]The case study was done when the author was a member of a research team operating out of the School of Education at Stanford University.

to understand them. His statements about *his aims and his* relations with his students are consistent with what his principal, his supervisor, and the members of the central staff of the school system say about him.

He told me that many of his teacher-training courses were "a waste of time." In probing this blanket indictment of professional educational preparation as he experienced it I discovered that he was dismayed and upset by certain points of view that he perceived as consistently appearing in his course work. He felt that his preceptors were trying "to give the school to the children," that they were more concerned with how children adjusted than what they learned, and that his instructors stressed cooperation, or at least group harmony, at the expense of competition. All of this he lumps together under the label "progressive education," which he rejects with feeling, but which he is content to leave as an unanalyzed abstraction.

He fits the criteria for the reaffirmative-traditionalist teacher type. He originated from a family culture where the traditional values previously described apparently existed in virtually pure form. He encountered the emergent-oriented values of the professional teacher subculture. He sensed the conflict, felt the threat, rejected the threatening alternatives, and sought refuge in the shelter of his original values.

The further presentation of data on this teacher and his classroom will include a few items selected from a considerable mass of information. We worked together for many months, and his file is extensive. But these few items will establish the pattern that permeated many of the interrelationships between him and his students.

One of our standard practices in case studies is to ask the teacher to fill out a form titled "Information Concerning the Student." It includes items on academic and social adjustment in the child's previous school, his home situation, approximate I.Q. test performance, special interests, hobbies, health history, his ambitions and plans for the future. The teacher is requested to fill out this form for each student without recourse to written records. He is scored on the number of items of information. A perfect score, indicating highest knowledge, would be ten.

This teacher averaged 3.2 for the forms filled out on all of his thirty-three students, which is lower, on the average, than the score attained by other teachers in our sample. The mean of his knowledge concerning children in his group originating from families of highest socioeconomic status was 4.9. His mean score for those of lowest status was 2.8. It is apparent that some bias is operating that tends to contradict his professed aims.

He was asked to list the names of those students in his class that he considered to be the best adjusted—emotionally and socially. Of the seven children he listed as best adjusted, only one child was included who originated from a family of less than middle-class status, and this child exhibited strong status-achievement drives. He was also asked to list the names of those students whom he considered least well adjusted. Of these seven children, only one came from a middle-class setting. The other six were from families of lower-class or special ethnic status. It is possible, of course, that he was correct in his appraisal, even from a psychiatric point of view. Other evidence concerning the behavior of these children indicates that he was not accurate in a number of instances. For our purposes at the moment what is significant is that the same bias in perception is revealed in this as was exhibited in his knowledge about students.

He was asked to list the 25 percent of his class group with whom he thought he had the most effective relationship. He listed eight children, and of these eight, five were from families of middle-class social status. He was also asked to list the 25 percent of his group with whom he felt he had the least effective relationship. All but one of these children were from families of lower-class status. Other evidence indicates that in this instance he appraised the situation more or less accurately. The pattern of selective perception, of differential bias in his interrelationships with children in his class group is, however, strengthened.

He was requested to name those children who were the most popular with or most accepted by their classmates. He listed eight, only one of whom represented a lower-class position. In only three instances did he name the same children that the students themselves did, according to sociometric information collected from the class. He was also asked to name those children to whom nobody in the class paid much attention. He listed six children, two of whom were middle-class in origin. The other four were from families of lower-class status. In four instances his perceptions matched those of the classroom group, but there were ten comparatively isolated children in that group, according to the sociometric data collected from the class. Of these ten, five were children originating from middle-class backgrounds, four of whom he missed in his appraisal. Again, there is a clear pattern of selective bias in his perception of the children in his classroom. It is difficult for him to implement his professed aims in the context of this pattern.

A few excerpts from anecdotal and verbatim records will strengthen the interpretation. One boy, who was quite isolated in the interaction among the boys in the class and who chose only girls in his own responses to a sociometric questionnaire was described by the teacher as a "real go-getter, one of the most magnetic personalities of any young child I have ever known. He has a very warm personality—truthful, sincere, with a good sense of humor. Tom gets along well with anyone, anywhere." This boy sometimes brought sample bottles of hair tonic, shoe polish, simple toys and gadgets to class in a small suitcase and tried to sell them to the other children. One day when I was observing, he was allowed to "make his pitch" before the class. He was, indeed, a motivated, magnetic, salesman, and probably will go far. The teacher apparently, perceived only this attribute—one that is congruent with some of his own achievement drives and their precedents in his family models. There is much else about this child that he needed to know in order to guide his development effectively.

In another instance of the same type the teacher described one girl as having a "horrible personality … egoistic, insincere, false. She never has a nice word to say about anyone but herself. I don't particularly care for Charlotte." She was the friendship choice of the "star-of-attraction,"—the girl most frequently chosen as a friend by the other girls in their sociometric responses. She was observed to interact effectively with most of the other girls. She had a high rating in status—reputation data collected from the class. She came from a broken home in a lower-class setting.

In his response to oral reports by the children about what they were reading in their spare time, his gestures, facial expression, bodily postures, comments and silences were all patterned in the framework of the same selective bias. He communicated approval of most of what the children of middle-class origins said, and of what they were reading. He communicated lack of interest, or suppressed distaste for what the children of lower-class origins said, how they said it, and of what they were reading.

I have almost too much data on this teacher and his classroom, and have had to struggle against the inclination to continue with examples that all substantiate the same pattern of bias and selective perception in his relationships with his students. He interacted effectively with only a minority segment of his classroom group—that segment which matched his own aspirations and values, derived from his own cultural setting. He opened doors for this selected group to channels of development they were already heading toward, and he sped them on their way. But for the larger number of his students, those who did not match his values and aspirations, he closed doors and left them waiting in the foyer of our culture.

Analysis of all of the data collected about this teacher and his operations in the classroom leads to the conclusion that his consistent selective bias was in part due to his own cultural background. But this pattern was accentuated by his reactive adjustment to the conflict between the culture he brought with him when he entered professional training to become a teacher and the special subculture he encountered there.

His exercise of the role of cultural transmitter was in contradiction to his own professed aims, and even to his own beliefs about what he actually did in the classroom. He was not giving all children an opportunity to participate; he did not understand their problems; he was not being fair and just to all his students; they were not all getting a "fair break." All these aims and beliefs were contradicted by his highly selective positive interaction with a small segment of his class. He was wearing cultural blinders that limited his perceptions to a single channel. His transmitting apparatus was sending out positive signals only to that segment responding within the frequency of that single channel.

## A CROSSCULTURAL PERSPECTIVE

Now I would like to apply a crosscultural perspective to this case and some of the inferences drawn from it. In one of my seminars we have been reviewing the available literature on the educative process in a wide variety of nonliterate, so-called "primitive" societies. One of the concepts we have found particularly useful is one we have termed "cultural compression." The meaning of the term is simple. It refers to any period of time in the life cycle of the individual when he encounters a culturally patterned reduction of alternatives for behavior, usually through restrictive cultural definitions of new roles appropriate to his particular stage of maturation. During these periods, culturally normative restrictions are placed upon him. They are the points in his development as a creature of culture when the norms of his group and society bear in upon him with the greatest intensity and where, as a consequence, he undergoes a change in social identity. I will apply this concept to the educational process in cultures other than our own, and then return to a brief reconsideration of the educative process in our society and the case of our teacher in this broadened perspective.

Cultural compressions may be detected in the life cycle in any society at a number of developmental stages. Toilet training and weaning are forms of cultural compression. So is induction to work. Culturally patterned preparations for assumption of adult roles are particularly critical points in the compressive sequence. In our examination of the literature available on forty nonliterate societies we have isolated a number of types of cultural compression sequence. We find that we can even draw graphs of them. Imagine two horizontal lines of equal length, one above the other. Place the newborn infant at one end between the lines and start him through his developmental stages. Contract the lines in such a way as to portray the points in his progressive experience where cultural restrictions are placed upon him in any specific cultural context. Expand them so as to portray the points in his experience where cultural restrictions are lifted as they no longer become appropriate to his age and status. This imagery should serve to indicate the kinds of models we have constructed. The specific types for different cultures are not relevant for our purposes here.

We find that the types differ sharply from each other in the sequence of cultural compressions during the prepubertal years. We find in all of them, however, that the channels of self and cultural development become progressively narrowed as time goes on. Eventually most alternative channels are eliminated, and only a single major one (but possibly several secondary ones) is provided for each sex in the more homogeneous societies. In order to insure that the cultural boundaries of this channel are internalized by the developing individual many societies introduce dramatically compressive restrictions at the time of puberty in the form of initiation ceremonies. In these societies this period is a time of very intensive training and of very severe restriction. Dramatic rituals, isolation from home and familiar surroundings and people, the use of forbidding strangers as instructors, heighten the effect of the restrictions and cultural transmissions that occur at this time. And there is only one correct major channel into which the initiate is compressed. A paper by C. W. M. Hart (Hart, 1963) has stimulated my thinking in this direction. He describes the initiation experience among the Tiwi of North Australia.

> So far his life has been easy; now it is hard.... The boy aged 12 or 13, used to noisy, boisterous, irresponsible play, is expected and required to sit still for hours and days at a time, saying nothing whatever but concentrating upon and endeavoring to understand long intricate instructions and "lectures" given him by his hostile and forbidding preceptors. Life has suddenly become real and earnest and the initiate is required literally to 'put away the things of a child, even the demeanor. The number of taboos and unnatural behaviors enjoined on the initiate is endless. He mustn't speak unless he is spoken to; he must eat only certain foods and often only in certain ways; at certain fixed times and in certain fixed positions. All contact with females, even speech with them, is rigidly forbidden, and this includes mother and sisters. He cannot even scratch his head with his own hand, but must do it with a special stick, and so on, through a long catalogue of special, unnatural, but obligatory behaviors covering practically every daily activity and every hour of the day and night.

Professor Hart continues in his description, but this will communicate what is meant by the notion of compression to a single channel.

This technique of cultural transmission apparently works very well in many small, nonliterate societies. They are comparatively homogeneous in value systems, there being a limited framework of values to which members of the society are committed. Specialization in roles and statuses is at a minimum compared to the situation in our society.

There are personality differences between members of my society, however "simple" it may be, but they cluster around the cultural promontories afforded by traditional values and prescribed roles. The society and its culture are tradition-oriented and unchanging, compared to ours. The highly compressive techniques are effective because the cultural boundaries and barriers imposed upon the growing individual are consistent with the character and limitations of the culture as a whole. Alternative channels for development are not needed as long as the equilibrium of the social system and the culture is not seriously disturbed.

It is easy to make the mistake of assuming that because these techniques of cultural transmission work well in comparatively simple nonliterate societies they will work for us also. Our society is extraordinarily complex with respect to the specializations required of individuals and the multiple roles and statuses provided for these specializations. And although our value system has some coherence, the alternatives and conflicts within it are impressive.

A single-channel type of cultural transmission is dysfunctional in our society. It is dysfunctional because we need variety of outlook, skills, and personality types in order to maintain our internal complexity. And if we are to adapt successfully to the rapidly changing conditions of existence forecast by the opening events of the atomic age and the first tentative steps towards the exploration of outer space and other worlds, we must provide, in our cultural transmission, for innovative channels of self and cultural development.

I think my point is clear. This teacher not only defeated some of his own educational aims in his classroom management, but he transmitted within only a single channel. He did not intend to do so, to be sure. This is precisely why his case is of interest to us. None of the illustrations of cultural transmission described were examples of wilful, intentional, misconstruing of the teacher's role. It is because cultural processes of this sort are difficult to perceive, particularly when one is caught up in them, that this topic is worthy of analysis.

## CULTURAL THERAPY

So that we do not lose focus, the major points that I have tried to communicate will be summarized briefly. I will then go on to a consideration of steps we might take towards a solution, and conclude with a statement of some unresolved dilemmas.

This chapter started with an analysis of conflicts in the patterning of American culture, and attempted to illustrate, through examples borrowed from the writings of Jules Henry and Dorothy Lee, and extracted from my own case records, how these conflicts were transmitted in our schools, with emphasis on the elementary years. I also tried to show how in the act of transmission, the professed aims of teachers were sometimes defeated and contradicted. I then moved on to an analysis of the conflict between the cultural values many teachers bring with them into professional training and those subsumed in the culture of the teacher-training institutions, and of the adaptive consequences of this conflict. The case study of the fifth-grade teacher was used to demonstrate the selective and goal-defeating process of cultural transmission that I believe to be characteristic of one of the adaptive types. I then shifted the emphasis from the transmission of culture conflicts to the problem of single-channel transmission and tried to demonstrate that this process is not only contradictory to the teacher's professed aims, but is also dysfunctional in our complex, changing society. Throughout, it has been maintained that as an agent of culture the teacher is not to be personally blamed for the consequences described.

We cannot let the matter rest there. It is true that the teacher is activating a precedent cultural condition in the process of transmission. It is also true that because this is so, changes are difficult to bring about, since the problem is of extraordinary scope. The total structure of our society and the patterning of our culture is involved. But because this is a problem in cultural process, I am going to propose a first step in solution that I will term "cultural therapy."

I did not describe my role in the teacher case studies used for illustrative purposes. This role has a direct bearing upon the notion of "cultural therapy." I was a member of a team that had a dual purpose—to collect case study data on the basic processes of education and to work in a close relationship with our teacher cases to improve their professional competence. We made no effort to select "problem" cases, and neither of these I have cited were defined as such. We merely operated on the assumption that all teachers were interested in improving their professional competence. Each member of the team took responsibility for certain cases, but we consulted with each other throughout both the research and consultative phases of the studies.

In the consultative phase of all cases we fed back to the teacher the data we had collected in the research phase. The completeness, timing, sequence, and interpretation of this "feedback" differed for each case. Some teachers can tolerate their objective image more easily than others. The fifth-grade teacher case was one who had a surprising capacity for such objective feedback except for a temporary resistance at first. He was very interested in improving his professional competence, partly because he was an ambitious man, and partly because he was a person who sincerely wanted to do the best he could for the children in his classes.

Over a period of several months I presented data to him and tried to guide him more or less gently to a broadened cultural perspective on himself, his students, and his teaching. At times, this being a mutual and cooperative relationship, he guided me, and in doing so contributed to my understanding of process in cultural transmission. We explored together his cultural background, his experience in the teacher-training institution, and the specific ways in which the dynamics resultant from this combination of cultural influences were expressed in his selective response to his students. Sometimes he was chagrined, sometimes depressed and self-doubting, sometimes angered, but always intensely interested and frequently very surprised. As a result, his perspective and understanding were broadened significantly, and he was able to interact more effectively with the broad cultural range represented by his students. He was able to do so because he had acquired a knowledge of his own cultural position, its influence upon him, the cultural range of his students, and his selective relationships within this range. I do not think he underwent a significant change in personality. It was not my intent, at least, to effect such a change. He did undergo a change in his cultural scope.

The use of the values—projective techniques in my education classes, and the analysis of data revealed by them in those classes, is an attempt to provide cultural therapy before the cultural patterns are activated in the classroom. I have no direct measure of their effectiveness. Students tell me, and give evidence in their behavior, of having experienced "cultural shock." They are able to place themselves in the matrix of values revealed in the analysis, and presumably are able to anticipate some of the ways in which their position may be a determinant in their exercise of the teacher's role, since this process is treated at length in class discussions and documented with many illustrations.

In both procedures—the "feedback" process in cooperative case studies and in the cultural analysis in the social foundations courses—the essential feature is that culture is treated as a third person. What I mean by this is that we are not dissecting the teacher's or the student's personalities; we are dissecting culture. The teacher's culture varies from the culture of others, but all variations reflect and are a part of the larger cultural context in which we all function. This makes a certain objectivity possible, which is usually impossible when the issue becomes more personal and the individual's emotional defenses are more directly aroused. The object of cultural therapy sees that his problem is not unique to him. It is shared in some degree with all of his colleagues—as a matter of fact, with everyone in his society. The "therapist" and the subject thus have the problem in common of understanding better how culture operates in and through all of us.

Cultural therapy is one direct measure we can take in our teacher-training programs to help reduce the self-defeating effect of cultural transmission in American schools. I hesitate to suggest the case study method as a direct measure because it takes a great deal of work to produce an effect on a single case. I am not optimistic about the probability that either approach will become widespread in the immediate future. We do not have the trained personnel to act as therapists. At this point I am not about to suggest that every teacher training institution start hiring anthropologists. Most anthropologists do not want to become therapists, even cultural therapists; they have other necessary and pressing work to do, and there are not enough to go around anyhow. With some help, the trainers of teachers can perform this function themselves, and the growing literature contributed by educators on the social and cultural process in American schools is an indication that this is already taking place.

## SOME UNRESOLVED DILEMMAS

Any highly schematic but exploratory analysis of the kind I have presented should be concluded with some unresolved dilemmas. In one sense I have had to attack an important source of some of the values I am trying to promote. I have argued for multiple channels of cultural transmission, and against single channel transmission. I have also tried to show how conflicts in our culture are communicated to children, to the defeat of many of the professed aims of teachers. Until we understand the dynamics of cultural transmission more fully than we can hope to now, one of the insurances against single-channel transmission is conflict transmission. Of course, the pursuit of this point of view would eventually lead us to a position at dead center, where we acknowledge the defeat of our declared educational goals as desirable. But assuredly it is true that much of the healthy variation in personalities in our society, and certainly some of the innovations that are produced in our culture, issue from the conflicts patterned into it.

Perhaps the way out of this dilemma is to acknowledge the conflicts in our culture more explicitly, even in the act of transmitting them. Some day we may reach the point in our self-knowledge where we can at least be selective of the kinds of conflicts we transmit, and control better than we do the negative and unanticipated results of our transmission.

But there is another dilemma. Presuming that we somehow learn to control the results of our intended transmissions with increased knowledge of the relationship between the teacher and his culture, and between the teacher, his culture, the students, and theirs, another order of question is raised—an ethical question.

The danger in knowledgeable and purposeful control is that this control could be used for purposes of inducing conformity, for purposes of transmitting values and patterns of behavior within a single channel. And with the trends toward conformity that seem well established in our culture, this seems highly possible.

We must exercise extreme care that a growing awareness of the cultural dimension, and particularly of the values dimension and its transmission is not misused, by accident or intent. What I am arguing for here is that the teacher, as a cultural transmitter, achieve sufficient awareness of the multidimensional processes involved so that fewer potentially creative channels of communication, of transmission, be blocked, with the consequence that more children can be effectively caught up in the educative process. But the ethical problem raised is unresolved. Here we must turn to the philosophers for help.

## REFERENCES

Hart, C. W. M. 1963. Contrasts Between Prepubertal and Postpubertal Education, pp. 400–425. In George Spindler (ed.), *Education as a Cultural Process*. New York: Holt, Rinehart & Winston.

Henry, Jules. 1963. In George Spindler (ed.), *Education and Culture*, pp. 215–233. New York: Holt, Rinehart & Winston.

Lee, Dorothy. 1963. In George Spindler (ed.), *Education and Culture, pp. 173–191. New York: Holt, Rinehart & Winston.*

# 3

# Education in a Transforming American Culture*

(1955)

*George D. Spindler*

The American public school system, and the professional educators who operate it, have been subjected to increasingly strident attacks from the public and from within its own ranks. My premise is that these attacks can best be understood as symptoms of an American culture that is undergoing transformation—transformation that produces serious conflict. I shall discuss this transformation as a problem in culture change that directly affects all of education and everyone identified with it.

The notion of social and cultural change is used persuasively, if carelessly, by too many writers to explain too much. Generalized allusions to technological change, cultural lag, the atomic age, and mass society, are more suggestive than clarifying. We must strike to the core of the change. My argument is that this core can best be conceived as a radical shift in values.

The anthropologist, and I speak as one but not for all, sees culture as a goal-oriented system. These goals are expressed, patterned, lived out by

*Reprinted, with revision, from *The Harvard Educational Review*, XXV, 1955, 145–156, with permission.

people in their behaviors and aspirations in the form of values—objects or possessions, conditions of existence, features of personality or character, and states of mind, that are conceived as desirable, and act as motivating determinants of behaviors. It is the shifts in what I believe to be the core values in American culture, and the effect of these shifts on education today, that I wish to discuss. These shifts in values will be seen as the conditions of life to which education and educators, whether progressives, experimentalists, conservatives, or in-betweens, must adapt—and to which they are adapting, albeit confusedly. My emphasis within the value framework will be upon shifts in the conception of the desirable character type, since education can never be freed from the obligation to support, if not produce, the features of personality and social character deemed desirable in society.

There is a body of literature on American culture. M. Mead (1942), C. and F. Kluckhohn (1947), C. Kluckhohn (1949), L. Warner (1953, 1959), G. Gorer (1948), D. Riesman (1950), M. Lantis (1955), S. Lipset and L. Lowenthal (1961). These writings range from the highly intuitive to the observation-based. Though there is consensus, and a surprising degree of it, on the part of these students of American culture, little they say can be or is intended by them to be taken as empirically demonstrated. These writings are useful as a starting point but most emphasize static patterning in values more than change in values. To extend the factual baseline I have been collecting relevant data from college students for the past eight years. The sample consists of several hundred students, ranging in age from 19 to 57 years, mainly participants in professional education courses, and representing socioeconomic strata describable as lower-middle to upper-middle class. The sample is as representative of this professional group and these economic strata as any regionally biased sample can be. I have used two simple value-projective techniques. The aim has been to find out what features of social character (the term I will use to designate those personality elements that are most relevant to social action) the students in the sample hold as being valuable and that presumably influence their behavior in classrooms. The first of these techniques is a series of 24 open-ended statements; such as "The individual is _____," "Intellectuals should _____." "All men are born _____." The second of these techniques is to require each student to write one brief paragraph describing his (or her) conception of the "Ideal American Boy." (sic !)

I have subjected the responses of the students in the sample to a straightforward content analysis—counting numbers of responses that fall into certain categories appearing from the data themselves. Perhaps some examples will illustrate both the techniques and the kinds of materials from which I am going to draw in the rest of this article.

From the open-ended sentence value-projective technique, results like these have been obtained: "All men are born _____," "equal" (70% of all responses), "wolves," "stupid," "dopes," "hot-blooded" (a miscellaneous negative category of 28%—provided mainly by females in the sample); "Artists are _____," "queer," "perverted," "nuts," "effeminate" (a negative-hostile category of 38% of all responses), "different," "people," "few," (a neutral category of 35%), "creative," "smart," "original," "interesting" (a positive category of 25%); "Intellectuals should _____", "be more sociable", "be more practical", "get down to earth" (a mildly derogative category of 36%), "keep it under cover", "drop dead", "shut up" (an openly hostile category of 20%), "apply their intellect", "study", "create", "think" (a neutral to positive category of 40%); Nudity is _____, "vulgar," "obscene," "profane," "repulsive" (a negative-moralistic category of 43%), "pleasant," "self-expressive," "beautiful," "healthy" (an enthusiastic–positive category of 20%), "depends on how interpreted", "all right in some places", "depends on who is looking" (a relativistic category of 30%).[1]

The values are self-evident, and do not call for discussion, as such, for the moment. What is more important is that this fairly homogeneous sample of students provides a wide range of response to each of these statements, excepting for the purposefully stereotyped "All men are born _____." And not only is there a wide range of response evidenced, but many of the categories of response to a single statement can be considered as contradictions with respect to each other. This suggests that although there are clear modalities of values in this sample, there are also differences between people and groups of people in respect to what they believe is good.

The material gathered together as results from the "Ideal American Boy" technique are even more suggestive. A sentence-content analysis reveals that the desirable features of character are ranked in the following order, from highest number of mentions, to lowest number: He should be *sociable,* like people, and get along well with them; he must be *popular,* be liked by others; he is to be *well-rounded,* he can do many things quite well, but is not an expert at anything in particular; he should be *athletic* (but not a star), and *healthy* (no qualifications); he should be *ambitious* to succeed, and have clear goals, but these must be acceptable within limited norms; he must be *considerate of others,* ever-sensitive to their feelings about him and about events; he should be a *clean-cut Christian,* moral and respectful of God and parents; he should be *patriotic;* and he should demonstrate *average academic ability,* and *average intellectual capacity.*

These are the characteristics of the ideal American boy seen as most important by a modal number (about 40%) of the students in the sample.

---

[1]Where percentages do not total 100 it is because various miscellanea are omitted.

Leadership, independence, high intelligence, high academic ability, individuality, are mentioned relatively infrequently (in about 20% of the descriptive paragraphs). But individuals do vary in the pattern of characteristics that are combined in the paragraph. Some emphasize the high achievement and individualized characteristics just mentioned. Some include elements from the modal list and combine them with these latter items. There have also been some shifts in the modal features of the ideal type over the eight years of data collection. But the characteristics listed above are mentioned most frequently.

The implications seem clear. The keynote to the character type regarded as most desirable, and therefore constituting a complex of values, is *balance, outward-orientedness, sociability,* and *conformity* for the sake of adjustment. Individuality and creativity, or even mere originality, are not stressed in this conception of values. Introspective behavior is devaluated (intellectuals are suspicioned by many). Deviancy, it seems, is to be tolerated only within the narrow limits of sociability, of general outwardness, of conformity ("Artists are perverts"). The All-American boy is altogether adjusted.

The materials just cited not only serve to illustrate the technique, but more important for present purposes, indicate rather clearly the fabric of the value pattern that seems to be emerging as the dominant core of the social character values in American culture (providing one can assume, as I am here, that the middle-class culture is the core of our way of life—the pattern of norms against which lower- and upper-class cultures are seen as deviations). From this point on, I shall use the implications of these data without further explication of the factual baseline. The purpose is to sketch in bold strokes the major dimensions of culture change in our American society and relate them to the contretemps of modern public education and educators.

The statements to be made now about American values, their shift, and the effect on education, are based upon the varying responses of different age groups in the sample, upon person-to-person variation in responses, and upon variations in response and particularly contradictions of response within single individual protocols (the total set of responses for a single individual). On the basis of these kinds of data, in the context of wider observations on institutions and culture patterns in the United States, it appears that a major shift in American values is taking place.[2] I find it convenient to label this shift as being from *traditional* to *emergent*, though no basic cultural change of this kind is actually linear. The values thus dichotomized are

---

[2]In my formulation of value trends and the interpretation of my data I have been particularly influenced by the writings of David Riesman.

listed under their respective headings below, with explanatory statements in parentheses.

## Traditional Values

*Puritan morality* (Respectability, thrift, self-denial, sexual constraint; a puritan is someone who can have anything he wants, as long as he doesn't enjoy it!).

*Work-Success ethic* (Successful people worked hard to become so. Anyone can get to the top if he tries hard enough. So people who are not successful are lazy or stupid, or both. People must work desperately and continuously to convince themselves of their worth.)

*Individualism* (The individual is sacred, and always more important than the group. In one extreme form, the value sanctions egocentricity, expediency, and disregard for other people's rights. In its healthier form the value sanctions independence and originality.)

*Achievement orientation* (Success is a constant goal. There is no resting on past glories. If one makes $9,000 this year he must make $10,000 next year. Coupled with the work–success ethic, this value keeps people moving, and tense.)

*Future-time orientation* (the future, not the past, or even the present, is most important. Time is valuable, and cannot be wasted. Present needs must be denied for satisfactions to be gained in the future.)

## Emergent Values

*Sociability* (As described above. One should like people and get along well with them. Suspicion of solitary activities is characteristic.)

*Relativistic moral attitude* (Absolutes in right and wrong are questionable. Morality is what the group thinks is right. Shame, rather than guilt is appropriate.)

*Consideration for others* (Everything one does should be done with regard for others and their feelings. The individual has a built-in radar that alerts him to others' feelings. Tolerance for the other person's point of view and behaviors is regarded as desirable, so long as the harmony of the group is not disrupted.)

*Hedonistic, present-time orientation* (No one can tell what the future will hold, therefore one should enjoy the present—but within the limits of the well-rounded, balanced personality and group.)

*Conformity to the group* (Implied in the other emergent values. Everything is relative to the group. Group harmony is the ultimate goal. Leadership consists of group-machinery lubrication.)

American culture seems to be undergoing a confused transformation, producing many disjunctions and conflicts, from the traditional to the emergent value systems outlined above. It is probable that both value systems have been present and operating in American culture for some time. But recently, and under the impetus of World Wars, the pressures exerted by the "radical right" and the "radical left," the external communist threat, atomic insecurities, and a past history of "boom and bust", the tendencies in the emergent direction have gathered strength and appear to be on the way towards becoming the dominant value system of American culture. At the same time, there is a minority resurgence of extreme versions of the traditional values as some people reaffirm allegiance to them as a reaction to the threat of rapid culture change.

Like all major shifts and schisms in culture, this one has consequences for people. Culturally transitional populations, as anthropologists know from their studies of acculturating Indian tribes, Hindu villages, and Samoan communities (among others), are characterized by conflict, and in most severe form—demoralization and disorganization. Institutions and people are in a state of flux. Contradictory views of life are held by different groups and persons within the society. Hostilities are displaced, attacks are made on one group by another. And this applies as well to the condition of American culture—the context of American education.

The traditionalist may view the emergentist as "socialistic," "communistic," "spineless and softheaded," or "downright immoral." The emergentist may regard the traditionalist as "hidebound," "reactionary," "selfish," or "authoritarian."[3] Most of what representatives of either viewpoint do may be regarded as insidious and destructive from the point of view of the other. The conflict goes beyond groups or institutions, because individuals in our transitional society are likely to hold elements of both value systems concomitantly. This is characteristic, as a matter of fact, of most students included in the sample described previously. There are few "pure" types. The social character of most is split, calling for different responses in different situations, and with respect to different symbols. So an ingredient of personal confusion is added that intensifies social and institutional conflict. I hypothesize that the attacks upon education, which were our starting point, and the confusion and failure of nerve characterizing many educators today, can be seen in clear and helpful perspective in the light of the conflict of traditional and emergent values, and particularly in the extremes of both forms that have been described. It is the heart of the matter. The task then becomes one of placing groups, institutions, and persons on a continuum of

---

[3]Irrespective of this kind of name-calling, the dichotomy of values employed in this analysis is not the same as "conservative" and "liberal" or politically "left" and "right." It is certainly very probable, for example, that some political liberals are traditionalists in respect to core cultural values.

transformation from the one value system to the other. A simple diagram will aid comprehension of what is meant.

The diagram conveys the information that different groups operating in the context of relations between school and community, educator and public, occupy different positions on the value continuum, with varying degrees and mixtures of traditional and emergent orientations. It should be understood that the placements indicate hypothecated tendencies, that no one group representing any particular institution ever consists of "pure" value types, but that there is probably a modal tendency for the groups indicated to place on the transformation, or continuum line, in the way expressed in the diagram.

| TRADITIONAL VALUES | | | EMERGENT VALUES |
| General public and Parents | | School administrators | Younger teachers |
| School boards | Students | Older teachers | Students   Some older teachers |

School boards are placed nearest the *traditional* end of the continuum because such boards are usually composed of persons representing the power, *status quo*, elements of the community, and of persons in the higher age ranges. They are therefore people who have a stake in keeping things as they are, who gained their successes within the framework of the traditional value system and consequently believe it to be good, and who, by virtue of their age, grew up and acquired their value sets during a period of time when American culture was presumably more tradition-oriented than it is today. They may be driven to extreme forms of traditionalism as a response to the pressures mentioned previously.

The general public and parent group, of course, contains many elements of varying value predilection. It is therefore unrealistic to place this public at any particular point in the value continuum. But I hypothesize that the public *tends* to be more conservative in its social philosophy than professional educators are. The placement to the left of center of the continuum takes on further validity if it is seen as a placement of that part of the public that is most vocal in its criticism of educators and education—since many of the criticisms made appear to spring out of value conflicts between traditionalist and emergentist positions. Parents complain that their children are not being taught the "three R's" (even when they are), that educators want to "socialize" the competitive system by eliminating report cards, that children are not taught the meaning of hard work. These all sound, irrespective of the question of their justification or lack of it, like traditionalist responses to change in an "emergent" direction.

Students are placed at two points on the transformation line because it is clear that those coming from traditionalist family environments will tend to hold traditionalistic values, but hold them less securely than will their parents (if our hypothesis for overall change is valid), while other students who come from emergent-oriented families will tend to place even further, as a function of their age and peer groups, towards the emergent end of the line than their parents would. This is only partially true, indeed, for such a rationale does not account for the fact that offspring in revolt (and many American children from 6 to 16 are in a state of revolt against parental dictums) may go to extremes in either direction.

School administrators, older and younger teachers, place at varying points on the emergent half of the transformation line. I have placed them there because I believe that the professional education culture (every institution has its own way of life, in this sense) that they have acquired in the schools and colleges of education has a clear bias towards an emergent-oriented ethos. Many of my educationist colleagues will reject this interpretation, and indeed, such interpretations are always guilty of over-generalization. Others will welcome such a characterization, but still question its validity. My case must rest on contemporary educational philosophy, theory, and practice. The emphasis is on the "social adjustment" of the individual, upon his role as a member of the group and community. Most of the values listed under the *emergent* heading are explicitly stated in educational literature as goals. Some of them, such as conformity to the group, are implicit. This value, in particular, grows out of the others, is more or less unintended, and constitutes a *covert* or *latent* value, by definition. This is, admittedly, a little like accusing a man of hating his mother, but not knowing it, and such accusations are usually rejected, or rationalized out of existence. But I believe that it is literally impossible to hold the other values in this system and avoid placing a strong emphasis on group harmony, and group control of the individual. My data, at least, gathered largely from students in professional education courses, indicate that this is the case.

But educators and schools do not all come off the same shelf in the supermarket. Older teachers will tend, I hypothesize, to hold relatively traditionalist views by virtue of their age, and time of their childhood training (when they acquired their basic values) a period in American culture when the traditionalist values were relatively more certain and supported than they are at present. Younger teachers were not only children and acquired their personal culture during a relatively more emergent-oriented period of American history, but they have been (I hypothesize) exposed to a professional education culture that has become emergent-oriented in its value position. They are therefore placed near the extreme of the transformation line in the emergent direction. Some older teachers, in reaction against traditional values, place near the emergent end of the continuum.

School administrators came from a different shelf in the same section of the supermarket. They, to be sure, range in age from young to old, come from different family backgrounds, and have been exposed in varying degrees to the professional education culture. But sociological and anthropological studies of the influence of status and role on behavior and perception indicate that these factors tend to override others, and produce certain uniformities of outlook. The school administrator's role is a precarious one—as any school principal or superintendent knows. He faces towards several different audiences, each with different sets of demands—school boards, parents, power groups, teachers, and students—as well as other administrators. He has to play his role appropriately in the light of all these demands. The fact that many cannot, accounts for the increasingly short tenure of personages like school superintendents. But to the extent that he plays *across the board* he will place somewhere towards the center of the line of transformation. Furthermore, his dependence upon the school board, and the power groups in the community, in many cases will tend to make his outlook relatively more conservative, and probably more traditionalistic, than that of his teachers—at least the younger ones. There are many exceptions, of course. I am only claiming *tendencies.*

My thesis, I hope, is clear by now. I am attempting to explain, or help explain, the increasingly bitter and strident attacks on schools and educators, and the conflict and confusion within the ranks. I have claimed that this situation can better be understood in the context of conflicts in core values. And I have tried to show the direction of the values shift in American culture and place the various actors in the drama upon a transformation line within this shift.

In this perspective, many conflicts between parents and teachers, school boards and educators, parents and children, and between the various personages and groups within the school system (teachers against teachers, administrators against teachers, and so on) can be understood as conflicts that grow out of sharp differences in values that mirror social and cultural transformation of tremendous scope—and for which none of the actors in the situation can be held personally accountable. This is the real, and perhaps only contribution of this analysis. If these conflicts can be seen as emerging out of great sociocultural shifts—out of a veritable transformation of a way of life—they will lose some of their sting. To understand, the psychiatrist says, is to forgive.

But now, though it seems indeed improper at this point, permit me to add another complication to an already complicated picture. I have tried to make it clear that not only are there variations in values held by groups and different parts of the social body and school institutions, but that there are also various values, some of them contradictory, held by single individuals as diverse streams of influence in their own systems. This is always true in rapid culture-change situations, as the anthropologist and philosopher know.

This means that the situation is not only confused by groups battling each other, but that individuals are fighting themselves. This has certain predictable results, if the anthropological studies of personal adaptation to culture change have any validity. And I believe that those results can be detected in the behaviors of most, if not all, of the actors in the scene. Let me try to clarify this.

I will deal only with teachers, as one of the most important sets of actors on this particular stage. I hypothesize that the child training of most of the people who become teachers has been more tradition than emergent value-oriented. They are drawn largely from middle to lower-middle social class groups in American society, and this segment of the class structure is the stronghold of the work-success ethic and moral respectability values in our culture (even in a culture that is shifting away from these values). Furthermore, it seems probable that a selective process is operating to draw a relatively puritanistic element into the public school teaching as an occupation. Self-denial, altruism, a moralistic self-concept, seem to be functional prerequisites for the historically-derived role of school teacher in American society (I might have said "schoolmarm").

If this can be granted, then only one other ingredient needs to be added to explain several persistent types of personal adaptation to value conflicts observable among school teachers. That ingredient is one already spelled out—the relatively heavy emphasis, within the professional education culture, on the emergent-oriented value system. Teachers-to-be acquire their personal culture in a more tradition-oriented family environment, but they encounter a new kind of culture when in training to become school teachers—in the teacher-training institutions. This is a particular kind of culture-conflict situation that anthropologists have recently begun to study, but mostly in nonWestern societies undergoing acculturation under the impact of the western way of life.[4]

On the basis of observations of teachers in coastal communities and in the middle west, I hypothesize that three types of adaptation to this personal culture-conflict situation and experience are characteristic.

*Ambivalent.* This type is characterized by contradictory and vacillating behavior, particularly with respect to the exercise of discipline and authority. The type tends to be *laissez-faire* in some classroom situations, and

---

[4]Acculturation is used here to refer to the changes brought about in the culture of groups or individuals as adaptation to a culture different from their own takes place.

authoritarian in others, depending upon which behavior is called into being as a defense against the threat of loss of control of self or of the classroom.

*Compensatory.* This type is characterized by one of two modes of behavior. The teacher overcompensates consistently either in the direction of the emergent or the tradition-centered values. In the first mode he (or she) tends to become a member of a *group-thinkism* cult—a perversion of progressive educational philosophy in action. The total stress is placed on social adjustment. Individuality is not sanctioned to any significant degree: Conformity to the group becomes the key to success. The type, in its extreme form, is a caricature of the emergent-centered value set. The second type compensates for internal culture conflict in the opposite direction, and becomes an extreme traditionalist. Tight dominance is maintained over children. Relationships with them are formalized and rigid. No deviation is allowed, so curiously enough, in this reactionary caricature of the tradition-centered values set there is convergence in the demand to conform—in one instance to the group, in the other to the teacher.

*Adapted.* This type can be either traditional or emergent value-oriented. But the compensatory and ambivalent mechanisms operating in the first two types are much less intense, or absent. The teacher of this type has come to terms with the value conflict situation and experience, and has chosen (consciously or unconsciously) to act within the framework of one or the other value set, or has achieved a workable synthesis of both. There is consequently a consistency of behavior, and the mode of classroom management and teacher–student relationship is not a caricature of either value system.

No one is in a position to say which of these types is represented in greatest numbers among American public school teachers today, and there are few "pure" types. Certainly there are many traditional and emergent-oriented teachers who have adapted successfully to the personal culture-conflict situation and discontinuity of enculturative experience described. But equally certainly there are many school teachers who fall more clearly into one or the other typologies. It would be asking too much to suppose that a cultural values-conflict situation as intense as the one transforming American culture could be handled without strain by a key agent of the culture- transmission process—the school teacher. But again, to understand is to forgive.

In any event, it seems clear that if conditions are even partially of the nature described, the group culture-conflict situation resulting in attacks by representatives of those groups upon each other is intensified and at the same time confused by the personal culture-conflict problem. Both processes must be seen, and understood, as the results of a larger culture-transformation process.

In conclusion to this incomplete analysis, let me make it clear that I am not attacking either the emergentists, or the traditionalists. Value systems must always be functional in terms of the demands of the social and economic structure of a people. The traditional mode has been functional in our society, and there is a staunchness, and a vitality in it that many of us view with considerable nostalgia. But rugged individualism (in its expedient, ego-centered form), and rigid moralism (with its capacity for displaced hate) become dysfunctional in a society where people are rubbing shoulders in polyglot masses, and playing with a technology that may destroy everything with a pushing of buttons. The emergentist position seems to be growing in strength. Social adaptability, relativistic outlooks, sensitivity to the needs and opinions of others, and of the group, seem functional in this new age. We need, as citizens, educators, anthropologists, and parents, to examine our premises more closely. The emergentist can become a group conformist—an average man proud of his well-rounded averageness—without really meaning to at all.

And lastly, I would like to reiterate the basic theme of this article. Conflicts between groups centering on issues of educational relevance, and confusions within the rank and file of educators, can be understood best, I believe, in the perspective of the transformation of American culture that proceeds without regard for personal fortune or institutional survival. This transformation, it is true, can be guided and shaped to a considerable degree by the human actors on the scene. But they cannot guide and shape their destiny within this transformation if their energies are expended in knifing attacks on each other in such a central arena as education, or if their energies are dissipated in personal confusions. I am arguing, therefore, for the functional utility of understanding, and of insight into the all-encompassing transformation of American culture and its educational-social resultants.

## REFERENCES

Gorer, Geoffrey. 1948. *The American People*. New York: W. W. Norton & Company, Inc.

Kluckhohn, Clyde. 1949. *Mirror for Man*. New York: McGraw-Hill Book Company, Inc.

_____, and Florence Kluckhohn. 1947. "American Culture: Generalized Orientations and Class Patterns." In *Conflicts of Power in Modern Culture, Seventh Symposium of the Conference on Science, Philosophy, and Religion*. New York: Harper & Row.

Lantis, Margaret (ed.). 1955. "The U.S.A. as Anthropologists See It." Special issue of the *American Anthropologist 57*: 1113–1295.

Lipset, Seymour, and Leo Lowenthal, eds. 1961. *Culture and Social Character: The Works of David Riesman Reviewed*. New York: The Free Press of Glencoe.

Mead, Margaret. 1942. *And Keep Your Powder Dry.* New York: William Morrow & Company, Inc.

Riesman, David, Nathan Glazer, and Reuel Denney. 1950. *The Lonely Crowd.* New Haven, Conn.: Yale University Press.

Ruesch, Jurgen, and Gregory Bateson. 1951. *Communication: The Social Matrix of Psychiatry.* New York: W. W. Norton & Company, Inc.

Warner, W. Lloyd. 1995. *American Life: Dream and Reality.* Chicago: University of Chicago Press.

_____. 1959. *The Living and the Dead: A Study of the Symbolic Life of Americans.* New Haven, Conn.: Yale University Press.

# 4

# Beth Anne:
# A Case Study of Culturally
# Defined Adjustment
# and Teacher Perceptions
## (1974)

*George D. Spindler*

*Editor's note: The study of Beth Anne was done in 1952. I used the case in my classes and distributed informal papers until I felt the material could be given wider distribution in the 1974 edition of* Education and Cultural Process: Anthropological Approaches, G. Spindler, ed.

This case study of Beth Anne will demonstrate how culturally unsophisticated perceptions of children by teachers may damage the "successful" middle-class child as well as the academically "unsuccessful" minority child in the school. The basic theme is the influence of the teacher's culture and the school upon perceptions and interpretations of children's behavior. For this purpose I am using a case study carried out in the 1950s when I was one of three people working in a school system under the aegis of the Stanford Consultation Service, directed by Dr. Robert N. Bush.

Our purpose as a service team was to perform various studies of whole class-rooms, teachers, individual children, other groups in the school, and even of whole school systems, as well as top supervisory personnel. Unlike the practice in a usual field study, we shared the data we collected and the analyses of those data with our informants. By so doing we hoped to share any benefits that might result from our research and direct them toward the improvement of the schools and the professional competence of teachers and related staff.

In this particular school, which we will call Washington Elementary School, we had entered to work with the whole staff of 12 teachers and the principal. First, we asked the assembled staff what it was they would like to study. They proposed a study of the "adjusted"—rather than the malad-justed—child in the classroom and in interaction with teachers and peers. We accepted this novel idea enthusiastically and proceeded to set up a mechanism whereby "adjusted" children could be selected for study. After some discussion the teachers helped out by deciding on several specific chil-dren. These children's classes were approached as a whole for volunteers for the study. Among the volunteers were the children picked out by the staff. The studies were cleared with their parents and we proceeded over a period of about three months to collect data and periodically to discuss these data and our interpretations with the assembled staff of the school. Beth Anne, a fifth-grade pupil, is one of the children studied.

## THE CLASSROOM AND BETH ANNE'S PLACE IN IT

The fifth-grade class consisted of 35 children ranging in age from 9 years, 8 months to 11 years, 8 months. The I.Q. range as measured by the California Mental Maturity Test appropriate to this age level was 70–140 with a mean of 106. There were three reading groups in the room, highly correlated with I.Q. scores as well as with reading achievement scores.

The classroom consisted of 20 children who could be described as Anglos whose socioeconomic status ranged from upper lower to upper middle (us-ing the scales drawn from the studies of H. Lloyd Warner and his associates). The other 15 children were from the minority groups represented in the community surrounding the school and included 3 blacks, 2 Filipinos, 3 Jap-anese-Americans, and 7 Mexican-Americans (the term "Chicanos" was not current at that time).

Beth Anne was 10 years and 3 months old, just 3 months below the aver-age for the whole class. She was in the top reading group and at the 95th per-centile with her I.Q. test score of 132.

Except for occasional minor illnesses Beth Anne was apparently in good health, according to her parents and to records from the school office. She was dark haired, clear skinned, well developed for her age, had regular fea-tures and almond-shaped, brown eyes, and wore braces on her front teeth. She always came to school extremely well dressed and was polite and considerate in her relations with her teachers; she appeared to be slightly reserved but equally considerate with her peers. The members of the team as well as the teachers in the school were impressed with her appearance and manners and regarded her as an exceptionally nice-looking child of good background.

Beth Anne was described by the teachers as an "excellent student," one of "the best students in the school," one who is "extremely conscientious," "cooperates well," "never has caused trouble in any of her classes," and who is "well liked by the other children." Further comments from the faculty were elicited in discussions of Beth Anne and the other children selected for study before the studies began.

Her former first-grade teacher said, "She was a very bright little child. perhaps not too friendly. At first she didn't respond too readily to me, but gradually began to work well and by the end of the year appeared to have made an excellent adjustment." Her present fifth-grade teacher said that "Beth Anne has attended very regularly this year. She is very interested in her class work and activities and performs at top level in everything. She even does excellent work in arithmetic and she plays very well with the other members of the class and in general with children of her own age." The principal said, "Her home would certainly be classified in the upper-middle bracket. The parents are middle aged, having married late. They have a very nice home and provide every cultural experience for the children." She went on to say that "one of the things that has concerned me a little, however, is a kind of worried look that Beth Anne has sometimes. It seems that if she doesn't understand the very first explanation in class, she is all concerned about it. She hasn't seemed so much that way this year but I have noticed it a lot in the past." Another teacher said, "Well, the mother has always been very interested in her children and has worked to give them many advantages. Beth Anne and her brothers and her parents go to many things and places together." Another teacher agreed, "Yes, they go to symphonies, I know. And they all went to the football game at Orthodox U."

Several times, and in different ways, we asked the teachers whether they regarded Beth Anne as a "well-adjusted" child. There were no explicit reservations expressed except for the comment by the principal about her "little worried look" and the comment by her first-grade teacher that at first "she didn't respond too readily." The teachers all expressed verbal agreement that she was indeed very well adjusted, both academically and socially. Several teachers went out of their way to say that she was not only accepted by her peers but was considered a leader by them.

## THE EVIDENCE

The study consisted of weekly classroom observations, watching playground activities, interviewing teachers, and administering psychological and sociometric tests. After having established the conditions of our study, our first step was to explain to Beth Anne what we would be doing and why. With her apparent enthusiastic consent, we proceeded then to a first interview followed by administration of the Rorschach projective technique and the Thematic Apperception Test (TAT). Within the following two weeks we also administered a sociometric technique to the classroom group. This technique included the questions, "Whom would you like best to sit next to?" "Whom do you like to pal around with after school?" and "Whom would you invite to a birthday party if you had one?" The sociometric maps of the choices expressed by the children were made up from the results elicited by these questions. They were quite consistent with each other. The sociometric map (sociogram) resulting from the responses to the first question is shown in Figure 4.1. We also administered a status-reputation technique that included 32 statements such as, "Here is someone who fights a lot," "Here is someone who never has a good time," "Here is someone who does not play fair," "Here is someone who is good looking," "Here is someone who likes school," "Here is someone who plays fair," and so forth. The children were to list three names in rank order following every statement. Following are summaries of these categories of data. With the wisdom of hindsight, I would not administer this technique again. It is potentially destructive to children's self-feelings and stimulates corrosive interpersonal evaluation.

## Observations

The reports by our three-man team of observers of Beth Anne's behaviors in the classroom and around the playground were monotonously similar. Beth Anne did not cause trouble. She was obedient, pleasant, and hardworking. She responded to questions in a clear voice and was noticeably disturbed when she was unable to provide the answer to a question in the arithmetic section. She read well and easily.

However, she interacted only infrequently with the other children in the classroom, either in the room or on the playground. She seemed quite reserved, almost aloof. Apparently she had a fairly strong relationship with one girl who looked and acted much as she did and who seems to have come from the same general social and cultural background.

Sometimes she chose to stay in the classroom when recess was called and would go out only at the urging of the teacher. She played organized games but not enthusiastically and seemed to find aggressive handling of a ball or other play equipment difficult.

## Psychological Test Results

The Rorschach and the TAT were administered the day after the preliminary interview with Beth Anne and before any other observations or other methods of data collection had been implemented. Without becoming involved with the many problematic aspects of their interpretation, I will summarize the results of these psychological techniques. In general we found these projective techniques to be of considerable use in our studies of individuals, though we regarded them with a certain flexibility.

*Thematic Apperception Test. Analysis*   Most of the pictures in the TAT are of people engaged in social interaction and the subject is asked to tell a story about each picture. This story should state what the people are doing and thinking, what probably happened before the situation pictured, and what probably will happen. Beth Anne did not like to tell stories of this kind. Picking up the TAT pictures, she stated perfunctorily who the people were and what they were doing and then laid them down with what appeared to be an impatient air of finality. She was not able to say more upon probing, though she appeared to be at least superficially eager to comply. The TAT record is consequently rather sparse, though it is revealing.

The resistance to letting her imagination guide her to a creative solution to problems of human relationships as suggested by the pictures seems to be the most important feature of her protocol. She does not seem to like to be in a situation where she has to turn to her own creativity and utilize her emotions for interpretation. She does not seem to be able to empathize freely with the people in the pictures, even when she sees them as children. When asked what they might be feeling or thinking, she answered "I don't know," and if pressed by the interviewer, "How should I know?"

It is hard to pick out the most revealing instance of this aspect of her personality from the large amount of evidence in the TAT protocol. Upon seeing a picture of a little boy sitting in front of a log cabin she said, "It looks like he lives in a log cabin." ("What is he doing there?") "He's probably sitting there thinking about something." ("What is going to happen?") "Probably he is going to do what he is thinking about after a while." ("What is he thinking about?") "I don't know what he's thinking about. He's just thinking about all the things there are to think about!" In my experience with the administration of this technique with children her age, this is an unusual response. Most children as intelligent as Beth Anne seemed to embrace the task of telling the story about each picture with considerable spontaneity and creativity. Not so Beth Anne, who did not seem to be able to let herself go.

In another instance, when she was presented with a blank card and told to put a picture there by telling a story, she said, "There's nothing to make up that I can think of." That appeared to be literally true. She did not seem to be able to dip into any reservoir of imagination.

Beyond this prevailing feature in her TAT protocol, we can say that she shows some overt hostility toward authority. She also shows a certain amount of depression that is fairly rare for children her age, and she is made quite uneasy by symbols of open aggression.

There is no direct evidence of what could be called a pathological character development. What seems to be apparent is a lack of spontaneity and a refusal or inability to use her imagination to interpret the behavior of others.

*Rorschach.*   Beth Anne gives evidence in her Rorschach protocol of possessing superior intelligence. She produced forty-eight appropriate responses, a result which is not only well above the average for her age group but higher than most adults achieve. She exhibits a high regard for detail and specification, but does not embark upon any flights of fantasy nor does she often put the details together to form an integrated whole perception.

Both qualitatively and quantitatively her protocol suggests that she is more constricted emotionally and intellectually than her superior productivity would lead one to expect. She has a well-developed perception of the concrete world about her, but these perceptions seem to stop at the level of concrete detail.

There is some evidence that she feels herself to be at times overwhelmed by forces beyond her control. There is also evidence that she has strong feelings that are not channeled into manageable interpersonal relationships or self-development.

It may be misleading to say that she lacks "creativity," but there is little imaginative spontaneity and little use of emotions for interpretive purposes. Beth Anne is what is sometimes known as a "tightrope" walker who sees what it is safe to see. She seems to avoid aspects of the inkblots that may have strong emotional implications for her and does not go deeply within herself for responses that would be emotionally meaningful. She avoids entanglements in emotionally laden material.

Furthermore, she seems to be fairly restricted in her ability to empathize with human motives or feelings. She does not seem to be able to put herself into another person's shoes, possibly because she has suppressed many of her own drives and feelings. At times, this may affect her intellectual performance, since she appears to be led off into inconsequential details and fails to see the larger whole.

Beth Anne is not likely to be a troublemaker. She conforms even at her own personal cost. She says "Thank you" every time a Rorschach card is handed to her and "Oh, pardon me!" when she drops a card an inch onto the desk and it makes a little noise. She seems very concerned about performing adequately and asks continually if she has given enough responses.

There is evidence that there are some definite problems in the handling of emotions. Generally speaking, the emotions seem to be suppressed or avoided, but when they are confronted they seem overwhelming. Given this

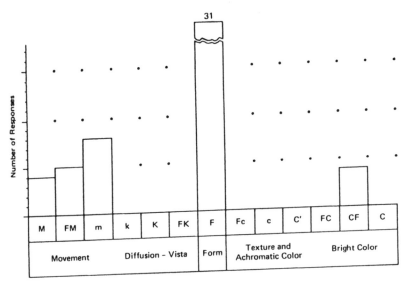

FIG. 4.1   Beth Anne's Rorschach profile.

evidence within the context of a personality adjustment that can be described as constricted and at the same time achievement-oriented, one would predict the probability of some form of hysterical behavior, probably in the form of conversion to somatic disturbances or to chronic invalidism. We shall see later that this prediction was supported.

The Rorschach psychogram is reproduced here (Fig.4.1). For those familiar with Rorschach interpretation, one can note the heavy emphasis on the "m" response and on the "F" category, the absence of textural or shading responses, the absence of controlled color responses, and the presence of several relatively uncontrolled color responses. This psychogram is accompanied by 6 percent whole responses, 51 percent large usual-detail responses, 20 percent small usual-detail responses, and 23 percent unusual-detail or white-space responses. Beth Anne's average reaction time for all responses was 11.5 seconds. As everyone who has worked with the Rorschach knows, not too much faith should be placed upon the formal psychogram. It happens in this particular case that the psychogram relates closely to interpretations that flow from the qualitative nature of the responses. This tends to support the interpretation but does not validate it.

Sociometric Results

The sociogram (Fig. 4.2) maps the results of class responses to the question, "Whom would you like to sit next to?" Without attempting an analysis of the classroom as a whole, I will only say that it is not unusual at this age level. There is a definite separation between boys and girls. While the boys tend to cluster around certain leaders or "stars of attraction," the girls usually relate to each other in smaller cliques or even dyads.

Beth Anne's position in the classroom group insofar as these data show is extremely marginal. She is the second choice of a girl whom she considers (inferred from other data) to be her best friend. She made no choices herself. Her social situation is not significantly altered according to the social mapping of the results of the responses to the other two questions, "Whom

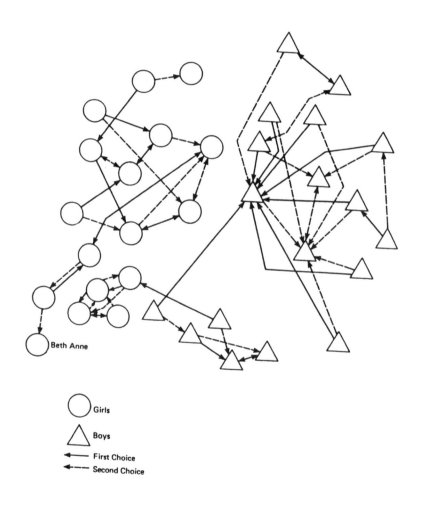

FIG. 4.2   Sociogram for Beth Anne's fifth-grade class.

would you like to pal around with after school?" and "Whom would you like to invite to a birthday party?"

Responses on the status-reputation test from the classroom group are impressively consistent with the results of the sociometric technique. Beth Anne is rated minimally: once for "Never having a good time" and once each for "liking school" and "being good looking."

The results from both techniques indicate that Beth Anne is marginal in the classroom group. She is given very little attention—either favorable or unfavorable. It is almost as though she were not there at all. These results are consistent with direct observations made of her behavior and interactions with other children in the classroom and on the playground during recess.

## Home Visit and Parent Interview

Her parents were informed that the study of Beth Anne was under way. They had given their enthusiastic permission for the study when they were told, as was true, that Beth Anne was selected as a particularly well-adjusted child for special study. After the data collected above had been discussed within our team, an appointment was made to discuss the material with the parents and I was elected as the team representative. By that time the study had become primarily mine, although all three members of the team had engaged in observations and we had discussed the data as they came in during weekly seminar sessions.

Beth Anne's home was decidedly upper middle class in furnishings and exterior appearance. The interior appointments were luxurious and a two-car garage with a beautifully landscaped lawn completed the picture. Her father's occupation as the manager of a large building materials manufacturing company was appropriate to the socioeconomic status assignment.

When I entered the house Beth Anne's mother was waiting for me and said that her husband would come soon because he was very interested also. We discussed their recent trip to Alaska until Mr. Johnson arrived. Mrs. Johnson's attitude seemed very cooperative, and in fact she appeared pleased that the school had arranged to have a home visit and interview.

As soon as Mr. Johnson arrived we began a cordial discussion over coffee. I wished to make it clear at the very beginning that we were not dealing with Beth Anne as a "problem" case, so I reviewed the circumstances of the selection. We were working with the faculties of several schools in the community in an attempt to improve understanding of the adjustments of children at different grade levels academically, socially, and emotionally. Having set the stage in this positive manner, I asked what aspects of our results they were particularly interested in. The father, a dynamic doer who wasted no time getting to the point, asked three questions as one, "What did you do, what did you find out, and what are you going to do about it?"

Rather than answer all these questions, I explained the techniques used in our study in some detail, including observations, sociometric materials, and projective tests. I explained why we used these techniques and what each contributed to a rounded picture of the child's adjustment. The parents seemed interested but obviously had some other concerns on their minds.

Mrs. Johnson queried, "Did you find that Beth Anne was temperamental or nervous at all?" I asked her to explain what she meant by that. She went on to explain that Beth Anne was "always complaining about her health. If any little thing is wrong with her, she wants to go to bed and ... she is always thinking that she is getting sick." She elaborated upon this at some length and then went on further to say, "She used to have a tic.... I guess that's what you would call it. When she was reading, and she reads a lot, she would draw her stomach up into a tight little knot and then let it go and the abdominal muscles would jerk back and forth." She continued, "I took her to the doctor, (of course he said that she was tense and nervous but not to worry about it, that it was just an abdominal tic. He said that she would get over it eventually and as a matter of fact she is better now." This condition had apparently become obvious about a year ago.

Using this as leverage, I asked the parents if she were not rather a perfectionist—if she didn't seem to feel that everything she did, particularly at school, had to be done perfectly. Both parents agreed quickly and rather enthusiastically that this *was* the case. They appeared to regard my question as somewhat of a compliment. Possibly they could regard the pattern I described as evidence of a high achievement drive. They confirmed the observation implicit in the question with several examples concerning her behavior at home, in her room, her dress, and maintenance of personal possessions. After some minutes of this, I asked them if they thought this perfectionism might not cost her too much in tension and loss of spontaneity. While both parents nodded assent to this, they did not agree as wholeheartedly as they did when I asked them if she were not a perfectionist. They apparently could accept the definition of Beth Anne as an achievement-oriented youngster, but they could not bring themselves to accept the possibility that the standards of achievement could be so high as to make the cost so great. I did not press the point. When a silence in the conversation developed, I did nothing to fill it.

At this point Mr. Johnson said, "There's something else.... I'm not so concerned about it but Mary [the mother] is.... " And then the mother took up the cue, saying, "There are several junior high schools here [and she named them], now you have had a lot of experience in schools, could you tell us which one is the best?" I replied by asking her what she particularly wanted of the school selected. She said, "Well, we've been wondering whether or not we should move to a different neighborhood when Beth

Anne is ready for junior high school. Washington School has been fine and we both appreciate all the things the teachers have done for Beth Anne, but you know there are all kinds of children over there—Mexicans, Italians, Chinese, Japanese, and even Negroes. Now, I believe in being democratic, but I feel that Beth Anne should associate with children that are, well ... more her *equals!* [emphasis hers]. When she gets into junior high school this will be more important than it is now, but she feels it even now. She came home just the other day and said, 'Oh Mother, do I *have* to dance with them?' I think she should go to a school that doesn't have such a mixed group, where the children are all more her kind ... don't you think so?"

In response I pointed out that the choice of a school was a decision that should be made by the parents in consultation with the child, and that what was important to one might not be important to another. Furthermore, it seemed to me that two points of equal importance in respect to a child's associates are, first, that the child be given a sense of belonging to a particular group and, second, that he or she should have broad experience with a wide variety of people from different backgrounds. This should enable the child to adjust well in any situation and to respect differences in others. When the parents pointed out that the two seemed contradictory I agreed, stating, however, that both could be accomplished if the parents' attitudes were supportive. To probe their attitudes a bit, I then suggested that they send their daughter to a private boarding school. Mrs. Johnson said that she wanted Beth Anne to be under her supervision, which would not be possible if she went away. However, she said, she wanted Beth Anne to be able to choose her own friends, with no attempt at reconciliation of the contradiction this posed with her other statements. I ended this phase of the discussion by saying that whatever the situation, Beth Anne's attitudes toward her classmates would reflect in significant degree what the parents thought.

I asked if there was any other specific topic they would like to discuss. The father asked how well Beth Anne was liked by her classmates. I replied, "She was not rejected more than a very few times by any other child; apparently they do not dislike her." While this did not tell the whole truth, it was at least in the direction of the truth, and I thought it was about as much as the parents could accept. I then asked if any of Beth Anne's friends were in her class, and Mrs. Johnson named three. My next statement was that Beth Anne was not chosen often either, and that in my opinion some of her classmates may have felt that she was critical of them. However, I told them also that the only negative trait on our status-reputation test was that she was rated as never having a good time. I could not explain the exact meaning of this, but assumed that it represented the children's feeling that she was serious about her school work. Before leaving I reassured them that "Beth Anne is a very excellent student and the teachers all like her a great deal."

With reference to the points they had brought up, I told them that it might be important to see that she is encouraged to relax a little more and enjoy life as it comes. I said I thought her school work would keep up since she is very intelligent, even though her parents make this appear less important. I left thanking them for their cooperation and saying that it was a pleasure to talk with parents who were as cooperative as they were. They both uttered the usual pleasantries and said that they very much appreciated my coming to talk with them.

## TEACHERS' RESPONSES TO THE EVIDENCE

By the end of our study period all of the evidence described above, plus many more details, had been shared with the staff. The teachers' responses could be described as ranging from surface compliance and agreement to deep covert resistance and resentment. I will draw a few representative comments from the tape taken during the final session with the faculty.

I have her in art for 80 minutes a week where we try to bring out creative ideas, but actually she never offers any ideas. She usually looks at me as if to say, 'Well, what do I do next?'"

"I know Beth Anne and her family quite well and she knows this, but she is aloof with me. Does she impress the rest of you that way?"

"She reads so much. I should think this would aid her imagination. She reads stories about girls, camping, fairy stories, everything that children her age and even older read."

"She belongs to a group that went to camp last summer, but I don't think she went. She does have that little frown or worried look. I remember it bothered you, Mrs. Smith."

"I suppose that when a teacher has 35 children she tends to think of normal and adjusted in terms of how well they conform."

"Well they do have a very nice home. The parents just returned from a month's trip to Alaska and they hired a trained nurse to stay with the children. They have always been very thoughtful about their welfare."

"Well she has certainly done outstanding work academically, all the way through since kindergarten right up to the present in this school."

"She was always absent a lot in third grade and she never was particularly friendly. I always felt that she looked down her nose at the other children in the class who weren't quite up to her ... I don't know whether she just didn't want to enter into things or whether she was fearful of making a mistake or what. Though she did good work, I always had a queer little feeling about her. I don't know just what it was."

"I don't think you have to worry about Beth Anne. She is going to arrive. Her family and their standing will see to that and she represents them very well."

"I agree. She'll be successful! She'll belong to a sorority."
"Well, anyway, she's a great reader!"

## INTERPRETATION

This case study virtually tells its own story and in that sense little interpretation is needed. Not all cases are as neat. This one was selected out of a much larger group—not for its representativeness but rather for its ideal typical characteristics. It pulls together in one configuration dynamic processes that are present in some form in many other cases. It seems to be in part a reversal of the relationship between the teacher and the fifth-grade class and the counselor and his class that I have discussed elsewhere (1959). It is actually only a variation in this relationship. In all of these cases and in many others that we studied during our several years of field research and consultation, it became apparent that teachers, usually quite contrary to their expressed intentions and ideals, were selecting children for the fruits of success in our social system or for the ignominy of defeat and alienation on the basis of undeclared, and probably unknown, cultural biases.

Beth Anne was selected by the teachers by consensus as exceptionally well adjusted. It is difficult to know exactly what "adjusted" means to anyone, though it was a term used very widely in the 50s and 60s in American public schools. These particular teachers said during our preliminary consultations that adjustment meant "conformity to the rules and regulations of the classroom," "success at school work," "the ability to achieve according to the expectations of parents and teachers," "an ability to get along well with one's peers," "a person who is not too conflict-ridden when he or she attempts to get along with their work and play," and "a child who works and plays well with others." The teachers were clearly not all of a single mind concerning what adjustment meant, but their definitions tended toward an adaptation to the situation as defined by teachers, by rules, and by the culture which the school represented. This is not unreasonable. In every cultural system those who accept the rules and achieve the goals laid down within the system are "adjusted" and those who do not are deviant, maladjusted, or criminal. The teachers' definitions do not pay much attention to what is inside Beth Anne's mind and, in fact, do not have much to do with Beth Anne at all. They have more to do with the school than with the child. This is understandable too.

However, we are faced with the fact that the teachers, even given their own criteria of adjustment, inaccurately perceived Beth Anne's situation. It is true that she achieved well according to the formal standards of academic performance. This achievement, however, was apparently at considerable psychic cost which was almost completely overlooked. Even more startling is the fact that the teachers misread her social adjustment. She did not "work and play well with others." In fact, she interacted with other children very little and was definitely marginal, really isolated within the classroom group.

Beth Anne's social marginality and isolation within the school was accompanied by severe internal distress in her own psychic system. She was compliant, a high achiever, but fearful of not achieving. She was unable to express her own emotions and had begun to evolve into a very constricted personality—all the more sad because she was such an intelligent girl. These processes had gone so far that a form of hysteric conversion had occurred. The prediction made on the basis of Rorschach evidence that the conversion would take the form of a somatic disturbance or possibly chronic invalidism was strongly supported. She wanted to stay in bed "on the slightest pretext" and suffered an "abdominal tic."

It would be easy to conclude that the teachers misperceive Beth Anne simply because she was academically successful—a high achiever in those areas where the teachers are directly responsible. This is, indeed, part of the cause for the misreading, but it is not a sufficient cause.

As I interpret the whole pattern of Beth Anne's adaptation and the perceptions of others of this adaptation, I see the teachers' perceptions as a self-sustaining cultural belief system. Beth Anne was selected not only because she was a high achiever but because in every other way she represented the image of what is desirable in American middle-class culture as it existed at the time of the study in the fifties and still exists today in slightly modified form. Beth Anne and her family represented success and achievement, the value of hard work, the validity of gratification delayed for future satisfaction, the validity of respectability and cleanliness, of good manners and of good dress as criteria for behavior. Beth Anne fit the criteria by means of which the teachers were selecting behaviors and children for the single channel of success and adaptation for which the school was designed as an institution representing the dominant mainstream culture.

I have characterized the belief in these values and selective criteria as self-sustaining because negative evidence was rationalized out of the system. Despite behaviors and attributes that any alert observer could have picked up in Beth Anne's case without the aid of outside experts or foreign instruments, Beth Anne was seen as one of the best-adjusted children in the school because she fit the belief system about the relationship between certain symbols, certain behaviors, and success as culturally defined.

This belief system, like most, can and does work. When belief systems stop working entirely they cease to exist, but they can continue to work partially for a very long time at great cost. In this case the cost to Beth Anne was profound. The culturally induced blindness of her teachers was in a certain real sense killing her and in ways no less painful than those in which minority children were and are being "killed" in many American schools.

## CONCLUSION

I am not blaming teachers personally for what I have described in this case analysis. The teachers, the children, the administrator, and all of the other actors on the stage are acting out a cultural drama. What I am striving for as an anthropologist of education is an understanding of this drama as a cultural process. As an anthropologist teaching teachers I want to promote *awareness* of this cultural process. None of the teachers that I have described here or elsewhere in my writings (Spindler, 1959) are people of bad intent. Most teachers are idealistic, many are quite liberal in their political and social beliefs, but they *are products of their culture* and live within the framework of values and symbols that are a part of that culture. By being made aware of what they are and do they can be freed from the tyranny of their cultures; in turn, they will be able to free children from the damaging effects of premature, inaccurate, or prejudiced estimates and interpretations of their behavior that are culturally induced.

This awareness is not easily gained. Though the teachers were exposed to intimate details of Beth Anne's case as these details developed, and though we exercised responsible skill and sensitivity in the dissemination of this evidence in open and closed discussions, the resistance of the teachers to the implications of the evidence was profound. The educative process had some effect, probably, but I doubt that it was very significant as far as the future behaviors of the teachers is concerned. Nor is a course or two in anthropology the answer. A year's fieldwork in a foreign community where one's assumptions, values, and perceptions are profoundly shocked by raw experience would make a significant difference, but not always in a direction that would be useful in the classroom. Matters have improved since the study of Beth Anne, but they have not improved enough. In my opinion a substantial part of the energy and time devoted to training teachers should be devoted to learning how to cope with the kinds of problems that I have been discussing in this and other case studies.

We were somewhat more successful with Beth Anne and her family as individuals than we were with the teachers. We explicitly recommended that the standards of excellence be lowered somewhat for Beth Anne and that she be given to understand that such achievements were not all that was important. Beth Anne seemed considerably improved according to a short follow-up observation the next year. But we cannot be sure of what happened. It may be that doing the study had a positive effect. Beth Anne at least knew that someone else had found out what it was like to be Beth

Anne, and her parents discovered that it was possible to face a problem that they intuitively felt to be there because an outside agency had detected the same problem.

## REFERENCE

Spindler, George Dearborn. 1959. *The Transmission of American Culture.* Cambridge, Mass.: Harvard University Press, for the Graduate School of Education.
Spindler, G. D. Ed. 1974. *Education and Cultural Process: Anthropological Approaches.* New York: Holt, Rinehart and Winston.

# 5

# Why Have Minority Groups in North America Been Disadvantaged by Their Schools?

(1974)

*George Spindler*

### IN HARLEM SCHOOL?

A description of a first-grade class in a Black ghetto in New York City follows. It is not a school in the poorest of the districts. It was considered typical for the grade.

> The teacher trainee (student teacher) is attempting to teach "rhyming." It is early afternoon. Even before she can get the first "match" (for example, book and look) a whole series of events is drawn out.
>
> One child plays with the head of a doll, which has broken off from the doll, alternately hitting it and kissing it.
>
> The student teacher tells a boy who has left his seat that he is staying in after school. He begins to cry. Another child teases that his mother will be worried

127

about him if he stays in after school. The boy cries even harder and screams at the teacher: "You can't keep me in until 15 o'clock."

A girl tries to answer a question put to the class but raises her hand with her shoe in it. She is told to put her hand down and to put her shoe on.

Another child keeps switching his pencil from one nostril to another, trying to see if it will remain in his nose if he lets go of it; he is apparently wholly unconcerned with the session in progress.

One child is lying down across his desk, pretending to sleep while seeing if the teacher sees him. Just next to him another child leads an imaginary band. Still a different child, on his side, stands quietly beside his seat, apparently tired of sitting.

While this is all going on the regular teacher of the class is out of the room. When she does return, she makes no effort to assist, or criticize, the student teacher. The student teacher later informed me that the regular teacher was not "just being polite." She rarely directed the student teacher, but simply let her "take over" the class on occasion. The student teacher also remarked that things were no different in the class when the regular teacher held forth.

Fifteen minutes had gone by, but little "rhyming" had been accomplished. A boy begins to shadow box in the back; another talks to himself in acting out a scene he envisions.

Still another child shakes his fist at the student teacher, mimicking her words: "cat-fat, hop-stop."

Two children turn to each other and exchange "burns" on one another's forearms, while another child arranges and rearranges his desk materials and notebook, seemingly dissatisfied with each succeeding arrangement.

A girl in the back has an empty bag of potato chips but is trying to use her fingers as a "blotter" to get at the remnants. She pretends to be paying attention to the lesson.

Another child asks to go to the bathroom, but is denied.

After a half-hour I left (Rosenfeld 1971:105).

As Gerry Rosenfeld, who taught in a Harlem school and did an anthropological field study there, pointed out, the schooling of these children is already patterned for them at the age of six or seven. "Not much is expected from them," they are from poor families, they are Black, and they are "disadvantaged." By high school many of them will be dropouts, or "push-outs," as Rosenfeld terms them. As they get older they become less docile than the children described above, and some teachers in ghetto schools have reason to fear for their own safety. The teachers of this classroom did not have reason to fear their pupils, but they were ignorant about them. Their preparatory work in college or in teacher training had not prepared them for a classroom of children from a poor ghetto area in the city. The student teacher knew nothing about the neighborhood from which the children in her class came. She knew only that she "did not want to work with 'these' children when she became a regular teacher" (Rosenfeld 1971:170).

As a teacher and observer at Harlem School, Rosenfeld found the teachers held an array of myths about poor children that they used to account for their underachievement and miseducation. At the benign liberal level there are beliefs about the nature of poverty and cultural disadvantage. These conditions become accepted as irrevocable givens. The child comes from such a background, therefore, there is nothing I, as a teacher, can do but try to get minimal results from this misshapen material. Among teachers who are explicitly bigoted in their views of the poor and Black, the explanations for failure may be less benign. According to Rosenfeld, and his observations are supported by others, an underlying ethos pervades the slum school which prescribes and accepts failure for the child.

> Assistant principals function not as experts on curriculum and instruction but as stock boys and disciplinarians. Boxes are constantly being unpacked and children are being reprimanded and punished. The principal seems more concerned with maintaining a stable staff, irrespective of its quality at times, than with effecting school-community ties and fashioning relevant learning programs. Education appears as a process where children are merely the by-products, not the core of concern. Guidance counselors and reading specialists are preoccupied with norms and averages, not with the enhancement of learning for all the children. Theirs is a remedial task, and where one would not exist, they create it. School directives and bulletins are concerned with bathroom regulations and procedures along stairways, the worth of the children being assessed in terms of their ability to conform to these peripheral demands (Rosenfeld, 1971:110).

The new teacher, however idealistic he or she may be at first, will be affected by the environment, and becomes a part of the social structure of the school. A socialization process occurs so that personal commitment and philosophy become ordered around the system. The clique structure among staff personnel also forces the newcomer to choose models and cultivate relationships. Communication must occur. There must be others with whom one can commiserate.

Teachers who keep their idealism, tempered as it is after a time by reality, turn more and more inward toward their own classroom. There one sees the results of the years of educational disenchantment. In the middle grades and beyond, the children are already 2 or more years behind standard achievement norms. The teacher realizes that for the children the school is an oppressive and meaningless place. He comes to understand also that children have developed counter-strategies for what they have perceived as their teachers' indifference, confusion, despair, and in some cases, outright aggression. But if the teacher persists in the effort to understand his or her pupils, eventually they become individuals. Most are alert and active. They are potentially high learners and achievers. Some are subdued and permanently detached. Some are irrevocably hostile towards schools, teachers, and White people. Others have surface hostilities but are willing to give trust and confidence when it is justified. Some are fast learners with strong curiosity and an eagerness to learn about the world. Others are apathetic or simply dull. Once the children become individuals, with sharp differences, they can no longer be treated as objects or as a collectivity.

The next step for the teacher who is going to become effective as a cultural transmitter and agent of socialization, as all teachers are, is to learn something of the neighborhood and of the homes from which the children come. But this is a step that is rarely taken. Rosenfeld describes the situation at Harlem School.

> Although Harlem School belonged to the neighborhood, it was not psychologically a part of it. On the contrary, teachers felt unwanted, estranged. Perhaps this was why few ventured off the "beaten paths" to the "hinterland" beyond the school, into the side streets and the homes where the children played out their lives. Some teachers at Harlem School had never been to a single child's household, despite the fact that they had been employed at the school for many years. Nothing was known of community self-descriptions, the activity and social calendar in the neighborhood, the focal points for assembly and dispersal, or the feelings of residents toward the "outside world." Teachers could not imagine that they could foster a genuine coming-together of neighborhood persons and themselves. They hid behind their "professionalism." They failed to realize that the apathy and disparagement they associated with parents were attributed by the latter to them. It is not to be underestimated how "foreign" teachers feel themselves to be at Harlem School, how disliked by the children. Why then do they remain on the job? Part of the answer is in the fact that the rewards of one's work are not always sought on the job itself, but in the private world. Teachers have little stake in the communities in which they work; that is why it may be necessary to link more closely teachers' jobs and children's achievement. It is my guess that all children (except those with proven defects) would achieve if teachers' jobs depended on this (Rosenfeld 1971:170).

It is clear that there are some parallels between the relationship of the school and teachers to the pupils and community in minority populations in the United States and the like relationship that has developed in many of the modernizing nations. Although there are profound differences in the two situations, the similarity is that the educational institutions in both cases are intrusive. These institutions stem from a conceptual and cultural context that is different from that of the people whose children are in the schools. This tends to be true whether "natives" or aliens are utilized as teachers and administrators for the schools. In the modernizing populations, as among the Sisala, the teacher, even though Sisala himself, is alien by virtue of his having been educated, removed from his community, socialized to norms, values, competencies, and purposes that are not a part of his community's culture (Grindal 1972). He is a member of a different class, for which there is as yet no clear place in the Sisala cultural system. He feels isolated from the community, and this isolation is reinforced by the character of the school in which he teaches. In Harlem School, or its prototypes, the teacher tends to be an alien whether he is White or Black. Even among Black teachers only some can maintain or acquire an identification with the people and community in which the school exists. The same processes of socialization and alienation that have taken place for the Sisala teacher have taken place for the Black teacher in the United States. This is particularly true for the Black teacher who comes from a middle-class background to begin with, then goes on to the university for advanced training. This teacher may be as far removed from the Black community in a slum school as any White teacher. Of course not all Black communities are in slums, but the slum school is the one we have been talking about.

## AT ROSEPOINT?

The interactions we are describing between school and culture occur elsewhere than in the urban slum. Martha Ward describes a community in what she calls Rosepoint, near New Orleans (1971). Rosepoint is a very small rural community, a former plantation occupied now by some of the people who worked on it, plus others. Rosepoint has its own culture—that of the Black South together with a heavy French influence characteristic of the area as a whole, and the unique ecological characteristics of a community built along a levee of the Mississippi River. Martha Ward was particularly concerned with language learning and linguistic features. She found that there were many substantial differences in speech and learning to speak between Rosepoint adults and children and White people. These differences contribute to the separation between community and school, which is the focus of our attention, because the school is taught mostly by Whites, although they are by no means the sole cause of this separation.

Rosepoint parents believe that most of the teachers in the schools their children attend—Black or White—are authoritarian and punitive. They also see that their children attending White schools for the first time are subjected to discriminatory practices, sometimes subtle, sometimes very obvious. There is little communication between the home and the school, whether primary or high school. Parents have little notion how the school is run, what their children are taught, or how to cooperate with the school or teachers. And the schools show no understanding of the social problems or cultural characteristics of Rosepoint. The conflicts are profound. The irrelevancy of the school for most Rosepoint children is measured by a high dropout rate and low rates of literacy. From about 11 years of age on, states Martha Ward, staying in school is a touch-and-go proposition, especially for males. She describes certain characteristics of the school environment and expectations that are at odds with those of the Rosepoint children.

> The school creates for the Rosepoint child an environment not as much unpleasant as unnatural. For years he has been determining his own schedule for eating, sleeping, and playing. The content of his play is unsupervised and depends on the child's imagination. His yard does not contain sand boxes, swings, clay, paints, nor personnel obliged to supervise his play. At school, however, play is supervised, scheduled, and centers around objects deemed suitable for young minds. There are firm schedules for playing, napping, eating, and "learning and studying" (with the implication that learning will occur only during the time allotted for it). The authority buttressing even minimal schedules is impersonal and inflexible with an origin not in face-to-face social relationships but in an invisible bureaucracy.
>
> Moreover, the Rosepoint home relies on verbal communication rather than on the written word as a medium. Adults do not read to children nor encourage writing. Extraverbal communication such as body movements or verbal communication such as storytelling or gossip are preferred to the printed page. The lack of money to purchase books, magazines, and newspapers partly explains this.... [sentence omitted] ... for children of a culture rich in ingroup lore and oral traditions the written word is a pallid substitute.
>
> Another conflict arising out of the home–school discrepancy is language—specifically, "bad" language. Remember, the Rosepoint child is rewarded for linguistic creativity ... [three sentences omitted]
>
> In the classroom such language has an entirely different interpretation on it. Some educators discretely refer to it as "the M-F problem."[1] [sentence omitted] A nine-year-old girl was given a two-week suspension from classes for saying a four-letter word. This was her first recorded transgression of the language barrier. The second offense may be punished by expulsion ... [two sentences omitted to end of paragraph] (Ward 1971:91–92).

The problems of Rosepoint and the schools that are intended to serve it are probably less overtly intense than those of Harlem School, its staff, and the community, but they are closely related to each other, and in turn to the problems of education among the Sisala, the Kanuri, and in Malitbog. The

---

[1]Refers to the use of obscenities in the school, including "Motherfucker."

school in all of these situations is intrusive and the teachers are aliens. Resentment, conflict, and failures are present in communication from all sides.

We should be very careful here to realize that what we have been describing is not a problem of Black minority populations alone. To some extent the disarticulation described between the school and community will be characteristic in any situation where the teachers and school stem from a different culture or subculture than that of the pupils and their parents. There is disarticulation between any formal school and the community, even where the school and community are not culturally divergent. Conflicts ensue when the school and teachers are charged with responsibility for assimilating or acculturating their pupils to a set of norms for behavior and thought that are different from those learned at home and in the community.

Education for minorities in North America is complicated by a variety of hazards. Harlem School operates in a depressing slum environment. No one wants to go there and the people there would like to get out. The conflicts and disarticulation germane to the school–community situation we have described are made more acute and destructive because of this. Rosepoint and its schools have their special circumstances also. The Rosepoint population has inherited the culture and outlook of a former plantation slave population. They are close to the bottom of the social structure. The teachers, particularly if they are White, have inherited attitudes toward Black people from the South's past. Let us look for a moment at a quite different place and people, the Indians of the Yukon Territory of Canada and the Mopass Residential School.

## IN THE MOPASS RESIDENTIAL SCHOOL?

The children who come to this school represent several different tribes from quite a wide area of northwestern Canada. Many of these tribal societies adapted quickly to the fur trade economy that developed soon after the first White men arrived and many became heavily acculturated to the other aspects of European culture. One could not say that on the whole the Native Americans of this area resisted the alien culture. In fact, they welcomed many of its technological and material advantages. As the northern territories have been opened for rapid development during the past decade, however, the Native Americans already there have found it increasingly difficult to find a useful and rewarding place in this expanding economy. The reasons for this are altogether the fault of neither the White Canadians nor the Indians, but certainly prejudice has played a role. One of the serious problems of the Indians, however, has been that, on the whole, they have had neither the skills that could be used in the expanding economy nor the basic education upon which to build these skills. The task of the school

would seem to be that of preparing young Native Americans[2] to take a productive and rewarding role in the economy and society now emerging in the
Northwest Territories. This is what it is like at Mopass Residential School,
according to Richard King, who taught there for a year and did anthropological observations during that period.

> For the children, the residential school constitutes a social enclave almost
> totally insulated from the community within which it functions; yet Mopass
> School reflects in a microcosmic, but dismayingly faithful manner the social
> processes of the larger society. Two distinct domains of social interaction ex-
> ist independently: Whiteman society and Indian society. Where these do-
> mains overlap, they do so with common purposes shared at the highest level
> of abstraction but with minimal congruence of purposes, values, and per-
> ceptions, at the operating levels of interaction. The Whiteman maintains
> his social order according to his own perceptions of reality. The Indian bears
> the burden of adaptation to a social order that he may perceive more realis-
> tically—and surely he perceives it with a different ordering of reality—than
> does the Whiteman. From his perceptions the Indian finds it impossible to
> accept the social order and, at the same time, impossible to reject it com-
> pletely. He therefore creates an artificial self to cope with the unique inter-
> active situations.
>
> In the residential school, the Whiteman staff and teachers are the end men of
> huge bureaucratic organizations (church and national government) that are
> so organized as to provide no reflection of the local communities. These em-
> ployees derive their social, economic, and psychological identity from the or-
> ganizations of which they are members.... [four sentences omitted]
>
> ... The children of the school are little more than components to be manipu-
> lated in the course of the day's work.... No job at school is defined in terms of
> outcomes, expected, or observable, in children (King 1967:170).

King goes on to describe the factionalism among the adult faculty and
staff in the school. He suggests that many of the people who take teaching
jobs in the residential school are deviant or marginal personalities, and that
the isolation of the school, and its nature as a closed system, tend to create a
tense interpersonal situation. The children have to adjust to this as well as
to the alien character of the institution itself.

The school children become uniquely adept at personality analysis, since
their major task is to cope with the demands of shifting adult personalities.
But this analysis is limited to their needs as the children perceive them in
specific situations (King 1967:88).

---

[2]The term *Native Americans* is preferred by many American Indians. We use Indian and Native
American interchangeably in recognition of this preference.

An artificial self is developed by the Indian child to cope with the total situation in which he finds himself. King says that the children sustain themselves with the conviction that their "real self" is not this person in the school at all. Through this, and other processes, the barriers between Whiteman and Indian are firmly developed

> not so much by a conscious rejection on the part of the Whiteman as by a conscious rejection on the part of the Indian child. The sterile shallowness of the adult model presented by the school Whitemen serves only to enhance—and probably to romanticize—memories of attachments in the child's primary family group, and to affirm a conviction prevalent among the present adult Indian generation that Indians must strive to maintain an identity separate from Whitemen (King 1967:88).

There is much more we could say about the social and learning environment that this school provided[3] the Indian children who attended it. King's case study should be read in order to understand it more thoroughly, for it is a startling example of miseducation and with the best of intentions on the part of the sponsoring organizations and the teaching and administrative personnel of the school itself. All the features of disarticulation, isolation and nonrelatedness we have ascribed to the other schools discussed are present, but in a special and distorted form because the school is a closed residential institution even more removed from the community that it is intended to serve than the other schools. It is also a church school, run by the Episcopalian church for the Canadian government. Its curriculum is even less relevant to the Native American children who attend it than the curriculum of the Sisala school was to the Sisala children, for it is the same curriculum that is used in other Canadian schools at the same grade level. It appears that the Mopass Residential School intends to recruit children into the White culture and a religious faith (because religious observances and education are a regular part of the school life). It fails in these purposes and, in fact, creates new barriers to this recruitment and reinforces old ones. More serious by far is the fact that it does not prepare the children who attend it to cope with the new economy and society emerging in the north. The children leave the school without necessary basic skills, alienated from what they see as White culture, alienated from themselves, and nonrelated to their own communities. This kind of schooling creates marginal people.[4]

---

[3]The school was closed in 1969. The "ethnographic present" is used in this description because it was in operation so recently and to be consistent with the other analyses.

[4]Mopass Residential School is neither better nor worse than other residential schools for Native Americans because it is Episcopalian, and certainly not because it is Canadian. Most of the same conditions exist in residential schools in both the United States and Canada, in Protestant, Catholic, and non-denominational schools.

## IS THERE A WAY OUT OF THE DILEMMA?

In the discussion so far we have dealt only with minority peoples who have had to operate in what some would describe as an essentially colonial situation. That is, they may have the theoretical rights of self-determination and self-regulation, but, in fact, do not and could not exercise these rights. There are now strong movements underway towards self-determination. Some are very militant, separatistic, and nationalistic. Others are more accommodative. But all share in striving for self-determination, and regulation of the schools is an important aspect of this determination. These people recognize, perhaps in different terms, what we have said—that education is a process of recruitment and maintenance for the cultural system. For minority people the schools have been experienced as damaging attempts to recruit their children into an alien culture. Their self-images and identities were ignored, or actively attacked.

There are some minority communities that have successfully resolved the problem. They have done so by creating and maintaining a closed cultural system that maintains a more or less defensive relationship toward the rest of the society. The Old Order Amish and the Hutterites are good examples of this solution. Both are nonaggressive pacifistic peoples, communal in orientation, and socioreligious in ideology and charter.

Amish communities are distributed principally throughout Pennsylvania, Ohio, and Indiana but are also found in several other states. The total Old Order Amish population is estimated at about 60,000. They are agrarian, use horsepower for agricultural work and transportation, and wear rather somber but distinctive dress. They strive to cultivate humility and simple living. Their basic values include the following: separation from the world; voluntary acceptance of high social obligations symbolized by adult baptism; the maintenance of a disciplined church–community; excommunication, and shunning as a means of dealing with erring members and of keeping the church pure; and a life of harmony with the soil and nature—it is believed that nature is a garden and man was able to be a caretaker, not an exploiter. The goals of education are to instill the above values in every Amish child and maintain, therefore, the Amish way of life. John Hostetler and Gertrude Huntington describe the concept of a true education from the Amish point of view.

> True education, according to the Amish, is "the cultivation of humility, simple living, and resignation to the will of God." For generations the group has centered its instruction in reading, writing, arithmetic, and the moral teachings of the Bible. They stress training for life participation (here and for eternity) and warn of the perils of "pagan" philosophy and the intellectual enterprises of "fallen man," as did their forefathers. Historically, the Anabap-

tist avoided all training associated with self-exaltation, pride of position, enjoyment of power, and the arts of war and violence. Memorization, recitation, and personal relationships between teacher and pupil were part of a system of education that was supremely social and communal (1971:9).

Realizing that state consolidation of schools constituted a severe threat to the continuity of their way of life and basic values, the Amish built the first specifically Amish School in 1925. By 1970 there were over three hundred such schools with an estimated enrollment of ten thousand pupils. When the population of the United States was predominantly rural and the major occupation was farming, the Amish people had no serious objections to public schooling. In the rural school of fifty years ago in most of the United States a curriculum much like that of the present Amish school was followed, the teacher was a part of the community, and the school was governed locally. Consolidation of schools in order to achieve higher educational standards shifted control away from the local area and the educational innovations that followed were unacceptable to the Amish. The Amish insist that their children attend schools near their homes so that they can participate in the life of the community and learn to become farmers. They also want qualified teachers committed to Amish values. Teachers who are merely qualified by state standards may be quite incapable of teaching the Amish way of life or providing an example of this way of life by the way they themselves live. The Amish also want to have their children educated in the basic skills of reading, writing, and arithmetic but training beyond that, they feel, should be related directly to the Amish religion and way of life. They do not agree with what they perceive to be the goals of the public schools, "... to impart worldly knowledge, to insure earthly success, and to make good citizens for the state." Ideally, from the Amish point of view, formal schooling should stop at about age fourteen, though learning continues throughout life. They feel that further schooling is not only unnecessary but detrimental to the successful performance of adult Amish work roles. The Amish pay for and manage their own schools in order to attain these goals (Hostetler and Huntington 1971:35-38).

Naturally, there have been serious conflicts with state authorities about the schools. Forcible removal of the children from Amish communities has been attempted in some cases, and harassment in legal and interpersonal forms has characterized the relationship of state authority to the Amish in respect to the problem of education. The Amish have doggedly but nonviolently resisted all attempts to make them give up their own schools, for they realize that these schools are essential to the continuance of their cultural system. They have made accommodations where they could, as for instance in providing "vocational" schooling beyond elemen-

tary school to meet state educational age requirements concerning duration of schooling.

The Amish story is one that anyone interested in the processes and consequences of separatism should know about. Hostetler and Huntington's
study is a good up-to-date overview that presents the case for the commu-
nity-relevant school clearly and objectively and with a sympathetic understanding of the Amish point of view and lifeway.

The Hutterite culture is similar in many ways to that of the Old Order
Amish, as seen from the outside, although the Hutterites are more communal in their economic organization and they used advanced agricultural ma-
chinery as well as trucks and occasionally cars. Hutterites are Anabaptists,
like the Amish and the Mennonites, originating during the Protestant Ref-
ormation in the sixteenth century in the Austrian Tyrol and Moravia. They
arrived in South Dakota in 1874 and have prospered since. There are about
18,000 Hutterites living on more than 170 colonies in the western United
States and Canada. They are noted for their successful large-scale farming,
large families, and effective training of the young.

Hutterites are protected from the outside world by an organized belief
system which offers a solution to their every need, although they, like the
Amish, have been subjected to persecution and harassment from the outside. The community minimizes aggression and dissension of any kind. Colony members strive to lose their self-identity by surrendering themselves to
the communal will and attempt to live each day in preparation for death,
and, hopefully, heaven. The principle of order is the key concept underlying
Hutterite life. Order is synonymous with eternity and godliness; even the
orientation of colony buildings conforms to directions measured with the
precision of a compass. There is a proper order for every activity, and time is
neatly divided into the sacred and the secular. In the divine hierarchy of the
community each individual member has a place—male over female, husband over wife, older over younger, and parent over child. The outsider
asks, "Why does this order work? How can it be maintained?" The implicit
Hutterite answer is that "Hutterite society is a school, and the school is a society." The Hutterites, like the Old Amish, do not value education as a
means toward self-improvement but as a means of "planting" in children
"the knowledge and fear of God" (Hostetler and Huntington 1967).

We will not go into detail concerning Hutterite schools. Although they
differ somewhat from the Amish schools in curriculum and style, particularly in being more strict and "authoritarian," the basic principles are the
same. The Hutterites also understand that they must retain control of their
schools and teachers if they are to retain their separatistic and particularly
their communal and socioreligious way of life. They do this by retaining a
"German school" that is in effect superimposed upon the "English school"

required by the state or provincial law. The two schools have rather different curricula and teachers and of the two the former is clearly the one that carries the burden of cultural transmission that recruits youngsters into the Hutterite cultural system and helps maintain that system most directly.

The Hutterites serve as another example of how to solve the problem faced by the Sisala, the people of Malitbog, the Kanuri, the children of Harlem School and their parents, the people of Rosepoint, and the children in the Mopass Residential School.

The problem all of these people face is how to relate a culture-transmitting institution that is attempting to recruit their children to a cultural system different from that of the community, class, area, or minority from which the children come. The school and teacher are alien in all of these cases, and they are charged, by governments or the dominant population, with the responsibility of changing the way of life by changing the children. Understandably the consequences are at least disruptive, and at worst tragic.

The Hutterities and Amish have done exactly what is logical according to the anthropologist viewing the relationship between education and culture. Realizing the threat to the continuity of their way of life from the outside world, particularly from schooling and transmission of concepts and views alien to their fundamental principles, they have taken control of their schools to whatever extent they can, given the exigencies of survival in contemporary North America. The schools are so ordered as to recruit and help maintain the traditional cultural system. They are successful. The way of life, beleaguered though it is in both cases, survives, in fact, flourishes.

It is important to understand, however, that, from another point of view, the cost of this success is too great. The result of success is a closed cultural system in a defensive relationship to the rest of society. That there are restrictions on personal behavior, sharp limits on self-expression, and confinement in the very thought processes and world view in both cases, is undeniable. The values of spontaneity, individual creativity, discovery and invention, pursuit of knowledge, and innovation, that are important to men and women elsewhere, are not values in these or any other closed cultural systems. There is also a kind of self-created disadvantage imposed by the Hutterites and Amish upon themselves. Since they lack higher education, in fact are opposed to it, and control as vigorously as possible the context of primary education, they cannot participate fully in the give and take of our dynamic society. True, they do not want to, but it is a hard choice, and one that could be very disadvantageous to any minority group. Somehow the modernizing peoples of the world emerging from a tribal and then colonial past, and the minority peoples in vast societies like the United States and Canada, must balance the consequences of a closed system and the educational institutions to support it, and an open system and the educational institutions to support it. It is clear, however, that it is necessary for all peoples to exercise and develop the rights of self-determination and self-regulation in education, as well as in other areas of life. It may be that this can be done without creating closed, defensive, and confining cultural systems. It may help for us all to realize that we actually have little control over what happens in our schools, no matter who we are. The educational bureaucracy in a complex urban system functions in some ways like an alien cultural system in relation to the local community, the children in school, and their parents, whether these parents and children are members of minority or majority groups. We all have this problem in common. In this age of cultural pluralism in the United States it is difficult to discern what else we all have in common. Perhaps it is possible to agree that there are some competencies all children should acquire, such as functional literacy, concepts of mathematical processes, and so forth, that are necessary if they are not to be severely handicapped in later life in a complex society. But in the area of specific values, ideologies, and worldviews we cannot repeat the mistakes of the past, when we assumed that the melting pot would melt all ethnic differences down to the same blendable elements. The cultures of the American Indians, Afro-American, Mexican-Americans, and Asian-Americans did not disappear as our ideology said they would. The challenge is to recognize and accept the differences without creating disadvantageous separatism or segregation, whether self-imposed or imposed from the dominant group. There are many paradoxes in the relationships we are discussing, and they are not easily resolved.

## REFERENCES

Grindal, Bruce T. 1972. *Growing Up in Two Worlds: Education and Transition among the Sisala of Northern Ghana.* CSEC. New York: Holt, Rinehart and Winston, Inc.

Hostetler, John A., and Gertrude E. Huntington. 1967. *The Hutterites in North America.* CSCA. New York: Holt, Rinehart and Winston, Inc. Revised edition 1996. Harcourt.

Hostetler, John A., and Gertrude E. Huntington. 1971. *Children in Amish Society: Socialization and Community Education.* CSEC. New York: Holt, Rinehart and Winston, Inc. Revised 1992.

King, A. Richard. 1967. *The School at Mopass: A Problem of Identity.* CSEC. New York: Holt, Rinehart and Winston, Inc.

Rosenfeld, Gerry. 1971. *"Shut Those Thick Lips!" A Study of Slum School Failure.* CSEC. New York: Holt, Rinehart and Winston, Inc.

Ward, Martha C. 1971. *Them Children: A Study in Language Learning.* CSEC. New York: Holt, Rinehart and Winston, Inc.

# The Transmission of Culture

## (1967)

*George D. Spindler*

This chapter is about how neonates become talking, thinking, feeling, moral, believing, valuing human beings—members of groups, participants in cultural systems. It is not, as a chapter on child psychology might be, about the growth and development of individuals, but on how young humans come to want to act as they must act if the cultural system is to be maintained. A wide variety of cultures are examined to illustrate both the diversity and unity of ways in which children are educated. The educational functions that are carried out by initiation rites in many cultures are emphasized, and the concepts of cultural compression, continuity, and discontinuity are stressed in this context. Various other techniques of education are demonstrated with selected cases, including reward, modeling and imitation, play, dramatization, verbal admonition, reinforcement, and storytelling. Recruitment and cultural maintenance are analyzed as basic educative functions. The chapter is not about the whole process of education but about certain parts of that process seen in a number of different situations.

## WHAT ARE SOME OF THE WAYS
## THAT CULTURE IS TRANSMITTED?

Psychologists and pediatricians do not agree on the proper and most effective ways to raise children. Neither do the Dusun of Borneo, the Tewa or Hopi of the Southwest, the Japanese, the Ulithians or the Palauans of Micronesia, the Turkish villagers, the Tiwi of North Australia, the people of Gopalpur, or those of Guadalcanal. Each way of life is distinctive in its outlook, content, the kind of adult personalities favored, and the way children are raised. There are also many respects in which human communities are similar that override cultural differences. All major human cultural systems include magic, religion, moral values, recreation, regulation of mating, education, and so forth. But the *content* of these different categories, and the ways the content and the categories are put together, differ enormously. These differences are reflected in the ways people raise their children. If the object of cultural transmission is to teach young people how to think, act, and feel appropriately this must be the case. To understand this process we must get a sense of this variety.

### This Is How It Is in Palau

Five-year-old Azu trails after his mother as she walks along the village path, whimpering and tugging at her skirt. He wants to be carried, and he tells her so, loudly and demandingly, "Stop! Stop! Hold me!" His mother shows no sign of attention. She continues her steady barefooted stride, her arms swinging freely at her sides, her heavy hips rolling to smooth the jog of her walk and steady the basket of wet clothes she carries on her head. She has been to the washing pool and her burden keeps her neck stiff, but this is not why she looks impassively ahead and pretends not to notice her son. Often before she has carried him on her back and an even heavier load on her head. But today she has resolved not to submit to his plea, for it is time for him to begin to grow up.

Azu is not aware that the decision has been made. Understandably, he supposes that his mother is just cross, as she often has been in the past, and that his cries will soon take effect. He persists in his demand, but falls behind as his mother firmly marches on. He runs to catch up and angrily yanks at her hand. She shakes him off without speaking to him or looking at him. Enraged, he drops solidly on the ground and begins to scream. He gives a startled look when this produces no response, then rolls over on his stomach and begins to writhe, sob, and yell. He beats the earth with his fists and kicks it with his toes. This hurts and makes him furious, the more so since it has not caused his mother to notice him. He scrambles to his feet and scampers after her, his nose running, tears coursing through the dirt on his cheeks. When almost on her heel he yells and, getting no response, drops to the ground.

By this time his frustration is complete. In a rage he grovels in the red dirt, digging his toes into it, throwing it around him and on himself. He smears it on
his face, grinding it in with his clenched fists. He squirms on his side, his feet
turning his body through an arc on the pivot of one shoulder.

A man and his wife are approaching, the husband in the lead, he with a
short-handled adz resting on his left shoulder, she with a basket of husked coconuts on her head. As they come abreast of Azu's mother the man greets her
with "You have been to the washing pool?" It is the Palauan equivalent of the
American "How are you?"—a question that is not an inquiry but a token of
recognition. The two women scarcely glance up as they pass. They have recognized each other from a distance and it is not necessary to repeat the greeting. Even less notice is called for as the couple pass Azu sprawled on the path a
few yards behind his mother. They have to step around his frenzied body, but
no other recognition is taken of him, no word is spoken to him or to each
other. There is no need to comment. His tantrum is not an unusual sight, especially among boys of his age or a little older. There is nothing to say to him or
about him.

In the yard of a house just off the path, two girls, a little older than Azu, stop
their play to investigate. Cautiously and silently they venture in Azu's direction. His mother is still in sight, but she disappears suddenly as she turns off
the path into her yard without looking back. The girls stand some distance
away, observing Azu's gyrations with solemn eyes. Then they turn and go
back to their doorway, where they stand, still watching him but saying nothing. Azu is left alone, but it takes several minutes for him to realize that this is
the way it is to be. Gradually his fit subsides and he lies sprawled and whimpering on the path.

Finally, he pushes himself to his feet and starts home, still sobbing and wiping
his eyes with his fists. As he trudges into the yard he can hear his mother
shouting at his sister, telling her not to step over the baby. Another sister is
sweeping the earth beneath the floor of the house with a coconut-leaf broom.
Glancing up, she calls shrilly to Azu, asking him where he has been. He does
not reply, but climbs the two steps to the threshold of the doorway and makes
his way to a mat in the corner of the house. There he lies quietly until he falls
asleep.

This has been Azu's first painful lesson in growing up. There will be many
more unless he soon understands and accepts the Palauan attitude that emotional attachments are cruel and treacherous entanglements, and that it is
better not to cultivate them in the first place than to have them disrupted and
disclaimed. Usually the lesson has to be repeated in many connections before
its general truth sinks in. There will be refusals of pleas to be held, to be carried, to be fed, to be cuddled, and to be amused; and for a time at least there
will follow the same violent struggle to maintain control that failed to help
Azu. For whatever the means, and regardless of the lapses from the stern
code, children must grow away from their parents, not cleave to them. Sooner
or later the child must learn not to expect the solicitude, the warm attach-

ment of earlier years and must accept the fact that he is to live in an emotional vacuum, trading friendship for concrete rewards, neither accepting nor giving lasting affection (Barnett 1960:4-6).

Is culture being transmitted here? Azu is learning that people are not to be trusted, that any emotional commitment is shaky business. He is acquiring an emotional attitude. From Professor Barnett's further description of life in Palau (Barnett 1960) we know that this emotional attitude underlies economic, social, political, even religious behavior among adult Palauans. If this happened only to Azu we would probably regard it as a traumatic event. He might then grow up to be a singularly distrustful adult in a trusting world. He would be a deviant. But virtually all Palauan boys experience this sudden rejection (it happens more gradually for girls)—not always in just this particular way—but in somewhat the same way and at about the same time. This is a culturally patterned way of getting a lesson across to the child. This culturally patterned way of treating the child has a more or less consistent result—an emotional attitude—and this emotional attitude is in turn patterned, and fits into various parts of the Palauan cultural system. What is learned by Azu and transmitted by his mother is at once a pattern of child training (the mother had it and applied it), a dimension of Palauan worldview (Palauans see the world as a place where people do not become emotionally involved with each other), a modal personality trait (most normal adult Palauans distrust others), and a pattern for behavior in the context of the many subsystems (economic, political, religious, and so forth) governing adult life.

Azu's mother did not simply tell him to stop depending upon her and to refrain from lasting emotional involvements with others. She demonstrated to him in a very dramatic way that this is the way it is in this life (in Palau it least). She probably didn't even completely rationalize what she did. She did not say to herself, "Now it is time for Azu to acquire the characteristic Palauan attitude that emotional attachments are not lasting and the best way to teach him this is for me to refuse to carry him." Barnett says that she "resolved not to submit to his plea." We cannot be sure that she even did this, for not even Homer Barnett, as well as he knows the Palauans, can get into Azu's mother's head. We know that she did not, in fact, submit to his plea. She may well have thought that it was about time for Azu to grow up. Growing up in Palau means in part to stop depending on people, even your very own loving mother. But maybe she was just plain tired, feeling a little extra crabby, so she acted in a characteristically Palauan way *without thinking about it* toward her five-year-old. People can transmit culture without knowing they do so. Probably more culture is transmitted this way than with conscious intent.

Discontinuity between early and later childhood is apparent in the Palauan case. Most cultures are patterned in such a way as to provide discontinuities of experience, but the points of time in the life cycle where these occur, and their intensity, differ widely. Azu experienced few restraints before this time. He did pretty much as he pleased, and lolled about on the laps of parents, kin, and friends. He was seldom if ever punished. There was always someone around to serve as protector, provider, and companion, and someone to carry him, usually mother, wherever he might go. Much of this changed for him after this day at the age of 5. To be sure, he is not abandoned, and he is still shielded, guided, and provided for in every physical sense, but he finds himself being told more often than asked what he wants, and his confidence in himself and in his parents has been shaken. He no longer knows how to get what he wants. The discontinuity, the break with the ways things were in his fifth year of life, is in itself a technique of cultural transmission. We will observe discontinuities in the treatment of children and their effects in other cultures.

## How Is It Done in Ulithi?

The Ulithians, like the Palauans, are Micronesians, but inhabit a much smaller island, in fact a tiny atoll in the vast Pacific, quite out of the way and fairly unchanged when first studied by William Lessa in the late forties (Lessa 1966). The Ulithians educate their children in many of the same ways the Palauans do, but differently enough to merit some special attention.

Like the Palauans, the Ulithians are solicitous and supportive of infants and young children.

The infant is given the breast whenever he cries to be fed or whenever it is considered time to feed him, but sometimes only as a pacifier. He suckles often, especially during the first three to six months of his life, when he may average around eighteen times during the day and night. The great stress placed by Ulithians on food is once more given eloquent expression in nursing practices. Thus, if both the mother and child should happen to be asleep at any time and it seems to someone who is awake that the baby should be fed, both are aroused in order to nurse the baby....

The care of the baby is marked by much solicitude on the part of everyone. One of the ways in which this is manifested is through great attention to cleanliness. The infant is bathed three times a day, and after each bath the baby is rubbed all over with coconut oil and powdered with tumeric. Ordinarily, bathing is done by the mother, who, as she holds the child, rocks him from side to side in the water and sings:

Float on the water

In my arms, my arms

On the little sea,

The big sea,

The rough sea,

The calm sea,

On this sea.

[three sentences omitted]

An infant is never left alone. He seems constantly in someone's arms, being passed from person to person in order to allow everyone a chance to fondle him. There is not much danger that if neglected for a moment he will harm himself (Lessa 1966:94-96).

Unlike the Palauans, the Ulithians do not create any special discontinuities for the young child. Even weaning is handled with as little disturbance as possible.

Weaning begins at varying ages. It is never attempted before the child is a year old, and usually he is much older than that. Some children are suckled until they are five, or even as much as seven or eight. Weaning takes about four days, one technique being to put the juice of hot pepper around the mother's nipples. Physical punishment is never employed, though scolding may be deemed necessary. Ridicule, a common recourse in training Ulithian children, is also resorted to. The child's reaction to being deprived of the breast often manifests itself in temper tantrums. The mother tries to mollify the child in a comforting embrace and tries to console him by playing with him and offering him such distraction as a tiny coconut or a flower (Lessa 1966:95).

Apparently this technique, and the emotional atmosphere that surrounds it, is not threatening to Ulithian children. We see nothing of the feelings of deprivation and rejection suffered by Azu.

The reactions to weaning are not extreme; children weather the crisis well. In fact, a playful element may be observed. A child may quickly push his face into his mother's breast and then run away to play. When the mother's attention is elsewhere, the child may make a sudden impish lunge at the breast and try to suckle from it. After the mother has scolded the weanling, he may coyly take the breast and fondle it, toy with the nipple, and rub the breast over his face. A man told me that when he was being weaned at the age of about seven, he would alternate sleeping with his father and mother, who occupied separate beds. On those occasions when he would sleep with his father, the latter would tell him to say goodnight to his mother. The boy would go over to where she was lying and playfully run his nose over her breasts. She would take this gesture good naturedly and encourage him by telling him he was virtuous, strong, and like other boys. Then he would go back to his father, satisfied with his goodness (Lessa 1966:95).

We also see in the above account of Ulithian behavior that transmission of sexual attitudes and the permissiveness concerning eroticization are markedly different than in our own society. This difference, of course, is not confined to relations between young boys and their mothers, but extends through all heterosexual relationships, and throughout the patterning of adult life.

Given the relaxed and supportive character of child rearing in Ulithi, it is small wonder that children behave in a relaxed, playful manner, and apparently grow into adults that value relaxation. This is in sharp contrast with the Palauans, whom Barnett describes as characterized by a residue of latent hostility in social situations, and as subject to chronic anxiety (Barnett 1960: 11–15).

Indeed, play is so haphazard and relaxed that it quickly melts from one thing to another, and from one place to another, with little inhibition. There is much laughter and chatter, and often some vigorous singing. One gains the impression that relaxation, for which the natives have a word they use almost constantly, is one of the major values of Ulithian culture (Lessa 1966:101).

Particularly striking in the transmission of Ulithian culture is the disapproval of unusually independent behavior.

The attitude of society towards unwarranted independence is generally one of disapproval. Normal independence is admired because it leads to later self-reliance in the growing individual, dependence being scorned if it is so strong that it will unfit him for future responsibilities. Ulithians talk a lot about homesickness and do not view this as improper, unless the longing is really for a spouse or sweetheart, the suspicion here being that it is really sexual outlet that a person wants. Longing of this sort is said to make a person inefficient and perhaps even ill. Homesickness is expected of all children and not deprecated. I was greatly touched once when I asked a friend to tell me what a man was muttering about during a visit to my house. He said he felt sad that I was away from my home and friends and wondered how I could endure it. Ulithians do not like people to feel lonely; sociability is a great virtue for them (Lessa 1966:101).

The degree and kinds of dependence and independence that are inculcated in children are significant variables in any transcultural comparison of cultural transmission. Palauan children are taught not to trust others and grow to adulthood in a society where social relationships tend to be exploitative and, behind a facade of pleasantness, hostile. Palauans are not, however, independent, and tend to be quite dependent for direction upon external authority (Barnett 1960:13, 15-16). The picture is confused in Palau by the greater degree of acculturation (than at Ulithi) and the threatening situations that the Palauans have experienced under first German, then Japanese, and now American domination. In American society, middle-class culture calls for independence, particularly in males, and independence training is stressed from virtually the beginning of childhood. But adolescent and adult Americans are among the most sociable, "joiningest" people in the world. Ulithian children are not taught to be independent, and the individual who is too independent is the object of criticism. Palauan children are taught a kind of independence—to be independent of dependency upon other people's affection—by a sudden withdrawal of support at about 5 years of age. But which is really the more "independent" adult? Palauans are independent of each other in the sense that they can be cruel and callous to each other and exploitive in social relationships, but they are fearful of independent action and responsibility, are never originators or innovators, and are dependent upon authority for direction. Ulithians are dependent upon each other for social and emotional support, but do not exhibit the fearful dependency upon authority that Palauans do.

This does not mean that there is no predictable relationship between the training of children in dependency or independence and the consequences in adulthood. It does mean that the relationship is not simple and must be culturally contextualized if it is to make sense.

Every society creates some discontinuities in the experience of the individual as he or she grows up. It seems impossible to move from the roles appropriate to childhood to the roles appropriate for adulthood without some discontinuity. Societies differ greatly in the timing of discontinuity, and its abruptness. The first major break for Azu, the Palauan boy, was at five years of age. In Ulithi the major break occurs at the beginning of young adulthood.

> The mild concerns of ordinary life begin to catch up with the individual in the early years of adulthood and he can never again revert to the joyful indifference of his childhood.
>
> Attaining adulthood is marked by a ritual for boys and another for girls, neither of which is featured by genital operations. The same term, *kufar, is* used for each of the initiations....
>
> The boy's *kufar* is much less elaborate and important. It comes about when he begins to show secondary sex characteristics and is marked by three elements: a change to adult clothing, the performance of magic, and the giving of a feast. All this occurs on the same day....

The outstanding consequence of the boy's ritual is that he must now sleep in the men's house and scrupulously avoid his postpubertal sisters. Not only must he not sleep in the same house with them, but he and they may not walk together, share the same food, touch one another's personal baskets, wear one another's leis or other ornaments, make or listen to ribald jokes in one another's presence, watch one another doing a solo dance, or listen to one another sing a love song (Lessa 1966:101-102).

Brother–sister avoidances of this kind are very common in human societies. There is a whole body of literature about them and their implications and consequences. The most important thing for us to note is that this is one of the most obvious ways in which restrictions appropriate to the young adult role in Ulithian society are placed on the individual immediately after the kufar. Transitional rites, or "rites of passage," as they are frequently termed, usually involve new restrictions of this sort. So, for that matter, do the events marking important transitions occurring at other times in the life experience. Azu lost the privilege of being carried and treated like an infant, and immediately became subject to being told what to do more often than demanding and getting what he wanted. One way of looking at Azu's experience and the Ulithian kufar is to regard them as periods of sharp discontinuity in the management of cultural transmission. Expressed most simply—what cultural transmitters do to and for an individual after the event is quite different in some ways from what they did before. Another way of looking at these events is to regard them as the beginning of periods of cultural compression. Expressed most simply—cultural compression occurs when the individual's behavior is restricted by the application of new cultural norms. After the kufar, the Ulithian boy and girl cannot interact with their mature opposite sex siblings except under very special rules. Azu cannot demand to be carried and is told to do many other things he did not have to do before.

In Ulithi the girl's kufar is much more elaborate. When she notices the first flow of blood she knows she must go immediately to the women's house. As she goes, and upon her arrival, there is a great hullabaloo in the village, with the women shouting again and again, "The menstruating one, Hooo!" After her arrival she takes a bath, changes her skirt, has magic spells recited over her to help her find a mate and enjoy a happy married life, and is instructed about the many *etap* (taboos) she must observe—some for days, others for weeks, and yet others for years. Soon she goes to live in a private hut of her own, built near her parent's house, but she still must go to the menstrual house whenever her discharge begins (Lessa 1966:102-104).

The discontinuity and compression that Ulithian young people experience after the kufar are not limited to a few taboos.

Adolescence and adulthood obviously come rushing together at young Ulithians, and the attitude of the community toward them undergoes a rapid change. The boy and the girl are admitted to a higher status, to be sure, and they are given certain rights and listened to with more respect when they speak. But a good deal is expected of them in return. Young men bear the brunt of the heaviest tasks assigned by the men's council. For their own parents they must help build and repair houses, carry burdens, climb trees for coconuts, fish, make rope, and perform all the other tasks commonly expected of an able-bodied man. Young women are similarly called upon to do much of the harder work of the village and the household. Older people tend to treat these very young adults with a sudden sternness and formality lacking when they were in their childhood. The missteps of young people are carefully watched and readily criticized, so that new adults are constantly aware of the critical gaze of their elders. They may not voice strong objections or opinions, and have no political rights whatsoever, accepting the decisions of the men's and women's councils without murmur. Altogether, they are suddenly cut off from childhood and must undergo a severe transition in their comportment towards others about them. Only in the amatory sphere can they find release from the petty tyranny of their elders (Lessa 1966:104).

## What Is It Like To Be Initiated in Hano?

Like the Hopi, with whom they are very close neighbors on the same mesa in Arizona, the Hano Tewa hold an initiation ceremony into the Kachina[1] cult at about nine years of age. In fact, the Tewa and Hopi share the same ceremony. Further examination of this occasion will be instructive. Up until that time Tewa children are treated about the way the Hopi children are. They are kept on a cradleboard at first, weaned late, by middle-class American standards, and on the whole treated very permissively and supportively by mothers, mother's sisters, grandparents, fathers, older siblings, and other people in and about the extended family household, admonished and corrected by the mother's brother, and half scared to death from time to time when they are bad by the Kachinas, or the threat of Kachinas. Of course nowadays the continuity of this early period is somewhat upset because children must start in the government day school at Polacca when they are about seven, and the teachers' ideas of proper behavior are frequently at variance with those maintained by Tewa parents. Excepting for school, though, Tewa children can be said to experience a consistent, continuous educational environment through the early years.

---

[1]This word is sometimes spelled Katcina, sometimes Kachina. Voth, used as the source for the description of the Hopi ceremony, spells it Katcina. Dozier, used as the source for the Hano Tewa, spells it Kachina. Either is correct.

Things change when the initiation takes place at about age nine. A cere-monial father is selected for the boy, and a ceremonial mother for the girl. These ceremonial parents, as well as the real parents and for that matter ev-eryone in the pueblo, build up the coming event for the child so that he or she is in a tremendous state of excitement. Then the day comes. Edward Dozier reports the initiation experience of one of his informants.

We were told that the Kachina were beings from another world. There were some boys who said that they were not, but we could never be sure, and most of us believed what we were told. Our own parents and elders tried to make us believe that the Kachina were powerful beings, some good and some bad, and that they knew our innermost thoughts and actions. If they did not know about us through their own great power, then probably our own relatives told the Kachina about us. At any rate every time they visited us they seemed to know what we had thought and how we had acted.

As the time for our initiation came closer we became more and more fright-ened. The ogre Kachina, the Soyoku, came every year and threatened to carry us away; now we were told that we were going to face these awful creatures and many others. Though we were told not to be afraid, we could not help ourselves. If the Kachina are really supernaturals and powerful beings, we might have offended them by some thought or act and they might punish us. They might even take us with them as the Soyoku threatened to do every year.

Four days before Powamu our ceremonial fathers and our ceremonial mothers took us to Court Kiva. The girls were accompanied by their ceremonial moth-ers, and we boys by our ceremonial fathers. We stood outside the kiva, and then two whipper Kachina, looking very mean, came out of the kiva. Only a blanket covered the nakedness of the boys; as the Kachina drew near our cer-emonial fathers removed the blankets. The girls were permitted to keep on their dresses, however. Our ceremonial parents urged us to offer sacred corn meal to the Kachina; as soon as we did they whipped us with their yucca whips. I was hit so hard that I defecated and urinated and I could feel the welts forming on my back and I knew that I was bleeding too. He whipped me four times, but the last time he hit me on the leg instead, and as the whipper started to strike again, my ceremonial father pulled me back and he took the blow himself. "This is a good boy, my old man," he said to the Kachina. "You have hit him enough."

For many days my back hurt and I had to sleep on my side until the wounds healed.

After the whipping a small sacred feather was tied to our hair and we were told not to eat meat or salt. Four days later we went to see the Powamu ceremony in the kiva. As babies, our mother had taken us to see this event; but as soon as we began to talk, they stopped taking us. I could not remember what had happened on Powamu night and I was afraid that another frightening ordeal awaited us. Those of us who were whipped went with our ceremonial parents.

In this dance we saw that the Kachina were really our own fathers, uncles, and brothers. This made me feel strange. I felt somehow that all my relatives were responsible for the whipping we had received. My ceremonial father was kind and gentle during this time and I felt very warm toward him, but I also wondered if he was to blame for our treatment. I felt deceived and ill-treated (Dozier 1967:59-60).

The Hano Tewa children are shocked, angry, chagrined when they find that the supernatural Kachinas they have been scared and disciplined by all their lives up until then, and who during the initiation have whipped them hard, are really men they have known very well in their own community, their clans, their families. To be treated supportively and permissively all of one's life, and then to be whipped publicly (or see others get whipped) would seem quite upsetting by itself. To find out that the awesome Kachinas are men impersonating gods would seem almost too much. But somehow the experience seems to help make good adult Hano Tewa out of little ones.
    If the initiate does not accept the spiritual reality of the Kachina, and will not accept his relatives' "cruel" behavior as necessary and good for him (or her), he can stop being a Tewa. But is this a real choice? Not for anyone who is human enough to need friends and family who speak the same language, both literally and figuratively, and whose identity as a Tewa Indian stretches back through all of time. Having then (usually without debate) made the choice of being a Tewa, one is a *good* Tewa. No doubts can be allowed.
    There is another factor operating as well. Children who pass through the initiation are no longer outside looking in, they are inside looking out. They are not grown up, and neither they nor anyone else think they are, but they are a lot more grown up than they were before the initiation. Girls take on a more active part in household duties and boys acquire more responsibilities in farming and ranching activities. And it will not be long before the males can take on the role of impersonating the Kachinas and initiating children as they were initiated. The ceremonial whipping, in the context of all the dramatic ceremonies, dancing, and general community uproar, is the symbol of a dramatic shift in status role. The shift starts with just being "in the know" about what really goes on in the kiva and who the Kachinas are, and continues toward more and more full participation in the secular and sacred life of the community.
    Dorothy Eggan sums it up well for the Hopi when she writes:

Another reorganizing factor ... was feeling "big." They had shared pain with adults, had learned secrets which forever separated them from the world of children, and now they were included in situations from which they had previously been excluded, as their elders continued to teach intensely what they believed intensely: That for them there was only one alternative—Hopi as against Kahopi.

Consistent repetition is a powerful conditioning agent and, as the youngsters watched each initiation, they relived their own, and by again sharing the experience gradually worked out much of the bitter residue from their own memories of it, while also rationalizing and weaving group emotions ever stronger into their own emotional core—"It takes a while to see how wise the old people really are." An initiated boy, in participating in the kachina dances, learned to identify again with the kachinas whom he now impersonated. To put on a mask is to "become a kachina," and to cooperate actively in bringing about the major goals of Hopi life. And a girl came to know more fully the importance of her clan in its supportive role. These experiences were even more sharply conditioned and directed toward adult life in the adult initiation ceremonies, of which we have as yet only fragmentary knowledge. Of this one man said to me: "I will not discuss this thing with you only to say that no one can forget it. It is the most wonderful thing any man can have to remember. You know then that you are Hopi. It is the one thing Whites cannot have, cannot take away from us. It is our way of life given to us when the world began" (Eggan 1956:364-65).

In many ways the preadolescent and adolescent period that we have been discussing, using the Ulithian kufar and the Hano Tewa initiation ceremonies as representative cases, is the most important of all in cultural transmission. There is a considerable literature on this period, including most notably the classic treatment given by Van Gennep (1960, first published in 1909) and the recent studies by Frank Young (1965), Yehudi Cohen (1964), Gary Schwartz and Don Merten (1968), and Whiting, Kluckhohn, and Albert (1958). Judith Brown provides a crosscultural study of initiation rights for females (Brown 1963). But these studies do not emphasize the educational aspects of the initiation rites or rites of passage that they analyze.

One of the few studies that does is the remarkable essay by C. W. M. Hart, based on a single case, the Tiwi of North Australia, but with implications for many other cases. Hart contrasts the attitude of cultural transmitters toward young children among the Tiwi to the rigorous demands of the initiation period.

The arrival of the strangers to drag the yelling boy out of his mother's arms is just the spectacular beginning of a long period during which the separation of the boy from everything that has gone before is emphasized in every possible way at every minute of the day and night. So far his life has been easy; now it is hard. Up to now he has never necessarily experienced any great pain, but in the initiation period in many tribes pain, sometimes horrible, intense pain, is an obligatory feature. The boy of twelve or thirteen, used to noisy, boisterous, irresponsible play, is expected and required to sit still for hours and days at a time saying nothing whatever but concentrating upon and endeavoring to understand long intricate instructions and "lectures" given him by his hostile and forbidding preceptors. [sentence omitted] Life has suddenly become real and earnest and the initiate is required literally to "put away the things of a child" even the demeanor. The number of tabus and unnatural behaviors enjoined on the initiate is endless. He mustn't speak unless he is spoken to; he must eat only certain foods, and often only in certain ways, at fixed times, and in certain fixed positions. All contact with females, even speech with them is rigidly forbidden, and this includes mother and sisters (1963:415).

Hart goes on to state that the novices are taught origin myths, the meaning of the sacred ceremonials, in short, theology, which in primitive society is inextricably mixed up with astronomy, geology, geography, biology (the mysteries of birth and death), philosophy, art, and music—in short the whole cultural heritage of the tribe; and that the purpose of this teaching is not to make better economic men of the novices, but rather " ... better citizens, better carriers of the culture through the generations ... " (Hart 1963:415). In this view Hart agrees (as he points out himself) with George Pettit, who did a thorough study of educational practices among North American Indians, and who writes that the initiation proceedings were " ... a constant challenge to the elders to review, analyze, dramatize, and defend their cultural heritage" (Pettit 1946:182).

Pettit's words also bring into focus another feature of the initiation rituals implicit in the description of these events for the Ulithians, Hano Tewa, and the Tiwi, which seems very significant. In all these cases dramatization is used as an educational technique. In fact a ceremony of any kind is a dramatization, sometimes indirect and metaphoric, sometimes very direct, of the interplay of crucial forces and events in the life of the community. In the initiation ceremonies dramatization forces the seriousness of growing up into the youngster's mind and mobilizes his emotions around the lessons to be learned and the change in identity to be secured. The role of dramatization in cultural transmission may be difficult for American readers to appreciate, because the pragmatization of American schools and American life in general has gone so far.

These points emphasize the view of initiation proceedings taken in this chapter—that they are dramatic signals for new beginnings and, at various times before and throughout adolescence in many societies, the intensification of discontinuity and compression in cultural transmission. Discontinuity in the management of the youngsters' learning—from supportive and easy to rigorous and harsh; compression in the closing in of culturally patterned demand and restriction as the new status—roles attained by successfully passing through the initiation period are activated. Of course this compression of cultural demand around the individual also opens new channels of development and experience to him. As humans mature they give up the freedom of childhood for the rewards to be gained by observing

the rules of the cultural game. The initiation ceremonies are dramatic signals to everyone that the game has begun in earnest.

## What Happens in Gopalpur?

In the village of Gopalpur, in South India, described by Alan Beals, social,
not physical, mastery is stressed.

Long before it has begun to walk, the child in Gopalpur has begun to develop
a concern about relationships with others. The period of infantile dependency is extended. The child is not encouraged to develop muscular skills, but
is carried from place to place on the hip of mother or sister. The child is rarely
alone. It is constantly exposed to other people, and learning to talk, to communicate with others, is given priority over anything else that might be
learned. When the child does learn to walk, adults begin to treat it differently.
Shooed out of the house, its training is largely taken over by the play group. In
the streets there are few toys, few things to be manipulated. The play of the
child must be social play and the manipulation of others must be accomplished through language and through such nonphysical techniques as crying
and withdrawal. In the play group, the child creates a family and the family
engages in the production of imaginary food or in the exchange of real food
carried in shirt pockets (1962:19).

Children in Gopalpur imitate adults, both in the activities of play and in
the attempts to control each other.

Sidda, four years old, is playing in the front of his house with his cousin,
Bugga, age five. Sidda is sitting on the ground holding a stone and pounding.
Bugga is piling the sand up like rice for the pounding. Bugga says, "Sidda, give
me the stone, I want to pound." Sidda puts the stone on the ground, "Come
and get it." Bugga says, "Don't come with me, I am going to the godhouse to
play." Sidda offers, "I will give you the stone." He gives the stone to Bugga,
who orders him, "Go into the house and bring some water." Sidda goes and
brings water in a brass bowl. Bugga takes it and pours it on the heap of sand.
He mixes the water with the sand, using both hands. Then, "Sidda, take the
bowl inside." Sidda takes the bowl and returns with his mouth full of peanuts.
He puts his hand into his shirt pocket, finds more peanuts and puts them in
his mouth. Bugga sees the peanuts and asks, "Where did you get those?" "I got
them inside the house." "Where are they?" "In the winnowing basket." Bugga
gets up and goes inside the house returning with a bulging shirt pocket. Both
sit down near the pile of sand. Bugga says to Sidda "Don't tell mother." "No, I
won't." Sidda eats all of his peanuts and moves toward Bugga holding his
hands out. Bugga wants to know, "Did you finish yours?" "I just brought a little, you brought a lot." Bugga refuses to give up any peanuts and Sidda begins
to cry. Bugga pats him on the back saying, "I will give you peanuts later on."

They get up and go into the house. Because they are considered to be brothers, Sidda and Bugga do not fight. When he is wronged, the older Bugga
threatens to desert Sidda. When the situation is reversed, the younger Sidda
breaks into tears (Beals 1962:16).

In their play, Bugga and Sidda are faithful to the patterns of adult control
over children, as they have both observed them and experienced them.
Beals describes children going to their houses when their shirt pockets are
empty of the "currency of interaction" (grain, bits of bread, peanuts).

> This is the moment of entrapment, the only time during the day when the
> mother is able to exercise control over her child. This is the time for bargain-
> ing, for threatening. The mother scowls at her child, "You must have worked
> hard to be so hungry." The mother serves food and says, "Eat this. After you
> have eaten it, you must sit here and rock your little sister." The child eats and
> says, "I am going outside to play, I will not rock my sister." The child finishes
> its food and runs out of the house. Later, the child's aunt sees it and asks it to
> run to the store and buy some cooking oil. When it returns, the aunt says, "If
> you continue to obey me like this, I will give you something good to eat."
> When the mother catches the child again, she asks, "Where have you been?"
> Learning what occurred, she says, "if you bought cooking oil, that is fine; now
> come play with your sister." The child says, "First give me something to eat,
> and I will play with my sister." The mother scolds, "You will die of eating,
> sometimes you are willing to work, sometimes you are not willing to work;
> may you eat dirt." She gives it food and the child plays with its sister
> (1962:19).

This is the way the child in Gopalpur learns to control the unreliable
world of other people. Children soon learn that they are dependent upon
others for the major securities and satisfactions of life. The one with a large
number of friends and supporters is secure, and they can be won and controlled, the individual comes to feel, through the use of food, but also by crying, begging, and working.

## And Among the Eskimo?

Eskimo children are treated supportively and permissively. When a baby
cries it is picked up, played with, or nursed. There are a variety of baby ten-
ders about, and after the first two or three months of life older siblings and
the mother's unmarried sisters and cousins take a hand in caring for it.
There is no set sleeping or eating schedule and weaning is a gradual process
that may not be completed until the third or fourth year.

How is it then that, as white visitors to Eskimo villages often remark, the
Eskimo have managed to raise their children so well? Observers speak warmly

of their good humor, liveliness, resourcefulness, and well-behaved manner. They appear to exemplify qualities that Western parents would like to see in their own children (Chance 1966:22). American folk belief would lead one to surmise that children who are treated so permissively would be "spoiled." Norman Chance describes the situation for the Alaskan Eskimo.

> Certainly, the warmth and affection given infants by parents, siblings, and other relatives provide them with a deep feeling of well-being and security. Young children also feel important because they learn early that they are expected to be useful, working members of the family. This attitude is not instilled by imposing tedious chores, but rather by including children in the round of daily activities, which enhances the feeling of family participation and cohesion. To put it another way, parents rarely deny children their company or exclude them from the adult world.
>
> This pattern reflects the parents' views of child rearing. Adults feel that they have more experience in living and it is their responsibility to share this experience with the children, "to tell them how to live." Children have to be told repeatedly because they tend to forget. Misbehavior is due to a child's forgetfulness, or to improper teaching in the first place. There is rarely any thought that the child is basically nasty, willful, or sinful. Where Anglo-Americans applaud a child for his good behavior, the Eskimo praise him for remembering....
>
> Regardless of the degree of Westernization, more emphasis is placed on equality than on superordination—subordination in parent–child relations. A five-year-old obeys, not because he fears punishment or loss of love, but because he identifies with his parents and respects their judgment. Thus he finds little to resist or rebel against in his dealing with adults. We will find rebellion more common in adolescents, but it is not necessarily a revolt against parental control.
>
> By the time a child reaches the age of four or five, his parents' initial demonstrativeness has become tempered with an increased interest in his activities and accomplishments. They watch his play with obvious pleasure, and respond warmly to his conversation, make jokes with him and discipline him. Though a child is given considerable autonomy and his whims and wishes treated with respect, he is nonetheless taught to obey all adults. To an outsider unfamiliar with parent–child relations, the tone of Eskimo commands and admonitions sometimes sounds harsh and angry, yet in few instances does a child respond as if he had been addressed hostilely....
>
> After the age of five a child is less restricted in his activities in and around the village, although theoretically he is not allowed on the beach or ice without an adult. During the dark winter season, he remains indoors or stays close to the house to prevent him from getting lost and to protect him from polar bears which might come into the village. In summer, though, children play at all hours of the day or "night" or as long as their parents are up....

Although not burdened with responsibility, both boys and girls are expected to take an active role in family chores. In the early years responsibilities are shared, depending on who is available. Regardless of sex, it is important for a child to know how to perform a wide variety of tasks and give help when needed. Both sexes collect and chop wood, get water, help carry meat and other supplies, oversee younger siblings, run errands for adults, feed the dogs, and burn trash.

As a child becomes older, more specific responsibilities are allocated to him, according to his sex. Boys as young as seven may be given an opportunity to shoot a .22 rifle, and at least a few boys in every village have killed their first caribou by the time they are ten. A youngster learns techniques of butchering while on hunting trips with older siblings and adults, although he is seldom proficient until he is in his mid-teens. In the past girls learned butchering at an early age, since this knowledge was essential to attracting a good husband. Today, with the availability of large quantities of Western foods, this skill may not be acquired until a girl is married, and not always then.

Although there is a recognized division of labor by sex, it is far from rigid at any age level. Boys, and even men, occasionally sweep the house and cook. Girls and their mothers go on fishing or bird-hunting trips. Members of each sex can usually assume the responsibilities of the other when the need arises, albeit in an auxiliary capacity (1966:22-26).

Apparently the combination that works so well with Eskimo children is support participation admonition support. These children learn to see adults as rewarding and nonthreatening. Children are also not excluded, as they so often are in America, from the affairs of adult life. They do not understand everything they see, but virtually nothing is hidden from them. They are encouraged to assume responsibility appropriate to their age quite early in life. Children are participants in the flow of life. They learn by observing and doing. But Eskimo adults do not leave desired learning up to chance. They admonish, direct, remonstrate, but without hostility.

The Eskimo live with a desperately intemperate climate in what many white men have described as the part of the world that is the most inimical to human life. Perhaps Eskimo children are raised the way they are because a secure, good-humored, resourceful person is the only kind that can survive for long in this environment.

### In Sensuron?

The people of Sensuron live in a very different physical and cultural environment than do the Eskimo. The atmosphere of this Dusun village in Borneo (now the Malysian state of Sabah) is communicated in these passages from Thomas Williams' case study.

Sensuron is astir an hour before the dawn of most mornings. It is usually too damp and cold to sleep. Fires are built up and the morning meal cooked while members of the household cluster about the house fire pit seeking warmth. After eating, containers and utensils are rinsed off with water to "keep the worms off" and replaced in racks on the side of the house porch. Older children are sent to the river to carry water home in bamboo containers, while their mother spends her time gathering together equipment for the day's work, including some cold rice wrapped in leaves for a midday snack. The men and adolescent males go into the yard to sit in the first warmth of the sun and talk with male neighbors. The early morning exchange of plans, news, and recounting of the events of yesterday is considered a "proper way" to begin the day. While the men cluster in the yard center, with old shirts or cloths draped about bare shoulders to ward off the chill, women gather in front of one house or another, also trading news, gossip, and work plans. Many women comb each other's hair, after carefully picking out the lice. It is not unusual to see four or more women sitting in a row down the steps of a house ladder talking, while combing and delousing hair. Babies are nursed while mothers talk and small children run about the clusters of adults, generally being ignored until screams of pain or anger cause a sharp retort of *kAdA!* (do not!) from a parent. Women drape spare skirts about their bare shoulders to ward off the morning chill. About two hours after dawn these groups break up as the members go off to the work of the day.

Vocal music is a common feature of village life; mothers and grandmothers sing a great variety of lullabies and "growth songs" to babies, children sing a wide range of traditional and nonsense songs, while adults sing at work in the fields and gardens during leisure and social occasions and at times of ritual. Drinking songs and wedding songs take elaborate forms, often in the nature of song "debates" with sides chosen and a winner declared by a host or guest of honor on the basis of "beauty" of tone, humor, and general "oneupmanship" in invention of new verse forms. Most group singing is done in harmony. Adolescents, especially girls, spend much of their solitary leisure time singing traditional songs of love and loneliness. Traditional verse forms in ritual, and extensive everyday use of riddles, folktales, and proverbs comprise a substantial body of oral literature. Many persons know much ritual verse, and most can recite dozens of stylized folktales, riddles, and proverbs.

Village headmen, certain older mates, and ritual specialists of both sexes are practiced speech makers. A skill of "speaking beautifully" is much admired and imitated. The style used involves narration, with exhortation, and is emphasized through voice tone and many hand and body gestures and postures. Political debates, court hearings, and personal arguments often become episodes of dramatic representation for onlookers, with a speaker's phrase listened to for its emotional expressive content and undertones of ridicule, tragedy, comedy, and farce at the expense of others involved. The verse forms of major rituals take on dimensions of drama as the specialist delivers the lines with skillful impersonations of voices and mannerisms of disease givers, souls of the dead, and creator beings.

By late afternoon of a leisure day people in the houses begin to drift to the yards, where they again sit and talk. Fires are built to ward off the chill of winds rising off the mountains, and men and women circle the blaze, throwing bits of wood and bamboo into the fire as they talk. This time is termed *mEgAmut,* after the designation for exchange of small talk between household members. As many as 20 fires can be seen burning in yards through Sensuron at evening on most leisure days and on many evenings after work periods. Men sit and talk until after dark, when they go into houses to take their evening meal. Women leave about an hour before dark to prepare the meal, smaller children usually eat before the adults. After the evening meal, for an hour or more, the family clusters about the house fire pit, talking, with adults often engaged in small tasks of tool repair or manufacture. By 8 or 9 PM most families are asleep; the time of retiring is earlier when the work days are longer, later on rest days (1965:78-79).

Children in Sensuron are, like Eskimo children, always present, always observers. How different this way of life is from that experienced by American children! Gossip, speech-making, folktale telling, grooming, working, and playing are all there, all a part of the stream of life flowing around one and with which each member of the community moves. Under these circumstances much of the culture is transmitted by a kind of osmosis. It would be difficult for a child *not to* learn his culture.

The children of Sensuron do not necessarily grow up into good-humored, secure, trusting, "happy" adults. There are several factors that apparently interact in their growing up to make this unlikely. In the most simple sense, these children do not grow up to be like Eskimo adults because their parents (and other cultural transmitters) are not Eskimo, Dusun cultural transmitters (anybody in the community that the child hears and sees) act like Dusun. But cultural transmitters display certain attitudes and do certain things to children as well as provide them with models. In Sensuron, children are judged to be nonpersons. They are not even provided with personal names until their fifth year. They are also considered to be " ... naturally noisy, inclined to illness, capable of theft, incurable wanderers, violent, quarrelsome, temperamental, destructive of property, wasteful, easily offended, quick to forget" (Williams 1965:87). They are threatened by parents with being eaten alive, carried off, damaged by disease-givers. Here are two lullabies sung to babies in Sensuron (and heard constantly by older children):

> Sleep, Sleep, baby,
> There comes the *rAgEn* (soul of the dead)
> He carries a big stick,

> He carries a big knife,
>
> Sleep, Sleep, baby,
>
> He comes to beat you!

or, as in this verse,

> Bounce, Bounce, baby
>
> There is a hawk,
>
> Flying, looking for prey!
>
> There is the hawk, looking for his prey!
>
> He searches for something to snatch up in his claws,
>
> Come here, hawk, and snatch up this baby! (Williams 1965:88).

None of the things that the adults of Sensuron do to, with, or around their children is to be judged "bad." Their culture is different from Eskimo culture, and a different kind of individual functions effectively in it. We may for some reason need to make value judgments about a culture, the character of the people who live by it, or the way they raise children but not for the purpose of understanding it better. It is particularly hard to refrain from making value judgments when the behavior in question occurs in an area of life in our own culture about which there are contradictory rules and considerable anxiety. Take, for instance, the transmission of sexual behavior in the village of Sensuron.

In Sensuron people usually deal with their sex drives through ideally denying their existence, while often behaving in ways designed to sidestep social and cultural barriers to personal satisfaction. At the ideal level of belief the view is expressed that "men are not like dogs, chasing any bitch in heat," or "sex relations are unclean." Some of the sexuality of Dusan life has been noted earlier. There is a high content of lewd and bawdy behavior in the play of children and adolescents, and in the behavior of adults. For example, the eight-year-old girl in the house across from ours was angrily ordered by her mother to come into the house to help in rice husking. The girl turned to her mother and gave her a slow, undulating thrust of her hips in a sexual sign. More than 12 salacious gestures are known and used regularly by children and adults of both sexes, and there are some 20 equivalents of "four-letter" English terms specifically denoting the sexual anatomy and its possible uses. Late one afternoon 4 girls between 8 and 15 years, and 2 young boys of 4 and 5 years were chasing about our house steps for a half hour, grabbing at each other's genitals, and screaming, *uarE tAle!* which roughly translated means, "there is your mother's vulva!" Adult onlookers were greatly amused at the group and became convulsed with laughter when the four-year-old boy improvised the answer, "my mother has no vulva!" Thus, sexual behavior is supposed to be unclean and disgusting, while in reality it is a source of amusement and constant attention....

Children learn details of sexual behavior early, and sex play is a part of the behavior of four-to-six-year-olds, usually in houses or rice stores while parents are away at work. Older children engage in sexual activities in groups and pairs, often at a location outside the village, often in an abandoned field storehouse, or in a temporary shelter in a remote garden (Williams 1965:82-83).

We can, however, make the tentative generalization that in cultures where there is a marked discrepancy between ideal and real, between the "theory" of culture and actual behavior, this conflict will be transmitted and that conflicts of this kind are probably not conducive to trust, confidence in self and in others, or even something we might call "happiness." We are like the people of Sensuron, though probably the conflicts between real and ideal run much deeper and are more damaging in our culture. In any event, the transmission of culture is complicated by discrepancies and conflicts, for both the pattern of idealizations and the patterns of actual behavior must be transmitted, as well as the ways for rationalizing the discrepancy between them.

## How Goes It in Guadalcanal?

Many of the comments that have been made about child rearing and the transmission of culture in other communities can be applied to the situation in Guadalcanal, one of the Solomon Islands near New Guinea. Babies are held, fondled, fed, never isolated, and generally given very supportive treatment. Weaning and toilet training both take place without much fuss, and fairly late by American standards. Walking is regarded as a natural accomplishment that will be mastered in time, swimming seems to come as easily. Education is also different in some ways in Guadalcanal. There is no sharp discontinuity at the beginning of middle childhood as in Palau, nor is there any sharp break at puberty as in Ulithi, or at prepuberty as among the Hano Tewa or Hopi. The special character of cultural transmission in Guadalcanal is given by Ian Hogbin:

> Two virtues, generosity and respect for property, are inculcated from the eighteenth month onward that is to say, from the age when the child can walk about and pat bananas and other things regarded as delicacies. At this stage no explanations are given, and the parents merely insist that food must be shared with any playmate who happens to be present and that goods belonging to other villagers must be left undisturbed. A toddler presented with a piece of fruit is told to give half to "Soandso," and should the order be resisted, the adult ignores all protests and breaks a piece off to hand to the child's companion. Similarly, although sometimes callers are cautioned to put their baskets on a shelf out of reach, any meddling brings forth the rebuke, "That

belongs to your uncle. Put it down." Disobedience is followed by snatching away the item in question from the child and returning it to the owner.

In time, when the child has passed into its fourth or fifth year, it is acknowledged to have at last attained the understanding to be able to take in what the adults say. Therefore, adults now accompany demands with reasoned instruction. One day when I was paying a call on a neighbor, Mwane-Anuta, I heard him warn his second son Mbule, who probably had not reached the age of five, to stop being so greedy. "I saw your mother give you those nuts," MwaneAnuta reiterated. "Don't pretend she didn't. Running behind the house so that Penggoa wouldn't know! That is bad, very bad. Now then, show me, how many? Five left. Very well, offer three to Penggoa immediately." He then went on to tell me how important it was for children to learn to think of others so that in later life they would win the respect of their fellows.

On another occasion during a meal I found Mwane-Anuta and his wife teaching their three sons how to eat properly. "Now Mbule," said his mother, "you face the rest of us so that we can all see you aren't taking too much. And you, Konana, run outside and ask Misika from next door to join you. His mother's not home yet, and I expect he's hungry. Your belly's not the only one, my boy." "Yes," Mwane-Anuta added. "Give a thought to those you run about with, and they'll give a thought to you." At this point the mother called over the eldest lad, Kure, and placed the basket of yams for me in his hands. "There, you carry that over to our guest and say that it is good to have him with us this evening," she whispered to him. The gesture was characteristic. I noted that always when meals were served to visitors the children acted as waiters. Why was this, I wanted to know. "Teaching, teaching," Mwane-Anuta replied. "This is how we train our young to behave" (1964:33).

It appears that in Guadalcanal direct verbal instruction is stressed as a technique of cultural transmission. Hogbin goes on to describe the constant stream of verbal admonition that is directed at the child by responsible adults in almost every situation. And again and again the prime values, generosity and respect for property, are reinforced by these admonitions.

The amount of direct verbal reinforcement of basic values, and even the amount of direct verbal instruction in less crucial matters, varies greatly from culture to culture. The people of Guadalcanal, like the Hopi, keep telling their children and young people how to behave and when they are behaving badly. In American middle-class culture there is also great emphasis on telling children what they should do, explaining how to do it, and the reasons for doing it, though we are probably less consistent in what we tell them than are the parents of Guadalcanal. Perhaps also in our culture we tend to substitute words for experience more than do the people of Guadalcanal, for the total range of experience relevant to growing up appropriately is more directly observable and available to their children than it is to ours.

> Girls go to the gardens regularly with their mother from about the age of eight. They cannot yet wield the heavy digging stick or bush knife, but they assist in collecting the rubbish before planting begins, in piling up the earth, and weeding. Boys start accompanying their father some two or three years later, when they help with the clearing, fetch lianas to tie up the saplings that form the fence, and cut up the seed yams. The men may also allocate plots to their sons and speak of the growing yams as their own harvest. The services of a youngster are of economic value from the time that he is pubescent, but he is not expected to take gardening really seriously until after he returns from the plantation and is thinking of marriage. By then he is conscious of his rights and privileges as a member of his clan and knows where the clan blocks of land are located. As a rule, he can also explain a little about the varieties of yams and taro and the types of soil best suited to earth.
>
> At about eight a boy begins to go along with his father or uncles when the men set out in the evening with their lines to catch fish from the shore or on the reef. They make a small rod for him, show him how to bait his hook, and tell him about the different species of fish—where they are to be found, which are good to eat, which are poisonous. At the age of ten the boy makes an occasional fishing excursion in a canoe. To start with, he sits in the center of the canoe and watches, perhaps baiting the hooks and removing the catch; but soon he takes part with the rest. In less than a year he is a useful crew member and expert in steering and generally handling the craft. At the same time, I have never seen youths under the age of sixteen out at sea by themselves. Often they are eager to go before this, but the elders are unwilling to give permission lest they endanger themselves or the canoe (Hogbin 1964:39).

The children of Guadalcanal learn by doing as well as learn by hearing. They also learn by imitating adult models, as children do in every human group around the world.

> Children also play at housekeeping. Sometimes they take along their juniors, who, however, do not remain interested for long. They put up a framework of saplings and tie on coconut leaf mats, which they plait themselves in a rough-and-ready sort of way. Occasionally, they beg some raw food and prepare it; or they catch birds, bats, and rats with bows and arrows. Many times, too, I have seen them hold weddings, including till the formality of the handing over of bride price. Various items serve instead of the valuables that the grownups use—tiny pebbles instead of dog's and porpoise teeth, the long flowers of a nut tree for strings of shell discs, and rats or lizards for pigs. When first the youngsters pretend to keep house they make no sexual distinction in the allocation of the tasks. Boys and girls together erect the shelters, plait the mats, cook the food, and fetch the water. But within a year or so, although

they continue to play in company, the members of each group restrict themselves to the work appropriate to their sex. The boys leave the cooking and water carrying to the girls, who, in turn, refuse to help with the building (Hogbin 1964:37-38).

Children seem to acquire the culture of their community best when there is consistent reinforcement of the same norms of action and thinking through many different channels of activity and interaction. If a child is told, sees demonstrated, casually observes, imitates, experiments and is corrected, acts appropriately and is rewarded, corrected, and (as in the Tewa-Hopi initiation) is given an extra boost in learning by dramatized announcements of status–role change, all within a consistent framework of belief and value, he or she cannot help but learn, and learn what adult cultural transmitters want him or her to learn.

## How Do They Listen in Demirciler?

In Demirciler, an Anatolian village in the arid central plateau of Turkey, a young boy, Mahmud, learns by being allowed in the room when the adult men meet at the Muhtar's (the village headman) home evenings to discuss current affairs.

Each day, after having finished the evening meal, the old Muhtar's wife would put some small earthenware dishes or copper trays filled with nuts or chickpeas about the room, sometimes on small stands or sometimes on the floor, and the old man would build a warm fire in the fireplace. Soon after dark the men would begin to arrive by ones or twos and take their accustomed places in the men's room. This was the largest single room in the village and doubled as a guest house for visitors who came at nightfall and needed some place to sleep before going on their way the next day. It had been a long time since the room had been used for this purpose, however, because the nearby growing city had hotels, and most of the modern travelers stayed there. However, the room still served as a clearing house for all village business, as well as a place for the men to pass the cold winter evenings in warm comfort.

The room was perhaps 30 by 15 feet in size, and along one side a shelf nearly 15 inches above the floor extended about 2 feet from the wall and covered the full 30 feet of the room's length. The old Muhtar sat near the center of the shelf, waiting for his guests to arrive. As the men came in, the oldest in the village would seat themselves in order of age on this raised projection, while the younger ones would sit cross-legged on the floor. No women were ever allowed to come into this room when the men were there. The Muhtar's wife had prepared everything ahead of time, and when additional things were occasionally needed during the evening one of the boys would be sent out to fetch it. Opposite the long bench was a fireplace, slightly larger than those in the kitchen of the other village homes, in which a fire burned brightly spreading heat throughout the room. The single electric bulb lighted the space dimly and so the shadows caused by the firelight were not prevented from dancing about the walls.

Mahmud would have been happier if the electric bulb had not been there at all, the way it used to be when he had been a very small boy. Electricity had been introduced to the village only a year ago, and he remembered the days when only the glow of the fire lighted these meetings.

As the gatherings grew in size, Mahmud heard many small groups of men talking idly about all sorts of personal problems, but when nearly all of the villagers had arrived, they began to quiet down.

The Hoca posed the first question, "Muhtar Bey, when will next year's money for the mosque be taken up?"

"Hocam, the amount has not been set yet," was the Muhtar's reply.

"All right, let's do it now," the Hoca persisted.

"Let's do it now," the Muhtar agreed.

And Mahmud listened as the Hoca told about the things the mosque would need during the coming year. Then several of the older men told how they had given so much the year before that it had been hard on their families, and finally, the Muhtar talked interminably about the duty of each Moslem to support the Faith and ended by asking the head of each family for just a little more than he knew they could pay.

Following this request there were a series of discussions between the Muhtar and each family head, haggling over what the members of his family could afford to give. Finally, however, agreement was reached with each man, and the Hoca knew how much he could count on for the coming year. The Muhtar would see that the money was collected and turned over to the Hoca.

The business of the evening being out of the way, Mahmud became more interested, as he knew that what he liked most was to come now. He had learned that he was too young to speak at the meetings, because he had been taken out several times the year before by one of the older boys and told that he could not stay with the men unless he could be quiet, so he waited in silence for what would happen next. After a slight pause one of the braver of the teenaged boys called to an old man.

"Dedem, tell us some stories about the olden times."

"Shall I tell about the wars?" the old man nearest the Muhtar asked.

"Yes, about the great war with the Russians," the youth answered.

"Well, I was but a boy then, but my father went with the army of the Sultan that summer, and he told me this story" (Pierce 1964:20-21).

Is there any situation in the culture of the United States where a similar situation exists? When America was more rural than it is now, and commercial entertainments were not readily available for most people, young people learned about adult roles and problems, learned to think like adults and anticipated their own adulthood in somewhat the same way that Mahmud did. Now it is an open question whether young people would want to listen to their elders even if there was nothing else to do. Possibly this is partly because much of what one's elders "know" in our society is not true. The verities change with each generation.

At the end of the "business" session at the Muhtar's home an old man tells a story. The story is offered as entertainment, even though it has been heard countless time before. Young listeners learn from stories as well as from the deliberations of the older men as they decide what to do about somebody's adolescent son who is eyeing the girls too much, or what to do about building a new road. Storytelling has been and still is a way of transmitting information to young people in many cultures without their knowing they are being taught. Any story has either a metaphoric application to real life, provides models for behavior, or has both features. The metaphor or the model may or may not be translated into a moral. The elders in Demirciler do not, it appears, make the moral of the story explicit. In contrast, the Menomini Indians of Wisconsin always required a youngster to extract the moral in a story for himself. "You should never ask for anything to happen unless you mean it." "He who brags bites his own tail." A grandparent would tell the same story every night until the children could state the moral to the elder's satisfaction (Spindler 1971). People in different cultures vary greatly in how much they make of the moral, but stories and myth-tellings are used in virtually all cultures to transmit information, values, and attitudes.

## WHAT DOES CULTURAL TRANSMISSION DO FOR THE SYSTEM?

So far we have considered cultural transmission in cases where no major interventions from the outside have occurred, or, if they have occurred, we have chosen to ignore them for purposes of description and analysis. There are, however, virtually no cultural systems left in the world that have not experienced massive input from the outside, particularly from the West. This is the age of transformation. Nearly all tribal societies and peasant villages are being affected profoundly by modernization. One of the most important aspects of modernization is the development of schools that will, hopefully, prepare young people to take their places in a very different kind of world than the one their parents grew up in. This implies a kind of discontinuity that is of a different order than the kind we have been discussing.

Discontinuity in cultural transmission among the Dusun, Hopi, Tewa, and Tiwi is a process that produces cultural continuity in the system as a whole. The abrupt and dramatized changes in roles during adolescence, the sudden compression of cultural requirements, and all the techniques used by preceptors, who are nearly always adults from within the cultural system, educate an individual to be committed to the system. The initiation itself encapsulates and dramatizes symbols and meanings that are at the core of the cultural system so that the important things the initiate has learned up to that point, by observation, participation, or instruction, are reinforced. The discontinuity is in the way the initiate is treated during the initiation and the different behaviors expected of him (or her) afterward. The culture is maintained, its credibility validated. As the Hopi man said to Dorothy Eggan, "I will not discuss this thing with you only to say that no one can forget it. It is the most wonderful thing any man can have to remember. You know then that you are Hopi I after the initiation]. It is the one thing Whites cannot have, cannot take from us. It is our way of life given to us when the world began." (See p. 328.) This Hopi individual has been *recruited* as a Hopi.

In all established cultural systems where radical interventions from outside have not occurred, the major functions of education are *recruitment* and *maintenance*. The educational processes we have described for all of the cultures in this chapter have functioned in this manner. Recruitment occurs in two senses: recruitment to membership in the cultural system in general, so that one becomes a Hopi or a Tiwi; and recruitment to specific roles and statuses, to specific castes, or to certain classes. We may even, by stretching the point a little, say that young humans are recruited to being male or female, on the terms with which a given society defines being male or female. This becomes clear in cultures such as our own, where sex roles are becoming blurred so much that many young people grow up without a clear orientation toward either role. The educational system, whether we are talking about societies where there are no schools in the formal sense but where a great deal of education takes place, or about societies where there are many specialized formal schools, is organized to effect recruitment. The educational system is also organized so that the structure of the cultural system will be maintained. This is done by inculcating the specific values, attitudes, and beliefs that make this structure credible and the skills and competencies that make it work. People must believe in their system. If there is a caste or class structure they must believe that such a structure is good, or if not good, at least inevitable. They must also have the skills—vocational and social—that make it possible for goods and services to be exchanged that are necessary for community life to go on. Recruitment and maintenance intergrade, as you can see from the above discussion. The former refers to the process of getting people into the system and into specific roles; the latter refers to the process of keeping the system and roles functioning.

## MODERNIZING CULTURES: WHAT IS THE PURPOSE OF EDUCATION?

In this transforming world, however, educational systems are often charged with responsibility for bringing about change in the culture. They become, or are intended to become, agents of modernization. They become intentional agents of cultural discontinuity, a kind of discontinuity that does not reinforce the traditional values or recruit youngsters into the existing system. The new schools, with their curricula and the concepts behind them, are future oriented. They recruit students into a system that does not yet exist, or is just emerging. They inevitably create conflicts between generations.

Among the Sisala of Northern Ghana, a modernizing African society, for example, there have been profound changes in the principles underlying the father–son relationship. As one man put it:

> This strict obedience, this is mostly on the part of illiterates. With educated people, if you tell your son something, he will have to speak his mind. If you find that the boy is right, you change your mind. With an illiterate, he just tells his son to do something.... In the old days, civilization was not so much. We obeyed our fathers whether right or wrong. If you didn't, they would beat you. We respected our fathers with fear. Now we have to talk with our sons when they challenge us (Grindal 1972:80).

Not all of the Sisala have as tolerant and favorable a view of the changes wrought by education, however:

> When my children were young, I used to tell them stories about my village and about our family traditions. But in Tumu there are not so many people from my village and my children never went to visit the family. Now my children are educated and they have no time to sit with the family. A Sisala father usually farms with his son. But with educated people, they don't farm. They run around town with other boys: Soon we will forget our history. The educated man has a different character from his father. So fathers die and never tell their sons about the important traditions. My children don't sit and listen to me anymore. They don't want to know the real things my father told me. They have gone to school, and they are now book men. Boys who are educated run around with other boys rather than sitting and listening to their fathers (Grindal:83).

That these conflicts should flare up into open expressions of hostility toward education, schools, and teachers is not surprising. A headmaster of a

primary school among the Sisala related to Bruce Grindal what happened
when a man made a trip to a village outside Tumu.

> He parked his car on the road and was away for some time. When he returned,
> he saw that somebody had defaced his car, beaten it with sticks or something.
> Now I knew that my school children knew something about this. So I gath-
> ered them together and told them that if they were good citizens, they should
> report to me who did it and God would reward them. So I found out that this
> was done by some people in the village. When the village people found out
> their children told me such things, they were very angry. They said that the
> teachers were teaching their children to disrespect their elders. It is because
> of things like that that the fathers are taking their children out of school
> (Grindal: 97-98).

The above implies that the new schools, created for the purposes of aid-
ing and abetting modernization, are quite effective. Without question they
do create conflicts between generations and disrupt the transmission of the
traditional culture. These effects in themselves are a prelude to change.
perhaps a necessary condition. They are not, however, the result of the effectiveness of the schools as educational institutions. Because the curricular content is alien to the existing culture there is little or no reinforcement
in the home and family, or in the community as a whole, for what happens in
the school. The school is isolated from the cultural system it is intended to
serve. As F. Landa Jocano relates concerning the primary school in
Malitbog, a barrio in Panay, in the middle Philippines:

> most of what children learn in school is purely verbal imitation and academic
> memorization, which do not relate with the activities of the children at home.
> By the time a child reaches the fourth grade he is expected to be competent in
> reading, writing, arithmetic, and language study. Except for gardening, no
> other vocational training is taught. The plants that are required to be culti-
> vated, however, are cabbages, lettuce, okra, and other vegetables which are
> not normally grown and eaten in the barrio. [sentence omitted]
>
> Sanitation is taught in the school, but insofar as my observation went, this is
> not carried beyond the child's wearing clean clothes. Children may be re-
> quired to buy toothbrushes, combs, handkerchiefs, and other personal items,
> and bring these to school for inspection. Because only a few can afford to buy
> these items, only a few come to school with them. Often the school require-
> ments are the source of troubles at home, a night's crying among the chil-
> dren.... [sentence omitted] In the final analysis, such regular school
> injunctions as "brush your teeth every morning" or "drink milk and eat leafy
> vegetables" mean nothing to the children. First, none of the families brush
> their teeth. The toothbrushes the children bring to school are for inspection
> only. Their parents cannot afford to buy milk. They do not like goats' milk be-
> cause it is *malangsa* (foul smelling) Jocano 1969:53).

Nor is it solely a matter of the nonrelatedness of what is taught in the school to what is learned in the home and community. Because the curricular content is alien to the culture as a whole, what is taught tends to become formalized and unrealistic and is taught in a rigid, ritualistic manner. Again, among the Sisala of Northern Ghana, Bruce Grindal describes the classroom environment.

The classroom environment into which the Sisala child enters is characterized by a mood of rigidity and an almost total absence of spontaneity. A typical school day begins with a 15- period during which the students talk and play, often running and screaming, while the teacher, who is usually outside talking with his fellow teachers, pays no attention. At 8:30 one of the students rings a bell, and the children immediately take their seats and remove from their desks the materials needed for the first lesson. When the teacher enters the room, everyone falls silent. If the first lesson is English, the teacher begins by reading a passage in the students' readers. He then asks the students to read the section aloud, and if a child makes a mistake, he is told to sit down, after being corrected. Variations of the English lesson consist of having the students write down dictated sentences or spell selected words from a passage on the blackboard. Each lesson lasts exactly forty minutes, at the end of which a bell rings and the students immediately prepare for the next lesson.

Little emphasis is placed upon the content of what is taught; rather, the book is strictly adhered to, and the students are drilled by being asked the questions which appear at the end of each assignment. The absence of discussion is due partially to the poor training of the teachers, yet even in the middle schools where the educational standards for teachers are better, an unwillingness exists to discuss or explain the content of the lessons. All subjects except mathematics are lessons in literacy which teach the student to spell, read, and write.

Interaction between the teacher and his students is characterized by an authoritarian rigidity. When the teacher enters the classroom, the students are expected to rise as a sign of respect. If the teacher needs anything done in the classroom, one of the students performs the task. During lessons the student is not expected to ask questions, but instead is supposed to give the correct answers to questions posed to him by the teacher. The students are less intent upon what the teacher is saying than they are upon the reading materials before them. When the teacher asks a question, most of the students hurriedly examine their books to find the correct answer and then raise their hands. The teacher calls on one of them, who rises, responds (with his eyes lowered), and then sits down. If the answer is wrong or does not make sense, the teacher corrects him and occasionally derides him for his stupidity. In the latter case the child remains standing with his eyes lowered until the teacher finishes and then sits down without making a response (Grindal 1972:85).

The nonrelatedness of the school to the community in both the content being transmitted and the methods used to transmit it is logically carried into the aspirations of students concerning their own futures. These aspirations are often quite unrealistic. As one of the Sisala school boys said:

> I have in mind this day being a professor so that I will be able to help my country.... As a professor I will visit so many countries such as America, Britain, and Holland. In fact, it will be interesting for me and my wife.... When I return, my father will be proud seeing his child like this. Just imagine me having a wife and children in my car moving down the street of my village. And when the people are in need of anything, I will help them (Grindal: 89).

Or as another reported in an essay:

> By the time I have attained my graduation certificate from the university, the government will be so happy that they may like to make me president of my beloved country. When I receive my salary, I will divide the money and give part to my father and my wife and children.... People say the U.S.A. is a beautiful country. But when they see my village, they will say it is more beautiful. Through my hard studies, my name will rise forever for people to remember (Grindal: 89).

As we have said, the new schools, like the traditional tribal methods of education and schools everywhere, recruit new members of the community into a cultural system and into specific roles and statuses. And they attempt to maintain this system by transmitting the necessary competencies to individuals who are recruited into it via these roles and statuses. The problem with the new schools is that the cultural system they are recruiting for does not exist in its full form. The education the school boys and girls receive is regarded by many as more or less useless, though most people, like the Sisala, agree that at least literacy is necessary if one is to get along in the modern world. However, the experience of the school child goes far beyond training for literacy. The child is removed from the everyday routine of community life and from observation of the work rules of adults. He or she is placed in an artificial, isolated, unrealistic, ritualized environment. Unrealistic aspirations and self-images develop. Harsh reality intrudes abruptly upon graduation. The schoolboy discovers that, except for teaching in the primary schools, few opportunities are open to him. There are some clerical positions in government offices, but they are few. Many graduates migrate in search of jobs concomitant with their expectations, but they usually find that living conditions are more severe than those in the tribal area and end up accepting an occupation and life style similar to that of the illiterate tribesmen who have also migrated to the city. Those who become village teachers are not much better off. One Sisala teacher in his mid-twenties said:

I am just a small man. I teach and I have a small farm.... Maybe someday if I am fortunate, I will buy a tractor and farm for money because there is no future in teaching. When I went to school, I was told that if I got good marks and studied hard, I would be somebody, somebody important. I even thought I would go to America or England. I would still like to go, but I don't think of these things very often because it hurts too much. You see me here drinking and perhaps you think I don't have any sense. I don't know. I don't know why I drink. But I know in two days' time, I must go back and teach school. In X (his home village where he teaches) I am alone; I am nobody (Grindal: 93).

The pessimist will conclude that the new schools, as agents of modernization, are a rank failure. This would be a false conclusion. They are neither failures nor successes. The new schools, like all institutions transforming cultural systems, are not articulated with the other parts of the changing system. The future is not known or knowable. Much of the content taught in the school, as well as the very concept of the school as a place with four walls within which teacher and students are confined for a number of hours each day and regulated by a rigid schedule of "learning" activities, is Western. In many ways the new schools among the Sisala, in Malitbog, and in many other changing cultures are inadequate copies of schools in Europe and in the United States. There is no doubt, however, that formal schooling in all of the developing nations of the world, as disarticulated with the existing cultural context as it is, nevertheless is helping to bring into being a new population of literates, whose aspirations and world view are very different than that of their parents. And of course a whole class of educated elites has been created by colleges and universities in many of the countries. It seems inevitable that eventually the developing cultures will build their own models for schools and education. These new models will not be caricatures of Western schools, although in places, as in the case of the Sisala or the Kanuri of Nigeria described by Alan Peshkin (Peshkin 1972), where the Western influence has been strong for a long time, surely those models will show this influence.

Perhaps one significant part of the problem and the general shape of the solution is implied in the following exchange between two new young teachers in charge of a village school among the Ngoni of Malawi and a senior chief:

The teachers bent one knee as they gave him the customary greeting, waiting in silence until he spoke.

"How is your school?"

"The classes are full and the children are learning well, Inkosi."

"How do they behave?"

"Like Ngoni children, Inkosi."

"What do they learn?"

"They learn reading, writing, arithmetic, scripture, geography and drill, Inkosi."

"Is that education?"

"It is education, Inkosi."

"No! No! No! Education is *very* broad, *very* deep. It is not only in books, it is learning how to live. I am an old man now. When I was a boy I went with the Ngoni army against the Bemba. Then the mission came and I went to school. I became a teacher. Then I was chief. Then the government came. I have seen our country change, and now there are many schools and many young men go away to work to find money. I tell you that Ngoni children must learn how to live and how to build up our land, not only to work and earn money. Do you hear?"

"Yebo, Inkosi" (Yes, O Chief) (Read 1968:2-3).

The model of education that will eventually emerge in the modernizing nations will be one that puts the school, in its usual formal sense, in perspective, and emphasizes education in its broadest sense, as a part of life and of the dynamic changing community. It must emerge if these cultures are to avoid the tragic errors of miseducation, as the Western nations have experienced them, particularly in the relationships between the schools and minority groups.

## CONCLUSION

In this chapter we started with the question, What are some of the ways culture is transmitted? We answered this question by examining cultural systems where a wide variety of teaching and learning techniques are utilized. One of the most important processes, we found, was the management of discontinuity. Discontinuity occurs at any point in the life cycle when there is an abrupt transition from one mode of being and behaving to another, as for example at weaning and at adolescence. Many cultural systems manage the latter period of discontinuity with dramatic staging and initiation ceremonies, some of which are painful or emotionally disturbing to the initiates. They are public announcements of changes in status. They are also periods of intense cultural compression during which teaching and learning are accelerated. This managed cultural compression and discontinuity functions to enlist new members in the community and maintains the cultural system. Education, whether characterized by sharp discontinuities and culturally compressive periods, or by a relatively smooth progression of accumulating experience and status change, functions in established cultural systems to recruit new members and maintain the existing system. We then turned to a discussion of situations where alien or future-oriented cultural systems are introduced through formal schooling. Schools among the Sisala of Ghana, a modernizing African nation, and a Philippine barrio were used as examples of this relationship and its consequences. The disarticulation of school and community was emphasized. The point was made that children in these situations are intentionally recruited to a cultural system other than the one they originated from, and that the school does not maintain the existing social order, but, in effect, destroys it. This is a kind of discontinuity very different than the one we discussed previously, and produces severe dislocations in life patterns and interpersonal relations as well as potentially positive change.

## REFERENCES AND FURTHER READING

Barnett, Homer G. 1960. *Being a Paluan.* CSCA. New York: Holt, Rinehart and Winston, Inc.

Beals, Alan R. 1962. *Gopalpur: A South Indian Village.* CSCA. New York: Holt, Rinehart and Winston, Inc.

Brown, Judith K. 1963. "A Crosscultural Study of Female Initiation Rites." *American Anthropologist,* 65:837–853.

Chance, Norman A. 1966. *The Eskimo of North Alaska.* CSCA. New York: Holt, Rinehart and Winston, Inc.

Cohen, Yehudi. 1964. *The Transition from Childhood to Adolescence.* Chicago: Aldine Publishing Co.

Deng, Francis Mading. 1972. *The Dinka of the Sudan.* CSCA. New York: Holt, Rinehart and Winston, Inc.

Dozier, Edward P. 1967. *Hano: A Tewa Indian Community in Arizona.* CSCA. New York: Holt, Rinehart and Winston, Inc.

Eggan, Dorothy. 1956. "Instruction and Affect in Hopi Cultural Continuity." *Southwestern Journal of Anthropology,* 12:347–370.

Grindal, Bruce T. 1972. *Growing Up in Two Worlds: Education and Transition among the Sisala of Northern Ghana.* CSCA. New York: Holt, Rinehart and Winston, Inc.

Hart, C. W. M. 1963. "Contrasts Between Prepubertal and Postpubertal Education." In G. Spindler (ed.), *Education and Culture.* Holt, Rinehart and Winston, Inc.

Henry, Jules. 1960. "A Crosscultural Outline of Education." *Current Anthropology* 1, 267–305.

————. 1963. *Culture Against Man.* New York: Random House.

Hogbin, Ian. 1964. *A Guadalcanal Society: The Kaoka Speakers.* CSCA. New York: Holt, Rinehart and Winston, Inc.

Jocano, F. Landa. 1969. *Growing Up in a Philippine Barrio.* CSEC. New York: Holt, Rinehart and Winston, Inc.

Lessa, William A. 1966. *Ulithi. A Micronesian Design for Living.* CSCA. New York: Holt, Rinehart and Winston, Inc.

Mead, Margaret. 1949. *Coming of Age in Samoa.* New York: Mentor Books (first published in 1928).

———. 1953. *Growing Up in New Guinea.* New York: Mentor Books (first published in 1930).

———. 1964. *Continuities in Cultural Evolution.* New Haven: Yale University Press.

Peshkin, Alan. 1972. *Kanuri Schoolchildren: Education and Social Mobilization in Nigeria.* CSEC. New York: Holt, Rinehart and Winston, Inc.

Pettit, George A. 1946. *Primitive Education in North America.* Publications in American Archeology and Ethnology, Vol. 43.

Pierce, Joe E. 1964. *Life in a Turkish Village.* CSCA. New York: Holt, Rinehart and Winston, Inc.

Read, Margaret. 1968. *Children of Their Fathers: Growing Up Among the Ngoni of Malawi.* CSEC. New York: Holt, Rinehart and Winston, Inc.

Schwartz, Gary, and Don Merten. 1968. "Social Identity and Expressive Symbols: The Meaning of an Initiation Ritual," *American Anthropologist, 70:* 1117–1131.

Spindler, George D., and Louise S. Spindler. 1971. *Dreamers without Power: The Menomini Indians of Wisconsin.* CSCA. New York: Holt, Rinehart and Winston, Inc.

Spiro, Melford. 1958. *Children of the Kibbutz.* Cambridge, Mass.: Harvard University Press.

Van Gennep, Arnold. 1960. *The Rites of Passage.* Chicago: University of Chicago Press.

Whiting, Beatrice B. (ed.). 1963. *Child Rearing in Six Cultures.* New York: John Wiley & Sons, Inc.

Whiting, John F., R. Kluckhohn, and A. Albert. 1958. "The Function of Male Initiation Ceremonies at Puberty." In E. Maccoby, T. Newcomb, and E. Hartley, (eds.) *Doings in Social Psychology.* New York: Holt, Rinehart and Winston, Inc.

Williams, Thomas R. 1965. *The Dusun: A North Borneo Society.* CSCA. New York: Holt, Rinehart and Winston, Inc.

Young, Frank. 1965. *Initiation Ceremonies.* Indianapolis: The Bobbs-Merrill Company.

# Part II

## COMPARISONS

# Part
# II

# COMPARISONS

This Part focuses on comparison, something we consider to be essential to an anthropological approach. Central Desert Aborigines (Australia) are compared to the Hutterites of North America to show that cultures may be constructed to produce success and not failure. Male and female responses to rapid culture changes are compared as an approach to understanding male and female adaptations to schooling. Roger Harker and the Schoenhausen school are juxtaposed to show how familiarity reduces the ethnographer's ability to perceive elemental cultural process. And the schools in Roseville and Schoenhausen are compared to highlight the dialogue that occurs in each about class control, discipline, learning, and authority.

# There Are No Dropouts
# Among the Arunta
# and Hutterites
## (1989)

*George and Louise Spindler*

We intend this chapter to be cross-cultural, holistic and anthropological in the traditional sense of the discipline. Much current work in school ethnography has been microanalytic rather than holistic and it has been confined to our own schools without comparative reference. Attention to the inner dynamics of the classroom, and even to smaller segments such as reading groups, has been productive. The broader comparative scope, however, can give us useful perspective on our schools and our assumptions about education. To do this we will regard schooling as a form of cultural transmission, and we will be particularly concerned with a special form of cultural transmission called 'initiation.' In the course of our analysis we will make various broad statements about education that express our understanding of the phenomenon. Though they may seem assertive, they are to be taken as tentative and subject to modification or replacement as our understanding grows.

## ASSUMPTIONS

All human societies purposefully educate their young. All humans, as advanced primates, are super-learners. They will learn anything and everything if not interfered with. Children in all societies, however, learn only certain things. All educational systems are intentional interferences with the learning process—so children learn what adults think they should learn, and do not learn what adults think they should not—presumably. Of course, what adults think they are teaching their children and what children actually learn may be rather different. The success of an educational system in the restricted sense of the term may be measured by the discrepancy.

In our cross-cultural studies we have called attention to a process we have termed 'cultural compression.' Humans spend a lot of time and energy compressing their offspring into the cultural mold. They do so because education, as cultural transmission, is the major mechanism of cultural survival. Cultural survival requires replication to the extent possible. Education, seen from this point of view, functions to recruit new members into society and maintain the cultural system (G. Spindler, 1970, 1974; G. and L. Spindler, 1982).

One of the major cultural compression, recruitment and maintenance processes worldwide is what anthropologists have called 'rites of passage' or initiation ceremonies (Van Gennep, 1960; Young, 1965). These may be seen as high points in cultural transmission and acquisition, where the moral force and social energies of the community are brought to bear on the initiate, to shape him or her into the desired and valued adult mold. They constitute the most explicit forms of intentional cultural transmission, the most formal expression of education—in most of the world's cultures.

These periods of initiation, of compressive cultural transmission, vary greatly in intensity and duration from society to society. In some cases, as among the Fore of the Highlands of New Guinea, there is scarcely notice of the transition of girls and boys into adulthood though much is made of funerals (Sorenson, 1967). As among others, such as the central desert people of aboriginal Australia (Spencer and Gillen, 1899, 1904), the Sambia of the New Guinea Islands (Herdt, 1981, 1987) or the Sebei of Africa (Goldschmidt, 1976, 1987), the initiations start early in life and continue in a highly compressive sequence of intensive periods of activity, in some cases lasting for a decade or more.

One of the primary mechanisms that make the initiation process effective as an educational device appears to be the resolution of dissonance, in the original sense of the term proposed by Leon Festinger (1957). That is, the experience of sudden compressive initiation, discontinuous with the previous experience of the child, creates anxiety and produces ambivalence toward the very cultural system and its representatives that are managing the initiation. This anxiety and ambivalence, which can be termed *dissonance* for our purposes, is resolved by the successful completion of the initiation sequence, and virtually all initiates do complete the process. The initiation proceedings are not designed to produce failure. They produce success. As this dissonance is resolved, the initiates identify with and internalize the attributes of the personnel, the values and symbols deemed important by the adult preceptors running the show. We may be able to convey the essential nature of this model of education by describing some of the sequences of initiations for the traditional Arunta of central desert Australia. We will use the ethnographic present in our description (Spencer and Gillen, 1899, 1904).

There are seven stages of initiation for Arunta males. We will not discuss the females; they are no less important than the males, but their initiation is focused mostly on one point in the life cycle—marriage. The males start their formal education at about age 10 and it continues into the 20s in most cases. The initiation begins with the Ambaquerka stage, when the boys are seized and taken from the bosom of their families by forbidding strangers. They are transported away into the night to an isolated camp in the bush. This separation from family and home is a persistent feature of initiations everywhere. While in the bush camp, the initiates are treated to considerable physical hazing, including being tossed in the air, smoked over fires and having some front teeth knocked out. While all this is happening, their preceptors are teaching them how important it is to keep secret all they learn, and giving them some glimpses into the structure of meaning surrounding creation and life. After a week the boys are returned to their home camp much chastened and enjoined not to talk about what has happened and to avoid all direct contact with their mothers and sisters. Secrecy and cross-sex avoidance are also near universals.

Within a year or two the young initiates will enter the next stage of initiation when a large gathering called a Corroboree is held. This stage of initiation, which includes a number of substages, culminates in circumcision, done with great ceremony, and as a kind of reinforcement of deep lessons learned and never to be forgotten concerning the time of origin—the dream time—and the Churingas—sacred objects connecting humans to the dream time. They also learn the obligations of kinship, as roles of instruction, support and hazing are distributed among kin. Among the Arunta kinship is very complex. During all the ceremonies the initiates huddle together, underfed, cold, scared, and denied anything resembling human status or participation in the normal round of Arunta culture. Nor are they permitted any casual social participation in their own peer group. Life is earnest, their preceptors severe and their future in seeming doubt.

To make matters worse, there is a constant battle being fought between the males at one end of the ceremonial grounds, where the initiates are literally held captive, and the females, including mothers and sisters, at the other end. The women surge forth, armed with shields and clubs, beat the men savagely and return triumphant to their end of the arena with the initiates they have recaptured. But soon the men invade the women's area, seize the initiates and return to their end. This happens several times. The boys are the object of a great deal of attention and conflict, all of it threatening.

During the days and nights of the initiation, for this particular stage, the boys are taught more and more about the dream time, the Churingas (sacred icons), and the network of kin obligations. They are also learning respect, obedience and gender roles. The physical hazing continues and one day, as the high point of the Ulpmerka stage, the initiates are seized, one by one, laid across a living table constituted of the backs of kneeling men, and circumcised with a chipped stone blade. They are not allowed a whimper or a cry. When finished, they have passed into the Arakatura stage and are semi-adult.

But the initiate still does not have full access to his Churingas or their totemic and sacred storage place, or to the innermost secrets of Arunta theology and cosmology. This will come later as he nears complete manhood and is admitted to the inner circle of power and knowledge. Another large Corroboree is held. Many rituals are held by the various totems and lineages assembled, but the most important is the staging of the final initiations for the 'graduating class.'

Again the males and females are segregated for ritual purposes during the days and nights of the ceremony. The symbolic battle for possession of the initiates goes on, the instruction in the esoteric and sacred aspects of Arunta culture continues under the most dramatic conditions imaginable. The climax is the subincision, when each initiate is again seized, laid down and held down on the living table of human backs, and his penis cut to the urethra its entire length. When this final event occurs the women wail, tear their hair and rub ashes on open wounds. The young men rouse from their state of shock and each grasps a boomerang furnished for that purpose, hurls it towards the female encampment, and sings a song directed at his mother which says, 'And now I am through with that place.' The boy has become a man and now has access to all of the secrets and power his culture affords. His dissonance is resolved. He is now Urliara—finished. He is committed forever to his culture, its values, beliefs and ideology and to male authority. Despite the onerous nature of the initiation, instruction and experience, and the dissonance aroused, all of the young initiates survive the ordeal and are dedicated to seeing that the next class of initiates gets the same treatment.

All of the initiates succeed, none fail, in this intensive, compressive school. To fail would mean at least that one could not be an Arunta, and usually this must mean death as well, but not death at the hands of another, but social death, which in most societies means physical death. The whole operation of the initiation school is managed to produce success. To fail to initiate the young males successfully is unthinkable. The continuity of culture would be broken and the society would disintegrate. There are no dropouts.

The Arunta are an exotic, traditional, non-Western technologically primitive people. It will be instructive to look at some similar processes among a Western culture group—the Hutterites (Hostetler and Huntington, 1980). They number some 20,000 people today, but only 300 when they fled to North America from Europe, persecuted for generations because of their anti infant-baptism beliefs. They live in communal colonies on the prairies of the western United States and Canada. They regard education as the most important instrument of survival, and they commit themselves unstintingly to its proper execution. Formal education among the Hutterites is functionally equivalent to the prolonged initiation in its multiple stages for the Arunta. The process starts with kindergarten at age 3, after a fairly unpressured early childhood. In kindergarten children do not play with toys or model clay. They sit at a table on long benches and learn to pray, sing hymns and repeat religious phrases. They may play at times with something like burnt matches in a box or a clothespin that they have brought with them. They do have naps and snacks, but by any mainstream standard the Hutterite kindergarten is a spare, compressive environment.

At age 6 they enter two schools—one the state or provincial mandated elementary school, the other their own German school—held before and after hours for the first school, and on Saturday. German school is run by a man who often walks about with a switch or strap and uses it when necessary. He never punishes in anger, only in sorrow, and to make good Hutterites. There is nothing personal about it.

At age 16, the children leave school and join the work force, traveling from colony to colony as a group. These are the 'foolish years' when courtship occurs and a certain amount of tomfoolery is tolerated, if not sanctioned. Girls paint their toes with fingernail polish, worn inside their heavy shoes, and boys affect a jaunty, if somewhat somber, cowboy style. These foolish years pass quickly and usually by the early 20s, though there are some holdouts, both sexes are asking for baptism, religious instruction and then marriage. After this the long road of Hutterite conformity follows until death.

Again, despite the massive interference, the heavy compression of Hutterite schooling, the system produces only success. There are no failures, and no dropouts. There is resistance, anxiety and dissonance along the way. As one young male Hutterite, whose name also happened to be George, said to me, 'George, you couldn't stand to be a Hutterite for three seconds!' Some of the young men delay baptism and marriage into the late 20s and even into the 30s but all finally succumb.

But the doubts are resolved by the process of education. Hutterite education is one long initiation process, as are all educational systems seen from the point of view we are presenting. The initiate is committed to the cultural system by experiencing its managed, intentional, compressive, educational interference with learning, and experiencing it successfully. The reward is becoming what one's preceptors want one to be—a Hutterite.

We will add only one other culture to our list of examples our own, as we experienced it. We are both 100 percent mainstream ethnic WASPS. We both went to school in places where there was ethnic and social class diversity. We both came from middle-class homes. My father was a professor in the local teachers' college. Louise's father was a self-made lawyer, a real estate developer and a politician. Our mothers were both homemakers but also active in social and community life. We both found the initiation ceremonies of our culture tedious at times. Our American initiation, our culturally constructed intentional interference in learning, begins early and lasts long. Much of it seems irrelevant, at least it did to us. The school was confining, it took up most of the day, it interfered with much else we wanted to do. But our success, like that of the Arunta and Hutterite children, was assumed and assured. We had special classes with special teachers. We skipped grades and participated in progressive educational experiments. When we performed poorly, our teachers made an effort to find out what was wrong and how it could be corrected. I went through high school with a cohort group of some 35 similar young people. We had all the best teachers and all the most interesting opportunities, much less available to the numerically dominant Polish Catholic majority of second generation immigrants. I (George) still found school oppressive and interfering, and I learned the more important lessons of carpentry, logic, esthetics and Latin from my father and not in the school. Louise minded it less, as girls usually do, though she claims her more positive attitude was due to the fact that she went to school in southern California, which was Lotusland in her day.

All of my cohort group in my small mid-Western community went on to college. Nearly all became professionals and have had successful American mainstream lives and careers. No one that I knew even considered dropping out of school, and all were confident that there would be a place in society for them at the end of the long initiation ritual we call schooling. Louise's experience was broadly similar.

## INTERPRETIVE CONCLUSION

The main point to our comparative analysis is a simple one and one that most of us recognize, and that is that school, just as in the Arunta and Hutterite cases, and in thousands of other cultures, is borne, endured, survived, accomplished, because it is geared to success, not failure, and because success means a place, a productive, acceptable place in the social, economic and honorific scheme of things. There is an assured and assumed continuity, whatever the compressions, constraints, threats and anxiety aroused may be. The system is self-sustaining. The outcome assures the reduction of dissonance and identification with desired goals; and the cultural system has recruited new members committed to its maintenance.

These are precisely the conditions that many minorities do not encounter and the experience they do not have (Jacobs and Jordan, 1987). The school experience early on defines them as potential failures or even learning disabled, and there is always the implication that even if they put up with such definitions and endure the school, they are not assured of a positive gain at the end. The long initiation ritual of the school is for many minorities a long drawn out degradation ritual. Their language is criticized, their style disparaged and their origins suspect. Often these intimations are very subtle, and corrections of behaviors and style are offered by teachers and sometimes by peers with the most worthy of explicit intentions.

Further, according to some analysts, certain indigenous minorities have developed a culture of resistance to schooling administered in its mainstream form (Erickson, 1987). This culture of resistance is formed out of the long experience of these minorities in an essentially racist society. As with all cultures, it may continue to persist when it is not an effective adaptation to reality. This cultural resistance casts the school and teachers as enemies, with whom cooperation is suspect and to whom submission is disloyalty to one's own peer group or even to one's home and family. It is as though some of the initiates in our schools had decided that they were being initiated into the wrong society, into the enemy camp.

Schooling in America is not experienced in the same way by all minorities, as everyone knows by now. Blacks, Mexican Americans and Native Americans are more frequently alienated by schooling than are Asiatics and many of the new immigrants such as the Punjabis. In fact, the latter two populations seem frequently to find the school experience a major instrumental path to success (Gibson, 1987). Increasing numbers of all minorities are achieving success in school and success, as measured by mainstream standards, in United States society, even at the same time as the proportion of dropouts is increasing in some areas.

The initiation rituals of the school in America must be endured, just like the initiations for the Arunta and Hutterites must be endured, if our children are to become functioning adults in our society. The initiation rituals of the Arunta and Hutterites are designed for, in fact guaranteed, success. Our initiation rituals seem designed to assure success for some, and failure for others (Goldman and McDermott, 1987).

Our analytic model suggests that success is what we need to study. The reasons for dropping out seem more apparent than the reasons for staying in. We need to examine the factors involved in the relative success of some groups, but we also need to examine more critically the factors involved in the school success of individuals. Nor should mainstream schools or mainstream children be neglected. There are many degrees of alienation expressed among mainstream children in even 'good' schools. What keeps mainstream children in school even under conditions of fairly heavy alienation? We might find that our prolonged initiation rituals, our intentional interferences with learning, have become less functionally related to life in our society and our time than we think. If the school can be made a pathway to success for everyone, there will be no dropouts.

## REFERENCES

Erickson, Frederick. 1987. 'Transformation and school success: The politics and culture of educational achievement.' *Anthropology and Education Quarterly*, 18, 4: pp. 313–34.

Festinger, Leon. 1957. *A Theory of Cognitive Dissonance*. Stanford, CA: Stanford University Press.

Gibson, Margaret. 1987. 'Punjabi immigrants in an American high school.' In G. and L. Spindler (Eds.). 1987. *Interpretive Ethnography of Education*. Hillsdale, NJ: Lawrence Erlbaum Associates.

Goldman, Shelley, V. and McDermott, Ray. 1987. 'The culture of competition in American schools.' In G. Spindler (Ed.), *Education and Cultural Process: Anthropological Approaches*, 2nd ed. Prospect Heights, Ill.: Waveland Press.

Goldschmidt, Walter. 1976. *The Culture and Behavior of the Sebei: A Study in Continuity and Adaptation* (with the assistance of Gale Goldschmidt). Berkeley, CA: University of California Press.

Goldschmidt, Walter. 1987. 'The Sebei: A Study in Adaptation.' In G. and L. Spindler (Eds.). *Case Studies in Cultural Anthropology*. Fort Worth, TX: Harcourt Brace.

Herdt, Gilbert, H. 1981. *Guardians of the Flutes: Idioms of Masculinity*. New York: McGraw-Hill.

Herdt, Gilbert, H. 1987. 'The Sambia: Ritual and gender in New Guinea.' In G. and L. Spindler (Eds.). *Case Studies in Cultural Anthropology*. New York: Holt, Rinehart and Winston.

Hostetler, John and Huntington, G. 1980. 'The Hutterites in North America.' In G. and L. Spindler (Eds.), *Case Studies in Cultural Anthropology*. New York: Holt, Rinehart and Winston.

Jacob, E. and Jordan, C. (Guest Editors). 1987. *Explaining the school performance of minority students*. Theme issue of the *Anthropology of Education Quarterly*, 18, 4: pp. 259–392.

Sorenson, Richard. 1967. 'Fore Childhood.' Unpublished doctoral dissertation, Stanford University.

Spencer, Baldwin and Gillen, F. J. 1899. *The Native Tribes of Central Australia*. Republished in 1965 by Dover Press, New York.

Spencer, Sir Baldwin, and Gillen, F. J. 1904. *The Northern Tribes of Central Australia*. Republished in 1965 by Dover Press, New York.

Spindler, George. 1970. 'The education of adolescents: An anthropological perspective.' In Ellis D. Evans (Ed.), *Readings in Behavioral Development*. Hinsdale, IL: Dryden Press.

Spindler, George. 1974. 'Cultural transmission.' In G. Spindler (Ed.), *Education and Cultural Process*, New York: Holt, Rinehart and Winston. Reprinted in G. and L. Spindler (1987) *Education and Cultural Process: Anthropological Approaches*, 2nd ed. Prospect Heights, IL: Waveland Press.

Spindler, George and Spindler, Louise. 1982. 'Do anthropologists need learning theory?' *Anthropology and Education Quarterly*, 13, 2: pp. 10–25. Reprinted in G. Spindler (Ed.), *Education and Cultural Process: Anthropological Approaches*, 2nd ed. Prospect Heights, IL: Waveland Press.

Van Gennep, Arnold. 1960. *Rites of Passage*. Chicago, IL: University of Chicago Press.

Young, Frank W. 1965. *Initiation Ceremonies: A Cross-Cultural Study of Status Dramatization*. Indianapolis, IN: Bobbs-Merrill.

# 8

# Das Remstal

(1990)

*George and Louise Spindler*

## Editor's Note

Das Remstal is the concluding portion of a longer article written for the
Festschrift for Melford Spiro, *Personality and the Cultural Construction of Society* (Jordan and Swartz eds. 1990). The purpose of the article is to explore the
applicability of an interpretation offered by Spiro of the shift that has occurred recently in the kibbutzim of Israel on the part of women from full participation in politics and production to more domesticated roles. He uses the
term "precultural" to describe tendencies in this direction in virtually all human societies (Spiro 1979). We explore the meaning of this term from the
viewpoint furnished by our data on male and female perceptions of change in
four different cultures, Menominee Indian, Blood (Kanai) Indian,
Mistassinee Cree and the Schoenhausen school population. The major thrust
of the portion of the article reprinted here is our attention to a remarkable
shift of instrumental choices that occurred over a period of ten years, that was
in opposition to massive reform efforts in Germany directed at education as
well as to agriculture, administrative units and industry. This shift in a conservative direction has implications for school policy and practice, since schools
were a major target of the reform. It appears that the school is, in concert with
public sentiment, in some degree of opposition to the intent of the reform.

Perhaps schools in general function to "put on the brakes" on the more extreme reform movements, irrespective of their origin. The gender differences related to change also alert analysts to possible differences in adaptation to changing situations females may take to change, in their own life span and in school policy, more readily than males.

## A DECADE OF CHANGE

In the spring of 1977 we returned to Germany to collect a new sample of responses to the Instrumental Activities Inventory and continue our ethnographic work in the Schonhausener Grundschule and the local community. During the nearly ten years since our first intensive study of the school and the collection of our first IAI sample in 1968, much had happened (G. and L. Spindler 1974). A sweeping educational reform had been implemented at both federal and provincial administrative levels. The effects of this reform had just begun to surface at the Grundschule during our 1968 field study. New reading books for the third and fourth grades had just appeared that stressed modern life, high technology, and the realism of contemporary urban life. They were in sharp contrast to the romanticized stories about life in the country and village that children had been reading for several generations.

This initial surfacing of reform soon extended to every sector of school life. The curriculum for all grades was completely revised, new textbooks, readings, and work manuals were supplied; a stream of directives to school personnel clarifying the new objectives issued from the ministries of education; and new teachers fresh from the teacher training institutions appeared in numbers.

The *Bildung Reform* (educational reform) was only a part of a vast effort to modernize and urbanize. Though West Germany had experienced the *Wirtschaftwunder* (economic miracle) and, thanks to the need to rebuild bomb-shattered industrial plants, had an essentially new production technology and industrial plant, the administrative structure of nonurban areas, the methods of agricultural production, transportation facilities, and residential construction had lagged. The great increase in the population of West Germany due to the tidal wave of migrants and escapees from the Soviet zone created problems of accommodation that had never been entirely resolved.

The population of the Remstal had increased threefold overnight, and rural areas and idyllic *Weinorten* (wine-producing villages, such as Burgbach and Schoenhausen) had been inundated, tripling and quadrupling in size. The final phase of accommodation to these dramatic changes took place during the near-decade between our 1968 and 1977 studies.

The decade between our first study and restudy was therefore one of great change and sweeping intentional modernization. The purpose of our restudy was to try to pin down the consequences of these changes in the functioning of the school as a mediator of change. The school is mandated to serve as such: a mediator. Its purpose is to prepare children for the conditions of life that they will experience in an urbanizing and modernizing environment.

In 1977 we again administered the IAI and carried out an intensive ethnographic study of the school and its immediate community context. Our assumption was that the changes, particularly the intentional educational reform, would affect the perceptions of instrumental alternatives in the intended direction—toward a more modern outlook. The Remstal IAI had been designed with this point in mind. The choices that respondents can make all lie between traditional-village and modern urbanized instrumentalities, as they are construed in the Remstal. We were jolted by the results, which showed the opposite to be true, though we did not appreciate their full significance until we had thoroughly computerized the data upon our return to Stanford.

These data and their significance extend well beyond the focus of this chapter on sex roles and adaptations to culture change. Our discussion will be highly selective and will keep to that focus.

*The 1977 Sample.*   In 1977 we collected responses to the IAI from 233 children (grades three-nine), age range 9–16 years, of whom 122 were again male, sixty-five parents, of whom thirteen were male, and nine teachers, of whom one was male. Innovations included the use of a control sample of sixty-five additional respondents from a nearby urban elementary school. In the sample all occupational, educational, cultural, and region-of-origin categories and degrees of urbanization present in the Schoenhausen community were represented.

Again, the responses were sifted for associations and differences between. these background factors and IAI choices. Again age and sex (and other variables) produced statistically significant results, with sex producing the most consistent differentiations. The differences within the new sample by sex were fewer than in 1968, for reasons we will clarify. The new (1977) sample was also tested against the old (1968) sample. And here were the surprises.

*The 1968 and 1977 Samples Compared by Sex.*   The first surprise revealed by our data analysis was that the 1977 sample as a whole, excluding the teachers, produced choices of instrumental alternatives that were more traditional land-village oriented than those produced by the 1968 sample. The overall sample trend toward more traditional choices (e.g., village residence, traditional dwelling, or Fachwerk Haus, old church, Weingärtner) was significant. It would be interesting to make many comparisons between the old and new sample and within the new sample between age groups. We will concentrate on the 102 children in the Grundschule, who are our core group, and their mothers.

First, let us take a look at the old (1968) sample of Schoenhausen girls. Within the 1968 sample there were statistically significant differences in the distributions of choices for boys and girls ranging from .01 to .0007 (using chi-square) for instrumental choices of village versus city; Fachwerk versus modern row house; Weingärtner versus white collar work; factory versus independent small shop; technical draftsman versus small farmer; traditional versus modern church; party at home versus party in a tavern (*Gasthaus*); participation in the Weinlese; and living in a *Bauernhaus*. In each instance the girls chose the modern, urban instrumentalities more frequently than boys did. We had anticipated this finding from our work with the Menomini, Blood, and Cree, and it fit our hypothesis for the 1977 sample.

When we computerized our results from the 1977 field trip, we were shocked when we compared boys and girls within the new sample (1977) from Schoenhausen. We again find differences, but their direction is *reversed*. Girls make the more tradition-oriented choices; boys make the more urban-oriented choices. The differences between sexes are statistically weaker than within the 1968 sample, for the sample as a whole is more traditional. Nevertheless, it is startling that the direction of choices is reversed for the two sexes.

The most interesting differences, however, appear when we examine the distribution of IAI responses for new (1977) girls as against old (1968) girls. The new (1977) girls chose the village over the city, the Fachwerk over the modern house, Weingärtner over working in an office, independent shop owner over factory worker, small farmer over machinist, large-scale farmer over technical draftsman, traditional over modern church, a party at home over one in a tavern, and participation (as against nonparticipation) in the harvest. The girls in 1977 unquestionably made an abrupt swing toward traditional instrumentalities.

When we examine the differences in distributions of responses for new (1977) as against old (1968) boys, we find a pattern that is statistically much weaker than for the girls but that is in the opposite direction. The new boys more frequently chose modern instrumentalities than the old boys did.

Particularly startling to us is the fact that, in three instrumental choices, the new (1977) girls almost totally reversed the distribution of responses as compared with the old girls. The three instances are the Fachwerk house, Weingärtner, and party at home. Nearly 100 percent of all new girls responding to the IAI made traditional choices in these areas, where a slight to heavy majority had made modern choices before (in 1968). These traditional/modern reversals are particularly significant because they are at the core of the village—land domestic complex. They are a statement of apparently near-universal agreement within the 1977 sample of girls that the traditional instrumentalities, particularly as they relate to domesticity and village—land lifestyle, are more desirable than modern instrumentalities. Comparisons of the distributions of IAI responses for older students (through the ninth grade and including several kinds of schools) show the same general trend toward more traditional choices for the 1977 sample, but the responses are less consistent, and the differences less marked. The realities of instrumental choices in an urbanizing environment have forced themselves upon the consciousness of these young people. In contrast, the Grundschule children in the third and fourth grade can express "pure" sentiments, largely unaffected by practical considerations, that in muted form are distributed throughout the sample as a whole.

The same statement can be made about the parents. Again, the 1977 sample tends toward more traditional instrumental choices than the 1968 sample of parents. New mothers are more traditional as a group. We also compared the sixteen working mothers with those who did not work and found no significant differences between the two groups.

*Summary of Statistical Differentiations.* We choose a prose style to report the results of statistical tests because we want to avoid pages of charts and columns of figures. To clarify the relationships we discovered, we summarize the main findings for the Remstal data.

1. A major mandated reform effort to modernize the agricultural, residential, administrative sectors in West Germany reached its major phase of implementation in the Remstal in the period between our first study of Schoenhausen in 1968 and our restudy in 1977.

2. The Schoenhausen sample as a whole in 1977 made more traditional instrumental choices than in 1968—the opposite effect from the one we had predicted.

3. Sex differences for the 1968 sample were highly significant, with females choosing modern instrumentalities more frequently than males.

4. Sex differences for the 1977 sample were still significant but less so than in 1968. Males chose more modern instrumentalities, and females made more traditional choices, in the 1977 sample, than in 1968, thus reversing the distribution of choices by sex.

5. Females in the 1977 sample chose traditional instrumentalities much more frequently than females did in 1968.

6.   Particularly significant, in both a statistical and interpretive sense, is the fact that three "reversals" occurred in distributions of instrumental choices for the females that relate most directly to the traditional land-village domestic complex

## DISCUSSION

There are parallels between the Remstaler and the kibbutzniks studied by Melford Spiro (1979). In both instances there was a dramatic movement toward a new articulation of political and economic life and new alignments of domestic life and the public domain. Granted, the movements are quite different, but they had in common at least the dislocation of traditional male–female relationships. In both cases the apparent response, after a significant pause, has been to reorient toward traditional roles and relationships.

Generalization tends to obscure critically important specifics. Nevertheless in both cases some point in change was apparently reached that became threatening—possibly for quite different reasons. The reorientation to traditional relationships can be seen as a response to that threat. Paradoxically, in all the cases we know directly, and in many that our colleagues have observed, women wanted change and perceived and valued instrumental opportunities available outside their immediate communities. When the changes actually occurred in the Remstal case, they eventually triggered a reorientation to a more traditional position. And our Remstal data do not make it seem that reorientation of sentiment was forced on women by men, though it is true that, as women actually experienced the new alternatives created by change, they encountered role structures that had not been transformed and that can be interpreted as disadvantageous to women. Modernization and development are often disadvantageous for women. They tend to suffer significant role loss as technological development and rationalization occur, and their special orientations, needs, and capacities are rarely taken into account. In the Remstal, the woman in the traditional Bauer or Weingarten family was a pivotal factor in survival and success. Women kept house, took care of children, fed livestock, prepared meals, and worked in the vineyard and fields. Male roles were extendable into female domains to some degree, but female roles extended into male domains much further. In public life, at formal church affairs, or in politics, males represented the family, but at home the picture of the all-dominating paterfamilias that seems widely shared by everybody but the natives themselves is laughably off the mark. Women worked very hard and long, but their lives were not dull. They were important and knew it. When the traditional land-village-family pattern is broken up, this importance declines. Some women become wage earners, like men, but generally not in equally permanent or prestigeful positions, or they become mistresses of small apartments or houses devoid of livestock and economically productive activity, and unrelated to either the community or the land around it. Interestingly, the one single anxiety explicitly voiced most frequently in the IAI protocols by female respondents of all ages in the Remstal was the fear of being socially isolated. Women and girls often supported their choices of Weingärtner, independent shop owner, farmer, traditional residence, participation in the harvest, and hosting at home with expressions to the effect that these settings would make it possible for them to work and be with their husbands and with their families and neighbors. No male respondent expressed any similar sentiment.

## CONCLUSIONS

One can argue that precultural, cultural, biogrammatic, socioeconomic, or political determinants influence males and females and their relationships in the directions we have discussed. It is difficult to explain with the same paradigm *both* the return to traditional sex-role relationships *and* the consistent tendency for females to want something different from what they have. The best explanation available seems to be the lower public prestige accorded women's roles in most, perhaps all, social systems, including changing systems. If there is residual dissatisfaction with one's lot all of the time, and acute dissatisfaction some of the time, one would understandably want a change. Once the change has been experienced, if the whole prestige system does not change, women will find competition with males, especially competition in the framework of identity, an uphill battle. There may then be a reversal of priorities and a return to domesticity and service.

It is also possible to posit that domestic and service roles are intrinsically rewarding in themselves, that they afford alternative satisfaction, and that when these rewards are threatened, there is a swing back to them. Our qualitative analysis of the Remstal females' IAI protocols supports the latter explanation, but the wider literature on women and culture change, particularly in complex societies, appears to support the former.

Probably, as with most issues in our convoluted field, both explanations are right, but the valence of one may be greater than the other at any given time in a particular culture change situation. Whatever the case may be, these are sociocultural explanations, and they are the ones with which we work.

We are left without a resolution of the biology versus culture argument. The problem here is that there really can be no biology versus culture issue. Human evolution could not likely occur without selection for complementary sex-linked capacities, and these capacities probably influence adaptation to continuing changes in the conditions of existence but never in "pure," or direct, biological form. There seems to be no logical or empirical way to separate biology from culture. Males and females have different external sex organs, reproductive systems, skeletal and muscular structures, endocrine systems, oxygen-using capacities, and perhaps even brains. One sex menstruates, becomes pregnant, gives birth, and lactates. The other does not. One sex is more resistant to disease, lives longer, is born more frequently, and survives to procreate more frequently unless there is cultural interference. But these differences gain meaning, among humans, in social contexts. They become, and always have been, *cultural translations*. There is nothing "precultural" for *Homo sapiens*, nor probably for any of our ancestral species, seen from this point of view. Panhuman universals, with considerable built-in variation, can be considered as antecedent to any one culture at any given time, but these universals are cultural translations in themselves. It does not seem strange that the translations should apply crossculturally, at least as a broad framework of similarity. It would be strange if humans in different communities did not pay attention to the biological differences (which are relatively invariant) between the sexes. Nor does it seem unreasonable to assert, as some theorists of psychodynamic inclination have, that men should compensate for their inability to reproduce. They ultimately depend upon women for survival, both for the community and for the individual. As the Papago women studied by Ruth Underhill told her when she asked them why they did not resent the male dominance of certain rituals and the exclusion of women from them: "Why should we envy men? We have the real power. We made the men!" (Underhill 1979:91–92; our paraphrase). Men dominate public affairs, including politics, religion, and warfare, for otherwise they are powerless. We need not accept this explanation, but it is an example of the way in which biological differences may influence a cultural translation that would have universal tendencies. Likewise, the conditions of survival for human communities through evolutionary time have doubtless influenced cultural translations of biological differences. Necessary specializations in food procurement and defense are alone enough to account for many similarities in cultural translation crossculturally.

We can and do work with the cultural translations, both as men and women and as anthropologists. Women respond differently to culture change and the images of change not because of some direct biogrammatic determinant(s) but because their social experience has molded them. And though our language and emphases are different, we and Mel Spiro are saying much the same thing.

We do know that women respond differently from men to culture change, and there is evidence in at least the Remstal and kibbutz cases that traditional sex-role orientations tend to reassert themselves after some level of significant disruption in these relationships has occurred. We think we see supporting evidence in many situations other than the ones we have cited in this discussion, including our own in the United States of the 1980s. We think there is a swing back to certain features of the traditional sex roles and relationships wherever change in these relationships has gone far enough and long enough. Our research task in this area as a discipline, we think, should be devoted in part to discovering what "far enough" and "long enough" mean under varying conditions and to what features of the traditional arrangements there is a return. Certainly there is never a whole recreation of the traditional system.

Whether or not one accepts the tasks as defined, one thing seems sure: Studies of adaptation to the changing conditions of life that fail to take into account male/female differences in perspective and response must be considered inadequate and potentially misleading.

## NOTES

Steven Borish regards the recent privatization of the kibbutz and the low prestige accorded service roles as pivotal; he develops his position both in his dissertation (Borish 1982) and in an as yet unpublished paper on the "problem" of women in the kibbutz. He contributed much to our thinking in prolonged discussions and criticized an earlier draft of this chapter. We are also indebted to our colleagues at Madison: Herbert Lewis, Arnold Strichon, and Susan Millar—and to Bernard Siegel at Stanford for careful readings and useful critiques of the first draft.

[1]We returned again in 1981 and 1985 to examine the role of the school in the transmission of culture under conditions of culture change and urbanization.

[2]This discussion includes reference to all four cultures included in the original article "Male and Female in Four Changing Cultures" (Spindler and Spindler 1990).

## REFERENCES

Borish, Steven. 1982. *Stones of the Galilee: A study of Culture Change on an Israeli Kibbutz* (PhD diss). Stanford University.

Spindler, George D. 1974. Schooling in Schoenhausen: A Study of Cultural Transmission and Instrumental Adaptation in an Urban German Village. In G. Spindler, ed. *Education and Cultural Process: Toward an Anthropology of Education.* New York: Holt, Reinhart and Winston. Pp. 230–272.

Spindler, George and Louise. 1990. Male and Female in Four Changing Cultures. In Dordan and M. Swartz, eds. *Personality and the Cultural Construction of Society.* Papers in honor of Melford E. Spiro. Tuscaloosa and London: University of Alabama Press. Pp. 182–200.

Spiro, Melford. 1979. *Gender And Culture: Kibbutz Women Revisited*. Durham: Duke University Press.

# Roger Harker
# and Schoenhausen:
# From Familiar to Strange
# and Back Again

## (1982)

*George and Louise Spindler*

### INTRODUCTION

Doing the ethnography of schooling is nearly as interesting as doing the ethnography of the Menominee, the Kanai (the Blood Indians of Alberta, Canada), or the Mistassini Cree hunters (near James Bay, Quebec). We have "done ethnography" with the first two intermittently for several decades (and intend to do more) and with the last one for a season. Our task in all these studies was complicated by the necessity of making the strange familiar. We observed and tried to understand behavior that seemed unusual, different, exotic, and at first inexplicable. We tried to make the strange familiar to our readers, as we translated our observations into logic and expressions understandable to them. We did a cultural translation. In the process, we did some violence to the cultural knowledge we had gained in our

201

fieldwork.[1] That is, we used our cultural categories, such as "religion," "ritual," "social organization," "kin terms," "acculturation," "psychological adaptation," and so forth, in translating our informants' cultural knowledge as they expressed it and practiced it into the language and cognitive categories of: (1) anthropology, (2) the English language, (3) the Euro-American culture. If we had used their language and their categories of thought and interpretation, no one would have understood us except those Menominee, Kanai, or Cree who spoke their own language and lived the traditional way of life. Making the strange familiar is the usual task of ethnography.

Making the strange familiar was not the problem in doing ethnography in schools in the U.S.A. When I (George Spindler) started fieldwork in 1950 in West Coast elementary schools, what I observed was indeed strange enough, but since it was a mirror of my own cultural strangeness I could not see it—at first. I came very near to quitting fieldwork on my first research assignment for the team I had been hired to participate in, working out of Stanford University under the direction of Robert Bush, Professor of Education.[2] I sat in classes for days wondering what there was to "observe." Teachers taught, reprimanded, rewarded, while pupils sat at desks, squirming, whispering, reading, writing, staring into space, as they had in my own grade-school experience, in my practice teaching in a teacher training program, and in the two years of public school teaching I had done before World War II. What should I write down in my empty notebook? In the fieldwork with the Menominee, with whom we had already spent three seasons, I couldn't write fast enough or long enough, and I spent hours each night working on my field notes. And when I could take pictures I took hundreds. It never occurred to me to take a picture in any of the classrooms I worked in during the 1950s, and for several weeks in the first classrooms my notebook remained virtually empty, except for some generalized comments such as "79.1 T [we used codes for everybody] seems nervous today"[3] or "Three girls whisper together until teacher glances in their direction and says 'Must you do that?'" The familiar was all too familiar.

As Margaret Mead (I believe) once said (approximately), "if a fish were to become an anthropologist, the last thing it would discover would be water." I was an American fish in my own element. The last thing I would discover would be the intricacies of communication and reinforcement of cultural values and class position that were the key to the classroom and what was happening there. But eventually I began to see the teacher and the pupils as "natives," engaging in rituals, interaction, roleplaying, selective perception, cultural conflict, sociometric networks, defensive strategies, and so on. I began the cultural translation from familiar to strange and back to familiar.

Doing the ethnography of schooling in the U.S.A. is, indeed, nearly as interesting as doing the ethnography of the Menominee, the Kanai, and the Cree—and a lot more difficult.

This chapter is devoted to a discussion of doing ethnography in two elementary schools, one in 1951 on the West Coast, the other in a village we called "Schoenhausen" in Southern Germany. George Spindler did the first work without the field collaboration of Louise Spindler, though one of the major research techniques utilized, the Expressive Autobiographical Interview, had been developed by her in the Menominee fieldwork and in her analysis of the data on Menominee women adapting to cultural change. The field research in Germany was done in two phases, one in 1967-1968, the other in 1977. During the first phase George and Louise were working in the villages of the Rems Valley near Stuttgart, including Schoenhausen, on a project on urbanization. In the 1977 study Louise Spindler was a full collaborator in the fieldwork in the school and in the data analysis and cultural translation phases following.

Each of the studies will be outlined briefly, then discussed. Each discussion will cover some points that the other does not, but both will include consideration of making the familiar strange, and vice versa.

## Roger Harker and His Fifth-Grade Classroom

I worked in depth with Roger Harker for six months. Although I did an ethnography of his classroom and the interaction between him and his pupils, I say I worked with him, because much of our study was collaborative, particularly during its later phases. This young man had taught for three years in the elementary school. He regarded his teaching as a kind of apprenticeship for an administrative role, which he shortly achieved with the enthusiastic support of his supervisors and principal. He volunteered for the study in order, he said, "to improve my professional competence." Only volunteers were accepted as subjects by the Stanford Consultation Service, but Professor Bush and other team members were so persuasive in the faculty meetings where the project was introduced that nearly all of the teachers and administrators present volunteered.

My collection of data fell into the following categories: (1) personal, autobiographical, and psychological data on the teacher; (2) ratings of him by his principal and other superiors in the superintendent's office; (3) his own self-estimates on the same points; (4) observations of his classroom, emphasisng interaction with children; (5) interviews with each child and the elicitation of ratings of the teacher in many different dimensions, both formally and informally; (6) his ratings and estimates for each child in his classroom, including estimates of popularity with peers, academic performance and capacity, personal adjustment, home background, and liking for him; (7) sociometric data from the children about each other; and (8) interviews with each person (superintendent, principal, supervisors, children) who supplied ratings of him.

I also participated in the life of the school to the extent possible, accompanying the teacher where I could and "melting" into the classroom as much as feasible. I was always there, but I had no authority and assumed none. I became a friend and confidant to the children. These are anthropological habits.

This teacher was regarded by his superiors as most promising "clear and well-organized, sensitive to children's needs," "fair and just to all of the children," "knowing his subject areas well." I was not able to elicit either with rating scales or in interviews any criticisms or negative evaluations. There were very few suggestions for change—and these were all in the area of subject matter and curriculum.

Roger Harker described himself as "fair and just to all my pupils," as making "fair decisions," and as "playing no favorites." This was a particular point of pride with him.

His classroom was made up of children from a broad social stratum—upper-middle, middle, and lower classes—and the children represented Mexican-American, Anglo-European, and Portugese ethnic groups. I was particularly attentive to the relationships between the teacher and children from these various groups.

One could go into much detail, but a few items will suffice since they all point in the same direction, and that direction challenges both his perceptions of his own behavior and those of his superiors. He ranked highest on all dimensions, including personal and academic factors, those children who were most like himself—Anglo, middle to upper-middle social class, and, like him, ambitious (achievement-oriented). He also estimated that these children were the most popular with their peers, and were the leaders of the classroom group. His knowledge about the individual children, elicited without recourse to files or notes, was distributed in the same way. He knew significantly more about the children culturally like himself (on items concerned with home background as well as academic performance), and least about those culturally most different.

The children had quite different views of the situation. Some children described him as not always so "fair and just," as "having special pets," as not being easy to go to with their problems. On sociometric "maps" of the classroom showing which children wanted to spend time with other specific children, or work with them, sit near them, invite them to a party or a show, etc., the most popular children were not at all those the teacher rated highest. And his negative ratings proved to be equally inaccurate. Children he rated as isolated or badly adjusted socially, most of whom were nonAnglo and nonmiddle-class, more often than not turned out to be "stars of attraction" from the point of view of the children.

Observations of his classroom behavior supported the data collected by other means. He most frequently called on, touched, helped, and looked directly at the children culturally like himself. He was never mean or cruel to the other children. It was almost as though they weren't there. His interaction with the children of Anglo-European ethnicity and middle and upper-middle social class background was more frequent than with the other children, and the quality of the interaction appeared to be differentiated in the same way.

This young man, with the best of intentions, was confirming the negative hypotheses and predictions (as well as the positive ones) already made within the social system. He was informing Anglo middle-class children that they were capable, had bright futures, were socially acceptable, and were worth a lot of trouble. He was also informing lower-class and nonAnglo children that they were less capable, less socially acceptable, less worth the trouble. He was defeating his own declared educational goals.

This young teacher did not know that he was discriminating. He was rated very positively by his superiors on all counts, including being "fair and just to all the children." Apparently they were as blind to his discrimination as he was. The school system supported him and his classroom behavior without questioning or criticizing him. And, of course, the dominant social structure of the community supported the school.

## Discussion of Roger Harker

### Dissemination

One of the problems we face as anthroethnographers is how to disseminate our findings in such a way that they penetrate the complex subculture of professional education. This "case study" (as I prefer to term what we usually do as ethnographers) of Roger Harker has been presented and interpreted before my classes at Stanford every year since 1952. It has also 'appeared, but only in partial form, in various publications, the most widely known of which is probably The Transmission of American Culture (G. Spindler 1959). Many of the people influential in the development of an anthropology of education took these classes (Harry Wolcott, Richard King, John Singleton, Richard Warren, earlier, and, more recently, Ray McDermott, Stephen Arvizu, David Fetterman, Jose Maceas, Christine Finnan, Patricia Phelan, Pat Hishiki, and others). From 1952 to the present more than 2,700 graduate students in education and a smaller number of graduate students in anthropology have taken courses or seminars in which

Roger Harker was presented. Through these channels Harker and his fifth-grade classroom have become a part of the lore, if not the scientific corpus, of educational anthropology.

It is probable that the teaching of the Roger Harker case has been more effective as a mechanism for diffusion into the culture of professional education than its publication. In our efforts to disseminate the results of anthroethnography we should not overlook the teaching channel. In some ways the classroom or seminar is the most salubrious setting for the transmission and diffusion of ethnographic case study material and the lessons to be learned from it. The classroom is more flexible and less permanent than the printed page. One can be wrong, find out, and correct oneself. Nuances can be better communicated, and there is less chance of damage to the object of study. I have never published the details of Roger Harker's autobiographic interview, for example, for I fear that without my being there to correct misunderstandings or warped interpretations, he might seem other than he is (or was).

My first point in this discussion is that the results of the ethnography we do should be taught as much as or more than published. My teaching career is based on case materials, from the Menominee, the Kanai, the Cree, Roger Harker, Miss Mildew, Burgbach, and Schoenhausen. I have published, and will publish, only a small portion of the material. Somehow this relationship between fieldwork and teaching is rarely made explicit, and yet most of our colleagues exploit their fieldwork in their teaching.

*Models and Interdisciplinary Translations*

I did not have a singularly anthropological theoretical model to guide my collection of data and interpretation in the study of Roger Harker and his classroom. My graduate training at Wisconsin and at UCLA was equally distributed in psychology, sociology, and anthropology. Not so strangely, the fieldwork and interpretation of the Harker case study were guided about equally by concepts and theory from each of these three fields. I conceived of Roger as engaged in three dimensions of action: projecting in his behavior a personality formed out of past experience and particularly from familiar socialization; acting out a role as teacher that he had developed from professional training, experience, and prior observation; and converting a culture that he had learned at home, in school, and from the peer group into action in the classroom. That these three dimensions are artifacts, what we usually term "constructs," is clear enough. They are cultural translations as well. One takes the "raw" data of observation and the emic data of interviews and biographies and translates it into categories that "make sense" of it.

The translation of Roger Harker has changed over the three decades that I have used this case study to demonstrate some of what seemed important in the anthropology of education as it developed through time. In 1952–1960 I saw personality factors as more important than role and cultural factors. The fact that Roger identified with his mother and older sister and was hostile to his father was indisputably demonstrated by his autobiographic interview, his thematic apperception test (TAT), and the Rorschach projective technique (the "inkblot test"). This seemed to help explain why he became an elementary school teacher, why he got along so well with an all-female faculty and school administration, why he rated girls in his class higher on all counts than boys, and why he was a little passive about his own goals and ambitions. The socialization–personality factor still seems to help explain these matters, but they don't seem as important now.

Since about 1958 I have been shifting toward greater emphasis on the social role and cultural transmitter dimensions. What loomed as more and more important—though it had been there and recognized from the start—was the selectivity with which Harker's culture, which was thoroughly Anglo middle-class, achievement-oriented, and respectable, was projected into his interactions with the children of various backgrounds in his classes and the positive sanction for this selectivity afforded by the school and school system.

More recently I have shifted further yet in a cultural direction and am more concerned with the kinds and specifics of cultural knowledge brought into the setting and acted out in the various scenes by the children, by Roger Harker, and by others who appear in the scenario. This development is essentially an extension of the second phase of translation I engaged in over the years.

It could be that these phases of cultural translation noted above are just different ways of talking about things. Sometimes, in my darker moments, I am sure of it. But almost certainly they are more than that. Roger Harker's case has grown and become more clear and more subtle as new constructions have been placed upon the data in the process of translation.

But what if the data for these multiple translations were not there? I spent six months, at least two days each school week, working with Roger. My file on him is about two feet long, but I have never used all the data in that file. The data I do use are detailed and comprehensive enough so that I can answer, at least well enough for my purposes, the new questions that the new constructs pose for me as I retranslate. This is an argument for the ethnographic stance. More observation, more interviews, more contextualization, more photos are collected on more kinds of events and circumstances than one sees a use for within the focus of a sharply delimited problem. I think there is also an argument, in the range of translations we are discussing, for an interdisciplinary orientation. It seems to me that Roger Harker, viewed as a socialized personality, a role-player, and a cultural transmitter, was well contextualized in theory as well as in the school system and community. Perhaps ethnography should be a part of a broad clinical approach as well as a procedure for doing highly focused microanalyses of sharply delimited event chains and interactions.

The techniques of data elicitation and collection used in the study of Roger Harker were marshaled, of course, by the three disciplines I drew upon. Psychology gave me the projective techniques (I had studied for two years under Bruno Klopfer in his advanced seminar at UCLA). Sociology gave me rating scales, Likert intervals, questionnaires, status reputation tests and sociograms, and a Warner-type rating procedure for a house-to-house survey of the school district as background information. Anthropology, especially the then-emergent psychological anthropology, gave me interviewing techniques, ethnographic observation of interaction in the classroom with special attention to nonverbal communication, the concept of culture and especially of covert or tacit culture, and Louise Spindler's Expressive Autobiographic Interview technique (the E.A.I.). The E.A.I. technique allows one to selectively elicit attitudes about and expressions of culture from respondents, but with a flexible, broadly chronological self-centered framework. It proved particularly crucial in Roger Harker's case study, because it was largely from the E.A.I. that I was able to place Roger with respect to sociocultural origins and specific cultural patterns identifying him as upper-middle class and achievement-oriented.

## Locked Into the System

My last major point in the discussion of the Harker case study is that he was locked into a self-reinforcing, self-maintaining sociocultural system of action, perception, and reward, and that in my interaction with him as a consultant (my role was both to do research and to consult with the teacher being studied) I had to make the familiar strange to him in order to have any effect. He was rated by administrators and by all supervisory personnel, on forms that our research team had prepared for this purpose, at or near the top of the five-point Likert-type scale. On all items they were unanimous in rating him as fair and just, not playing favorites, and fair in all decisions concerning students. He was perceived as an alert, dedicated, unprejudiced teacher, fair in all respects. He was rated as one who had the best interests of his students at heart and made every effort to understand their problems and bring out the best in them. He perceived himself in exactly the same terms and with the same degree of approval, and he even predicted, on a form that we converted to this purpose, that his superiors and supervisors would perceive him this way. This pattern of self-reinforcing estimates is clearly established in the case material, both through responses on rating forms and in follow-up interviews with each respondent.

Just as unimpeachable is the evidence for his pattern of perceptions and estimates that show something very different operating in the classroom. Roger Harker, with the best of intentions, was highly biased and very selective in his interactions with and knowledge about the children in his classes. He was never cruel or overtly racist. But he matched, albeit unconsciously, the children like himself—middle class, achievement-oriented, and "respectable"—to all that was good and desirable. The children perceived this, but not even those whom he disadvantaged could hate him for it, because he was such a nice, kind person.

There were three cultural dimensions operative in the classroom. Roger Harker had his version of this culture: who was liked or disliked and by whom, who was "respected," who was maladjusted, who was succeeding and who wasn't, who was known for being fun, hardworking, or mean, etc. The children had quite another version, encompassing the same items, though differently phrased. And there was a third cultural dimension—the tacit culture of the children to the effect that the teacher was selective and prejudiced in his interaction with children. This was reflected in such phrases as "he has pets and favorites," "doesn't talk to me," "can't go to him with my personal problems," produced by children in interviews and a teacher rating form.

Roger could not see the strangeness of his selective perceptions, interactions, and approval because this pattern was customary and familiar, not only to him, but to his superiors, and probably to all the teachers and other professional school personnel with whom he came in contact. His "normal" environment was assimilationist, racist, and mainstream. This environment was "normal" at that time for the American school system as a whole. A great accumulation of studies indicates that the situation has not changed much. Roger Harker's case study could be replicated many times over today.

There was no way Roger Harker by himself could see and change what he was doing. If it had not been for intervention that came quite unexpectedly from the outside to challenge the interlocking and self-sustaining system of perceptions, beliefs, and rewards of which he was a part, it is most unlikely he would have changed.

## Cultural Therapy

Part of my role was to do what came later to be called "cultural therapy." it consisted of feeding back to Roger what I had collected, collated, and translated about him. He saw where and how his perceptions and understandings were skewed, and quite out of line with both reality as I perceived it and the realities of classroom life as the children perceived them. At first he was disbelieving and hostile. Eventually he assimilated what was being pre-

sented. The process was one of cultural translation for him as well as for myself. I was collating data and translating observations into a cultural
framework called "social science." By doing this I objectified the relationships in his field of action. He could accept this objectification where he
would have rejected translations in his own idiom. I also translated into the
children's perceptions so he could understand the tacit culture of his own
classroom.

In these ways I made the familiar culture of Roger Harker's classroom,
the school, and his interactions with children strange. As he said in one of
our "therapy" sessions, "It seems so strange to me now that I could be doing
that [selectively interacting with the children as described]. Why couldn't I
see it for myself?"

### Schoenhausen Grundschule: Study and Restudy

#### Introduction

We now turn to quite a different study, with different concepts, methods,
and results. However, the case study of Roger Harker and his classroom and
the study of Schoenhausen Grundschule have something in common. They
are both studies, in different ways, of resistance to change. In Roger
Harker's case he was a part of a self-reinforcing system that selected children out for the class and caste roles they would play in society. In the
Schoenhausen school this was true as well, but an educational reform had
been phrased less in terms of equal opportunity than in terms of modernization. Germany is not as multicultural and multiethnic as is our society,
though there are more differences than one might at first suspect.

Schoenhausen is an urbanizing German village of about 3,000 population in the Rems Valley, near Stuttgart.[4] It has one elementary school
(Grundschule) with six full-time teachers, a Rektor (similar to a principal)
and two others who teach music and religion on a part-time basis, and about
150 students in grades 1 through 4. Our purposes in the original study in the
winter and spring of 1967-1968 were to observe cultural transmission as it
occurred in the school and relate it to children's perceptions of instrumental alternatives (such as occupations, habitat, religion, recreation, and sex
roles) available in their environment and leading to lifestyles of greater and
less urbanization. We were also concerned with the assimilation of children
whose parents had migrated during the massive relocation after World War
II from culturally and linguistically quite different areas of Germany.

#### The 1967–1968 Study[5]

In the first study, I (George Spindler) participated in as many of the school
activities as possible, including nature hikes, trips to local historical centers,

excursions, staff and parent meetings, and so forth, and observed in all of the classrooms of the six teachers then at the school. This enabled me to write an ethnography of the educative process focusing on the transmission of culture and particularly on the transmission of values. To study the perceptions of instrumental alternatives related to urban versus traditional lifestyles, I adapted a research technique called the Instrumental Activities Inventory (I.A.I.), which we had developed in our studies of acculturation among American Indians (G. & L. Spindler 1965). The "inventory" consists of 37 line drawings of activities, such as working in the vineyard, living in a traditional Bauernhaus (farmer's house), baking bread in the communal oven, working in a factory, working as an independent shopkeeper or craftsman, a chemist, a lawyer, or a doctor, etc. The "instrumental activities" also include avocations, hobbies, and even choices of "activities" such as having an intimate dinner at home for friends or throwing a party at a tavern or other public place. This series of 37 line drawings was first administered individually to 30 children representing the age range I anticipated working with (9 to 18 years). On the basis of this pilot study, 17 drawings were selected, which were then converted to 35mm slides that could be shown with projectors to groups of approximately 30 each, beginning with the third grade. In this group administration of the Instrumental Activities inventory most of the 17 drawings were shown in contrastive pairs, forcing choices between urban-oriented and tradition-oriented activities—for example: living in a traditional Fachwerkhaus (exposed beam construction) versus living in a modern single-family row house; working in a factory versus working in the vineyard; being a big farmer (Grossbauer) versus being a chemist; going to a newly built, very modern church versus attending an ancient, very traditional church. Drawings of a Grundschule, a modern Bauernhaus, and the Weinlese (wine-grape harvest) were shown by themselves and respondents indicated whether they liked the school, wanted to live in the house, or wished to participate in the Weinlese, and why. Each respondent also wrote a short essay commenting on two statements, one favorable to urban life and one favorable to village life.

The essay statements and the I.A.I. line drawings were administered to all children in the third and fourth grades in the Grundschule, to children in the fifth, sixth, seventh, and ninth classes in the Hauptschule that most Schonhausen graduates attended (and to 15 Gymnasium students on an individual basis), to 31 parents of children in the Schoenhausen Grundschule, and to the teachers in that school.[6] The data thus obtained were treated statistically for differences in distributions of responses between class groups, and for relationship to sex, age, occupation of father, geographical origin of each parent, educational level of parents, and a host of other background variables. Age and sex proved to be the most powerful.

The results of the I.A.I. administration showed an interesting mix of idealization of rural village life—being a vintner or farmer and working in and with nature—and pragmatism about occupational choices and lifestyles. Certain values evoked as support for given instrumental choices appeared consistently in support of the rural village lifestyle ("fresh air," "less traffic," "more person-to-person contact," etc.) and dominated alternative values supporting more urban lifestyles ("live closer to work," "more shops," "more to do"). There appeared to be an idealized identification with the small village and land-related activities. This identification, however, did not interfere with the making of pragmatic instrumental choices. It did seem to serve some useful stabilizing functions during the urbanization process.

The results obtained with the I.A.I. were related to the ethnography of the school and its classrooms. Although the cultural transmission process in the school was tilted toward village-land tradition it was also pragmatically oriented and gave children a wide range of skills and understandings that were very effectively transmitted. I concluded that part of the effectiveness of cultural transmission in the school was the emphasis on excursions and visits to local historical sites and the attention to the local environment and geographical area (its present state as well as its history) in the Heimatkunde (study of the homeland) and Naturkunde (study of nature) classes.

A content analysis of textbooks and other teaching materials used in the Grundschule indicated that they were consistent with these and other emphases in cultural transmission as detected in the ethnographic study of the classroom and related activities (G. Spindler 1974a).

## The 1977 Field Study

In March, 1977, we returned to Schoenhausen to repeat the study described briefly above, although with some changes in research design. The purpose was to study the effects of the elimination of Heimatkunde and Naturkunde programs from the Grundschule curriculum, the total replacement of village and land-oriented texts with urban-oriented ones, and other extensive changes resulting from sweeping federal and provincial educational reforms initiated by the ministries of education. We wished to find out whether these had resulted in: (1) changes in the cultural transmission process in the classroom and other teacher-managed learning situations (e.g., excursions); (2) changes in perceptions of instrumental alternatives related, as before, to urban versus village-land traditional lifestyles.

We both participated extensively in the life of the school and observed for many hours in each of the classrooms in the Schoenhausen Grundschule. The I.A.I. was again administered, to all children in the third and fourth-grade classes in the school, to all teachers in the school, to 60 parents of children in the school, and to graduates of the Schoenhausen

Grundschule attending secondary schools in the area. In addition, 65 children attending an urban Grundschule nearby were administered the I.A.I. as a comparative control group.

The protocols collected from these 296 respondents were coded and computerized. Statistical tests of difference were applied to the 1968 and 1977 samples. The results were: (1) The children attending the Schoenhausen Grundschule produced a profile of I.A.I. responses exhibiting strong continuity with that produced by the children nearly a decade before. Again, they idealized the village-land tradition but made pragmatic choices of occupational alternatives that often appeared to violate this romanticized identity. (2) The children attending the more urban Grundschule (80 percent lived in high-rise apartments in a very densely populated urban area) exhibited more urban-oriented choices and perceived the advantages of urban living significantly more frequently than did the children in the Schoenhausen sample. Nevertheless, a majority of the children attending the urban school engaged in the same romantic idealization of village-land-traditional life as did the Schoenhausen children. (3) Age and sex again overrode any other background factors in relationship to choices of instrumental alternatives. (4) Older children attending the advanced schools (Realschule, Hauptschule, or Gymnasium) made urban-oriented choices more frequently, but retained the pattern of values idealizing the traditional village-land complex. (5) Television viewing was included as a variable, with respect to both program choice and number of hours of viewing per week, for every child in the sample. Television viewing, insofar as it varied within our sample, was not a significant factor influencing I.A.I. choices. (6) Most important in the framework of our purposes was the surprising finding that children in the 1977 sample made significantly more tradition-oriented land-village instrumental choices than did the children in 1968. This was true picture-by-picture of the I.A.I. and also by statistical comparison of a combined modernization score for each protocol. No significant differences between 1968 and 1977 samples of teachers appeared. Teachers, however, tended to be more oriented towards traditional instrumental choices and values than either children or parents in both the original and restudy samples. The 1977 parents' sample showed significantly more land-village choices than the parents' sample in 1968. The educational reform apparently had no effect on children's perceptions of instrumental choices available to them in their changing environment, unless the swing towards traditional values exhibited by both parents and children is a reflection of resistance to the declared policy directed at change.

The 1977 classroom observations were similar in nature to those carried on in 1968, but this time we included certain observational techniques that were not used the first time. For example, we charted the movements of teachers about the classroom. The "travel maps" resulting from this activity showed that teachers had characteristic paths and rest stations in their classrooms, from which they only occasionally deviated. This in turn influenced which children they attended to the most frequently.

We also taped most of the classes that we observed. It was not our purpose to collect the content of all verbalizations in this way, but rather to collect data on the ebb and flow of classroom activity-noise level, degree of teacher dominance, distribution of student response, etc. These tapes, when correlated with our written notes and travel maps, produce a fairly complete nonvisual record of the classroom activity.

In order to supplement this nonvisual record, we took several hundred still photos, using a 35mm compact camera with a 40mm semi-wide lens and highspeed (400 ASA) color film. We have found that a series of 25 slides from an hour of classroom instruction adds a vital dimension to our observations. Of particular interest is the styling that becomes more obvious with the visual material. Teachers assume characteristic postures, use characteristic gestures, project varying degrees of intensity, travel about the classroom differently, and so on.

Another dimension was added to our classroom observations in the 1977 study through the use of movie film. We shot over 2000 feet of sound-color film, covering all classrooms in the Schoenhausen Grundschule, but particularly the three teachers we were concentrating on—the teachers of the third and fourth grades. We also filmed playground activity, excursions, and community scenes. We used a simple fixed-focus super8mm existing light sound and color camera to avoid technical complications that would have distracted from our observations in other media, which we were carrying on simultaneously (this is where two observers were essential). The filming was done in the last two weeks of our observational period. This permitted us to film behavioral sequences that we felt sampled critical areas of teacher–student behavior. We tried to collect key behavioral episodes that would show variations in individual teaching styles. We were at least partly successful. The film sequences provide support for our inferences about style drawn from the nonvisual data and from the 35mm timed shots. For example, the film, together with the 35mm still shots and our notes, shows how teachers act when they retire to their "stations," such as a seat in a certain part of the room or a certain window ledge against which they lean, when temporarily turning over the class to student activity. One teacher tries to retain active command, albeit unintentionally, as bespoken by head and body posture and gestures. Another withdraws so completely, with only changes in facial expression as the children proceed, that she seems to disappear. Or the visual material shows how teachers behave when they invade student territory, out of their usual travel route. One teacher leans into the territory as though there were an invisible electric fence marking the boundary; another crouches down, making herself smaller and less distinguishable; and so forth.

## Discussion of the Schoenhausen Study

### Cultural Conservatism and the Grundschule

Despite sweeping curricular reforms, an almost complete turnover of teachers, and increasing urbanization of the environment, there is strong continuity, and in fact a marked conservative swing, in instrumental perceptions and supporting values exhibited by the Schonhausen children over almost a decade. Antecedent factors, such as the diverse geographic and cultural origins of parents, religious affiliation, and degree of urbanization of family of origin, exert little differential influence on instrumental choices and supporting values. There appears to be a regional culture complex that can be called "Remstal" or "Schwäbisch" that is persistent through time and that tends to homogenize, with the aid of the school, the perceptions and evaluations by children. This regional culture is land and small community oriented. Despite sweeping urbanization and industrialization, the Rems valley remains a major wine-producing area. And the Schwäbisch are famous for their stubborn conservatism.

The precise role of the school in the process is still difficult for us to define. On the one hand the fact that the curriculum, textbooks, and personnel were radically changed between our 1968 and 1977 studies, without any discernible effect on children's I.A.I. choices or supporting values, suggests that the influence of the school is unimportant. On the other hand, the diversity of cultural background represented by the families (about 40 percent are from other parts of Germany, including the former East Zone, now the D.D.R., and the outlying settlements, such as Sudetenland and Bessarabia) in the face of the homogeneity of instrumental perceptions and values exhibited in their children's responses suggests that some institution or experience setting is having an effect on these children.

Culture must be transmitted and acquired. We think that the teachers are transmitting a conservative cultural orientation and encouraging its acquisition in their classrooms and in their management of extra-classroom activities and relationships with children, irrespective of formal structural changes and educational reforms, and irrespective of individual differences in teaching styles. The school, of course, is a part of a larger, mutually reinforcing cultural whole.

The relative cultural conservatism in I.A.I. choices displayed by the teachers in both 1968 and 1977 samples (even though the overall profile is balanced between urban and village-land preferences) suggests that the school has been a steady influence in the direction of traditional values.[7]

## Contextualization

Fieldwork in the Rems Valley has been a major preoccupation for us since 1967, though we began in the fall of 1959 when we were appointed faculty for Gruppe III at Stanford in Germany. We did not return to this undergraduate study center until the winter of 1967, but then spent at least one academic quarter each year there until it was closed, for financial reasons, in 1976. The 1977 restudy of the Schoenhausen school was carried out independently of any Stanford program, as was the 1968 study, but in all of the other years we had the benefit of the fieldwork of our students who were learning anthropology by doing it. *Burgbach: Urbanization and Identity in a German Village* (G. Spindler 1973) is a product of this fieldwork. These undergraduate students did excellent ethnography, and in doing so were sensitized to German culture and, reflexively, to their own, in a way that is not possible by any other means. For us as professional research anthropologists this arrangement had great benefits, in that we had a more thorough contextualization for our own more focused work than would have been possible otherwise. We had a team, for almost a decade, of over 400 field ethnographers.

When we presented our research at a University of Wisconsin Symposium recently, a sociological colleague asked—somewhat tartly, we thought, how far we thought we had to go to contextualize adequately. The only response we could think of was "as far as time and resources permit."

## Substitute Change Versus Change in Principle

There cannot be too much context information, as we see it. One keeps finding surprises. For example, we discovered that one of the most important forces for continuity in the traditional way of life in the Remstal villages was substitute change (as against change in principle).

Tractors were substituted for drayage animals, electric power was substituted for human muscle to turn turnip and hay choppers, rototillers were substituted for the hoe, and so on. These changes of apparent significance technologically were actually forces for conservatism. They made doing the old tasks easier and more efficient and therefore kept traditional patterns of land use and residence associated with them intact long past the time this complex would have disappeared without this help. It was not until a sweeping consolidation of land ownership and a total physical recontouring of the vineyards—a change in principle—was implemented that the traditional pattern was broken. This occurred during our residence in Germany and we were able to record the consequences (G. Spindler 1973).

The function of substitute change in stabilizing traditional cultural complexes was something we first discovered in the context outside of the school. As we proceeded with our study, this discovery became the base for a hypothesis relevant to schooling. Of course, we did not have the results of our application of the I.A.I. indicating a conservative swing until we returned from the field, but our ethnographic work told us that despite a new curriculum, new textbooks and readings, new state directives, and new personnel (six teachers had been replaced) not much had really changed.

We will mention only one example. Heimatkunde had been eliminated by the reform. It had been the object of scathing criticisms by professional educators, sociologists, and folklorists. *Das Bild der Heimat im Schullesebuch* by Jörg Ehni, for example, analyzed many of the readings used in elementary school to show how a "false" sentimentality and distorted romanticism were presented to children in the established curriculum, and particularly by Heimatkunde. This was regarded as inappropriate in an age of transformative modernization. Some analysts went further to argue that the sentimental attachment to the home, village, and local area fostered a kind of amoral localism that had been one of the factors permitting the rise of Hitler and the Nazis.

A subject called *Sachskunde* had been substituted for Heimatkunde in the new curriculum. Sachskunde was to emphasize urban life, civic affairs, Germany and Europe, governmental processes, and an objective view of social life. The curriculum for Sachskunde is quite specific. We observed Sachskunde lessons and interviewed teachers about them. We accompanied classes on local excursions. We watched children roleplaying the presentation of a petition for a public playground–park to the Bürgermeister and Town Council. The conclusion we drew was that the substitution of Sachskunde for Heimatkunde and those aspects of Naturkunde that were concerned with nature and the local area was not at all a change in principle. Though it was so intended, it was converted to a substitute change in the process of instruction and classroom management. The examples used during Sachskunde sessions, the excursions, the roleplaying, were heavily in favor of the local community. There was much lost. The richness of local history and folklore and the appreciation of the manifestations of nature literally outside of the school windows were reduced and made diffuse. In essence, however, Sachskunde became a kind of Heimatkunde. As one teacher said when we asked her what happened to Heimatkunde, "Oh, we do most of that now, but we call it Sachskunde."

No change in principle had occurred. A new subject matter category had been implemented as a curriculum change appropriate to the new age, but it served largely as a mechanism of stabilization and continuity. It was a substitution, not a transformation.

Another kind of continuity was revealed in our ethnographic work, but we did not fully understand it until we returned home and analyzed our films of classroom behavior. In fact, for a while we were fairly confused about some observations we had made of teachers in their classrooms. It had to do with making the strange familiar—quite the opposite of what G. Spindler had to do in the study of Roger Harker.

## Teaching Styles and Central Questions

Our classroom observation and recording techniques were described in the summary of the Schoenhausen study. At the end of the first two weeks of observation we had decided that each of the six teachers whose classrooms we visited had a very distinctive teaching style but that the three on whom we were concentrating represented the whole range. One, the Rektor, a middle-aged male and a very experienced teacher, orchestrated his classroom every moment. He spent most of the time in the front of the room lecturing and demonstrating. He aroused interest, called on students, most of whom were trying to get his attention so he would call on them, paced back and forth, and used vigorous gestures and bodily movements to make points. When he was not lecturing or demonstrating, the class was working on assigned projects while he moved among them examining their work, correcting, and urging them on. He never relinquished overt control and virtually never rested. We began to call him the "Conductor" (as of an orchestra).

Another teacher, young, female, and with four years of teaching experience, seemed totally different in her classroom behavior. She rarely lectured; her arm and head gestures were subtle and close to the body. She never paced about in or orchestrated from the front of the room. Her rest stations, where she stopped in repose, observing but not overtly controlling, were window-side-front (to the left of the students) or in the back of the room in either corner. She turned the class over to the children, or seemed to, for group work and particularly for roleplaying, her favorite technique for getting the children involved and teaching them to think through the workings of everyday situations—working in a newspaper office, learning etiquette, petitioning the mayor, reenacting history, and so forth. We began to think of her as the "Fader," because she literally seemed to fade from the scene. One had to look for her in the classroom at times.

The style of the third teacher, also young and female and less experienced, was somewhere between the two just described. She spent most of her time in front of the classroom, lectured and demonstrated with more emphasis and gesturing than the other female teacher but much less than the Rektor, and moved among the children occasionally when they were working, but more often remained in the front of the room while children came up to her with their work. She never used roleplaying as a teaching technique during our periods of observation.

All three teachers seemed highly effective. Children were eager to learn and on the whole cooperative and involved. The work they did, much of which we examined, seemed substantially above grade level for American elementary school children in substance and competence, though not as diverse and individualistic.

We were so impressed with the differences in teaching styles among these three teachers whom we had observed and recorded with field notes, travel maps, audio recording, and 35mm shots that we began to wonder how we could ever pose our central question: How is culture transmitted in the school and how does this transmission relate to the perceptions and choice of instrumental alternatives leading to more urban or more traditional life-styles? If there were such great differences in transmitting styles, we could hardly use our observations as an argument for some relatively uniform influence of the school.

## Making the Strange Familiar Through Film

When we began filming in classrooms during the last two weeks of our field-work, we concentrated on behavioral episodes that would document the observed differences in teaching styles. We succeeded, for when the films are shown everyone immediately sees the differences and describes them approximately as we have. We know this because we have shown the films to 209 graduate students in education, nearly all of them experienced teachers, in three different classes at Stanford and at Wisconsin, to a seminar in ethnography, and to individual colleagues. The students in our classes wrote out their observations. They saw something we did not, however, and this something turned us around in our interpretations.

We had been so impressed with the diversity in styles that we could not see the commonalities. We began to form our perception of the differences during the first days of fieldwork, and everything we observed and recorded seemed to confirm these perceptions. When we started filming, we filmed in order to record the differences. It was not until more than a year after our return home, following repeated reviewings of the films and finally the observations by our students and colleagues who had not been in the field with us, that we began to see the commonalities.

The features that the three teachers have in common in their classroom management are perceived as follows:

- There is strong task orientation. A clear instructional goal is laid out, worked on, and completed. Work is immediately turned in to the teacher at completion.
- The materials used, as well as the task definition, are uniform. All children do the same lesson at the same time.
- There are clear definitions of limits in tolerated behavior at all times, even when teachers appear to relinquish control.
- The classrooms are clearly teacher-centered, teacher-controlled, teacher-directed, and teacher-disciplined.
- There is little fostering of self-responsibility or autonomy.
- The relationship to authority is fixed and constant, even when it appears superficially not to be.
- Teacher approval rather than peer approval is sought by children, and given; it is the major sanction.
- All three teachers appear to assume that if they do not control the classroom, disorder will result.

All of these commonalities were detected and recorded by most of the people who observed the films, with no previous suggestions or information about the classrooms viewed except for general statements about when and where the work was done, general background on the Rems Valley area, and an overall statement of the purpose of the project as a whole.

The differences in style impressed us so strongly that we could not see the commonalities, but why? As we reconstruct the situation, we think we were so overwhelmingly impressed because we were in an exotic setting. "Exotic" is too strong a word, but it conveys our meaning. German culture, language, and social behavior are much more like our own than, say, traditional Kanai culture, but they are still different enough so that despite regular visits lasting months for many years we never lost our sense of being in a "foreign" country. In ways we do not fully understand, this directed our attention to the differences rather than the commonalities—in fact, to the exclusion of the commonalities. We acquired a "mindset" early in the fieldwork and used our recording techniques to record what our mind-set told us was there.

We had to make the strange familiar back home, in our own setting, by reviewing our recorded data and the films of classroom behavior and showing the films to others, to make this possible.

This episode in our field experience convinced us that one of our common professional problems in ethnographic cultural translation may be that we are prone to making the strange even stranger than it really is. Perhaps it is this occupational hazard that has made cultural anthropology as a discipline more oriented toward differences in humankind than toward basic commonalities.

Of more direct importance to the anthroethnography of schooling was the fact that without our films and, of course, our slides, audiotapes, field notes, etc., to review again and again and display to others, we would not have been able to correct the deficiencies in interpretation produced by our fieldwork mind-set. Anthroethnographers must be collectors of more than they know uses for at the time.

Further, this episode underlines the unique importance of films (and videotapes). There is no parallel to the capturing of experience on sound-color film. The gestalt of movement, gesture, voice level, pitch, pause, facial expressions, and interactions with children is there to review again and again.

To be sure, the camera is selective. One of our frustrations is that we would be pointed in one direction while something was happening in six other sectors. We tried to pan and move from event to event quickly. Our films have a great deal of information in them. They are also the world's worst cinema. They are jerky and spasmodic and make one dizzy. They also miss much and highlight selectively. Nevertheless, they are indispensable.

Our use of the camera in the field, incidentally, was quite different from the kind of use often advocated and practiced by many careful ethnographers. The work done by Frederick Erickson using videotape depends on a continuous, unmanned, and less selective record of classroom activity. The videotape is the primary source of data in this and some similar studies and is microanalyzed. In our usage, the camera is an extension of the field-worker's eye, after enough fieldwork has been done to sensitize one to what is happening and what is important. We carried the super-8mm camera and compact 35mm camera everywhere we went for two weeks, and when we saw something we thought should be filmed, we filmed it. That our mind-set caused us to film classroom episodes that make the stylistic differences loom large in our film record is not to be gainsaid. It is a tribute to the value of the relatively complete record film makes possible, even when shot selectively, that we could recover the commonalities underlying differences that we did. We have also found a source of renewed inspiration and a continued flow of new information in the film shots of playground activity, street scenes in the village, vineyard operations, panned shots of the whole valley from vantage points high above it, Sunday walkers, sports contests, and much more. We are still doing fieldwork years later as we view the films.

## Qualitative Versus Quantitative Methods: Strange Bedfellows?

It has been said by some colleagues, in papers at professional meetings and in print, that quantitative and qualitative methods are incompatible. We reject this notion. In all of our nonschooling ethnographic fieldwork we have used quantitative methods and statistical analyses extensively. In both the original and the restudy phases of the Schoenhausen study such methods and analytic procedures are a central part of the methodology.

Confining our remarks to the Schoenhausen study, we make the point that the major instrument, the Instrumental Activities Inventory, elicits *emic* understandings with *emic* stimuli, and yet the responses can be treated quantitatively. It is the native's view and his or her cultural knowledge that we are eliciting with an instrument composed of stimuli that are formulated in native terms. The translation into social science occurs after the native responses are elicited, and is facilitated by the fact that the instrument is etically organized as well. That is, the conceptual structure that lies behind the I.A.I. model is drawn from theories and research on culture change and cognitive control. This conceptual structure remains constant. It remained essentially the same in our application of the instrument with the Kanai and the Cree, and in Germany. But the emic stimuli, the line drawings themselves, are made relevant to the local culture, and to the local version of modernization.[8] The line drawings of which the I.A.I. consists are accurate representations, taken directly from 35mm shots and modified by stripping out background "noise," of activities and settings in the immediate environment of the respondent. Furthermore, these drawings were critiqued during their development, by natives, on native terms, both for selectivity and for realistic accuracy. The instrument elicits qualitative data (choices of instrumental activities and statements of supporting values) that can be coded and treated nonparametrically.

The statistical treatment of the I.A.I. data provides a framework within which certain phases of the ethnographic study proceed, but the ethnographic study determines what will be in the instrument. Without the I.A.I. data we would not have known any of the things we listed as major conclusions of the study. Without the ethnography we would never know how these results could have come about. Qualitative and quantitative techniques are in no way incompatible. They provide information on different dimensions of the same phenomena, *if* the instruments used for quantification are heuristic to the setting and are formed out of field experience.

## Fieldwork and Sex

As a last point in the discussion of the Schoenhausen study we wish to take up the matter of sex in the classroom. It is usually the case that there are two sexes present, and yet most classroom ethnographies have been done by either a man or a woman or two persons of the same sex. In our experience in the Schoenhausen school we found that as a man–woman team we had access to many more aspects of school life than did G. Spindler alone in the 1968 study. Since most of the teachers were then, and are now, female, there were some awkwardnesses for a lone male. It was not possible, for instance, for George alone to enter and feel comfortable in the teachers' room where all teachers assembled before, in between, and after classes. The Rektor never entered the room himself. As a man-woman team, and particularly as a married team, we found that most of the awkwardness in research evaporated and an easy give-and-take developed that was invaluable as a source of insight and information regarding the operation of the school and the attitudes of individual teachers.

In the classroom, and on excursions, it was very useful to have both sexes represented on the team. Louise Spindler saw behavior that George did not see the first time and did not record. For example, the Rektor tended to favor girls in his classroom interaction. This is probably quite usual for male teachers, but though George had perceived it in the study of Roger Harker it did not appear in his observations in Schoenhausen in either 1968 or 1977. This was noted and recorded extensively by Louise.

There were many other instances where the presence of both sexes was important. In general, George Spindler had relatively low direct contact with the girls, but they clustered around Louise Spindler at every opportunity, allowing for free interviewing and exchange.

Even if both sexes are not doing ethnography in the same situation at the same time, it does seem important that at least two persons be present. Observers on both sides of the room see and record many events and interactions that one would miss. Two people can also do different things at the same time. One can photograph while the other writes notes. One can interview a teacher while the other observes and records the interaction, even filming it. There were many situations in and around the Schoenhausen school where the presence of two fieldworkers seemed indispensable.

In the social life outside the school, with teachers and townspeople alike, the married couple relationship was very important, since most of the parents and teachers were married. We formed friendships and made contacts that would have been difficult for a single person.

## Conclusion to This Chapter

It seems useful to summarize the major methodological points that we have made in the discussion of Roger Harker and of the Schoenhausen school.

1. Teaching should be considered (more than it is) as a means of diffusing ethnographic innovations into professional education.
2. Collecting enough data in scope and depth so that it can be used in different cultural translations is highly desirable.
3. Ethnographers may profitably draw from an interdisciplinary corpus of concepts and research techniques.

4. Contextualization can usefully extend as far as time and resources permit and often provides the base from which relevant hypotheses can be drawn.

5. Securing as complete an audiovisual record as possible is important, because this record can be analyzed and interpreted in different ways again and again.

6. Qualitative and quantitative methods and data are not opposed, but on the contrary are complementary.

7. Instruments, when used, should be emically relevant, oriented to the views and cultural knowledge of the natives.

8. It is desirable to have both sexes or at least two observers on the ethnographic team.

9. Making the strange familiar will remain a basic task in transcultural ethnography. Making the familiar strange will continue to be a basic problem in the anthroethnography of schooling in our own society.

## NOTES

[1] The Menominee fieldwork is described in the chapter by George and Louise Spindler in G. Spindler, ed. 1970a.

[2] The team was called the "Stanford Consultation Service." Its purposes were to offer in-service, individualized consultation and at the same time to do basic, case-study-oriented research in classrooms, schools, and school systems. It was supported by the Rosenberg Foundation during its initial phases. On the team were a sociologist, a psychiatrist, Professor Bush, and various graduate students working on dissertations in education and sociology.

[3] See L. Spindler, *Menomini Women and Culture Change*, 1962.

[4] "Schoenhausen" is a fictitious name. Though the Rektor and other participants in the study have no objection to our using the real name of the community, we feel it is best to cloak its identity.

[5] The results of this study are published in one paper (G. Spindler 1970b), a chapter in a collected volume on education and cultural process (G. Spindler 1974), another chapter in a monograph on urbanization and identity in a German village (G. Spindler 1973), and in an analysis of long-term research on the psychology of culture change and urbanization (L. Spindler 1978). Our purposes in the restudy of 1977 were focused on studying the effects of sweeping educational reform that had been instituted since our first study. Louise Spindler did not work in the school in the 1967-1968 study, although she was active in its community phases. She was a full partner in the 1977 restudy.

[6] There are several kinds of secondary schools in Germany. The Hauptschule is not university-preparatory; the Gymnasium is.

[7] We wish to extend our special thanks to the teaching staff in the Schoenhausen Grundschule, particularly its Rektor. The parents, the graduates of the

Grundschule attending other schools, the children themselves, and the personnel of the urban control school also deserve our warm gratitude. Doubtless we
were extended special privileges and courtesies, because we were foreigners, that
might not have been as enthusiastically rendered to a native researcher. We are
in deep debt to all of the people who so generously helped us and we only regret
that the anonymity that we hope to preserve for the school and community
makes it impossible to thank them publicly by name. We should also like to express our gratitude to the National institute of Mental Health, the WennerGren
Foundation for Anthropological Research, the Human Factors Programme of
NATO, and the Spencer Foundation for the support of the 1977 study. The
1968 study was supported by the National Science Foundation and by the
School of Education at Stanford University.

[8]See G. Spindler 1974b for a statement of the model and G. and L. Spindler 1965 for
the application to the Kanai study.

## REFERENCES

Ehni, Jörg. 1967. *Das Bild der Heimat im Schullesebuch.* Volksleben, Vol. 16.
Tübinger: Tübinger Vereinigung für Volkskunde.
Spindler, George. 1959. *The Transmission of American Culture.* The Third Burton
Lecture in Elementary Education, Harvard University. Cambridge, Mass.: Harvard University Press. Abridged version in G. Spindler, ed., 1963. *Education and
Culture: Anthropological Approaches,* pp.148–172. New York: Holt, Rinehart and
Winston.
_____. 1970a. (reissued 1986). *Being an Anthropologist: Fieldwork in Eleven Cul-
tures.* Prospect Heights, IL: Waveland Press, Inc.
_____. 1970b. "Studying Schooling in Schoenhausen." *Council on Anthropology
and Education Newsletter,* 1:1–6.
_____. 1973. *Burgbach: Urbanization and Identity in a German Village.* New York:
Holt, Rinehart and Winston.
_____. 1974a. "Schooling in Schoenhausen: A Study of Cultural Transmission
and Instrumental Adaptation in an Urbanizing German Village." In G. Spindler,
ed.., *Education and Cultural Process: Anthropological Approaches,* 2/e. Prospect
Heights, IL: Waveland Press, Inc.
_____. 1974b."From Omnibus to Linkages: Models for the Study of Cultural
Transmission." *Council on Anthropology and Education Newsletter,* 1(4).
Spindler, George, and Louise Spindler. 1965. "The Instrumental Activities Inventory: A Technique for the Study of the Psychology of Acculturation." *Southwest-
ern Journal of Anthropology,* 21:1–23.
_____. 1978. "Schooling in Schoenhausen Revisited." *Anthropology & Education
Quarterly,* 9:181–182.
_____. 1978."Die Vermittlung von Kulturellen Werten and Spezifischen
Anpassungmechanismus in einen Dorf mit zunehmend städtischen Gepräge."
In M. Matter (ed.), *Rheinisches Jarhbuch für Volkskunde,* pp. 85–96. Bonn:
Universität Bonn.

Spindler, Louise. 1962. *Menomini Women and Culture Change*. American Anthropological Association, vol. 64, no. 1, memoir 91. See also her doctoral dissertation, *Women and Culture Change: A Case Study of the Menomini Indians*, 1956, her M.A. thesis, *The Autobiographical Approach to the Study of Acculturation of Menomini Indian Women*, 1952, Stanford University, and chapter ll in G. Spindler ed., 1970, *Being an Anthropologist*, New York, Holt, Rinehart and Winston, for further information on the development and use of the expressive autobiographic interview.

_____. 1978. "The Psychology of Culture Change and Urbanization." In G. Spindler (ed.), *The Making of Psychological Anthropology*. Berkeley: University of California Press, 174–200.

# 10

# Cultural Dialogue and Schooling in Schoenhausen and Roseville: A Comparative Analysis

(1987)

*George and Louise Spindler*

*Our study examines schooling crossculturally by looking at two examples of school culture. We suggest that the recent movement in educational anthropology and ethnography away from crosscultural or comparative focus to concerns with classrooms, schools, and schooling in our own society may have contributed to a blurring of focus on culture itself. We define what is meant by the study of culture and then discuss our current research in Schoenhausen, Germany and Roseville, United States (these place names are pseudonyms). Because we see education as cultural transmission, we want to look at the learning that takes place in classrooms as the result of calculated intervention. We use ethnography, the instrumental activities model, and films as evocative stimuli in reflective crosscultural interviews.*

In "Roots Revisited: Three Decades of Perspective," presented as the retiring president's talk at the Council on Anthropology and Education meetings in 1983, four concerns were listed that were originally pronounced in the 1954 Stanford Education–Anthropology Conference (Spindler 1955, 1984). They are: (1) the search for a philosophical as well as theoretical articulation of education and anthropology; (2) the necessity for sociocultural contextualization of the educative process; (3) the relation of education to "culturally phrased" phases of the life cycle; and (4) the nature of intercultural understanding and learning.

We intend to take up the latter in this article. We will not give even passing attention to the history of the search for intercultural understanding, even as exemplified in our own work and in the volumes that have appeared under our joint editorship, but will concentrate on the research that we are engaged in currently. We are doing a controlled comparison of two elementary schools, one in Germany (Schoenhausen) and one in the United States (Roseville). We will discuss some of the results of this research and the methods employed, focusing on the use of film as a record of activity and as stimuli for interviews. We will also touch briefly on culture as dialogue and education as a calculated intervention in learning, since these processes are what we think we are studying when we do ethnography in schools (Spindler and Spindler 1987b).

As rephrased in "Roots Revisited," drawing from Cora DuBois's paper on intercultural understanding for the 1954 conference, the concern was with how such understanding is acquired and how its acquisition could be promoted—how one can be taught, and learn, to understand a culture other than one's own (DuBois 1955). The discussion turned to how we learn our own culture, and to concepts, such as analogical learning, that seemed to be at the root of this acquisition. Such concerns bring us immediately into central problems of learning, of teaching as the transmission of culture, and the nature of culture itself.

The argument we wish to promote in this article is that these concerns are central to the anthropology of education; in fact, they are the *sine qua non* of our discipline; they have become less central in our work and talk as educational anthropologists during the past decade or so, and we should make them central once again.

There is no way that we can sensibly review the work of others to support the contention that these concerns about intercultural understanding have diminished in recent decades—and still accomplish what we wish to in this article. We refer you to the excellent and extensive review of current ethnographic work on education as a part of qualitative research by Goetz and LeCompte (1984), David Fetterman's edited volume on evaluative ethnography (1983), George Spindler's edited volume on the ethnography of schooling (1982), and Elizabeth Eddy's review of educational anthropology in the *Anthropology and Education Quarterly* (1985). It seems clear, too, from these and other materials, that we educational anthropologists and ethnographers have shifted decisively to concerns with classrooms, schools, and schooling in our own society; we have lost or blurred our focus on culture, and a clear crosscultural or comparative focus is notable for its absence. Of course, implicit crosscultural and comparative dimensions do appear in many current writings dealing with schooling in multicultural America, but they are rarely in sharp, explicit focus. Some of our colleagues, such as Marian Dobbert and her associates, are including explicit crosscultural dimensions in their projects (Dobbert et al. 1984). We are speaking of broad trends.

There are many possible dimensions of crosscultural understanding and the learning and teaching of culture. To clarify what we are talking about we want first to define what we think we are studying when we study culture, then discuss our current research in Germany and the United States.

## WHAT IS CULTURE?

Culture, cultural process, and cultural knowledge appear in various guises. We need to define what we study when we study culture.

One often refers to an "American" culture (Spindler and Spindler 1983; Varenne 1987). Objections are immediately raised. America is multicultural. America is too diverse to be called a culture. Despite these objections, we say there is an American culture. We claim that there is an American culture, because ever since preRevolutionary times we have been dialoguing about freedom and constraint, equality and difference, cooperation and competition, independence and conformity, sociability and individuality, Puritanism and free love, materialism and altruism, hard work and getting by, and achievement and failure. It is not because we are all the same (we are not) or that we agree on most important matters (we do not) that there is an American culture. It is somehow that we agree to worry, argue, fight, emulate, and agree or disagree about the same pivotal concerns. The fact that these concerns arrange themselves in oppositional pairs is no accident. That is the nature of culture, according to anthropological structuralists. This is the dialogue of American culture. It gives meaning to our lives and actions as Americans.

In any social scene within any setting, whether great or small, social actors carry on a culturally constructed dialogue. This dialogue is expressed in behavior, words, symbols, and in application of cultural knowledge to make instrumental activities and social situations "work" for one. We learn the dialogue as children and continue learning it all of our lives, as our circumstances change. These are the phenomena that we believe we study as ethnographers—the dialogue of action, interaction, and meaning. We observe behavior and we interview any "native" who will talk with us. When we are in classrooms, we observe the action and talk to students and teachers, principals, counselors, parents, and janitors. We observe, formulate and ask questions, observe some more, record behavior by various means, including film or video, and ask yet more questions, until the patterns of behavior and native explanations for them coalesce into repetitive sequences and configurations. We try to determine how teaching and learning are supported and constrained by understandings, many of them implicit, that govern the interaction of teachers and students. The dialogue around what is to be taught, and how much of it is to be learned, how the teaching and learning will be conducted, and how it is actually conducted is what we try to record and interpret as ethnographers of education. Educational anthropology is more than ethnography, but ethnography is the business end of the relationship and has a massively determinate influence on what our discipline is and will be (Spindler and Spindler 1987c).

## WHAT IS EDUCATION?

We see education as cultural transmission, and, of course, cultural transmission requires cultural learning, so learning and transmission are never separated, except by convention (Spindler and Spindler 1982a; Wolcott 1982). Further, we see that aspect of cultural transmission in which we are most interested—education in the broad sense, schooling in the narrower sense (inducting initiations, rites of passage, apprenticeships, as well as schools)—as *calculated interventions* in the learning process. We are not interested in all learning that takes place as children grow into adults, get older, and finally die. We are interested in the learning that takes place, whether intended or unanticipated, as a result of calculated intervention. It is our unique subject matter as educational anthropologists, and without a unique subject matter, as well as a methodology, there is no discipline. With this we turn now to our own research.

## SCHOENHAUSEN, GERMANY AND ROSEVILLE, U.S.A.

Our most recent research in Germany was in the spring of 1985, but we need to say a few words about our previous work there since we began in the spring of 1968. In the previous field trips to Germany, we established the sociocultural baseline of the Grundschule (elementary school) in the village community of Schoenhausen, and that of Schoenhausen in the Rems Valley region stretching southeast from Stuttgart (Spindler 1973, 1974; Spindler and Spindler 1978). A migration and assimilation model guided our earlier work, as we researched the adaptation of children of the migrants to West Germany after World War I and the assimilation of these children in the Rems Valley schools of Schoenhausen and Burgbach. The second phase of our research explored the effects of a massive educational reform over a period of nearly a decade (1968–1977), using both ethnography and the instrumental activities model as methods (Spindler and Spindler 1982a, 1982b). It is relevant to this discussion, particularly because it is an indication of the great staying power of culture, that our results indicate that there were no essential changes in the basic elements of cultural transmission in the school as a result of the very extensive and expensive reform and no significant shift in choices of life styles or instrumentalities leading to them, except that they tended to become more conservative (Spindler and Spindler 1987a). The third phase of our work focused on teachers' styles in classrooms and instructional management. We found that though there were as many different styles of teaching as there were teachers, the underlying interactions and organization of cultural experience remained quite constant (Spindler and Spindler 1982b). The fourth and present phase of research is devoted to a comparative study of the influence of deep cultural structure on the classroom behavior of teachers and children. To this end we have carried out field research in the Roseville elementary school in Wisconsin in the autumns of 1983 and 1984 and in the Schoenhausen school in the spring of 1985 (Spindler and Spindler 1987a).

Since we wanted to make a controlled comparison, we needed a community and school comparable in size to Schoenhausen—one serving a nonurban district and that was preparing children for both rural and more urban careers. The fact that Roseville's population is predominantly ethnically German was an added bonus.

The concern with the influence of culture on schooling has, of course, been present from the beginning of our research in Schoenhausen, but until 1983 we lacked a specific site from the United States for cross-cultural comparison. The site at Roseville has afforded us an invaluable perspective. Comparison of the cultural influence in the two schools will be carried forward in a chapter by us in our forthcoming volume *Toward an Interpretive Ethnography of Education at Home and Abroad* (Spindler and Spindler, eds. 1987). We will summarize the differences.

## Some Emergent Cultural Differences Between Schoenhausen and Roseville

*Schoenhausen behavior patterns:* active, teacher-centered, frontal focused. Intense competition for teacher approval. Intense, high-key and noisy. Chaotic when teacher absent. High, uniform standards collectively attained. Individual brought up to class standard with individual help by teacher.

*Roseville behavior patterns:* Low-key, small group discussion and individual work occur simultaneously, less overt, "feverish" competition. Teacher approval not the main reward—rather, the chance to work on something one chooses to do, when the required work is finished. Peers teach each other. Less teacher-centered. Less noisy. Classroom remains in order and children continue working when teacher absent.

*Schoenhausen cultural knowledge:* "Katzenjammer Kids" assumption: children are naturally lively and mischievous. When external authority is not present and monitoring activity is not being carried on, children will naturally break loose. Teacher is instigator and leader of learning activity. Class hours must be filled with directed activity. Uniform collective achievement is the aim. The individual is given attention so that he or she can be brought up to group standards.

*Roseville cultural knowledge:* Self-control is to be expected. Authority is (relatively) internalized. Teachers expect classrooms to stay in order when absent from the room. Misdemeanors are regarded as a violation of an understanding reached between teacher and child, and as an exhibition of immature behavior. Individuals are the end goal of teaching and learning. The group exists in order to make individual life and achievement possible—as contexts with sufficient order to permit the pursuit of individual goals. Individuals will naturally vary with respect to both quality and quantity of production.

These behavioral and ideational characteristics were established by many hours of classroom observation, the repeated review of films, and interviews with teachers *before* our most recent field research in the spring of 1985. The results of this research gave us additional data and an understanding of a somewhat different viewpoint.

## METHODOLOGY

Our methodology was enhanced in the Schoenhausen school in the 1977 field trip by our first use of film to record key episodes in classroom behavior. The permanent record of action in these films permitted us to review repeatedly what we had observed, and made it possible to determine whether others noted the same behavior and interpreted it as we did. We have shown these films to groups of students and colleagues for this purpose. A high degree of agreement in noting and interpreting behavior has been consistently exhibited.

Another potential use of these films occurred to us, and in the 1981 field research we screened the films of their own classrooms for the Schoenhausen teachers and recorded their reactions. That experiment was a partial success. The individual teachers viewing films of their own classrooms and others' teaching were very interested but not particularly articulate in explaining what they did or how they felt about various episodes. Group showings were more productive. Teachers commented excitedly about the behavior of individual children and the class as a whole, as well as the teaching methods used in both their own classrooms and those of their colleagues. Intense discussions ensued that gave us a more intimate look into teacher perceptions, understandings, and assumptions—into the knowledge (and we term it *cultural knowledge*) that they employ in the management of themselves and their classrooms as teachers. Although we had conducted formal interviews with each teacher and repeatedly observed in their classrooms, we derived an inside perspective that was different enough to be significant. We term this usage of the use of films as *evocative stimuli* for interviews and discussion.

## The Use of Film in Reflective, Cross-Cultural Interviewing

In our 1985 trip our procedure was different. We had filmed all of the classrooms in the Roseville school (KG through 8) as well as activities in the gym, playground, the Christmas program, and during lunchtime, during our two autumns of field research (1983 and 1984). We had already shown the Schoenhausen films to the Roseville teachers before we left for Germany and recorded their reactions.

When we arrived in Germany in April, 1985, we immediately met with the equivalent of our superintendent of schools for the area (*Regierungschuledirektor*), two members of his staff, and the principal (*Rektor*) of the Schoenhausen school to discuss our plans for research and to receive permission to carry it out. The Schuledirektor and his two staff members were so interested in the possibility of viewing films from a small American elementary school that they requested an immediate screening.[1] This was arranged for our third night in Germany. The attending group included all of the five Schoenhausen teachers, the Rektor, ourselves, and the Schuledirektor and his two associates. The proceedings were recorded and constituted in fact our first data gathering session for our 1985 field trip. In the discussion that ensued, which lasted for more than an hour (excluding time for the refreshments of wine, sausage, and various tasty small eatables), the Schuledirektor asked many questions, then launched upon a statement that summed up his reaction. That reaction was that the Roseville classrooms seemed orderly and the children appeared cooperative, but the dispersion of activity in the room and the relaxed quality of it could only mean that *Leistungsfahigkeiten* (productive efficiency) was not being attained. He went on to explain vigorously how classrooms in the German schools were focused on the attainment of the goals specified in a *Lehrerplan* (curriculum plan) for Baden Wurttemberg (the *Land* of which Schoenhausen is a part), with the overall aim that a common standard for all should be achieved. He asked if Roseville teachers had such a plan, and how it was created if there was one. When he learned that there was, and that the Roseville teachers themselves, together with personnel from the superintendent's office, had developed it, he expressed surprise. The Lehrerplan for Schoenhausen issues from far above in the hierarchy.

The Schoenhausen teachers and Rektor perceived the Roseville classrooms as self-disciplined, relaxed, *freiwillig* (free-choice oriented) and the children and teachers in them as considerate and friendly with each other. The Rektor, in particular, was impressed with the relaxed, "conversational," quality of relationships between children and teachers. They also wondered, however, about the goals that were being attained. Both the teachers and the Schuledirektor perceived the same general qualities in the actions filmed in Roseville classrooms but reacted to them somewhat differently.

These perceptions and reactions, produced so quickly in the earliest phase of our work period in Germany, proved to be themes around which all subsequent responses to the Roseville films revolved. The self-discipline, relaxation, cooperation, consideration, dispersion, and free choice of learning activity were seen by every respondent. Teachers said that they would like to try *freiwillig* (self-determined free-choice) choices of activities in their classrooms but feared that it would be very difficult for some children to do so and that disruption and disorientation might occur, which would interfere with teaching and learning. With highly specific goals to reach during every hour of instruction, as laid out in the state lesson plan, with instruction limited to 8:30–11:30 A.M. six days a week, they could not afford to lose any time and had to keep instruction on track, they said. They also expressed concerns that if every minute of the class hour was not filled with intensive direct learning activity, there would be disruption, if not chaos.

These same general perceptions and reactions were shared by the children in grades 1 through 4 who also saw the films and discussed them. The teachers guided discussions with the children after they had viewed the films. Children agreed that the *freiwillig* character of the Roseville classrooms was intriguing but the chances of its working in Schoenhausen were slim. They said that if a person were to walk around the room to go get some materials to work on, on their own, somebody would be sure to stick out their foot and trip them. They also noted many other things, such as black caps on some of the girls (Brownie Day), *Popkorn Tag* (once a week), American flags and clocks in every room, that adult viewers tended to ignore or overlook. They were enthusiastic about the gym and its use for recesses as well as P.E., and wondered at the school lunch program. It was interesting to see how children's perceptions were both the same as and different from those of adults.

We used the Roseville films, then, as background stimuli for interviews about classroom procedure and rationale, with all of the teachers, the Rektor, and the children of the Schoenhausen school. Our actual interviewing procedure was, however, dependent upon having *both* the Schoenhausen and Roseville experience present in the discussion as a constant frame of reference. We wanted each interview to engage with an active comparison of the two and for the teachers to reflect on the similarities and differences. (We term this procedure *reflective* crosscultural interviewing).[2] To this end, we filmed each class of every teacher. We held one interview before the filming, in which the teacher presented her lesson plan for the hour we were to film and explained how she would carry it out and how it would fit into the master curriculum guide for Baden Wurttemberg. The plans also included a statement of the theme, such as "the significance of water," a goal, such as "to gain understanding into the process of water circulation in nature," and the *Stunden Verlauf* (course of the hour), the instructional procedures for the period. These procedures always included: (1) the presentation of the problem for the hour; (2) some preliminary demonstration by the teacher; (3) group participation in the activity; (4) written work (*Fixierung*-reinforcement); and (5) summation. All activities included all children at the same time and were distinctly teacher-managed.

After this interview, each period was filmed, following the lesson plans so that each phase of the lesson was recorded.

After the films were developed, usually three days after filming, a second interview was held. We met in the Rektor's apartment, where we could view the films in comfort. The interviews centered, in each phase of the lesson, on purposes, rationale, and the successes and failures of instruction, and explored the educational philosophy of the teacher. The discussions ranged over many topics, some personal, some professional, but all of them rich.

The major difference between the 1985 interviews and the ones conducted in previous years was the constant comparison between Roseville and Schoenhausen, which was explicit in most comments of the teachers about everything. The Schoenhausen teachers saw themselves as goal-directed, and viewed the goals as specifically defined by the general curriculum plan. They felt free to use almost any method to attain those goals, but as centering instruction on teacher leadership and monitoring of all activity. They saw themselves as trying to fill every period right up to the last moment with intense directed activity, preplanned around specific learning goals, and working with the class as a collectivity as well as with individuals, so that all children attain the goal. They did not generally regard this need to fill every class period with teacher-directed activity as an undue imposition of authority but as a necessity imposed by the statement of goals in the *Lehrerplan.*

There are many other elements that emerged in the interviews. We will mention only the statement in some form common to all, and that is that they would enjoy trying some of the freedom and self-direction obvious in the Roseville films, but they would not be able to meet their designated goals if they did, and they did not think that some of the children would be able to adjust to such freedom and exercise of free will without disrupting others.

## To Sum Up

The following are characteristic of the Schoenhausen school and of the norms maintained by the school director's office as perceived by teachers, the Schuledirektor, and in their own way, by the children: (1) clearly rationalized and specific instructional goals issuing from the upper level of the educational hierarchy; (2) the striving to achieve those goals in the class time allotted; (3) the maintenance of collective achievement standards; (4) the efficient, goal-directed, use of time with no time left over for the exercise of free will and/or disruption; (5) the teachers as constant and active centers of all learning activity; (6) intensive, dynamic activity on the part of children, which if uncontrolled, often becomes disruptive and chaotic; (7) the reliance on external, higher authority for goal definition; (8) the wish to experiment with more free choice, coupled with the "knowledge" that it would not work.

These perceptions are similar to the observations made by us prior to the 1985 trip, but they center more on the goal for teaching and learning and the necessity of constant, directed classroom activity to attain those goals. Our observations and interpretations focus more on the noisy, to us at times chaotic, behavior that takes place when teacher monitoring ceases or has not yet begun. Our interpretive agenda includes an inference that in Schoenhausen, external authority must be imposed to maintain order and that this is assumed to be a "natural" condition, while in Roseville, self-control is assumed to be the basis of order, and its development is a major aim of education. There are various levels of manifest and latent, explicit and implicit meaning in both statements of the principal actors in these two sites and in our interpretations that need to be worked out as we proceed in our analysis. Nevertheless, taken together they constitute a fairly coherent description of the two situations and the culturally constructed dialogue that takes place within them.

We maintain that these characteristics, both as observed by us through 1985 and as generated by teachers in reflective interviews, are deeply embedded in German culture and social institutions, just as the characteristics described for the Roseville classroom are deeply embedded in American culture and social institutions. They are not amenable to change in the same way that clothing, speech, or even food habits are. They represent long-term, stable aspects of German and American cultural tradition. They are only partly amenable to manifest, intentional control by the teachers, principals, or higher authority. The school is governed by and transmits these cultural characteristics without their explicit statement as a declared, intentional manifesto.

We do not contend that the Roseville school is typical of American elementary schools any more than we contend that Schoenhausen is typical of German elementary schools. Both are, however, culturally normative institutions charged with the responsibility for maintaining culturally defined standards and expectations. Dialogue in the classrooms, in administrative direction, and in interaction with the community, is, respectively, an American dialogue and a German dialogue. The dialogues and the cultural norms and pivotal concerns that they project vary by region, class, ethnicity, and degree of urbanization, but they revolve around some distinctive commonalities in each cultural framework. That, at least, is our working hypothesis at present.

## Work To Be Done

We hope to extend the research in both Germany and the United States. In both countries we need to observe, film, and interview teachers in one of the more urbanized schools of the area. Such schools are available in close proximity to both Schoenhausen and Roseville. We can thus keep the general cultural area and its population components constant.

## FINAL COMMENT

This discussion began with an argument that cross-cultural, comparative research had lagged during the last decade or so and that this was potentially injurious to the state of our discipline. We offered the comments on our research in Schoenhausen and Roseville to give some content to the concept, "crosscultural, comparative research," as well as to introduce some developments in theory and methodology that we have found intriguing.

While it is true that there is an implicit cross-cultural and comparative perspective in much of the interpretation done by anthropologists in educational settings, wherever they are, including in our own country, there are advantages to be gained by making the cross-cultural and comparative features explicit and as controlled as possible. As stated, we selected the Roseville school and community because it was as close a parallel to the

Schoenhausen situation as it was possible to attain in the United States. No attempt at control can be perfect, but we agree with Fred Eggan (1954), in his classical article on controlled comparisons, that controls are necessary in order to produce the most useful kinds of comparisons. In our case, the controls were exercised over size of school and population of district from which each draws, the rural character of the environment from which the schools draw, the task of the schools, involved as they are in preparing children for a wide spectrum of careers in the rural-urban sector, and finally even in ethnicity, since many of the children in Roseville are of German descent. It might be more important to control other factors in other studies. But these served our purposes.

The "reflective, cross-cultural interview procedure" stimulated teachers to make many explicit statements that were culturally meaningful without self-consciousness. It isn't that they were self-consciously talking about either German culture or American culture, but rather about the things they did and the reasons that they did them, that were American or German. We found it difficult under other circumstances to get teachers to talk this way, even though we were on intimate territory in both situations with the teachers and administrators. The kinds of talk that we wanted to hear flowed spontaneously and easily and with great involvement on the part of our informants. We feel that this was possible because every statement made was bracketed by observations and images formed from direct, personal exposure to the living documentation of behavior on film.

We found it rewarding, not only to collect such stimulating interview material and to further observe the action in both schools, but also to feel that the teachers themselves benefitted from the experience. Many teachers in both Schoenhausen and Roseville have commented upon how the cross-cultural exposure (though they didn't phrase it just this way) caused them to look at their own practices with a new perspective. The Roseville teachers began to wonder if they were expecting too much of their children in respect to self-discipline, self-control, and consideration of others. They also began to reflect upon their teaching goals and how they could best attain these goals with out diminishing the desirable features of free choice and independent work. The Schoenhausen teachers similarly reflected upon their management of classrooms and instructional materials, and wondered about ways that they might be able to increase independence, free choice, and self-discipline. They also questioned the need for such a tight, goal-oriented curriculum and about the ways in which the goals themselves were formed. This "consciousness-raising" is a by-product of the procedure but could well serve as a major purpose in a more applied research context.

## NOTES

*Acknowledgments.* The earlier phases of the research in Schoenhausen were supported by the National Science Foundation, the National Institute for Mental Health, the Stanford School of Education Research Fund, and the WennerGren Foundation for Anthropological Research. The latter phases of the research were supported by the Spencer Foundation of Chicago and the Center for Educational Research at the University of Wisconsin, Madison. We gratefully acknowledge this support. We would also like to name the faculty and staff of both the Schoenhausen Grundschule and the Roseville Elementary School (the names of the schools are pseudonyms). We do wish, however, to express our deepest gratitude to all of these people who have been so extraordinarily helpful and hospitable. At no time did we experience any feelings of rejection, hostility, or negativism. On the contrary, we were welcomed into classrooms, conferences, private conversations, and to homes and public places as friends and colleagues, as well as researchers.

A version of this article was presented at the 84th annual meeting of the American Anthropological Association in Washington, D.C., at the invited session "Retrospective and Prospective on Educational Anthropology: Four Views," organized by Cathie Jordan. A shorter version of this article appears in *Education and Cultural Process* (Spindler, ed. 1987).

[1]We used super8 mm sound-color film throughout our work in both Schoenhausen and Roseville. Videotape would be less expensive and sometimes easier to use in classes and other public demonstrations. We did not use it because of problems with compatibility of equipment overseas. For use in our own seminars at Stanford and Wisconsin, it is much easier to lug around a 25-pound 8 mm projector than it is to arrange for video display equipment to be brought in. For public displays, it is also true that film offers better resolution than video. The filming itself was usually done with G. Spindler from the outside edges of the classroom group, focusing on the whole group and teacher behavior, and L. Spindler on the inside of the group, focusing on person-to-person interaction.

[2]"Reflective interviewing" is not to be confused with "reflexive narrative" ethnography. Although the two have something in common in that both modes involve reflection on experience, *reflective interviewing* is intended to elicit less personal reactions and "reflections" and is directed at both the reflection of culture in the responses of the informant and the reflections of the informant on behaviors that have pointed cultural implications. (See Ruby 1982.)

## REFERENCES

Dobbert, Marion Lundy, Rivka A. Eisikovits, Mary Anne Pitman, Jan K. Gamradt, and Kyungsoo Chun. 1984. Cultural Transmission in Three Societies: Testing a Systems-Based Field Guide. *Anthropology & Education Quarterly* 15:275–311.

DuBois, Cora. 1955. Some Notions on Learning Intercultural Understanding. In *Education and Anthropology*. George D. Spindler, ed. pp. 89–105. Stanford: Stanford University Press.

Eddy, Elizabeth M. 1985. Theory, Research, and Application in Educational Anthropology. *Anthropology & Education Quarterly* 16:83–104.

Eggan, Fred. 1954. Social Anthropology and the Method of Controlled Comparison. *American Anthropologist* 56:743–763.

Fetterman, David M. 1983. *Educational Ethnographic Evaluation*. Beverly Hills, CA: Sage Publications.

Goetz, Judith P., and Margaret LeCompte. 1984. *Ethnography and Qualitative Design in Educational Research*. New York: Academic Press.

Ruby, Jay, ed. 1982. *A Crack in the Mirror: Reflexive Approaches in Anthropology*. Philadelphia: University of Pennsylvania Press.

Spindler, George D. 1973. *Burgbach: Urbanization and Identity in a German Village*. New York: Holt, Rinehart and Winston.

——— 1974. Schooling in Schoenhausen: A Study of Cultural Transmission and Instrumental Adaptation in an Urbanizing German Village. In *Education and Cultural Process: Toward an Anthropology of Education*. George D. Spindler, ed., pp. 230–272. New York: Holt, Rinehart and Winston.

——— 1984. Roots Revisited: Three Decades of Perspective. *Anthropology & Education Quarterly* 15:3–10.

Spindler, George D., ed.

——— 1955. *Education and Anthropology*. Stanford: Stanford University Press.

——— 1982. *Doing the Ethnography of Schooling: Educational Anthropology in Action*. New York: Holt, Rinehart and Winston.

——— 1987. *Education and Cultural Process: Anthropological Approaches, 2d ed.* Prospect Heights, IL: Waveland Press.

Spindler, George D., and Louise Spindler.

——— 1978. Die Vermittlung von Kulturellen Werten und Spezifischen Anpassungmechanismus in einem Dorf mit zunehemend städtischen Geprage. In *Rheinisches Jahrbuch für Volkskuncle*. M. Matter ed., pp. 85–96. Bonn: Universität Bonn.

——— 1982a. Do Anthropologists Need Learning Theory? *Anthropology & Education Quarterly* 13:109–124.

——— 1982b. Roger Harker and Schoenhausen: From Familiar to Strange and Back Again. In *Doing the Ethnography of Schooling: Educational Anthropology in Action*. George D. Spindler, ed., pp. 20–47. New York: Holt, Rinehart and Winston.

1983. Anthropologists View American Culture. *Annual Reviews of Anthropology*, 13:49–78.

1987a. Schoenhausen Revisited and the Rediscovery of Culture. In *Toward an Interpretive Ethnography of Education at Home and Abroad*. George D. Spindler and Louise Spindler, eds., pp. 143–170. Mahwah, NJ: Lawrence Erlbaum Associates.

1987b. Editorial Introduction to Part 1, Ethnography: An Anthropological View. In *Toward an Interpretive Ethnography of Education at Home and Abroad*. George D. Spindler and Louise Spindler, eds., pp. 1–10. Mahwah, NJ: Lawrence Erlbaum Associates.

1987c. Teaching and Learning How to do the Ethnography of Education. In *Toward an Interpretive Ethnography of Education at Home and Abroad*. George D. Spindler and Louise Spindler, eds., pp. 17–36. Mahwah, NJ: Lawrence Erlbaum Associates.

Spindler, George D., and Louise Spindler, eds., 1987. *Toward an Interpretive Ethnography of Education at Home and Abroad*. Mahwah, NJ: Lawrence Erlbaum Associates.

Varenne, Herve. 1987. *The Symbolization of America*. Lincoln, NE: University of Nebraska Press.

Wolcott, Harry F. 1982. The Anthropology of Learning. *Anthropology & Education Quarterly* 13:83–108.

# Part III

## ETHNOGRAPHY IN ACTION

# Part
# III

# ETHNOGRAPHY IN ACTION

This part is devoted to the explicit exposition of ethnographic methods, though actually every piece in this book is a demonstration of method. We describe procedures in teaching ethnographic methods to graduate students in education (mostly). Our emphasis is experiential. That is, each major step is demonstrated with simulation. Then, students perform the procedure themselves and the results are critiqued. Sensitization procedures are used to alert students to the pitfalls of crosscultural observation and interpretation. And, most important, we are able to use methods to make hidden assumptions and covert cultural knowledge explicit. This is a theme throughout the book that is more apparent at some times than others.

# Teaching and Learning How To Do the Ethnography of Education

(1988)

*George and Louise Spindler*

## WHAT IS ETHNOGRAPHY?

In this chapter we have two purposes. One is to state what we think ethnography is and what ethnographers study. The other is to describe how we try to teach it. By trying to teach ethnographic methods and the concepts and values that lie behind them, as well as doing ethnography, we come to an understanding of how ethnography is a certain kind of inquiry, guided by assumptions and purposes that are different than most methods in the social sciences and education.

Ethnographers attempt to record, in an orderly manner, how natives behave and how they explain their behavior. And ethnography, strictly speaking, is an orderly report of this recording. Natives are people in situations anywhere—including children and youth in schools—not just people who live in remote jungles or cozy peasant villages. We and many of our colleagues in educational anthropology have been concentrating lately on

247

schooling as cultural transmission but we do not regard the ethnography of schooling as essentially different than ethnography anywhere.

## Credentials

Though our most recent ethnographic field work has concentrated on schools and their contexts in Germany and America (G. & L. Spindler 1982) our first field work was with the Menominee Indians of Wisconsin (1948–1954). We did further field research with the Blood Indians of Alberta, Canada (1958–1964) and the Cree of Mistassini Lake, Quebec (1966). Louise Spindler (1978) reviews this research in a retrospective chapter. Our work in Germany began in 1959, resumed in 1967, and has continued intermittently ever since. The earlier phase, centering on "Burgbach," an urbanizing village in the Rems Valley, in southern Germany, an area remarkable for its fine wines, is represented in G. Spindler's case study (1973). Our research in the Schoenhausen school in a nearby community began in 1968 (G. Spindler, 1974a) and has continued in field trips in 1977, 1981, and 1985. G. Spindler also did extensive research during the 1950s on California schools with the Stanford Consultation Service headed by Dr. Robert N. Bush.

Altogether we have made 28 field trips, only a portion of which have been represented directly in publication. Like many anthropologists, we would rather *do* field work than write it up. Our field experience, however, is what we teach from as we teach others how to do ethnography.

## Toward a Good Ethnography

Teaching anything requires that the teacher have a model in mind for what is taught. Our model of an ethnographic approach has grown out of our own field experience and the influence of our anthropological and educationist colleagues.

This model is not easily classified as "ecological," "ethnoscientific," "semiotic," "psychodynamic," or "interactionist," for it combines, in a pragmatic working combination, elements from all of these current models. We study human behavior in social contexts, so we are interested in social interaction and the ways in which these environmental contexts impose restraints on interaction. We are interested in the meaning that social actors in contexts assign to their own behavior and that of others. We are concerned with the way in which people organize information relevant to their behavior in social contexts. And we try to understand how individuals emotionally load their cultural knowledge, thereby assigning priorities that are not a direct function of the taxonomic ordering of that cultural knowledge.

We have elsewhere (G. Spindler, 1982a, 1992) set forth the criteria for a good ethnography. They are summarized next.

## Criteria for a Good Ethnography    /0  Crtterian

Criterion I.  Observations are contextualized, both in the immediate setting in which behavior is observed and in further contexts beyond that context, as relevant.

Criterion II.  Hypotheses emerge in situ, as the study goes on in the setting selected for observation. Judgment on what may be significant to study in depth is deferred until the orienting phase of the field study has been completed. (We assume that the researcher will have searched the literature and defined the "problem" before beginning fieldwork, however much the problem may be modified, or even discarded, as field research proceeds.)

Criterion III.  Observation is prolonged and repetitive. Chains of events are observed more than once to establish the reliability of observations.

Criterion IV.  The native view of reality is attended through inferences from observation and through the various forms of ethnographic inquiry (including interviews and other eliciting procedures).

Criterion V.  Sociocultural knowledge held by social participants makes social behavior and communication sensible. Therefore, a major part of the ethnographic task is to elicit that knowledge from informant-participants in as systematic a fashion as possible.

Criterion VI.  Instruments, codes, schedules, questionnaires, agenda for interviews, and so forth, should be generated in situ as a result of observation and ethnographic inquiry.

Criterion VII.  A transcultural, comparative perspective is present though frequently as an unstated assumption. That is, cultural variation over time and space is considered a natural human condition. All cultures are seen as adaptations to the exigencies of human life and exhibit common as well as distinguishing features.

Criterion VIII.  Some of the sociocultural knowledge affecting behavior and communication in any particular setting being studied is implicit or tacit, not known to some natives and known only ambiguously to others. A significant task of ethnography is therefore to make what is implicit and tacit to informants explicit.

Criterion IX.  Since the informant (any person being interviewed) is one who knows and who has the emic, native cultural knowledge the ethnographic interviewer must not predetermine responses by the kinds of questions asked. The management of the interview must be carried out so as to promote the unfolding of emic cultural knowledge in its most heuristic, *natural* form. This form will often be influenced by emotionally laden preoccupations that must be allowed expression.

Criterion X. Any form of technical device that will enable the ethnographer to collect more live data—immediate, natural, detailed behavior will be used, such as cameras, audiotapes, videotapes, and field based instruments.

The most important requirements for an ethnographic approach, as we see it, is that behavior in situations must be explained from the native's point of view, and both the behavior and explanation must be recorded as carefully and systematically as possible, using whatever aids are expedient, such as note taking, tape recorders, and cameras. This obviously requires the ethnographer to be present in the situation (ceremonials, chief's council, school board meeting, classroom, etc.) when behavior is happening, and be able to ask questions of the natives about their behavior. There is a constant interaction between observation and interview. One observes, begins to formulate questions, asks questions and gets some answers, observes some more with perceptions sharpened by new cultural knowledge, refines questions, focusing them on relationships that appear to be particularly critical, observes some more, looking for repetitions of behavioral pattern with more focus than initially, and so on, and on.

## Ethnographers Are Pesky People

Ethnographers are pesky people. Resentment and rejection are conditions of life in the field. Sensitivity about and respect for the people one is observing and questioning are essential. One doesn't climb into bed with lovers to observe lovemaking. One might well interview lovers *about* lovemaking—if they can and will talk about it. A lot of ethnographic information is second-hand, in the sense that one cannot observe directly what is happening but people talk about something that happened. Validity is affected. One compensates by trying to find a number of people who will talk about the behavior hidden to the ethnographer, hoping to elicit recognizable explanatory elements from some or all of these respondents.

## Tacit Rules

There is always the problem that much of behavior is guided by applying tacit, usually undeclared rules. For example, when Americans enter an elevator, they behave in certain predictable ways. They avoid direct eye engagement with strangers. They stand facing the door. Males keep their hands clasped in front of them or straight at their sides, and avoid touching others. Women tend to clasp handbags. People don't start conversations with strangers. Conversations begun by a pair before entering an elevator cease temporarily, or are carried on sotto voce. There are more rules for elevator behavior, but these will suffice.

We are rarely conscious of all these rules governing elevator behavior. We know about them, and with skillful interrogation one can usually elucidate them. The ethnographer of elevator behavior can, after riding elevators under varying conditions—crowded, uncrowded, with other persons of the same and opposite sex, several stories' duration, one person, party crowds, business men and women, with an operator and without, etc.—by a skillful combination of casual and more formal interviewing, construct a reliable ethnography of elevator behavior that tells us how people act, and how people explain these actions. We have behavior patterns and native cultural knowledge.

## Inferential Interpretation

There is a problem, however. When we interview elevator natives, we find that they can tell us what one does on an elevator. That is, they have the requisite cultural knowledge to behave appropriately in the elevator context under varying conditions, and they know that they have it. When we ask *why* they behave the way they do, our informants are likely to get quite vague; "It makes one uncomfortable," or "I'd be embarrassed," or "It isn't polite," or even "It could be dangerous" (to talk to strangers, eye engage, touch, etc.).

What we don't know is why our informants feel like this. Why are they embarrassed or uncomfortable in elevators when people violate the rules? We don't get the deeper rationale by eliciting the cultural knowledge that informants bring into situations. We find it necessary to infer an explanation, and this is where theory, preference, and prejudice take over.

The rationale that most American anthropologists prefer is cultural. "In Western culture, personal space is important, so people keep a minimum of space between themselves and others. Elevators create situations where personal space may be violated, therefore one takes precautions to reduce that violation to a minimum." Neat enough. But why do Americans need this personal space? "Well, you see, in American culture, independence and privacy are valued, and personal space is an expression of this." But, why Americans and not Arabs or Senegalese? "People in every culture have concepts of personal space, but they differ. Perhaps American concepts of personal space reflect self-expression and individuality that developed with the

westward expansion, the frontier, and the space and opportunity." Inference upon inference!

Inference, construction of explanations, and models of explanation that
go far beyond the original observations and the elicitation of native cultural
knowledge make interesting reading. In fact, this is what we find most interesting. We evaluate our great anthropologists such as Clifford Geertz, Anthony Wallace, Gregory Bateson, Margaret Mead, Clyde Kluckhohn, Evans
Pritchard, Malinowski, by the inferences they draw and how they present
them to us. Nevertheless, they had a solid base of ethnographic study from
which to build their inferential structures of explanation.

The problem is that ethnography provides the raw material for
inferencing but inferencing must be minimized while doing ethnography
and writing an ethnographic report. The ethnographer collects observations from as intimate a perspective as possible. These observations are collected repetitively—so we are sure which behaviors are patterned and
which may be fortuitous one-time events. And the ethnographer elicits cultural knowledge from natives who will explain, and perhaps, if occasion demands, defend their behavior. A true ethnography is an orderly compilation
of observations and native cultural knowledge. Inference is at a minimum,
though some is necessary, even to know what questions to ask our informants. Doing ethnography and making ethnographic reports requires that
we hold our inferences in check and use them parsimoniously.
Ethnographic interpretation requires us to do more.

### Where Are the Ethnographies?

"What are some examples of ethnographies that meet your criteria?" our
students ask. Ethnographies, in the pure sense, rarely see the light of day.
What we read are mostly case studies with an ethnographic base or significant ethnographic dimension. Most of the chapters in this volume are case
studies with a strong ethnographic base. They are case studies in interpretive ethnography. The problem for the reader is often how to separate ethnography and inference.

When we teach how to do ethnography, we stress again and again this
separation between ethnography and inference. This separation is an ideal,
incapable of full realization, but it guides our behavior as teachers of
ethnographic methods.

Inference is necessary. However, the ultimate purpose of ethnography is
to provide reliable source material for analysis. Analysis is inference governed by systematic models, paradigms, and theory. We try to teach how to
analyze ethnographic data in our training seminars as well. It is impossible
to document this adequately in a few short pages. Reading good case studies, including the ones in this volume, with an eye to the distinction be-

tween what we have described as ethnography and what we have described as inference will be informative.

We turn now to a description of how we try to teach ethnography in our training seminars.

## TEACHING ETHNOGRAPHY

We teach our students to do *anthroethnography*, meaning that the major concepts, models, techniques, and purposes of "our" ethnography issue from the discipline and theory of cultural anthropology. Anthropology, however, is notoriously eclectic, so we can dip into our neighboring disciplines as needed.

We began collaborative ethnographic training with educators in 1978 with an intensive 2-week seminar for the Milpitas school district near Stanford. Since then, we have refined and developed the model that emerged in that very experimental and intensive 2 weeks during seven semesters at the University of Wisconsin at Madison and six summer quarters at Stanford.

Of course, we had taught field methods in our anthropology graduate courses for many years, particularly in advanced seminars in psychological anthropology. Perhaps the most intriguing experience with training novitiates was at the Stanford Center in Germany, where over 400 undergraduates did field work under our supervision in the Remstal (Spindler, 1973). Training graduate students in education, however, has been especially rewarding. These mature and usually professionally experienced people have a clear purpose in learning to do ethnography. They want to use it to gain understandings of education-related phenomena that conventional correlational and experimental research methods have not illuminated.

Our first seminar meeting is devoted entirely to one or two reports by graduate students in anthropology who have recently returned from the field and are writing their dissertations. They are happy to talk about their experiences, and their enthusiasm is infectious. Without any preliminary coaching from us, excepting a very general format, they describe what problem they went to the field with, how the problem changed as they became familiar with the situation, what difficulties they encountered in role taking and responding to the expectations of natives, problems of entré, ethical concerns, sampling procedures, relations with key informants, observing, and recording.

Seminar participants ask questions. As the discussion proceeds, the characteristics of an ethnographic approach to research emerge with great clarity. Researchable problems emerge in the field as one gains experience there. The ethnographer must constantly be on the alert to avoid prejudgement of the significance and meaning of behavior. Repetitive observation over time is necessary. Native cultural knowledge can and must

be elicited by casual observation, by eavesdropping, as well as in defined interview situations. One is a participant observer, sometimes intimately involved in native life, but one never becomes a native—not at least as long as
one remains an ethnographer.

These inductively derived insights into the ethnographic enterprise are
very convincing. Students read the "criteria for good ethnography" appre-
ciatively.

Our second seminar meeting is devoted to a cultural sensitization demonstration (G. Spindler, 1974b). The technique has proved invaluable as a
way of showing students, through their own responses to the alien cultural
situations exhibited to them with 35mm slides, how their perceptions reflect their cultural experiences. It is humbling to realize that one does not
"see" a prominent manure pile in front of a *Bauernhaus* (farmer's house) because there is no cultural category for such a relationship in his or her own
culture. It is equally humbling to realize that one has described a terraced
German vineyard as a series of defensive barricades against advancing enemy troops because of a cultural category in one's own cultural repertoire
that defines things German as militaristic. No respondent ever makes all
possible errors, but all respondents make some of them. Each slide is reviewed after the initial administration and the kinds of errors usually made
are pointed out. This is a first lesson in withholding judgment, avoiding intuitive leaps, and holding one's cultural categories in check. Our next seminar meeting or two is devoted to a continuation of this lesson in quite a
different form.

Consistent with our conviction that a problem of first magnitude for
most of us in doing ethnography in schools is that they are all too familiar to
us (G. & L. Spindler, 1982), the next demonstration-experiment uses two
episodes from a film on aborigines of the central Australian desert. The episodes, lasting about 2 minutes each, are of ceremonial activity involving
only adult males, and of subsistence activity using digging sticks and involving only females and young children. The film is run twice, without sound
and without introduction except for some general guidelines about observing and taking notes.

Students take notes, then write a one-page summary of them, with only
the instruction that they stick to their observations and avoid interpretations of the significance of what they observed. They then exchange their
summaries with other students and note differences between them. The
summaries are turned in and we analyze them thoroughly, tabulating content, descriptive terms, and, particularly, noting premature interpretations,
eticisms and divergences among the students in what was observed.

Students are asked to generate questions for interviews. The interviews
follow, usually in the next session of the seminar, with George acting as a

knowledgeable old male aborigine and Louise as a recently married woman. Ground rules are established for the conduct of the interviews. The informants' responses are based on in-depth ethnographic knowledge of the traditional central desert culture. Both informants behave as informants usually do. They obfuscate, mislead, divert, provide ambiguous answers, get "turned off" by some queries, respond "emically," and so on. Students take notes, get frustrated, hurt, and excited. After an hour, sometimes more, of interview, they write up their second summary, not more than two pages in length. These summaries are analyzed carefully for content, sequence, emphasis, overall integration, and unwarranted interpretive generalizations. Divergences between students' summaries are noted and discussed. A discussion of the relationship between cultural knowledge and behavior follows. The concept of "idioverse" (Schwartz, 1978) is introduced. This concept calls attention to the fact that knowledge held by any one informant is idiosyncratic to some degree and that many natives in different sectors of the cultural topography must be observed and interviewed. We also introduce the problem of cultural translation from the culture of the native to that of the ethnographer.

In several different forms this procedure is followed throughout the seminar. One of the most productive sequences focuses on materials from our long-term field work in Schoenhausen. We use both slides and Super 8mm films as resources. We start with social settings in the village and its surrounding fields and vineyards, and move finally into the elementary school classrooms. Students are told nothing about the scenes except some general orientation to time and place. Meanwhile, they have had demonstrations of interviews by the instructors, as well as the central desert "experience." They observe, take notes, summarize, interview, observe again, take notes, interview, write up, for as many sessions of about 1 hour each as we have time for in our semester or quarter format of one 3-hour meeting each week. We term this procedure the "ethnographic interview reinforcement technique." We actively critique each product, both individually and collectively.

## The Expressive Autobiographic Interview (E.A.I.)

Another interview technique that we have found very fruitful in our field research in all of our cultural settings, including schools in Germany and America, is the expressive autobiographic interview (E.A.I.). This technique is a cross between a structured expressive interview and a chronological autobiography—in abbreviated form. The interviewer interrupts with questions at critical points, critical to his or her interests (i.e., prepuberty, early school, first contact with the opposite sex, marriage, death, kin relations, etc.), while the interviewee is relating his or her life events.

The emotional atmosphere established in the confidential framework of the life story seems appropriate for questions of almost any type. The respondent introduces you to his or her family, reveals incidents loaded with sentiment, touches upon the main areas of friction and conflict in his or her life, expresses attitudes towards parents, siblings, friends, and authority figures and talks about areas inaccessible to direct questioning. One purpose in using the technique is to elicit materials concerning a person's special cultural knowledge, beliefs, and attitudes concerning the people and the world around him or her. The informant is often unaware of the kinds of values and attitudes communicated in his or her E.A.I. responses. These kinds of data usually cannot be secured by direct questioning. Answers to direct questions too often refer to the "ideal," what one should do or what it is thought the interviewer would like, rather than to the actual expected behavior of the informant. The E.A.I. is a record of behavioral events plus the informant's attitudes towards them.

Another purpose in using the technique is to elicit materials to help clarify a person's identity, confusion of it, or lack of it. Whether it is male, female, neuter, middle-class American (upper or lower), Native American traditional, modern Chicano, etc., the materials from the E. A. I. help place a person in the larger cultural context. By way of illustration, we cite below two excerpts from interviews conducted by Louise Spindler with Menominee women.

> (*Question*): What were your parents like? (The respondent is an elite, acculturated woman.)
>
> My parents believed in self-support, work from sunrise to sunset. They didn't believe in vacationing. If you don't work you can't eat, they said. I'm like that too. I feel these people around here weren't brought up right. My parents always believed in 6 days of work and 1 day of rest.

A culturally transitional Menominee woman replied, in answer to the question: "How did you meet your husband?":

> My mother introduced me to Shumasen's (a shaman) son, John. It always seemed kinda funny that my mother liked all those things—Indian dances and medicines, when my grandmother was a good Catholic (referring to her mother's involvement with a native doctor and learning special native medicines). I don't know where I belong. I don't go to church, and I use Indian cures for different things. I can't go to church now. If I should die I suppose I would be buried out in that potter's field (an unkept area in the cemetery for the "pagans").

It is clear from these two brief excerpts that the first woman identifies with the mainstream American work ethic and that the second is unsure of her identity and is suspended between two cultural worlds. Other matters of a more intimate and potentially threatening nature such as witchcraft, sex, community politics, scandals, crimes, and so forth, are often discussed with an abandon that almost never characterizes other formal interview situations.

There is always the problem of ethics in using personal materials of this type. The interviewer should establish good rapport with the informant before asking intimate questions, and then request permission to use the data. Anonymity must be assured by disguising the identity of the interviewee. Certain intimate details may be omitted, and trivial data disguised to throw curious readers off the track. Still, we have avoided publishing expressive autobiographic interviews in their entirety in outlets accessible to the general public.

We further demonstrate the E.A.I. by role playing Roger Harker, our classic case. Roger is a fifth grade teacher who faces a mix of students of diverse ethnic and social class origins (G. & L. Spindler, 1982). He is a "classic" middle-class WASP. His cultural repertoire is very different from that of about half of his students. He interacts intensively with children who share his cultural background, and almost not at all with children who are significantly culturally deviant from his own. His selectivity is impressive and makes an excellent case for a cultural explanation of behavior.

George Spindler plays Roger Harker and Louise interviews him, using the verbatim transcript of the original E.A.I. collected by George Spindler in the case study of Roger Harker and his classroom. Students in the seminar take notes. Afterwards, the cultural profile of Roger is developed, and predictions of his classroom behavior are made. Then, the actual behavior is presented in some detail using extensive ethnographic data and various rating scales developed during the project. One particularly productive exercise is to test retrospectively the predictive power of a psychological model of interpretation as against a cultural model. In Roger's case it is apparent that a cultural model works best. We are able to explain his selective interactions with students. We are able to present the psychological as well as the cultural model because we have not only the E.A.I., but in addition the results of projective tests and psychiatric interviews administered to Roger.

## Other Methods

This is not all there is to the seminar, although these are important aspects. These procedures allow us a control over experience and learning that to us seems essential. Because each student is required to write two "miniethnographies" the learning is immediately applied. By the time students do their own ethnographic "sorties" into the local environment they are well-trained in observation and interviewing. More importantly, they have learned to defer judgment, avoid premature interpretation and generalization, and confine *ethnography* to observation of behavior, eliciting the cultural knowledge of natives, and writing "close to the ground."

We also spend the first 30 minutes, sometimes more, of each period discussing questions students have turned in from their reading, both in our text (G. Spindler, 1982b) and from an extensive annotated bibliography. Students write reactive rather than critical reviews on each piece read, and we select issues and questions from these reviews for discussion. Much of this discussion centers on theory.

And we present and defend major research projects of our own, particularly on the Menominee, and Schoenhausen, with comparative materials from American schools. Though we stress the ethnographic component, we also develop strategies for quantitative design and show how the ethnographic and statistical analyses complement each other.

## Quantitative Versus Qualitative

The quantitative versus qualitative argument that has erupted recently is not a valid argument. Some people seem to regard ethnography as in confrontation and conflict with statistically oriented research design. To us this is nonsense. We usually publish results in both forms simultaneously. The chapter on schooling in Schoenhausen in this book and in previous publication (G. Spindler 1974a) are good examples. We used an eliciting instrument, the Instrumental Activities Inventory, to collect comparable data from several hundred "informants." The responses are in the form of declared choices between instrumental alternatives significant in the social setting of the respondent, and also in the form of explanation of the choices made. The choices are easily quantified, the explanations less so, but still entirely possible. The quantification and the application of inferential statistics, testing the probability that a given relationship between distributions of instrumental choice and age, sex, occupation, residence, origin, education, etc., is due to chance, provides us with invaluable generalizations that are impossible with ethnographic data alone. The quantitative data, and its analysis and testing, also provide us with parameters within which our ethnography must be understood.

For example, it was imperative that we have I.A.I. data from 1968 and from 1977 in the Schoenhausen study. The quantification and statistical testing of these data showed us that perceptions of traditional versus modern-urban instrumental alternatives had shifted radically during the near decade in the opposite direction than our hypothesis had indicated. We had expected a major school reform to produce changes toward urbanization and modernization. Instead, the changes were in the direction of traditional life-ways. Our ethnographic data assumed a new significance once this parameter was established. We could understand a growing persuasion on our part that not much had changed in the school at levels of meaning deeper than curriculum, textbooks, classroom organization, and personnel. Heartened by the confirming evidence of a traditional reorientation, we looked deeper into the cultural transactions taking place in the classroom. The quantitative, statistically analyzed data not only reinforced inferences emerging from our ethnographic work in the school, it forced a rethinking of the significance of dramatic variations in teachers' styles of classroom management, for these styles did not appear to affect student perceptions of cultural alternatives. In fact, the quantitative data forced us to rethink the role of the school as an agency of change, the role of the teacher as a cultural transmitter, and in general acted as a needed control on the process of analytic inference from our ethnographic data.

The Menominee case presentation also allows us to demonstrate the relevance of quantification and inferential statistics to establish parameters for ethnographic inquiry. In the context of the training seminar, the most important attribute of this study is to show how important it is to establish intracommunity differences and avoid the assumption of homogeneity. The Menominee data also show us how important it is to separate the responses of males and females. Far too often, ethnographers have not systematically taken into account the differences between the sexes in their adaptation to the exigencies of everyday life, ideology, and particularly to culture change and modernization (G. & L. Spindler 1990).

The Menominee case study also demonstrates the relationship between autobiographic data gained from 16 E.A.I. collected from women by Louise Spindler and eight collected from males by G. Spindler, and both the statistical and ethnographic data. It is clear that the autobiographic data bore deep into the strata of personal meaning and experience in the community, where neither quantitative indices nor ethnographic data are as likely to go.

## Other Concerns

As a final product, students have two choices—they can expand upon the two miniethnographies they have carried out and written up, doing more fieldwork and developing a problem orientation as they narrow the focus of their work; or they can write a dissertation proposal, well researched and referenced, with a significant ethnographic component.

Throughout the seminar the principles we have stated as criteria for a good ethnography are stressed operationally again and again. We move from observation to interview in order to determine not only what people do in their various social settings but why they do it. The "why," of course, has many dimensions. Situational determinants are always operative. Our focus is upon the relation between cultural knowledge—as it is used *in situ,* its ordering by the informant, and, separately, by the ethnographer—and observed behavior. Behavior, for us, is the "tip of the iceberg," to use Spradley's phrasing (Spradley, 1979, 1980).

This viewpoint immediately pulls one into complex and enormously compelling questions about behavior and mental organization that involve the basic questions facing our discipline. We do not fully accept an ethnoscientific or ethnosemantic model of cultural knowledge but we start with it. One of our most productive engagements with the data in our various observation–interview experiments is to show that informants associate cultural domains and their contents in ways that are not predictable from taxonomically ordered domains. They emotionally "load" these associations and they transform the logical structures of taxonomies because of their own personal experiential careers.

## Analysis

It would be easier to teach how to do ethnography if we could regard ethnography as a set of techniques removed from theory. It seems to us that there is a tendency in some current "qualitative design" writing to do just that. The result can be a kind of mindlessness that puts neither the theoretical nor applied concerns of educators or anthropologists ahead very far.

We have already sketched the outlines of the theoretical underpinnings of our ethnographic research and for our teaching of ethnographic methods. This underpinning is decidedly eclectic—both an advantage and a disadvantage. We try to make the sources of theory explicit as we proceed through the various stages of our training seminar. There is a further problem, however, with which we must cope. "What do we do with all this stuff?" students ask. They find that the *analysis* of ethnographic data, beyond its orderly collation and presentation, is the hardest part of the whole enterprise. Analysis, of course, is directed toward goals that are usually shaped by both theoretical and practical concerns. For social scientists the former may be most important. For educators in school systems and classrooms, the latter goals may dominate. In either case it is necessary to take systematic steps to move from data to generalization. We develop analytic procedures, with examples from our own field work and from the experiences that the students have had as they collected and tried to cope with their own ethnographic data during the course of the seminar. The first step is to generate some *grounded inferences* from collected observations. Grounded inferences are statements of relationships between variables that stay close to the action and frequently become hypotheses for further exploration. For example, a statement about the use of readings about the local environment and the taking of trips to local historical sites in the Schoenhausen Elementary School (G. Spindler, 1974a), to the effect that both experiences support a localized identity orientation, is a grounded inference. It is also a hypothesis that can be tested by further analysis and data collection. We collected data on identity, as in our Schoenhausen study (G. Spindler, 1974a), to make the connection. In the process of further analysis and data collection, however, we discovered that though the localized identity was strong and apparently reinforced by elementary school reading texts and trips in the immediate locality of the school, this identity did not appear to interfere with the making of pragmatic choices in the direction of urbanization and modernization.

However, we want to go further. We want to produce generalizations that are not limited to our particular community or area of study. For example, in our Schoenhausen study, we observed in depth certain parts of curriculum and practice termed *Heimatkunde* (lessons about Homeland). *Heimatkunde* was eliminated in the curriculum in the reform of the 1970s. *Sachkunde* (lessons about current affairs) was substituted as desirably more urban and modern in orientation. Our observations show that *Sachkunde* was reinterpreted by the teachers in actual practice as *Heimatkunde*. We generated from this several generalizations about cultural persistence and about substitute as against transformative change that are potentially applicable to all cultural innovations and all culture change situations. We try to lead students inductively through the mazeway of data presentation in the seminar to grounded inferences and analytic generalizations of this type. For many, this is the most difficult part of ethnographic training.

Analysis and generalization are heuristically difficult, but the difficulty is exacerbated by the fact that the concepts, models, and theory from which we draw in these seminars come from anthropology, and most of our students are unfamiliar with them. This makes it more difficult for us as well, but it is surprising how quickly students acquire an understanding of concepts and theory if they are applied to data that have become meaningful to them through a direct experience.

## CONCLUSION

No one chapter can completely cover two complex topics such as the nature of ethnography and the teaching of it. There is much else, about movement from opportunistic topographical interviews through several levels of focus, to the highly focused, problem-oriented interview; about various stages in reconnaissance; the differences between ethnography and ethnology; more about interpretation; and particularly, ethics; that we would enjoy discussing. All of our efforts are directed toward understanding what ethnography is, what ethnographic methods can do, and what stands behind them. Through our attempts to teach ethnographic methods to mature professional people with little or no background in anthropology, we have come to see ethnography in a new light. We have discarded some standard assumptions about ethnographic method in anthropology. For example, we are cautious about the use of "key informants." We have, however, retained an essentially anthropological orientation, and have drawn more from culture as a frame of reference than from any other. The training experience in our seminar centers on sensitization to cultural influence on the native behavior and on the perceptions of the observer of that behavior. We look at cultural process in social contexts, such as classrooms, as exhibiting universal features, yet unique to each situation. We see cultural process as a continuing adaptation to the changing conditions of existence for any group. Culture is never static, as we conceive of it. It is ever changing but exhibits remarkable persistence.

We try to create, in each seminar, the conditions for discovery learning. Every seminar session is an inductive learning experience—if we are successful. Our powers of observation and interpretation develop, not from our being told what has to be learned, but from finding out what seems to work. The receptive student, sensitized by this process, is, we believe not only an ethnographer of human behavior, but a better teacher, administrator, counselor, or supervisor. We think doctors, lawyers, businessmen, and anyone else who deals with people on a daily basis would also benefit from this kind of experience.

## REFERENCES

Schwartz, T. 1978. Where is the culture? Personality as the distributive locus for culture. In G. Spindler (Ed.), *The making of psychological anthropology*. Berkeley: University of California Press.

Spindler, G. 1973. *Burgbach: Urbanization and identity in a German village*. New York: Holt, Rinehart and Winston.

Spindler, G. 1974a. Schooling in Schoenhausen: A study of cultural transmission and instrumental adaptation in an urbanizing German village. In G. Spindler (Ed.), *Education and cultural process: Toward an anthropology of education*. New York: Holt, Rinehart and Winston.

Spindler, G. 1974b. Transcultural sensitization. In G. Spindler (Ed.), *Education and cultural process: Toward an anthropology of education*. New York: Holt, Rinehart and Winston.

Spindler, G. 1982a. The criteria for a good ethnography of schooling. In G. Spindler (Ed.), *Doing the ethnography of schooling*. New York: Holt, Rinehart and Winston.

Spindler, G. (Ed.). 1982b. *Doing the ethnography of schooling*. New York: Holt, Rinehart and Winston.

Spindler, G., & Spindler, L. 1982. Roger Harker and Schonhausen: From the familiar to the strange and back again. In G. Spindler (Ed.), *Doing the ethnography of schooling*. New York: Holt, Rinehart and Winston.

Spindler, G.. & Spindler, L. 1990. Male and female in four changing cultures. In M. Schwartz & D. Jordan (Eds.), Personality and the cultural construction of society: Festschrift for Melford Spiro. Tuscaloosa and London: University of Alabama.

Spindler, L. 1978. Researching the psychology of culture change and urbanization. In G. Spindler (Ed.), The making of psychological anthropology. Berkeley: University of California Press. Paperback edition, 1980.

Spradley, J. P. 1979. The ethnographic interview. New York: Holt, Rinehart and Winston.

Spradley, J. P. 1980. Participant observation. New York: Holt, Rinehart and Winston.

Wolcott, H. (Ed.). 1983. Teaching fieldwork to educational researchers: A symposium. Anthropology and Education Quarterly, 14(3), 171–218.

# Transcultural Sensitization

## (1974 and 1997)

### George D. Spindler

This chapter discusses the ways common errors in transcultural observation and interpretation can be anticipated and how sensitivity concerning them can be acquired. The source of data for this discussion is a sensitization technique first administered in the winter of 1968 to Stanford undergraduate students at one of the university's overseas centers, Stanford in Germany. The same technique has been used in advanced education classes at Stanford University on the home campus during most years since 1970. I am not concerned in this chapter with the differences between groups, but rather with the educational purpose of the technique and the kinds of perceptual distortions consistently revealed by it. Whether applied at Stanford in Germany or Stanford in California, the technique has been used in my classes as a way of sensitizing students to the kinds of errors one is likely to make when perceiving and interpreting behavior in cultural contexts other than one's own. Some 800 students have responded to the technique to date. The perceptual/interpretive errors they make are remarkably consistent from group to group.

There is a substantial literature in psychology, and some in anthropology, concerned with cultural variability in perception. Very little, however, has been written about the very complex process of perceiving and interpreting

265

culturally relevant material across cultural boundaries in the manner described here. The interpretive principles applied in this chapter are implicit in much of the reported experience of anthropologists in the field (Spindler 1997), but they have not, to my knowledge, been explicitly stated or applied in the specific ways developed here.

At Stanford in Germany there were usually about 80 students, mostly sophomores, in attendance at any given time. For 6 months they carried on with their regular academic work while learning the language of and becoming exposed to the history, politics, and economics of their host country. The program was designed to enable nearly all interested Stanford students to have an overseas experience irrespective of their major concentrations or future professional plans. The students live together in the various centers (there are also centers in France, Italy, England, and Austria), but do a great deal of traveling and are in constant contact with the population of the areas in which the centers are located.

Whenever I have been in residence, students at Stanford in Germany have done field research in the Remstal, the area near the study center, on the continuity of the folk culture in the small villages and on the urbanization and industrialization overtaking these villages. This field research has, in turn, been related through classroom discussions and lectures to basic generalizations and interpretive principles in cultural anthropology. The purpose of my courses in anthropology as I taught them at Stanford in Germany has been to help develop a cognitive organization for observation and participation in a culture foreign to the student.[1]

German culture cannot be considered, from the anthropological point of view, to be radically divergent from North American culture. Though there are substantial cultural differences between the various European countries and North America, in the larger sense they must all be seen as versions of the same general culture. There are, however, sufficient differences to make the deeper adjustment and accurate perceptions of the European culture problematic for North Americans unless they have systematic help. Contact, even prolonged, does not necessarily result in adjustment on this deeper level. Learning to speak the language is a major step in this direction but does not guarantee accurate perceptions and understandings. Human beings tend to interpret new experience in the light of past experience unless there is decisive intervention in the interpretive process. The anthropology instruction at Stanford in Germany was designed as such an intervention.

---

[1]The fieldwork was of such high quality that I was able to utilize it extensively in a Case Study in Cultural Anthropology (G. Spindler and student collaborators 1973).

The first step in this intervention, as I came to understand and practice it in my instruction, was to alert students to the types of perceptual distortions to which they would be subject and which could be corrected in some degree by transcultural sensitization. The specific way in which we went about this, and some general conclusions concerning the major types of distortions, are the subject of this chapter.

## The Technique and Its Results

The technique consists of the administration of ten 35 mm color slides selected from several hundred I had taken of the Remstal and its internal cultural variations. During the first week overseas the slides are shown and the students are asked to write their responses to each of the pictures and turn them in to me. I use those responses in a simple inductive content analysis, the results of which I utilize in class discussions. A description of the pictures—several of which are included in this text—and their culturally appropriate interpretation, together with the major categories of student reaction to them follows.

*Picture No. 1.*        The first slide is of a small area of vineyards (*Weinberge*) near the Stanford in Germany center. This area is subdivided into many small plots, most of which are not larger than a tenth of an acre. Each plot is terraced and there are poles and wires for the support of the grapevines.

The picture is very clear and presents no structural or spatial ambiguity. Students are asked to describe what they see in the picture, what it is used for, and what its possible significance might be in the cultural system of the Remstal.

The slide shows very clearly the small, terraced plots of vineyard characteristic of the area. The important point is that the plots are so small and their distribution so fragmented that mechanized cultivation is impossible. Consequently, traditional labor methods are still used for cultivation of the crop and upkeep of the poles and wires. This is a significant support, though one of several, for the entire traditional complex of viniculture and the way of life associated with it.

Students see a very wide range of possibilities in this picture. The majority see it as connected with agriculture, although usually not as vineyard plots but as an irrigation project, feeding troughs for cattle or pigs, a soil conservation project, erosion control, or cribs for grain storage. A sizable minority (about 35%) see it as something entirely unrelated to an agricultural operation, such as Roman ruins, rows of chairs for a mass audience, a religious congregation, a guarded border, fields destroyed by war, or gun emplacements.

The problem in accurate perception seems to be that there is no exact counterpart in the culture of the viewers for what is seen on the screen. Though vineyards are known in California, hilly, small, terraced plots of this kind are unknown. Further, there is no functional complex in the culture of the viewers into which this perception fits, even if the perception is accurate. The small size and fragmented distribution of the plots of vineyard have no meaning. Consequently, students seldom see the plots as vineyards, and only a few perceive their functional relevance. In general, the range of interpretations is wide and the level of inaccuracy high. Only about 10% of the students grasp the cultural significance of what is observed.

*Picture No. 2.*     This is a picture of a middle-aged woman in dark clothing bending over and tying grapevines onto a wire trellis on a sunny, early spring day (Fig. 12.1). Students are asked to describe what the subject is doing and why her activity might be functionally significant. They are also asked to indicate what they think the subject is thinking and feeling. The type of labor performed here is skilled labor, which frequently is obtained, within the traditional economic framework, from the membership of the extended family. This validates these relationships, thus helping to maintain the family and values associated with it. The necessity of such intensive hand labor in the small distributed plots is one factor that has kept traditional folk-oriented adaptation intact up to the present time in this area of Germany.

FIG. 12.1   Woman pruning grapes.

Most students see that some form of agricultural activity is involved in this picture. Only a small proportion (5%–15%) expressed an understanding of the significance of the intensive hand labor. Again, as there is no functional counterpart for this kind of work in North American culture, few students can see its cultural or economic significance.

The interpretations of what the subject is thinking and feeling run through a wide gamut, but the modalities that appear have mostly to do with fairly grim states of mind. "Tired," "old," "tedious," "boring," "aching back," "aching bones," "tired muscles," are the responses that predominate. Though the bones and muscles of German women who work in the Weinberge do ache, the interpretation of this sensation is quite different in the traditional subculture of the Remstal than in middle-class America. Labor and its discomforts are regarded as positive and old women complain about no longer being able to work in the Weinberge.[2] Students project from their own culture the meaning of experience appropriate to the activity as perceived.

*Picture No. 3.* This is a visually ambiguous picture. It shows an older female teacher helping a child of about 9 years of age into an old church tower where they are to examine four very large cast bells about which she had lectured in *Heimatkunde* (homeland) just before the trip to the tower. There are heavy beams in the picture and the surroundings are generally dark and dusty looking. Students are asked to indicate what is "going on" in the picture. Actually, all that is happening is that the teacher is helping the child off the top rung of the ladder into the upper part of the tower where the bells are. Cultural significance is not in question here.

About one third of the students see the teacher as assisting the child in some way, and about one third see her as punishing the child. The other third of the responses are distributed over a wide range. Those who see the teacher as assisting the child refer to help given in going under a fence, coming out of a mine shaft, a cave, an earthquake-stricken building, or a collapsed basement in a deteriorated slum, or out of a bomb shelter; or, in entirely different directions, as assisting her to go to the toilet or even as preventing suicide. Those who see the teacher as punishing the child usually refer to whipping in a woodshed, spanking because the child had gone some place where she should not have, or being caught because she tried to run away. The interpretations in the third category are too variegated to sample adequately. Most of the interpretations in all categories are irrelevant to the actual situation as it occurred.

It seems clear that the range of possible perceptions and interpretations eases as the situation observed becomes more ambiguous. Ambiguity may

---

[2]Case endings are not observed in the use of German terms in order to avoid confusing the reader who does not know German.

be either a product of cultural irrelevance or lack of clarity in spatial or structural relations. Both forms of ambiguity enter into the interpretation of this picture, but the latter are probably most important in this case. Spatial and structural relations are not clear, which is why this picture was selected. The act of climbing into an old church tower to examine bells that have been discussed in class is uncommon in both American and German culture, so the spatial and structural ambiguity is compounded. Perceptions and interpretations, therefore, tend to be fanciful and more or less irrelevant to reality. In actual fieldwork, or in ordinary contact within a foreign culture, situations where ambiguity prevails abound.

*Picture No. 4.*     This slide (Fig. 12.2) shows a small bake house *(Backhaus)* in which shifts of several village women bake bread and *Kuchen*[3] together at certain hours each week. The small brick building is technically clear, as is the fire in the furnace inside. A woman is standing by the door with the long ash stirrer in her hand. Students are asked to indicate what it is they are seeing and what its significance could be in the culture of the Remistal. The significance of the Backhaus is not only in the fact that women bake their weekly bread there but in that it is a social gathering and

FIG. 12.2   The Schoenhausen Backhaus.

---

[3]Various kinds of baked sweet dough usually served with fruit toppings and whipped cream.

gossip center for the more conservative women of the village. It thus is a contributing element of social control, as there everyone is talked about and judgements passed on their behavior.

About 30% of the students see this as a Backhaus, but virtually none have ever perceived the function of this place as a communication and so-cial-control center. The range of interpretations for the other 70% of the students is quite wide, including such perceptions as small-town industry, refinery, one-room house with a coal fireplace, fireplace in an inn, a kiln for making pots, an incinerator, and so forth.

Again, there is no exact cultural counterpart to the Backhaus in U.S. cul-ture, though the general form of the structure and even its purpose may not be unknown. The picture is technically clear. The only ambiguity is the cul-tural one, which seems to produce a wide range of interpretations as to what is in the picture, and the absence of a cultural counterpart in the culture of the viewer leads to interpretations of significance irrelevant to the local situation.

*Picture No. 5.*     This picture shows a man pumping a liquid of some sort into a trough which empties into a long barrel-like container laid lengthwise on a trailer hauled by a small tractor. The man is actually pump-ing liquid from a pit under the manure pile which is found in front of each *Bauernhaus.*[4] The liquid is then taken in the barrel up to the Weinberge and distributed between the rows of grapevines. This is a substantial contribu-tion to the enrichment of the soil, made possible by the total economic-eco-logical unit represented by the Bauernhaus. The animals live on the ground floor and the people above them. There is a functional interdependence be-tween the Bauernhaus and the Weinberge other than that created by the ac-tivities of the people themselves.

Only 5% of the students in any of the samples have ever seen this as a pump for liquified manure or anything like it. Interpretations range wide: a cement mixer for fixing broken sidewalks for building houses, crushed grapes being pumped into a container, water for spraying, loading coal, de-livery of a pillar, tar for street repairs, pumping insecticide into barrels, filling old barrels with new wine, washing gravel, loading pipe onto a truck, erect-ing the base for a monument, rinsing off a grinding stone, locating a plumb-ing fixture, and so forth.

Again, the picture is very clear technically. There is no visual ambiguity because of structural or spatial relationships. The ambiguity is culturally in-troduced. There is no counterpart for the pump or for the use of liquid ma-nure in agricultural operations in the experience of the majority of American students. They produce, therefore, a wide variety of interpretations.

---

[4]The traditional structure, quite large, housing humans, cows, pigs, and chickens, hay, and imple-ments used in maintaining agricultural activity.

*Picture No. 6.*    This is a picture of a small boy helping his father pick black currants (Fig. 12.3). It is a pleasant picture filled with sunshine, green leaves, bursting clusters of currants, and a basket heaped with the fruit. Students were asked to indicate what is going on in the picture and how the boy feels and thinks about it. Children in this area of Germany are not required to work until they are ready to do so because their parents want them to enjoy working in the fields and the Weinberge. Most children enjoy helping their parents and older siblings in this way.

About 90% of the students see this as an activity connected with the harvesting of grapes or currants. Most, however, see the boy as wishing he could join his comrades in play, hoping that the work will be finished so he can leave, wondering if he is going to grow up to do a tedious and boring job like his father, restive under his father's hand, wishing the sun were not so hot, resigned to the work, feeling hot and scratchy, wishing there were an easier way to do it, feeling restless, resenting the drudgery, and so forth.

Again, students tend to project their own experience or the stereotype of that experience within American culture into the perception and interpretation of events or situations in another culture. Working in the field under the hot sun, perhaps especially with one's father, is perceived as boring, tiresome, and so on, and one "naturally" wants to escape to play with peers, as a projection, it appears, of attitudes common in U.S. culture. Though it is likely that

FIG. 12.3    Boy picking grapes with his father.

some Remstal children feel this way, it is doubtful that many do, given the particular cultural antecedents to the event and its interpretation in this culture.

It is clear in responses to this and other pictures that when motivations and feelings are identified, the range of perceptions and interpretations increases and the potential irrelevancy of these perceptions likewise increases, irrespective of the technical clarity of the stimulus.

*Picture No. 7.* This slide shows a not atypical Bauernhaus with large double doors through which animals and hay pass through to the ground floor where the animals are kept, the manure pile surrounded by its square concrete retaining wall in front with the pump in the center, and two stories and attic under a heavy tiled roof (Fig. 12.4). The Bauernhaus is the traditional structure housing the extended family and livestock and is an especially significant representation of the traditional agricultural "folk" adaptation. People live in these houses within the villages and farm the many scattered strips of flat land and small plots of Weinberge from it. The Bauernhäuser, small plots, Weinberge, manure pile, and so forth, constitute a whole functioning culture complex. It is a way of life that is disappearing but is still very much in evidence.

Students see the Bauernhaus as a warehouse, a gasoline station, a tavern, combined hotel and restaurant, a shop or general store, a feed store, suburban home with a two-stall garage, factory of some kind, store with a loading

FIG. 12.4   A Bauernhaus.

platform, cheese factory, a garage where cars are fixed, a house of prostitu-
tion, a winery, an apartment house, a bakery and family home combined,
and an equipment repair shop. Only about 10% of the students in the various groups ever saw this structure as a regular domicile, and only about half
of those saw it as a structure sheltering both man and beast within the general complex described.

As in the other cases, the responses to this picture contained a wide variety of culturally ready categories imposed from the perceiver's culture upon
the situation presented from another culture. Ambiguity is created not because of lack of clarity in spatial or structural relations (the picture is clear
and focused), but rather because there is no specific cultural category in the
perceiver's culture for the perceived event, object, or situation. Nor is there
any functional complex in which the perceived situation would fit even if it
were perceived relevantly.

*Picture No. 8.* This slide shows a male German teacher of about forty
years of age standing before a fourth-grade class in the *Grundschule* (elementary school). He is standing in a more or less relaxed posture with his hands
behind his back looking at the class. The children are grouped around the
tables facing him. The classroom is entirely ordinary. Specific clues to the effect that this is a German classroom are lacking, so students are told that it is.
The students are asked to indicate what kind of a classroom atmosphere
probably exists here and what kind of a teacher this man is. The teacher,
Herr Steinhardt from the Schoenhausen School, is not a "permissive"
teacher but certainly is not an authoritarian one. I have observed many
American Classrooms that were much more strictly run than his. The nature of the school and educational philosophy are described in chapter 10.
The children were allowed considerable freedom of movement and expression. Their grouping at tables rather than in traditional, formal rows of sta-
tionary seats is symptomatic of this freedom.

The student respondents saw Herr Steinhardt as formal, strict, and orderly, authoritarian, austere, autocratic, dominating, arrogant, stern, me-
ticulous, demanding, stiff, detailed, traditional, old-fashioned, "uptight,"
and as a "pompous authoritarian" in about 80 percent of all responses to this
picture. The classroom was seen consistently in the same framework, that
is, one demanding submission from the children, as having an orderly, "di-
dactic," "rigid," "alienating," highly disciplined atmosphere.

It is apparent that students responding to this picture have projected a
stereotype that is patterned in their own culture about a situation in another culture. American students have stereotypes about how German
classrooms are run and what German teachers are like. These stereotypes

are projected. The range of perceptions and interpretations is not broad, but the irrelevancy of those offered is marked.

*Picture No. 9.*    This slide shows the same classroom 10 seconds after the slide in Picture No. 8 was taken. The teacher is in a more dynamic posture with hand raised and a lively expression on his face, and the children are raising their hands; some are half risen from their seats. Students are asked to indicate whether this slide causes them to change their interpretation of the first picture of this classroom.

About 50% of the respondents say that the second picture does not cause them to modify their first perceptions significantly. The other 50% describe the classroom as less autocratic than they had thought, less rigid, more free, and more democratic.

It is significant that approximately one half of the students modify their interpretations in the direction of greater freedom in the classroom. This illustrates the importance of time sampling in any particular sequence of behavior, and is also an important element in transcultural sensitization.

*Picture No. 10.*    This slide shows several boys walking into the *Schönhausen* School with Herr Steinhardt standing out in the school yard with one hand raised pointing toward the door (Fig. 12.5). His posture is rather relaxed and his hand and arm are not in a stiff position. Students are

FIG. 12.5    Boys walking into Schoenhausen school.

asked to indicate what they think the boys are thinking and feeling as they enter the classroom and school.

About one half of the students in the various groups to which these pictures have been shown see the boys as feeling reluctant, fearful, anxious, resigned, and resentful. About one-third see the boys as eager to enter, excited, anticipatory, wanting to get started, happy, and fascinated. The rest produce a fairly wide range of responses, including "not rushing but ok," "amenable but not eager," "not thinking or feeling very much," being rewarded for obedience, feeling cheated because the recess break has been cut short, and so forth.

A substantial number of American student respondents appear to draw from their own experience with school. They are probably not only drawing directly from this experience but also from stereotypes about what this experience is like, particularly for boys in U.S. culture. Stereotypes of German classrooms and teachers, and American student responses to these stereotypes, as well as the influence of one's school experience and stereotypes relating to that experience in U.S. culture, are intermingled. This happens frequently in transcultural perception and interpretation.

## CONCLUSION

It should be remembered that the procedures described previously are carried out as a part of an instructional program and not primarily for purposes of research on perceptual distortion. With the exception of the groups at Stanford in California, all of the students were at Stanford in Germany and were about to enter or had already entered into fairly intensive contact with German people and German culture.[5] The cultural sensitization procedure was carried out in order to enrich their overseas experience by making them more sensitive and acute observers, and also to increase the probability of success in fieldwork in the Remstal area.

The pictures were all presented on a large screen with a 35 mm projector. The responses, as stated, were written by each student and collected at the end of the period. The instructor did a content analysis, resulting in the categories of response described before. These results were presented to each class in two 50-minute discussion periods during which the pictures were again shown and considerable detail presented by the instructor about the content and significance of each slide. Certain general principles of perceptual distortion in transcultural observation and interpretation were derived

---

[5]Two of the Stanford in Germany groups had actually been in Germany for one academic quarter at the time the technique was administered. It is interesting that the same types of perceptual errors were displayed by these groups as by the others. The students had no anthropological training during the first quarter.

inductively in these discussions. I summarize these general principles briefly, as they have already been anticipated in the discussion of the pictures and student responses to them.

It appears that perceptual distortion in transcultural observation increases when:

1. There is no clear counterpart for the perceived object or event in the observer's culture. Responses to the picture of the Bauernhaus, the liquid manure wagon, and the Weinberge all fall into this category. None of these objects, events, or situations occur in North American culture.

2. There is no functional complex into which the object, event, or situation, even if accurately perceived, fits, so the significance is lost or skewed. This applies clearly to the Weinberge and the Backhaus and, to some degree, to most of the rest of the presented pictures. The Weinberge cannot be understood even if seen as Weinberge unless one understands that the size of the plots and their distribution, as well as their terracing, prevents the application of large-scale mechanical power to their maintenance, and that this in turn is related to the necessity for intensive hand labor, in turn related to the extended family as a source of labor and eventually to the utility of the Bauernhaus and the whole traditional complex. Neither can the Backhaus be understood even if perceived as a house where bread and cakes are baked unless it is seen as a communication and gossip center. This same line of reasoning can be applied to a number of the other pictures and responses.

3. There is a stereotype of experience related to the event, object, or situation patterned in the observer's own culture. This seems clear in the interpretation of the boys' feelings as they leave the school yard to go into the school. Boys would rather play, it is said. The school is confining. This is an image of school in American culture, according to the respondents themselves as they retrospected about their reactions to the pictures and their own experience. The same principle applies to the projection of aching backs and bones, the tediousness of labor, and the desire to escape from it in the interpretation of the picture of the women working in the vineyards and the picture of the small boy helping his father pick currants.

4. There is a stereotype of the experience or meaning of the event, object, or situation as it is presumed to exist in another culture. German teachers and classrooms are believed, in American culture, to be authoritarian, strict, and disciplined. This stereotype is applied to the picture of Herr Steinhardt, with the result that the responses are largely irrelevant to the actual situation portrayed in the picture.

5. There is ambiguity due to lack of clarity in the structural or spatial relations surrounding or involved in the event, object, or situation. This applies particularly to the situation where the teacher is helping a child up the last part of the ladder into the loft of the church to see the bells. The range and irrelevancy of responses is great and seems to be a function of the fact that no one understands exactly what is being seen. Potentially meaningful cues are seized upon, such as the heavy structural beams in the tower, the general dinginess of the surroundings, or the white bandage on the child's hand. There is not only spatial and structural ambiguity involved here but also cultural ambiguity, because the situation is unfamiliar in American culture.
6. There is projection of emotional states ascribed to subjects in another culture. This applies to all situations in which student respondents were asked to indicate what they thought people in the pictures might be thinking or feeling. The emotional states projected are clearly functions of the patterning of experience and beliefs about experience in North American culture. They tend to be quite irrelevant to the specific situations represented in the pictures.
7. There is a single time sample of the action. This applies most directly to the two pictures of the classroom, but it could apply to any of the situations. In order for interpretations to be relevant (i.e., accurate), they must be based upon a sampling of parts of the whole cycle of activity, whatever it is.

## Implications

The processes engaged in by students responding to the pictures described previously are similar to those experienced by the field anthropologist. They are also similar to those experienced by the teacher faced with a classroom full of children, particularly when they are from different social classes or ethnic groups than his own. Furthermore, the children also represent a youth subculture different from that of the teacher. Teachers make the same types of errors described in this analysis, and for the same reasons the Stanford students made them. Some of these errors are mainly humorous, others suggest why there is constant, serious, often tragic, misinterpretation and noncommunication in classrooms where cultural differences are sharp.

By applying what we know about culture and about the problems of the anthropologist in the field to the analysis of materials that may be brought into the classroom from another culture, such as the slides I used, we may anticipate the kinds of errors that are likely to occur in transcultural perception and interpretation, control them better, and develop some relevant skills in observation. I have called this a *transcultural sensitization process.*

Something similar, I suggest, should be a part of all teacher-training programs. It is one way that an anthropological perspective may help improve teaching.

## REFERENCES

Spindler, George and students. 1973. *Burgbach: Organization and Identity.* New York: Holt, Rinehart and Winston.

Spindler, George. 1987, 1997. Transcultural Sensitization. In G. Spindler (Ed.), *Education and Cultural Process* (2nd and 3rd edition). Prospect Heights, IL: Waveland Press.

# Crosscultural, Comparative, Reflective Interviewing in Schoenhausen and Roseville

(1993)

*George and Louise Spindler*

## Voices

'Voices', for us, means the voices of our 'native' informants in the Schoenhausen and Roseville elementary schools, the sites of our comparative research. The voices include those of the administrator, the children, and, most importantly in this exercise, the voices of two teachers teaching in comparable schools, one in Germany, the other in the United States. The voices in our study are elicited by using evocative stimuli in the form of films taken by us in the Schoenhausen and Roseville schools. We have arranged for textual space so that informants have their own voices, and made the dialogue between ethnographer and informants explicit, as appropriate to a study in modernist format. Our analysis is directed at culturally phrased assumptions apparent in the voiced discourse of the informants. The voices of the ethnographers, ourselves, are heard in the quest for assumptions in the discourse phrased by the natives, but our voices are muted, since we try to elicit the discourse in such a manner that it is self/other reflective. Our method is therefore called the "Crosscultural, Comparative, Reflective Interview."

## The Research Sites

Schoenhausen is a village of about 2,000 in a semirural but urbanizing area in *Land* Baden Württemberg, Southern Germany. Schoenhausen was known, and still is to some extent, as an ausgesprochener Weinort (emphatically a winemaking place). The native-born are swaebisch and protestant. Most of the 'newcomers' originally migrated from the former east zone, Sudetenland, or other areas from which Germans were expelled or from which they fled after World War II. They are somewhat more urbanized as a rule, and more often than not Catholic (Spindler, 1974). The Grundschule (elementary school) is charged with the responsibility for educating all of the children and preparing them for a changing Germany and world. Its 127 children are distributed in four grades staffed by six teachers and a Rektor (Principal), and various other special services personnel. The Schoenhausen Grundschule has enjoyed a good relationship with the community and with the parents whose children attend it. Partly, at least, this relationship is due to the benign influence of the Rektor (Principal) who has been in that position since the beginning of our study in 1968.

The Roseville elementary school, located in central Wisconsin, includes kindergarten through eighth grade and is somewhat larger than the Schoenhausen school but is comparable in every other respect. The school district is rural but has many commuters that work in nearby towns, some of them as much as forty or fifty miles distant. The majority of children attending the school come from small dairy farms. This school also enjoys good relationships with its community and with the parents who eagerly attend school functions whenever possible. The Principal is himself a farmer as well as an educator and is well-liked. The predominant ethnicity of the Roseville School District is German (Spindler, 1987, 1987b and 1990).

## Purpose

Our purpose in this chapter is to demonstrate one particular kind of research technique and the text that it produces—the crosscultural, comparative, reflective interview (CCCRI). The technique has been discussed only briefly in our own publications and demonstrated somewhat more extensively in a study in which a Japanese and an American preschool furnished the cultural 'brackets' in the form of films (or video) from each location, for interviews with teachers (Fujita and Sano, 1988, 1997). Our research in Schoenhausen began in 1968, and continued in 1977, 1981 and 1985. In each of the field visits we had specific research objectives that are discussed in 'Schoenhausen Revisited and the Discovery of Culture' (Spindler, 1987a). Our overall objective was to explore the role of the school in cultural change in comparable areas in Germany and the United States.

As with all instruments or special techniques used in our research, the CCCRI developed out of field experience *in situ*. It was fully applied for the first time in 1985 though we had used films as evocative stimuli (Collier & Collier, 1986) in interviews before that, though not in an explicitly comparative and reflective framework.

The interviews conducted with teachers, children and administrators were directed at cultural differences and similarities, both between Schoenhausen and Roseville and among the named 'audiences.' Figure 13.1 expresses the overall relationship in both sites.

The diagram shows us that all three kinds of natives in the Schoenhausen and Roseville elementary schools shared some perceptions and assumptions and diverged in others. The divergence appears to represent positional differences. Both the 'shared' and 'divergent' sectors may be considered cultural phenomena. The anthropologist is not a native, but participates in the situation, perceives, and assumes. His and her (G. & L. Spindler) perceptions and assumptions are no less influenced by position as well as by shared experience and participation in the dialogue of the two research sites.

The CCCRI are designed to stimulate dialogue about pivotal concerns on the part of natives in comparable cultural systems. Some form of audiovi-

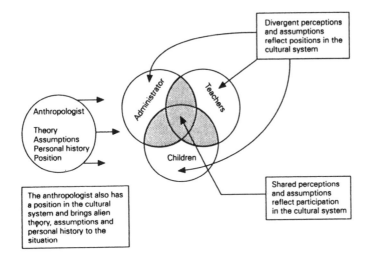

FIG. 13.1 Positionality in the Schoenhausen CCCRI.

sual material (in this instance films of classrooms) representing two cultures (conceivably more) is used to 'bracket' the interview. That is, the interview is conducted as an inquiry into the perceptions, by the native, of his/her own situation and that of the 'other,' and the assumptions revealed in reflections about those perceptions. We regard both the perceptions and assumptions as cultural phenomena.

We believe that a 'complete' ethnography should include explicit recognition of this complex dialogue in both its shared and divergent aspects.

## THE CROSSCULTURAL, COMPARATIVE, REFLECTIVE INTERVIEW (CCCRI)

The basic procedure for the CCCRI is simple—we filmed in Schoenhausen and we filmed in Roseville and we showed the teachers, the children, and the administrators in both sites the films from both places.[1] We conducted interviews about what they saw in their own classrooms and in those of the 'other' and how they interpreted what they saw. These interviews are of a different quality than anything that we had collected previously. They are reflective in depth and with a subtlety that had heretofore been lacking, and they are cultural translations by natives. The observed differences in the action in the two settings, Schoenhausen and Roseville, caused teachers and children to reflect back on their own behavior at the same time that they were pronouncing perceptions of the behavior of the other. In a sense they were experiencing what we have experienced as ethnographers. After working in the Schoenhausen school in 1968, 1977 and 1981 our visits to the Roseville school, beginning in 1983, caused us to reexamine what we were observing in Schoenhausen. This reorientation was fully implemented in our 1985 visit. We had come to accept the 'normal,' as familiar, and it had become increasingly difficult to 'see' what it was we were observing. The Roseville experience sharpened our perceptions and caused us to think about them in a different way. In order to observe anything, anywhere, it seems necessary to make it a little 'strange' (Spindler, 1988)[2]

---

[1]We used Super 8 mm sound and color film rather than video and though we have converted some of the files to video cassettes we still use film for most viewings in our own classroom, since resolution and screen size are so much better.

[2]In some recent reading in education we found to our surprise that there is a well developed 'reflective teaching' orientation that has developed in educationist circles (Ross & Weade, 1989). As we briefly explored this literature we had the feeling that one way of enhancing the desired reflective process on the part of teachers would be to create cultural 'brackets' for the reflection in some manner similar to the procedure we carried out for Schoenhausen/Roseville. Even the relatively small differences in classroom management between Germany and the United States caused teachers to 'stand on their heads' to look again at their own practice. In both of our research sites it was rewarding to hear teachers say that they felt that they had gained insight into their own practice as a consequence of this crosscultural reflective activity. Though improvements in practice were not one of our explicit objectives, it is always good to feel that beyond merely not doing harm          (continued on next page)

The rest of this chapter will be devoted to an examination of some texts produced by the crosscultural, comparative, reflective interviews. Though we have extensive interview material from all of the teachers, the administrator, and from the children in both school settings, we will present only two interviews from teachers, one in Schoenhausen and the other in Roseville, provide some excerpts from the perceptions of the children when they saw the films of their counterparts and provide a brief excerpt from a longer monologue by a high official in the school district of which Schoenhausen is a part, when he saw the Roseville films. The reactions of the children follow, excerpted from group interviews conducted in the Schoenhausen and Roseville schools. The children will be followed by the administrator, and finally the two teachers, Mrs. Schiller (Roseville) and Frau Wanzer (Schoenhausen).[3]

## DIVERSE REFLECTIONS

### Children's Reactions to Films

*Schoenhausen.* We showed the films of Roseville classrooms to the first and second grades combined and the third and fourth grades combined, in separate screenings, in the Schoenhausen Grundschule. These are the same films that the teachers and administrators viewed. The Schoenhausen first and second graders seem barely able to control their enthusiasm at the prospect of spending an hour looking at films from America. The teachers keep saying 'still!' and 'ssshhh!' and 'wiederstill!' The noise level is very high and one has the impression of tremendous vitality. The teacher and then George Spindler describe the kinds of films they are going to see and what we would like them to do. The first film shown is of a first and second grade class in Roseville on the history of exploration in the United States. Some of the children are seated at a table in the front of the room with the teacher discussing the exploration of the Mississippi River Valley while other children are seated at their desks or moving quietly about the classroom as they pursue individual tasks. After the film is shown the Schoenhausen children bounce up and down on their seats, snap their fingers, and shout for attention. 'What did you notice?' says the teacher. The children respond, 'Some

---

[2] *(continued from previous page)* one may be doing some goods with one's research activity. Though improvements in practice were not one of our explicit objectives, it is always good to feel that beyond merely not doing harm one may be doing some good with one's research activity. Another effort to help teachers to reflect on their own activity in the classroom is represented by 'cultural therapy,' as conducted with individual teachers in conjunction with ethnographic studies of their classroom (Spindler, 1989).

[3] Our first reflective interviews were conducted in Schoenhausen in 1985 and had been preceded by interviews in Roseville, before we had read Marcus, Clifford, or others engaged in 'postmodernist' criticism of traditional positivist realist ethnography. We have been influenced, however, by our recent reading of their critical writings in the interpretation of what we were doing.

of them could work at a table with a teacher and others could sit alone.'
'They could work with another person if they wanted to.' 'They could go to
the closet and get things to use if they wanted to and there were some of
them listening to tape recorders.' The teacher admonished them, 'I can't
hear unless you're a little more quiet!'—but the noise level continues at
what to us seems a very high level. The second film, is shown, also of a first
and second grade classroom in *Roseville*.

The children are shown working on preparations for Thanksgiving so
they are moving about the classroom a great deal but in the subdued way in
which children move in Roseville classrooms. The Schoenhausen children
are beside themselves! 'Waaagh!' 'Wooooo!' 'Huhuhuuuuuu!' They are
shouting, jumping up and down, and snapping their fingers. The teacher
again attempts to still them, but with only moderate success. 'Some of them
are black-haired!' 'The children are not fighting with each other!' 'There's
nobody tripping anybody else when they move around!' 'There's 'keine
Streiten' (no fighting).' 'The teacher stays up front with the group.' 'She
doesn't even look at the others!' 'Doch, doch!' 'The seats are all rooted to
the floor!' 'They could run around anytime they wanted to!' 'They were at
various places.' 'They were rühig (quiet) even though they run from place to
place (verscheidene Zonen).' 'What were they doing with the paper?'
'What's in those bags?' (We explained that the film had been taken on 'popcorn day' when children could buy popcorn for 10 cents a bag if they wanted
to and that the colored paper being cut up was in order to make tails for
Thanksgiving turkeys that would be put up on the bulletin board). 'They
picked up all the paper that they dropped on the floor!' 'They were quiet in
the classroom all the time.' 'They talked only in English.' 'They didn't fight
at all.' 'They weren't loud.'

Films of comparable classrooms in Roseville were shown to the
Schoenhausen third and fourth grade classes. We went through the same
procedure of explanation and then showed the first film. The reactions to
the films were very similar to those furnished by the first and second grade
children though the older children were somewhat more reflective. They
felt that the Roseville system would not work for them because there would
be 'too much fighting' in the Schoenhausen school. They would not learn as
much without a teacher present to help them 'at all times.' 'Learning with a
teacher is much simpler than having to learn by yourself.' 'You couldn't have
somebody walking around the classroom anytime they felt like it because
somebody would be sure to trip them.'

*Roseville.*   We followed the same procedure in the Roseville school,
showing the children films of their grade counterparts in Schoenhausen. We
had already showed them films of their own classrooms. The children filed

into the gymnasium where the film showing was to take place and where bleachers had been set up for grades 3 through 6. They took their places quietly and talked to each other in whispers. The teachers did not have to call upon them to be quiet or to focus their attention on the films. We showed three films in sequence and we present here only a few of their comments. 'I'd rather live away from school. I like riding on the bus!' 'We have more recesses and they are a lot of fun and we have a gym. Did they have a gym?' 'I like having desks like ours where there is a special place to keep one's own things. I wouldn't like to get a table with other kids.' 'I like being in school a long time each day.' (We had explained that the German school day was much shorter than theirs). 'We like staying in school for lunch, it's fun.' 'It's too noisy in those (Schoenhausen) classrooms. How could you learn anything if it was so noisy?' I couldn't work by myself if there was so much noise all the time.' (A few said that they would like to be able to talk out loud and run around the room sometimes and make more noise in general but the consensus was that the Schoenhausen classrooms were too noisy). 'I like being able to choose things that I want to do.' 'The teacher isn't always telling us what we have to do.' 'None of them wore hats!' 'Two of them looked like Bernie and Travis (children in Roseville).' 'The top of their desk was messy, there were markers lying all over.' 'The moving chalkboard is really neat.' 'I wouldn't want to live so close to the school. I like to ride on the bus.' 'It would be nice to have sinks in the classroom like that.' (The Schoenhausen classrooms all have sinks towards the front). 'Our school is more modern and has a nice gym.' 'The town is very old.' (We had showed one film of the Schoenhausen environment). 'I like modern buildings.' 'I'd like to be able to make all the noise I want' (chorus) 'No Way!' 'My ears would go woof woof!' 'There is just too much noise.'

## Interpretation

Children notice the same features that adults notice, but from a different perspective, quite naturally, since they are children, but they are natives of the same system that the teachers are. The Roseville children perceive the noise level and activity of the Schoenhausen children as greater than in their own classroom and most place a negative value on it. They appreciate the long school day, the lunch period, and living out in the country not 'packed in' with other families in houses. They also recognize the facilities such as the gymnasium and the modern school building as being positive attributes. They are, surprisingly, not particularly attracted by the route of apparent freedom to talk out loud or to engage in vigorous physical activity at times and felt that this could actually be injurious to learning. They do not reflect in the same way that the teachers do on the significance of these differences but merely accept them as given. They are much more attentive to details of the environment and details of behavior. Schoenhausen children attend to the popcorn day, the black hair, the desks, picking up paper, and not fighting when they move around. They perceive the quiet order of the Roseville classrooms and feel that it would not work that way in their own school.

These are the real conditions of the childrens' lives in the school. These conditions are perceived through cultural screens provided by life in Roseville and life in Schoenhausen. How far this goes into what we could think of as 'American' culture or 'German' culture is beyond the scope of our intent at the present. What is most important for our purposes is that there is, as will be seen, considerable similarity in teacher perceptions, administrative perceptions, and those of children of the same situations, but there are important differences that reflect the positions of the teachers, administrator, and the children, respectively.

The reflections of the Schulamtdirektor (Superintendent of Schools) follow.

## The Schulamtdirektor Speaks

We showed the films we have described to the Schulamtdirektor, his staff and the Schoenhausen teachers the third evening that we were in Germany in 1985. The Schulamtdirektor had expressed his strong interest in seeing the films when we explained our mission on the first day of our presence in Germany. We excerpt, following, a few translated statements from his much longer reaction.

It is difficult for me to see whether these films (of either Roseville or Schoenhausen) are typical of either the school or of other schools in a broader area. If they are typical we come to a situation. I must say that there is between the school in Roseville and that in Schoenhausen a clear difference. A decisive difference. Our teachers, our understanding about school, are situated in a specific system. This system is influenced directly from above, from the school system viewpoint. One always understands that there is a curriculum plan prepared beforehand from above that is binding. And it gives a clear statement of what instruction means. A very clear statement. Instruction is, as we understand it, as a rule joined with a certain theme. Instruction is joined with a certain class. Instruction is linked to a certain preparation, a certain goal and a certain realization of these goals. Indeed there are always variations but these variations are always within the framework of these intentions. It binds the teachers and the school children in their relationship. The teacher is always at the front. The children sit before him. That can vary of course but as a rule that's the way it goes. The teacher instructs everyone at the same time. There are certain themes that can be followed in groups but these are brought together in a successive sequence. One hears what has been done and what will be done. It is the art of the teacher to bring together these results in order to bring all of the children along, insofar as possible, in the same way. The teacher brings everything together under the same label, tries to reach the same goal, so that in every hour a little piece of the mosaic (of learning) is laid down. And so goes the work in a given hour and in the next hour, week for week until finally the teacher with the children reaches a specific goal. This is characteristic for German instruction and for our understanding of instruction. If I am to take these pictures of (Roseville) that we have seen as typical, and you say that they are, then it is very difficult for me to understand how instruction and progress can move together. There are many questions, many. For example, are the children able to reach, to proceed in similar steps towards learning goals? We have certain disciplines, as in Deutsch, in Mathematik, in Sachuntterickt. Is there something like that comparable here? How does the teacher handle the problem of having one group further along and the other hanging along behind? I am not one to think that there is only one way to get to Rome. But without doubt for us a goal (Ziel) is a goal and without doubt a goal is to be attained. The overall goal is to maintain regular progress in the class. When a child, for example cannot reach the goal then there is a possibility to repeat or to go to a special school. Naturally one will in instruction always seek to stimulate and follow children's personal motivation, but Leistungsfähigkeit (productive efficiency) for the group is the purpose—not the self-purpose of the individual. Everything goes back again into the group. This is certainly the art of the teacher.

The Schulamtdirektor goes on at length about the relationship of goals for the school, for instruction, for each hour of instruction. He points out that there have been changes in this curriculum plan through the years in Germany but that there always is a plan and it is given to the teachers. He feels, paradoxically, that he had greater freedom as a younger teacher than teachers have today. He is particularly impressed with the apparent freedom of the teachers in the Roseville school to teach at their own pace and manner and that the curriculum plan is generated by the teachers themselves. It is clear that the Schulamtdirektor perceives the Roseville classrooms in ways parallel to the way the Schoenhausen children do and in the same general frame of reference as Frau Wanzer does in the following interview (and Frau Wanzer represents quite well the other teachers in the Schoenhausen school). This convergence of perceptions from children, teachers and the higher administration impresses us. If we think of culture as a screen through which one perceives 'reality' then a part of this screen is shared by these participants in the Schoenhausen and Roseville process. At the same time, however, it is important to recognize that the teachers, children, and the administrator are each speaking from their particular positions. Their perceptions converge, but they are not identical. The positions, and the perceptions flowing from them, are also culture. Diversity and commonality are both subsumed by cultural structure and process.

Our next step is to present the text from interviews of two teachers, one from Roseville, the other from Schoenhausen.

## Two Teachers

### Mrs. Schiller, Roseville Elementary School

The interview begins with a summary, by us (GLS) of what we had seen and filmed in Mrs. Schiller's classroom yesterday (and later showed in Germany). As usual, there were a group of children (twelve) at the big table at the front of the room, in this instance, learning how to tell time. Mrs. Schiller seemed completely absorbed in this activity and didn't even glance at the children in the back of the room working at their desks or moving quietly about the room to get materials or books from the big closet or shelves lining the walls. Four children, in two pairs, were using flashcards for drill in arithmetic, two others had headsets on and were listening to tapes. Some were pasting paper 'feathers' on the tails of paper turkeys (it is close to Thanksgiving). Yet others appear to be working on workbook lessons.

Mrs. Schiller has seen some of the same films of Schoenhausen and Roseville as the children, other teachers, and the Schulamtdirektor had.

GLS:            It's remarkable that the children work on their own as they do. How do you prepare them to do this?

Mrs. Schiller:  I'm not sure I do prepare them. They have to trust me. We try to develop a relationship, that has to happen first. Then I try to figure out which kids won't get along—there are some I would never put next to each other. I separate those—but basically we have really good kids.

GLS:            How do they know what to do?

Mrs. Schiller:  Well, you're probably thinking of the silent reading period that is never silent at this grade level. They want to share. They can move around, use the flashcards, whatever. I'm just glad they want to come to school and share in the activities like that.

GLS:            They seem so, so independent. They are teaching each other! How do they know how to do that?

Mrs. Schiller:  I suppose some need help and others know when they need it so they just do it.

GLS:            It's not something you establish?

Mrs. Schiller:  No, I don't. It begins as soon as they grow up a little (in first grade). This one needs math, this one reading. You know, we're pretty high in math here, but low on reading pretty much in the whole area. Jack (the Principal) has ten of his students (from the seventh and eighth grades) come in and each one takes one of my children and reads a story to them, and the little ones read back, too. It is a great help. I can tell when we discuss the readings later. They are well informed. (Mrs. Schiller spoke at length about one problem child and his mother who won't come to school to consult with her.)

GLS:            Now, with respect to your underlying objectives as a teacher, that is Linda Schiller as a teacher, not necessarily what you get in the education courses, what would you say your basic purpose is?

Mrs. Schiller:  To teach them to be an individual, to be all they can, to the limits of their abilities and if I can get them to be a happy person, as well as get them to do their best, then I think I have done my job. (Mrs. Schiller talks more about the problem child and his mother. The mother was going to sue because Mrs. Schiller had him repeat the first grade. What she tried to do was to help the child to learn all he could in order to overcome his reading difficulty.)

GLS:            Now let's go back a little to this management process. It strikes me (GS) as rather incredible that you have some kind of understanding that they are supposed to go about their activities on their own—individually—and pick up on the things they do without wasting a great deal of time or being disruptive in the class. It seems to me that there's something pretty deep going on here. It doesn't work that way in Schoenhausen.

Mrs. Schiller:  You don't feel that if I went to Germany I could operate a classroom the way I do now here? If I got them at the same age level?

GLS:            It would be a remarkable experiment! The kids tend to act up when adults are not around. But here in Roseville wouldn't you be able to walk out of the classroom, go down to the office, leave your class for five minutes or more?

Mrs. Schiller:  Well, yes. I left the first graders alone up in front without any assignment just the other day and Jeremy grabbed the pointer and started 'A,B,C,D' etc. and the whole class repeated, and then went on through the alphabet several times. And I said, 'That was so nice. You did not waste time!' And then I had to go to the art room and Christopher, my repeater, (a child who was 'held back' a year) called all the children in the first grade to the desk to get their math books out and be ready and he stood at the board to write names down if they were talking, so they were all ready, waiting for the class to get started. When they do things like that, I praise. We don't have any time to waste and so I was happy to have the first graders ready to go when the bell rang.

GLS: There were so many different things going on in the class we observed yesterday. It was fascinating to try and film them—this little group here, this one here, another someplace else. I (GS) have a logistics question. How do the children know when and how to find what they need?

Mrs. Schiller: Well, it would be great if we could do more of this kind of free choice, but a lot of it is more structured. The head office would like us to do more of the things the kids want to do themselves.

GLS: But how do they know, when they do, what they do?

Mrs. Schiller: Well, it's just the choice. The flashcards, are there somewhere, the charts, the tape recorders, you know they're, they're really all little teachers, it's just built in. They come up and ask, 'Can I do the flashcards? Can I use the charts? Can I use the tape recorder?' Especially if it's a first grader that needs help and then a second grader can teach them. They love to do that.

GLS: But you arrange the materials for their use somehow?

Mrs. Schiller: Well, they ask if they can do it.

GLS: But you keep the materials in the classroom and they know where they are? Access to them is just them asking you?

Mrs. Schiller: Yes, and it's their choice of friends that they want to work with or whoever they want to share with.

GLS: Where have you taught before? (Mrs. Schiller named several places—all larger and more urban than Roseville.) Do you think it was this way in those communities also?

Mrs. Schiller: Yes, I really do. I have a lot of faith in kids. I think kids are neat! If you have high expectations, 98% of the time they will fulfill your expectations.

GLS: What would you feel like if you went out in the hall or someone called you to the phone and you came back after 5 minutes and found things in considerable disorder?

Mrs. Schiller: Well, I would tell them right out, 'I am very disappointed! I had this important phone call and you couldn't sit for 5 minutes while I answered it.' I would let them know it hurt me personally. It's a kind of personal thing. Oh, yes! You start building that up the first day of school. Then they feel 'we can't hurt our teacher.' Oh, yes, that happened today! I had to take a workbook to a parent who was taking her little girl to the dentist so she could work on it if she had to wait and the class had the same assignment. When I came back to my room they had all finished that page that was assigned and they went right on to the next one. I praised them again 'it was really nice that I could count on you, and I could come back to a nice quiet class.' And of course they all beamed. They just love praise!

GLS: Do you think you are different than other teachers here or elsewhere?

Mrs. Schiller: Perhaps. I have so many sisters that are all teachers and my mom is a teacher. I have my own philosophy. I don't think children need to finish every page of the workbooks, etc. It's so important for these children living in a rural area to social-ize with each other so I try never to keep a child in during re-cess or after school to do makeup work on a workbook. They need socialization. And I will not be a grouch. I'm not really strict. Some people would probably say that I was lax.

GLS: Were you struck with any specific feature when you looked at the German films?

Mrs. Schiller: Well, one thing was the discipline. When they were running around the room and making a lot of noise it was going fur-ther than it would here. But I do feel like we can learn even though we're a little noisy.

GLS: You know, we found that each of the teachers in the Schoenhausen school had a regular sequence of operations that they planned out in every classroom and every hour. Would you say that there was a sequence here and in your classroom?

Mrs. Schiller: Well, we have a curriculum, but we can handle it any way we want. I don't go through the same sequence every day. It would be too boring!

GLS: You mentioned a 'curriculum'—in Germany the teachers have a 'Lehrerplan,' that defines subjects and sequences and amount of time that should be spent on certain themes. Is that what you mean by curriculum?

Mrs. Schiller: There is a little book here on the shelf that happens to be for the third and fourth grade (she hands it to us).

GLS:                    Where does this come from?

Mrs. Schiller:   The teachers put it out.

GLS:                    You mean—the teachers here?

Mrs. Schiller:   The whole district of Arcadia (the larger area around Roseville) teachers from Roseville had input.

GLS:                    Does it tell you how to teach?

Mrs. Schiller:   No, it doesn't tell you that. We are still queens in our own classrooms and there's plenty of freedom.

GLS:                    Now we have seen a number of reading books and some periodicals that are used in your classes. Where do these materials come from?

Mrs. Schiller:   One is the *Weekly Reader*, and there's *Sprint*, and we pick our own books—there's a Reading Committee, a Math Committee, and so forth, appointed from teachers. We look over the books that the various publishers furnish and pick out the ones we want. We pick, say, three books. They are sent out to schools and then the teachers all vote on them. The ones that get the most votes are the books that we use.

GLS:                    Well, thank you very much for your time and all the insight you've given us. It's been a real pleasure to talk with you and we'll be doing it again, we hope.

Mrs. Schiller:   It's been very enjoyable for me and I've learned a lot looking back on my own teaching practices and classroom management. Looking at the Germans, at the films from Germany, really stirred up my thinking.

## Frau Wanzer, Schoenhausen Grundschule

For the first few minutes we talked about what we wanted to do in her classroom, indicating that we would like to present a systematic view of her classroom on film, to the Roseville teachers, in our exchange activity. To help do this, we suggested that she spend some twenty minutes before the class that we were to film explaining her procedures and goals, and that we, in turn, would explain this to the Roseville teachers. She had seen the Roseville films at the same time as the Schulamtdirektor.

Frau Wanzer:   Ja! It would perhaps have been good if for the films you showed us (of the Roseville classrooms) they had this introduction. Für Mich in jeden Fall (for me in any case), it was really difficult to see what was intended. Perhaps that was also the ground for the feeling that many of us had, 'Was lernen sie eigentlich? (What are they learning really?)'

GLS: We explained that the films shown were typical for this class and that the 'freiwillig' (free will) character of the classroom activity was indeed characteristic.

Frau Wanzer: I can scarcely understand how the teacher working at the table with some of the children would work on without looking to see what the other children were doing in the rest of the room. How do the children working alone know what they are supposed to do? But it had to function well. They were seemingly satisfied and they weren't causing any difficulties. Bei uns gibt es (with us there are) Schwierigkeiten (difficulties) und Streiten (strife or fighting). This was apparently not the case (in the Roseville school)! Probably they (the children) are accustomed to this.

GLS: Frau Schiller is very proud that her classroom is productive. The 'freiwillig' character also impressed us. 'How do the children know exactly what there is for them to do?' we asked Frau Schiller. She answered 'I do nothing—the materials are there and the children seek them out for themselves, but they usually ask me if they can use them.' 'Naturally, the children have specific lessons, but when they are finished—they can do what they will.'

Frau Wanzer: Sie können tuen was sie wollen! (They can do what they want!)

GLS: They have various opportunities—such as tapes, computers, the library, flashcards, charts and posters, etc.

Frau Wanzer: Da ist natürlich ein grosser Unterschied (There is naturally a great difference) to our school. They (Roseville) have much more time to work, much more. With us one hour equals forty-five minutes and one must in this time reach a goal. In America they have so much time and so when they are finished with their lessons they can do what they want, but with us there is no time. The more gifted children finish, but many do not and then they must be helped to reach the goal for the lesson. (She talks about helping the slower children and how the more gifted children get less attention than they deserve. She also talks about the learning-disabled children—how some of them can reach only minimum goals defined in the curriculum plan [Lehrplan]).

GLS: To go back a little, so there is for every hour a specific goal you must reach?

Frau Wanzer: Ich habe in mein Lehrplan (I have in my curriculum plan) the goal that I must reach—the goals that I must reach. Every hour has a part goal. I must find out as the hour progresses if I'm going to have enough time to reach that goal. It depends on whether the hour goes well or badly—how much time I will spend. For example, there is the topic of 'Where do we get our water?' It's fascinating. In the Lehrplan there are ten hours given for this subject, but the children are so begeistert (enthusiastic), they want to know so much! It takes much more time than the ten hours foreseen in the Lehrplan. Then I must narrow down the amount of time spent on other subjects such as plants or animals, all within the Sachunterricht (home, community, civic affairs, etc.) curriculum.

GLS:    You speak of a Lehrplan. Is that local or Baden Württemberg?

Frau Wanzer:    Ja, the Baden Württemberg plan.

GLS:    The Lehrplan appears to be very tight. If you had more time would you have freiwillig (free choice) periods?

Frau Wanzer:    Ja, bestimmt (Yes, certainly).

GLS:    How would you handle it?

Frau Wanzer:    I would arrange materials beforehand that zu eine bestimmten Thema gehört (that belong to a specific theme). But in the framework of this theme, the children could do what they wanted. But I wouldn't just leave it up to them to choose from unorganized material. I would have the fear that they would choose things that were just play. And I have the impression that the children are so müde (tired), so lustlos; (without drive) that they wouldn't do anything strenuous. They spend all afternoon and evening before the TV. This is very practical for the parents, but not good for the children. I am afraid that if I ask them to do whatever they wanted they would do gar nichts (nothing at all)! For instance, I told them 'Everyone bring a favorite book and we'll make a big library and we'll have a free reading period.' Well, two-thirds of them read with pleasure and one-third did nothing at all and disturbed the others.

GLS:    So how would you proceed? Would you have them work in groups?

Frau Wanzer:    Ja, for example, with respect to animals that we don't have in Germany, such as camels and lions, etc., I would have four tables arranged and I would furnish each of them with books and materials, such as pictures, before the children arrive. And then they could work on whatever they chose—a lion or a camel or whatever—of the four possibilities. And then ten minutes before the end of the period I would have them report, each group, to another group. This kind of procedure will work, but völlig frei (fully free)? Das macht nichts (that makes nothing—that's of no use)! We have a time problem and when I only have three hours per week for Sachunterricht, there is simply too little time for this kind of free choice situation.

GLS: We would like to ask another kind of question. We have the impression that here in the Schoenhausen Grundschule, or for that matter in any of the schools in the nearby towns that we have visited, that when you leave the classroom, Sie erwarten dass die Kinder unruhig und eben chaotic werden (that you expect that the children will become restless and even chaotic).

Frau Wanzer: Erwartet (expect)! Ich hoffe sie bleiben ruhig! (I hope they remain quiet!). But there are always those two or three children that are poorly socialized and get everyone else stirred up. There is, for example, in my class, a child that has terrible personal problems. He strikes out and shouts at other children and they tell him he's crazy and, he's very sensitive. He comes from a family with no father—a damaged home environment—he is terribly sensitive and disruptive.

GLS: Would you expect the children to work on their lessons when you leave them?

Frau Wanzer: This is my goal!

GLS: How often is it reached?

Frau Wanzer: In the course of the school year—in the first grade—hardly. In the second year it goes somewhat better. By the fourth year they can work for longer periods. You have to handle this sort of thing in little doses.

GLS: What would you do if you heard a disturbance in the room when you returned?

Frau Wanzer: I would talk to the class. I would attempt to reach an understanding. Scolding does no good. Sometimes I have said that I am traurig (sad).

GLS: Would you say you were beleidigt (hurt)?

Frau Wanzer: No, never beleidigt, nur (only) traurig.

GLS: Do you make the children feel guilty (schuldig)?

Frau Wanzer: I feel that guilt is not understandable for children of this age. How can they understand who is guilty, the one who started the trouble or the one who responded to the trouble and carried it on further?

(We carried on discussions of this kind with Frau Wanzer several times and her interpretation of her own behavior in the classroom and that of the Roseville teachers that she had seen on film was consistent. She saw the Roseville classrooms, as did the other teachers, as tending towards being directionless and without specific goals and not organized for the attainment of whatever goals existed. She did find the quiet orderliness of the Roseville schools impressive and as exhibiting good 'teamwork.')

## Interpretation

Frau Wanzer and Mrs. Schiller are two experienced teachers of about the same age, teaching the same grades, about many of the same things, in quite similar schools in parallel communities in Germany and in the USA. And yet their handling of their classrooms and the assumptions that guide their behavior are significantly different at some critical points. And their perceptions of each other's classrooms reflect these differences. Mrs. Schiller's classroom is relaxed, quiet, low-keyed, and diverse. Children carry out various activities on their own, in addition to those carried out by the teacher and the small group she is leading through a specific learning task. There is little or no disruptive behavior. These qualities, confirmed in many sessions of observation by us, are apparent in the films we showed to all of the Schoenhausen teachers, the Principal, the Schulamtdirektor (Superintendent of Schools) and his assistants.

Frau Wanzer perceives Mrs. Schiller's classroom as undirected, as almost goalless. At the same time, she acknowledges that there appears to be good 'teamwork,' but that this method would be unlikely to work this well in Schoenhausen Grundschule.

These perceptions are apparent in the interview. Frau Wanzer's assumptions are apparent: that if children are undirected they, or at least a significant proportion of them, will do nothing at all, become disruptive, or will choose to play rather than work. She also reports that when children have clear directions on an interesting topic they can become very enthusiastic about learning and will work hard at it.

Frau Wanzer explains the differences observed in terms of time, which is short in Schoenhausen, and the fact that the curriculum plan there defines the goals to be reached quite precisely. She does not see these as cultural attributes, but as given, practical, preconditions to whatever she does, and the children do, in her classroom.

The differences run deep. Mrs. Schiller assumes that her goal is to help each individual develop to his or her fullest degree—to the limit of their individual capacities. Frau Wanzer assumes, as does the Schulamt-direktor, that her purpose is to help each child attain the standards set forth in the Lehrerplan—that some will meet them fully and others only minimally. Frau Wanzer takes for granted the existence of a Lehrerplan and that it is furnished to the school by the State school system, and that it will guide her management of her instruction directly. Mrs. Schiller takes for granted the fact that teachers from the school district develop their own curriculum and that it is only an approximate guide. Frau Wanzer assumes that the children eventually learn to continue working when she leaves the classroom, but that one can't expect too much of the younger first and second graders. Mrs. Schiller expects her first and second graders to be responsible for keeping a quiet, ontask classroom when she is gone for a few minutes. Frau Wanzer would 'talk' to her class if there were a disruption, but she would not act 'hurt,' only 'sad,' and she would not try to make her children feel 'guilty.' Mrs. Schiller would develop personal liking and trust with her children, would be 'hurt' if they misbehaved, and would leave them all feeling guilty if they did. And the two teachers have quite different conceptions of guilt. For Frau Wanzer guilt has to be established—there is a perpetrator, a reinforcer, and perhaps a victim. For Mrs. Schiller there is a feeling state—guilt is internalized. The children feel guilty about their irresponsible behavior and hurting their teacher.

These are the assumptions, as we see them, that lie behind both the behaviors of the two teachers in their classroom, and their perception of each other's behaviors *in situ*. These are cultural differences, we believe, that are expressed in, and derived from, the German and American historical experience respectively. The case for this extension would have to extend substantially beyond the scope of this chapter. We, therefore, confine ourselves to the observation that in Schoenhausen and Roseville respectively, these are assumptions that we regard as cultural, in the sense that they are pervasive within the dialogue of the school and school system and antecedent to the operations of the specific teachers and children we have observed.

## Conclusion

The crosscultural comparative reflective interview procedure furnishes clear evidence that the various audiences viewing the action all saw the same things in the films of classrooms. The children and teachers in Roseville saw the children in the Schoenhausen classrooms as noisy and enthusiastic. The children and teachers in Schoenhausen saw the Roseville classrooms as quiet and orderly. Each acknowledged that their own classrooms were more 'noisy' or more 'quiet', as well as seeing the other in those terms.

The crosscultural comparative reflective interviews also gave us clear evidence of the ways in which position affects perceptions. The Schulamtdirektor, the children, and the teachers 'saw' the same features of behavior in the 'others' setting, but emphasized these features differently, and the children actually 'saw' some things the adults did not. The Schulamtdirektor viewed the action from the top down, from the perspective of a system. The children interpreted the classroom action and setting from their perspective—desks, lunch, clothes, popcorn day, teacher's position in the classroom, blackboards, and so forth, but still 'saw' the quiet and order in the Roseville classroom and the noise level and boisterous activity in the Schoenhausen classrooms. The teachers, represented by Mrs. Schiller and Frau Wanzer, interpreted behavior in their own and the other's classroom with clearly different assumptions about what each expected of children and what their purposes as teachers were. These assumptions, we hold, are cultural.

All of the principals cited above are 'natives,' and they tell their 'story' in their own way. The foreign observers, ourselves, the ethnographers, also 'saw' and 'interpreted.' We 'saw' the same features of classroom activity and our interpretations are not wildly different from those of the natives at any point, but they are influenced by our anthropological goals, our persistent search for 'culture,' in its various expressions. The interested reader may find confirmation of the above in our publications (Spindler, 1987a & 1987b).

What we have presented in this chapter is, in contrast to a 'realistic' text, a modernist text. Modernist texts are designed to feature the eliciting discourse between ethnographer and subject or to involve the reader in the work of analysis. The experience represented in the ethnography must be that of the dialogue between ethnographer and informants, where textual space is arranged for informants to have their own voices (Marcus & Fischer, 1986, p. 67). We have featured both the eliciting discourse and involved the reader in the work of analysis.

Doing this (above) is regarded by Marcus (and others) as a 'radical shift' in perspective—as a 'derailment of the traditional object of ethnography.' Part of its challenge to traditional ethnographic realism is that it avoids the assumption of shared cultural coherence. The texts we have presented in this chapter both demonstrate shared culture and culture differentiated by position. We believe that an adequate ethnography must represent both. We do not feel, however, that this 'derails' ethnography, but, rather, enhances it, by making ethnography a more accurate representation of social and psychocultural reality.

In all of our ethnographic work we have paid attention to differences in culture in relation to gender (Spindler, 1990), sociocultural adaptation (Spindler, 1978), social class and ethnicity and cosmopolitan/hinterland differences (Spindler, Spindler, Trueba & Williams, 1990) and we have consistently tried to let the voices of informants, of the 'natives,' be heard. What we have done differently in the research leading to this chapter is to place the dialogue between informant and ethnographer in the framework of an 'own' and 'other' reflection upon audiovisual representations of similar situations (classrooms) in our two field sites. The dialogue is thus culturally bracketed and the conversation becomes reflective, but the reflectivity is not focused on the ethnographer, as it often is in the 'new' ethnography, but on the informant. The 'native' is doing his/her own cultural analysis by engaging in discourse about the self and other. Under ideal conditions the ethnographer is almost a bystander.

What is left unresolved for us is how the elicited dialogues represent 'German' culture and 'American' culture. We have recently represented the latter as a 'cultural dialogue' (Spindler et al., 1990) and we can understand certain of Mrs. Schiller's interpretations as expressions of (for instance) individualism, achievement and internalization of authority and guilt, that are a part of this dialogue. We can understand some of Frau Wanzer's discourse, and that of the Schulamtdirektor, as expressing certain aspects of a long-term German dialogue about authority, efficiency, collective effort and the attainment of standards. To claim that the little elementary schools in Roseville and Schoenhausen somehow express the national Zeitgeist goes further than most of us want to go, and yet there are some tantalizing connections. The action in these classrooms and the interpretations by the 'natives' seem to be the 'tip of the iceberg.' The parts of the iceberg under the water is the enormous complexity of the national whole and its history. Just how to make the analytic connections remains unresolved. Neither our concepts, nor our vocabulary are sufficient. However, the value of methodology we have presented here does not rest on being able to solve this problem.

The results of our research also have some implications for the debate swirling in anthropological circles about objectivity, positivism, humanism, and the effect of the position of the ethnographer on observation and interpretation (O'Meara, 1989; Spaulding, 1988; Rosaldo, 1989; Marcus and Fischer, 1986; Clifford and Marcus, 1986). The agreement about what is observed ('seen') is greater than one would presume from the doubts cast on the possibility of objectivity in ethnography. Irrespective of position in the situation (for example, child, teacher, administrator, or anthropologist) we all 'saw' the same basic features of action and setting. At the same time it is important to acknowledge that position of the observer vis a vis the action, actors, and setting, as well as training and personal experience, do affect the interpretation (and cultural translation) represented in the writing of ethnography.

Acknowledgments

We wish to thank the faculty and staff of both Roseville and Schoenhausen Elementary Schools and the Schulamtdirektor and his staff, of the Schoenhausen area. They could not have been more gracious or more help-ful. We also wish to thank Mimi Navarro and Diane Johnson for their indis-pensable help in the development of the article from a voice on tape to a finished product. We are grateful to Hector Mendez, University of Califor-nia at Santa Barbara, for his expert use of the computer in producing Figure 13.1. We appreciate the perceptive readings of the first drafts of this chapter by Christine Finnan, Ray McDermott, and Bernard Siegel, and the re-sponses of the many who attended a conference on education in a multicul-tural world sponsored by the Division of Education at the University of California at Davis, organized by Marcelo Suarez-Orozco and Henry Trueba, where we first presented this paper on 12 October 1990. And we are beholden to the Spencer Foundation and the Center for Educational Re-search at the University of Wisconsin, Madison, for crucial funding.

## REFERENCES

Clifford, J. and Marcus, G. (Eds). 1986. *Writing Culture: The Poetics and Politics of Ethnography*. Berkeley, CA, University of California Press.

Collier, J., Jr. and Collier, M. 1986. *Visual Anthropology*. Albuquerque, NM: Univer-sity of New Mexico Press.

Fujita, M. and Sano, T. 1988. 'Children in American and Japanese daycare centers: Ethnography and reflective crosscultural interviewing.' In Trueba, H. and Delgado Gaitan, C. (Eds), *School and Society: Learning Content Through Culture*. New York, Praeger, pp. 73–97.

Fujita, M. and Sano, T. 1997. 'Daycare teachers and children in the United States and Japan: Ethnography, Reflexive Interviewing, and Cultural Dialogue.' In Spindler, G. (Ed), *Education and Cultural Process*, 2nd edition. Prospect Heights, Waveland Press.

Marcus, G. E. and Fischer, M. (Eds). 1986. *Anthropology as Cultural Critique: An Ex-perimental Movement in the Human Sciences*. Chicago, IL, University of Chicago Press.

O'Meara, T. 1989. 'Anthropology as empirical science.' *American Anthropologist*, 91, pp. 354–369.

Rosaldo, R. 1989. *Culture and Truth: The Remaking of Social Analysis*. Boston, MA, Beacon Press.

Ross, D. and Weade, G. (Eds). 1989. 'The context of reflection.' *International journal of Qualitative Studies in Education*, 2, pp. 273–275 (special issue on reflective teaching).

Spaulding, A. C. 1988. 'Distinguished lecture: Archaeology and anthropology.' *American Anthropologist*, 90, pp. 263–271.

Spindler, G. 1973 *Burgbach: Urbanization and Identity in a German Village*. New York, Holt, Rinehart & Winston.

Spindler, G. 1974. 'Schooling in Schoenhausen: A study of cultural transmission and instrumental adaptation in an urbanizing German village.' In Spindler, G. (Ed.) *Education and Cultural Process: Toward an Anthropology of Education*. New York, Holt, Rinehart & Winston, pp. 230–273.

Spindler, L. 1978. 'Researching the psychology of culture change and modernization.' In Spindler, G. (Ed.), *The Making of Psychological Anthropology*. Berkeley, CA, University of California Press, pp. 174–198.

Spindler, G. and L. 1987a. 'Schoenhausen revisited and the discovery of culture.' In Spindler, G. and L. (Eds), *Interpretive Ethnography of Education at Home and Abroad*, Hillsdale, NJ, Lawrence Erlbaum Associates, pp. 143–67.

Spindler, G. and L. 1987b.'In prospect for a controlled crosscultural comparison of schooling: Schoenhausen and Roseville.' In Spindler, G. and L. (Eds), *Education and Cultural Process: Anthropological Approaches*, Prospect Heights, IL, Waveland Press, pp. 389–400.

Spindler, G. and L. 1989. 'Instrumental competence, selfefficacy, linguistic minorities, and cultural therapy.' *Anthropology and Education Quarterly, 20*, pp. 36–50.

Spindler, G. and L. 1990. 'Male and female in four changing cultures' in Jordan, D. and Schwartz, M. (Eds), *Personality and the Cultural Construction of Society*. Tuscaloosa, AL, University of Alabama Press, pp. 182–200.

Spindler, G. and Spindler, L. 1988. 'Roger Harker and Schoenhausen: From the familiar to the strange and back again.' In Spindler, G. (Ed.), *Doing the Ethnography of Schooling: Educational Anthropology in Action*. Prospect Heights, IL, Waveland Press, pp. 20–46 (first published in 1982 by Holt, Rinehart & Winston.)

Spindler, G. and L. with Trueba, H. and Williams, M. 1990. *The American Cultural Dialogue and its Transmission*. London, Falmer Press.

Stocking, G. W. 1983. *Observers Observed: Essays on Ethnographic Fieldwork*. Madison, WI, University of Wisconsin Press.

# Part IV

# AMERICAN CULTURE

# Part
# IV

# AMERICAN CULTURE

## Chapter 14

## Chapter 15

## Chapter 16

This part moves from a traditional representation of American culture in the form of values around which consensus has developed as anthropologists have written about American culture since de Toqueville to a processual analysis of how the culture is transmitted in real situations, and finally to an interpretation of current right wing actions that seem to constitute a reactive movement. The implications for education are pursued.

# 14

# Consensus and Continuity
# in American Culture
## (1983)

### George and Louise Spindler

An analysis of all of the global earlier works on American culture, such as those by Mead, Kluckhohn, Gorer, Ruesch & Bateson, Hsu, Spindler, and Gillin—and there are others—reveals certain commonalities in their characterizations. Though each author phrases the qualities of the culture being analyzed somewhat differently, these observations converge into a fairly coherent list of features. The precise nature of these features, as concepts, is more difficult to define than their content. We will furnish them as descriptive statements of belief and value in presumably pivotal areas of American culture. They are a kind of statement of cultural ideology. They include:

*Individualism.* The individual is the basic unit of society. Individuals are self-reliant and compete with other individuals for success.

*Achievement orientation.* Everyone is concerned with achievement. Achievement, when recognized as success, is a measure of one's intrinsic worth.

*Equality.* Although born with different attributes and abilities, everyone stands equal before the law and should have equal opportunity to achieve, utilizing one's individual ability and energy in a self-reliant manner.

*Conformity.* Everyone is expected to conform to the norms of the community or group. Conformity and equality are closely related in that equal can be translated as "the same as."

*Sociability.* Friendliness and the ability to get along well with others, to make friends easily, to be open to others are desirable qualities.

*Honesty.* Keeping contracts is moral. It is also good for business. It is the "best policy."

*Competence.* One should be able to do things well in order to succeed, but one should also be able to take care of oneself and those dependent upon one … to be independent.

*Optimism.* The future is hopeful. Things will work out for the best. Improvement is possible, even inevitable if one works hard and is competent.

*Work.* Work is good, not just a necessary evil. Idleness is bad and leads to dissolute behavior. Working hard is the key to success, even more than ability.

*Authority.* Authority, from within a hierarchy or as represented by external power or even expertise, has negative value excepting under special conditions.

In 1952 we began administering a simple open-ended sentence "values test" to Stanford students in our classes that was organized around these points of consensus. We have continued to do so intermittently since that time and have published interpretive summaries of the results in 1955 and 1974. We regard the responses from our now rather large sample as expressions of cultural ideology. Over the now 30-year period for which we have data, certain response modalities have exhibited a high degree of consistency. Others have exhibited significant shifts.

Those features exhibiting the most continuity through time are: equality; honesty (as the best policy); the value of work coupled with clear goals; the significance of the self-reliant individual; and sociability—getting along well with others and being sensitive to their needs and appraisals. Those features exhibiting the greatest shifts in meaning and value are: optimism about the future; tolerance of nonconformity; and the value of material success.

The changes in response modalities over time exhibit a trend that can be described as progressively less traditional, if we take the statement of cultural ideology furnished above as our starting point. More tolerance for nonconformity, more interest in self-development than rugged individualism, more concern for other people and their needs, a more relativistic conception of order and morality, less certainty that the time-honored formula of work to get ahead will indeed work at all, more suspicion of authority—the changes have been consistently in these directions. That is, they were until the late 1970s and early 1980s. Now there is a swing back to the traditional formulas. Work, success, achievement, and individualism are stated in the 1979–1982 sample in ways very similar to the 1952 sample.

That the modalities of responses we have collected from Stanford students are not as biased by that provenience as one might expect is indicated by large samples from elsewhere in California and the east coast, and selective samples of minority groups. It is interesting that the latter in general, both at Stanford. and elsewhere, express a more traditional profile than do mainstream students. The results of a survey of 200,000 freshmen at 350 colleges by the American Council of Education support our Stanford data. Though the eliciting device is not the same, many of the categories of belief and value overlap.

The Stanford data appear to tell us something about American culture, or at least its ideology. We may hypothesize that the core features of this profile are those that have exhibited the greatest continuity. But even the changes that have occurred over this 30-year period have occurred around pivotal areas defined by the list of consensi furnished above. This is not surprising, since the eliciting frames were set up around them, but we also asked respondents to describe in one paragraph their ideal person. Their responses in this sector are also phrased around the cultural pivots of the consensus list. The results of this research (originally intended as a teaching device, not a research) appear to correlate well with the insights of the earlier anthropological workers. For whatever reason, these anthropological observers and interpreters of the American scene seem not only to have agreed with each other but to have hit upon some significant features.

Our next step in the search for global cultural continuities will be to examine some of the observations made by both foreign and native interpreters of the American scene well before there was an anthropology. We will not be able to linger over their very interesting observations and the wonderful prose they were expressed in, but will summarize briefly the essence of some of their interpretations.

The best known of these observers is undoubtedly Alexis de Toqueville, who wrote about the Americans in 1831 when we were 24 states and 13 million people. He saw our ancestors as independent, resistive of authority, dedicated to justice, preoccupied with material success, and worried about being different than one's neighbors. Though de Toqueville admired much of what he saw in Americans, he was uncompromisingly critical of what he interpreted as our need to conform and believed that it was so pervasive that it threatened two other values that Americans held dear—individuality and freedom.

An earlier observer, M. G. St. Jean de Crevecoeur, wrote about America before there were states, when the colonies were at the point of revolution. His observations were made during his tenure as a farmer in Orange county, New York, from 1765 to the outbreak of the war against domination by the British crown. He described the Americans of that time as deeply egalitarian, patriotic and very identified with being American, freedom-loving and independent, industrious, valuing competence, and agrarian.

Harriet Martineau, an English reformer, traveled in the United States for 2 years beginning in 1834. She, like de Tocqueville, perceived elements of both individualism and conformity, though she saw them less as universal American attributes and more as regional, the easterners, being more the conformists. She saw "the workings of opinion" as the "established religion" of the United States, taking precedence over even the pursuit of wealth and overshadowing even the love of freedom and the regard for the individual.

We cannot leave the historical dimension behind us without a glance into Frederick Jackson Turner's famous frontier hypothesis. The hypothesis, somewhat simplified, is that the opportunities and imperatives of the frontier, constant to the time of his writings (beginning in 1893), were the cause of individualism, intolerance of restraints, inquisitiveness, masterful grasp of material things, buoyancy and exuberance marking the American character. Among the factors most important was the availability of free land, which supported incessant expansion and constant movement. This "hypothesis," at least the characterizations of the American character it was purported to explain, relates well to the profile of attributes delineated, though it emphasizes individualism, optimism, and materialism (and material success) and de-emphasizes conformity.

There were other earlier observers that one would cite in a more extended sampling of interpretations, including Thomas Jefferson, who saw America as a country of farmers and wanted to keep it that way, and Baron J. A. Graf von Hübner, who saw our individualism as a not unqualified success. The three summarized are sufficient for our purposes. It is clear that what they describe for the America they knew, now 100 to more than 200 years past, does not sound unfamiliar in the framework of pivotal attributes that anthropologists writing in the 1940s and 1950s produced, or that we were able to delineate with our Stanford and related samples.

## INDIVIDUALISM AND CONFORMITY: A KEY OPPOSITION

A key concept which emerges from the writings of both the anthropologists of the earlier period and historical observers such as de Toqueville is that of individualism. Turner was only one of the last of the historical observers to focus upon this attribute. In one way or another, individualism figures largely in the formulations of Crevecoeur and Martineau as well as de Toqueville and is never absent from the interpretations of any of these historical observers.

Individualism is still a major focus in many current writings. Hsu, both in his earlier publications and in his chapter in the Smithsonian volume, Kin and Communities, as well as in his extensively rewritten and expanded third edition of Americans and Chinese, makes individualism a key factor in American life, past and present. In fact, he sees most of our major problems such as juvenile delinquency and corruption in government, racial tensions, prejudice, and preoccupation with sex as consequences, of "rugged individualism." The American version of individualism stresses "militant" self-reliance, competition, and rejection of authority. The individual becomes isolated and, as a consequence, insecure. This insecurity in turn leads to preoccupation with sex, because sexual contact is at least some form of communication and involves some cooperation. Insecurity also leads to conformity, for the isolated individual can only be reassured by being like others, even though this may not lead to meaningful communication.

Hsu's analyses are notable both for their extensive and complex interweaving of seemingly unrelated patterns of behavior and belief and also for the fact that they are comparative. He contrasts American and traditional Chinese cultural foci. American culture is individual-centered while the Chinese culture is situation-centered. Individual achievement, with consequent isolation, is valued in the first, whereas mutual dependence that produces collective achievement is valued in the latter. It is a lesson in integrative analysis to read Hsu's works and observe how he weaves these key constructs into interpretations of art, sex, home life, school, social class, marriage, heroes, government, religion, old age, crime, violence, economics, and industry.

Hsu's comparative stance is productive, whether or not one accepts all of his interpretations and particularly his single-mindedness with respect to "rugged individualism" as the root of all evil. Much of the literature by anthropologists, in fact, suffers from a lack of comparison to any other culture or situation. This is true in all sectors of the anthropological attempt to make sense of our culture, from the global interpretive essays on American culture or national character to the limited context studies of the "new" anthropology. There are exceptions, to be sure, and the social histories such as Hatch's and Wallace's suffer less because a historical analysis is inherently comparative through time.

The opposition between individualism and conformity in American culture and character has been a preoccupation with many writers other than anthropologists. We have declared this review to be limited to anthropological writings, but we cannot consider individualism and conformity without mentioning David Riesman. His constructs of inner- and outer-directed character types are the most complete single "theory" of individualism and conformity. His analysis, cast as it is in character types, is likely to be rejected by most contemporary anthropologists who want to limit their analyses to cultural phenomena in the form of symbols and signs and social meaning, largely through analysis of language, as in the work of Varenne, Perin, and in a somewhat different way, Spradley. The material determinism of a Marvin Harris will also eschew characterological approaches. Nevertheless, there is probably no single work by a contemporary social scientist on American culture that has been so influential as Riesman et al's *The Lonely Crowd*, first published in 1950. Riesman, however, was not solely character-oriented, nor was he also much concerned with the kind of society and institutional settings that called for these kinds of characterological attributes. *Individualism and Conformity in the American Character*, edited by Rapson is particularly valuable as an integrative collection and interpretation of major writings in the topic up to the publication date, 1967. David Potter, the historian, Francis Hsu, and the sociologists Seymour Lipset and David Riesman, as well as the early observers of the American scene that we have mentioned, are included.

In the first analysis of the data from Stanford students in the mid-1950s, a movement in American culture from "traditional" to "emergent" value orientations was posited. Traditional orientations centered upon hard work, success, individual achievement, future orientation, and absolute morality. Emergent orientations centered upon conformity to the group, sociability, hedonistic present orientation, sensitivity to others, and relativistic, situation-centered morality. These clusters were not unlike Reisman's constructs but centered more on social contexts.

Over the years of continuing data collection and reflection, however, it has seemed more likely that the "traditional" and "emergent" constructs are not so much a statement of change as a statement of strain within the American cultural system. The same can be said of Riesman's constructs and in fact of the whole individualism/conformity dialogue. If our culture is as loosely bounded as Merelman suggests, furnishing no firmly bounded contexts in which roles can be played, membership had, and stable identities formed, we would expect individualism to become a creed and conformity to immediate social pressure to be its companion. There would not be much else with which people might do their social work and character building. When we examine carefully what the observers said in the early period of our history, we are led to the conclusion that America has always been loosely bounded. The traditional boundaries of European society were what people coming to America were trying to escape from, and the expanding society (not necessarily simply the frontier society) in which they found themselves never recreated the bounded societies from which they originated.

The most recent anthropological analysis of the individual/conformity duality is contained within Varenne's discussion of Appleton. Varenne does not directly discuss conformity, but rather community, symbolized and reaffirmed in governmental and administrative activities and meaningful to individuals as a relationship created by love. Individuals are, however, rarely firmly committed to community, and when individual satisfaction, free choice, or particularly "happiness" is threatened by commitment or membership, the individual withdraws to find new alignments. The emic concept of individualism is the ability to make free choices. There is, there-fore, a constant opposition between individual and community, even though the existence of one depends upon the other. Both the individual and the community are considered from the native's viewpoint. In this sense, neither may exist in structural terms with which Lloyd Warner would be comfortable. On the other hand, Warner, believing himself that social classes existed and had clear boundaries, may have in part created them.

G. Spindler found essentially the same individual vs community (broadly interpreted) relationship in a controlled comparison of German and Ameri-can G.I.s as they responded to the hierarchical structures of the Wehrmacht and the U.S. Army respectively in World War II. The American G.I. persis-tently asserted his individualism and resisted submersion in the hierarchical order by rejecting authority and engaging in activities that were declared court-martial offenses. German soldiers were much more incorporated in the structure and resisted authority less. American G.I.s also withdrew their love of the group more quickly under combat conditions than did the Ger-mans when the survival of ego was threatened.

However phrased, it appears that individualism, and the opposition (and complementarity) of the individualism/conformity duality, is a central fea-ture of American culture. The recognition of it has been surprisingly constant for about two centuries. Although modes of interpretation have changed, there is considerable continuity. If we did not have the writings of the early historical observers and the analyses of a few anthropologists whose natal cul-ture was not American (Gorer, Hsu, Varenne), we might question whether this emphasis was not a projection of our own "imbeddedness" in our culture, since American analysts, it is said, tend to reduce all social phenomena to in-dividual psychology. We need both history and cultural variety on the part of observers to make social interpretation work.

## DIVERSITY, CONFLICT, AND ACCOMMODATION

So far in this review we have used broad and undifferentiated terms, such as "American culture" to refer to what we are discussing and what anthropolo-gists have addressed themselves to, even when they were working in limited contexts or communities. The only diversity we have encountered is the di-versity of individual choices. But the United States of America is consid-ered to be diverse regionally, structurally, and culturally. Yet as one crosses the country by auto and stops in small towns, uses roadside conveniences, and samples local affairs via newspaper and radio, one is impressed with the uniformity of the American scene.

Diversity in the USA may be less ethnic or regionally cultural, although to be sure there is some significant variation, than it is interactional. That is, various groups conflict with and make various accommodations to the "establishment," or "mainstream," or the "power structure," or "the man," or "the white man," or their parents, and in so doing create a certain shallow, often transient diversity.

There is ample evidence to support the perception of diversity in American culture. Strickon, for example, in his work on ethnicity in rural populations in Wisconsin, establish a convincing thesis that ethnicity in this state at least has depth (Strickon, 1975). Ethnicity is expressed in trust relationships, intermarriage, celebrations, and in economic activity, and has played a significant role in the development of the region up to the present. Meyerhoff tells poignantly how a California coast community of Jewish retirees celebrates its culture. Yinger reviews and interprets countercultures as confrontations with established norms. Yanagisako shows how Japanese–American Nisei preserve certain aspects of Japanese kinship and combine them with mainstream American elements so that the cultural structure of Japanese–American kinship "is pervaded at all levels by people's conceptions of their social (ethnic) identity." Her analysis is presented as a challenge to Schneider's assertion that at one level of analysis, that is, in the system of distinct features that define a person as a relative, the cultural order, there is uniformity (he acknowledges variation at other levels).

Similar analyses of differences in the ordering of kin at the cultural level for other ethnic groups in America might well show significant variation. Ethnicity, however, much less this kind of study of ethnic variation, has not been the major focus of anthropological work in this country. Examination of a current, seemingly well-balanced textbook on American ethnicity shows the anthropological contribution to be relatively small compared to that of other social scientists (Bahr, Chadwick, and Stauss).

The interpretation of American kinship and culture by Schneider sheds light on both diversity and uniformity. He early characterized American kinship as diverse but centering on basic unity, and he has enlarged upon this core position in a succession of papers and books. No review of his comprehensive writings can be attempted here. While other analysts have produced interesting works on American kinship; they have relatively infrequently attended to the larger cultural arena of which kinship is a part. Schneider's works, in contrast, have been much involved with the larger problem. Particularly interesting is his delineation of cultural "galaxies," such as kinship, nationality, ethnicity, and religion, defined by a common cultural code for conduct: in this instance diffuse, enduring solidarity. The variability is in the "substance" for each unit in the galaxy, so kinship is distinguished by blood, community by locality, etc. This galaxy in turn is contrasted to one constituted of work, commerce, and industry, with a cultural code of enlightened self-interest, personal advantage, and dominant rationality. Schneider's model of kinship in American culture has not gone unchallenged, as Scheffler's and Yanagisako's arguments demonstrate.

It is interesting that the individual/conformity-community poles we discussed previously can fit within the structural opposition of these two galaxies. Some interpretive orientation of this general type appears to be cast up in attempts to analyze the core features of American culture. The uniformity of American culture may extend well beyond the surface features one so easily observes, and in fact may even pervade the dialogue of diversity. It is interesting that Henry produced a similar interpretation when he distinguished a cluster of features centering around "drive," such as achievement, competition, profit, mobility, and expansion, and another cluster centering on "love," such as kindness, quietness, simplicity, etc. The continuity of interpretations, in variable terminology and with different analytic models, is impressive.

The problem of greatest interest is not whether there is diversity or uniformity in American culture. Surely there are both. There are discernible variations in behavior and symbol for each of the approximately 30 ethnic groups in the USA. There are also variations, often of more significance, in region and social class and age group despite impressive uniformity at the level of commercial and pop culture, mass media, clothing, highway strip culture, and possibly even core values. Religious cults, sexual habits and preferences, and family culture add to the diversity.

The problem is, to what are variations attributable, and how deep do they go? No single factor explanation will suffice because most of the core problems of sociocultural dynamics are involved. However, there are at least two seemingly useful models that we term the residual and interactional. The first assumes that cultural patterns, including phenomena that range from highly specific behaviors to very diffuse symbols such as "love" and solidarity, are simply inherited from a past when the differentiation was greater, whatever it is. The other deals with variation, particularly in ethnic, religious, and social class components, as produced and reinforced as various elements in society interact with each other.

The two processes are apparent in our analysis of contemporary Menomini Indian culture, as they are in other studies of Indian–White confrontation and adaptation. Our data, collected over a period of some years, show that there are several major adaptive components among the Menommi. These components have psychocultural as well as sociocultural depth. Each of these components is a product of long-term interaction with the mainstream American power structure, economy, churches and religious orders, the education establishment, world view, and prejudice. The underlying processes of contemporary Menomini adaptation may be described as reaffirmative, compensatory, syncretic, anomic, marginally constructive, segmentalized, and so forth. These processes are stabilized in the form of actual groups such as a native-oriented enclave, a peyote cult, etc. Similar adaptive responses appear in various contexts, not only in studies of American Indians, but in studies of other ethnic groups. The same general line of interpretation can also be applied religious movements, sects and cults and to the flux and flow of political behavior.

Taken from this point of view, diversity in American culture is a product of confrontation, conflict, and accommodation between populations such as ethnic and mainstream elements initially marked off by historically derived distinctions. Though some groups or movements such as hippie communes, Moonies, Jonestown, the Birch Society, etc. have little specific historic depth, they do have historical antecedents in American society. Conflicts and accommodations appear, and then are stabilized in various institutional and cultural norms. The processes of interaction reinforce initial differences selectively, and then add new ones. There is, in fact, the possibility that the long-term and continuing process of conflict and accommodation is necessary to the maintenance of the American cultural system. Only by a contrast to diversity and cultural "disorder" can American order and unanimity be recognized and defended.

When ethnic discourse is examined, as Ruskin and Varenne have done for Puerto Rican Americans, the focus on interaction may be taken yet further. They acknowledge ethnicity in the USA as a factor contributing to diversity and point out that immigration is continuing and that ethnic enclaves are being replenished. What they are interested in, however, is the possibility that the experience of ethnicity "particularly as it is mediated by the structural discourse people must use to express it," is in fact a "fully melted" American experience. The American ethnic discourse is similar to discourses Americans will use in other contexts such as religion and politics. It will center on individualization, psychologization, the need for unanimity, and conformity. Ruskin and Varenne take off in their analysis from the seminal work of Schneider who points to the possibility that such homologies would be found between cultural content domains. Their results so far have been inconclusive, but the model is congruent with what we have termed an interactionist explanation of American cultural diversity. If ethnicity is indeed mediated by a structural discourse that is culturally American, the experience of ethnicity itself is decidedly American even though differences are recognized, and in fact exist.

## THE PROBLEM OF WOMEN

Though the literature on sex roles in the USA is now extensive, there are few interpretive analyses and even fewer empirical studies by anthropologists. There are some studies of minority women, but not even the most recent and major collected volumes or texts include serious attention to mainstream American culture, although suggestions for the improvement of women's status in this country and elsewhere are not lacking. The task of anthropologists working with sex roles is apparently self-defined as cross-cultural. Naomi Quinn has provided a knowledgeable review of such studies. The *Wilson Quarterly* provides a useful though nonprofessional review essay on some of the research on "Men and Women." Though research in other cultures by anthropologists is cited, there is no identifiable piece by anthropologists cited on any part of the USA. In the influential Rosaldo Lamphere collection there is only one of 16 chapters devoted to an American population.

How does Woman, the "other" or the "second" sex, fit into American culture? The "problem" of women may be considered a subset of the problem of diversity in American culture. Anthropologists have until recently neglected women in their research. Because the majority of anthropologists have been males, it is not surprising that they have attended to the highly visible public roles played by males in most societies. And in classic analyses of American culture by sociologists and historians, it has been assumed that since American men have been dominant status-wise, the characteristics of American men were the characteristics of the American people, including women. In his frontier hypothesis, Turner was referring only to male values. Riesman's concept of a shift from inner to outer orientation is quite inapplicable to women, who have always been "outer-oriented" to children and family. At best, the woman's world is difficult for a male to research. Now that female anthropologists are focusing on women in cross-cultural studies and are therefore calling attention to the infrastructures of society instrumented mainly by women, we can expect eventually to reexamine role relationships in American society from a cross-cultural viewpoint. Jane Collier, for example, views women as political strategists who use resources available to them in support of interests often opposed to those of men. Women's strategies, she claims, are important components of the processes by which social life proceeds. This kind of approach could well be the focus of some anthropological work on American women, particularly because they have, in part, moved out of infrastructural roles.

Florence Kluckhohn, a sociologist with strong anthropological leanings, has presented one of the few organized macromodels of differences in male and female roles in mainstream American culture. Using her "Values Orientation" schema, she showed that women's roles historically have expressed as "variant" rather than "dominant" values in American culture. She posited that individualism—with man as autonomous free agent—was a dominant male value, while women as wives and mothers were oriented toward group goals. Where the valued personality type for males was the "Person of Action," "the Doing Personality," for women it was the philanthropist type, dedicated to community improvement and family morality. And while the time orientation for males has been the future, for practical reasons for women it has been the present. Some such form of cultural analysis, with appropriate modifications, might be applicable to the contemporary scene.

Some of the best work by anthropologists on women's roles in American society has been done on black women. Carol Stack's *All Our Kin* presents a vivid, cutting analysis of urban black domestic relationships. Stack suggests that the characterization of urban black families as matrifocal is static and misleading. She views black women as strategists, coping with problems of poverty, unemployment, and oppression in a resilient manner. She illustrates with personal histories the ways women form alliances, relying on an enduring network of kin among whom goods and services are exchanged. Other studies also illustrate the resiliency and creative aspects of the strategies used by black women in rural as well as urban settings. American Indian women as members of a minority group have also received a share of anthropological attention. Estelle Smith's study of Portuguese-Americans and Agnes Aamodt's study of neighboring among Norwegian-American women extend our knowledge of ethnicity and women's roles. Sylvia Yanagisako's analysis of women-centered kin networks shows that Japanese–American centrality of women in kinship is similar to that of other middle-class Americans.

Women's adaptations to culture change have occupied some attention. A published symposium chaired by Ann McElroy and Carolyn Mathiassen includes chapters on changing sex roles among the Oglala Sioux, Native-American women in the city, Mexican-American women in the mid-west, the Eskimo, and on the Iroquois as well as on women in Africa, Sri Lanka, and Iran. In our own research, starting with the Blood, Menomini, and Cree Indians, and in our recent studies on urbanizing villages in southern Germany, we have been careful to include matched samples of both sexes in our research design and data collection. Females are less tradition-oriented, less reserve or village-oriented, and more outside- and urban-oriented than are males in all four samples. Sex was the single most significant antecedent variable in our quantified data analysis. Some parallel results might be expected were the same research design applied to other American minorities and to selected mainstream groups. The two sexes apparently do respond to culture change, urbanization, and modernization differently, and some features of their difference may well be generalizable transculturally. Such generalization would have practical as well as theoretical significance.

Elizabeth Moen and co-workers in their study of women and economic development in two Colorado mining towns, show that the social and ultimately economic costs of ignoring women in development planning are substantial. As the two case studies reveal, the parallels between the effect of economic development on women in the Third World and in these two western American towns are striking. Most development planning has been conceptualized and applied as though women did not exist, or were like men.

A community study of southwestern Saskatchewan women by Seena Kohl offers a useful model for studies needed on American women. Kohl provides the rich historical background of the community and traces the key roles women have played in its formation and maintenance. She describes three generations of development. Kohl regards the view taken of women in agricultural enterprises as "crypto-servants" as misleading. She found that women were full participants in the developments which laid the base for contemporary agriculture in the area. Women were the most important components of the developing social order and were highly valued as such. They were and are, as household managers, the "gatekeepers" for consumption wants. The situation among agrarian communities in the western United States seems similar enough to warrant some generalization.

Beyond empirical studies of ethnic and particularly mainstream sex roles there is a strong need for an ethnography of the feminist movement itself in the United States. This study should be done by researchers with both the traditional social science perspective and by those involved in feminist studies, where a sense of oppression and a deep concern for change are integral to their work. A more interactive and sharing pattern than is usually the case might be required in the research role in a change-oriented feminist setting, as Light and Kleiber's study of women's health collective suggests.

In such an ethnography of the movement there would also have to be attention to working-class and minority women who tend to identify more strongly along class and race lines than on the basis of sex. Many feel little in common with affluent housewives and professional women and students in the liberation movement. They feel that their men need rights as much as the "already privileged feminists" Working-class women often feel that men are put down as much as women, and black women insist that their own emancipation cannot be separated from that of their men.

Studies of women's roles and especially their roles in change in the USA may lead to some surprises. Most anthropologists who dared to predict the course of sex role changes in the future of the USA have predicted more identity, or sameness, in sex roles for men and women, more public roles for women, and more domestic engagement for men. As Spiro's revisit to the Kibbutzim of Israel shows, a return, in some unpredictable degree, to more traditional sex roles may occur when some as yet undifferentiated point is reached in liberation. Our own most recent work in Germany shows something of the kind occurring there as well. The current conservative swing in the USA already seems to be carrying sex roles along with it to some extent. One thing is clear, the differences between men and women go deep in culture and social contextualization, however deep they may or may not be in biology. How these major forces co-mingle and separate in sex-linked behavior will continue to be a major focus of study by all the disciplines for a long time to come.

## LANGUAGES IN THE USA

The title of this brief section is taken from a recent collection edited by Ferguson & Heath. We offer the following comments as a reminder that language is an integral part of culture and can be treated as a significant dimension of American culture. Of five recent edited collections on American culture discussed in the next section, however, only two include explicit attention to language. Possibly this is the case because the greater part of the work on language in the USA has been done by nonanthropological linguists.

American English appears to be an expression of a loosely bounded or open culture. Tendencies to eliminate the past tense in conversation, disregard distinctions between adjectives and adverbs, absorb words and phrases from Black English, Italian, Jewish, etc, use exaggerated terms, abbreviate extensively in both writing and speaking, compound parts of words into new words, and use contact words extensively characterize current mainstream language use.

There is, however, little solid evidence of language homogenization in the USA. In fact, variety in social dialects may be on the increase as special groups and lifestyles have developed in urban contexts. Though regional and social class distinctions in language are much less than in Great Britain, dialectic diversification is continuing.

In addition to life styles and interest groups, ethnicity is a major source of diversification. Much more work has been done on the speech usages of ethnic minorities; this is appropriate, since some 28 million Americans have a language other than English as a mother tongue or live in households where some other language is spoken. Ethnic diversity is currently being renewed with the influx of refugees and migrant workers as well as the many thousands from Great Britain and Europe seeking improvements in material well-being. Only a small portion of this study had been carried out, however, by anthropological linguists. Black English has received the most attention.

Anthropological linguists have long been interested in the classification of and relationships among American Indian languages, but few have been concerned with the social significance of contemporary Native American language use. Some work, however, has been done recently on the social contexts of speech acts.

Some recent studies in the special languages of occupational groups suggests that this is a rich field that can profitably be worked further and will contribute to our understanding of increasing diversification.

It seems apparent that all dimensions of the study of language should be studied as a part of a larger concern with American culture. Some of the questions raised in this review concerning uniformity and diversity can be pursued profitably in studies of language usage.

## COLLECTIONS AND CASE STUDIES

Courses on American culture, devised and taught by anthropologists, have apparently proliferated on American campuses, to judge from the appearance of several major collected volumes and texts for class use, starting with Jorgenson & Truzzi's *Anthropology and American Life* in 1974, the first to appear since the special issue of the AAA in 1955 (Lantis). Montague & Arens' *The American Dimension* has already appeared in two editions (1976 and 1981). Others include Spradley & Rynkiewich's *The Nacirema*, Holmes' *The American Tribe*, and most recently Kottak's *Researching American Culture*. Each of these volumes except the latter contains a sample of published articles and some original pieces. Several include material researched and written by undergraduate students. This trend was pioneered by Spradley and McCurdy with a 1972 text that outlines an approach to ethnographic research employing an ethnoscientific model and includes twelve mini ethnographies by undergraduate students.

The range of topics and approaches subsumed by the collected volumes prohibits coherent review in short compass. Though many of the pieces included in each of the collected volumes are of first class quality, some lack enough depth to be taken seriously by undergraduate users. There is a tendency at times to produce scintillating observations without much hard evidence to support them. Anthropologists still seem prone to take American culture less seriously than they do those of others. Doubtless some of this can be traced to an attempt to titillate and stimulate student interest and probably some of it is successful in so doing. In our experience in a course at Stanford on American culture that we initiated in 1973 and that has enjoyed a growing undergraduate enrollment, the more in-depth analyses with substantial evidence to support them are the most effective. We find also, with other instructors, that students thrive on instruction in and application of ethnographic methods to their own surroundings in field studies they can carry out themselves.

The other major indication of a growing interest in anthropology at home for instructional use is the appearance of case studies on various segments of American culture. The most recent include Applebaum's study of construction workers, Gamst's on locomotive engineers, Williams' of a black urban neighborhood, and Wong's of the New York Chinatown. The first American culture case study in the series edited by the Spindlers appeared in 1969 with Keiser's first edition of *Vice Lords*. The first studies of a segment of the mainstream appeared in 1972, with the publication of Pilcher on longshoremen and Partridge on a hippie ghetto. Other widely used case studies on segments of American culture include Madsen & Guerrero on Mexican Americans in South Texas, Hostetler & Huntington on the Hutterites and on the Amish, Hicks on an Appalachian community, Daner on the Hare Krishna, Jacob's on a retirement community, Rosenfeld on a slum school, Wolcott on an elementary school principal, Davidson on Chicano prisoners, Aschenbrenner on black families in Chicago, Dougherty on rural black women, Kunkel on a rural black community, Safa on the poor of Puerto Rico, and Sugarman on a drug therapy center.

A number of the case studies published on American Indians are explicitly oriented to interaction with the mainstream American culture, including Garbarino on the Seminole, McFee on the Blackfeet, Hoebel on the Cheyennes, Spindlers on the Menominee, Downs on the Washo and the Navajo, and most recently Grobsmith on the Lakota Sioux.

Thirty case studies on segments of American culture appeared in the series between 1969 and 1983. Though their publication by a major commercial publisher is evidence that academic concern with American culture by anthropologists has been taken seriously, it is noteworthy that the sales of these studies have never approximated the volume of sales of other studies in the series devoted to remote non-Western cultures. The wisdom of their publication from a profit-oriented point of view has always been questionable, however useful they may have been to instructors in the emerging curricula of anthropological American studies. Because of their marginality in this framework, many of these studies will shortly become unavailable for multiple class use. In our experience, case studies are essential instructional materials. They provide a relatively in-depth look into the phenomenal variety of American culture(s). They exemplify the cross-cultural view, but within the boundaries of American culture and society, that anthropologists have claimed as their special advantage in examining behavior elsewhere.

## CLOSING REMARKS

We have not attempted in this review to cover everything written on American culture by anthropologists and have touched on very little written by others. American anthropologists have made a significant effort to study their own culture. The pace of such efforts has increased of late and will probably continue to accelerate. The boundaries between "foreign," "overseas," "exotic," or even "primitive" or "nonliterate" and "at home" or "in our own culture" are disappearing as the world culture becomes more uniform at one level and more diverse at another. Within the USA the diversification is particularly impressive. All of the skills and insights gained by anthropologists in cultures away from home can be used to good advantage at home. Anthropologists attend to symbols, ceremonies, rituals, communities, language and thought, beliefs, dialects, sex roles and sexuality, subsistence and ecology, kinship, and a multitude of other topics in ways that historians, sociologists, political scientists, and psychologists will not, because of the heritage of experience with "other" cultures from primitive to peasant to urban away from home.

## REFERENCES

Aamodt, A. 1981. *Neighboring: discovering support systems among Norwegian American women.* See Messerschmidt, 1981.

American Anthropologist. 1955. *The U.S.A. as anthropologists see it.* See Lantis, M., ed.

Applebaum, H. 1981. *Royal Blue: The Culture of Construction Workers.* New York: Holt, Rinehart & Winston.

Aschenbrenner, J. 1975. *Lifelines: Black Families in Chicago.* New York: Holt, Rinehart & Winston.

Bahr, H. B., Chadwick, J., Stauss, R. 1979. *American Ethnicity.* Lexington, Mass: Heath.

Boas, F. 1928. *Anthropology and Modern Life.* New York: Morton.

Braroe, N. 1975. *Indian and White: Self Image and Interaction in a Canadian Plains Community.* Stanford, Calif: Stanford University Press.

Burling, R. 1973. *English in Black and White.* New York: Holt, Rinehart and Winston.

Cazden, C., John, V., Hymes, D., eds. 1972. *The Functions of Language in the Classroom.* New York: Teachers College Press.

Collier, J. 1974. *Women in politics.* See Rosaldo, M.,M. Lamphere, eds., pp. 89–96.

Crevecoeur, M. G. St. Jean de. 1904. Letters from an American Farmer. New York: Fox, Duffield.

Crevecoeur, M. G. St. Jean de. 1967. *The American, this new man.* See Rapson, R. ed. 11917. pp.15–18.

Daner, F. 1976. *The American Children of Krisna.* New York: Holt, Rinehart & Winston

Davidson, R. T. 1974. *Chicano Prisoners: The Key to San Quentin*. New York: Holt, Rinehart & Winston.

Davis, A., Gardner, B., Gardner, M. 1941. *Deep South: A Social Anthropological Study of Caste and Class*. Chicago: Univ. Chicago Press.

de Beauvoir, S. 1953. *The Second Sex*. New York: Knopf.

DeVos, G. 1980. Ethnic adaptation and minority status. *J. Cross Cult. Psychol.* 10 1–12.

DeVos, G. 1981. Adaptive strategies in American minorities. In *Ethnicity and Mental Health*, ed. E. E. Jones, S. Korchin.

Dollard, J. 1937. *Caste and Class in a Southern Town*. New Haven: Yale Univ. Press.

Dougherty, M. 1978. *Becoming a Woman in Rural Black Culture*. New York: Holt, Rinehart and Winston.

Downs, J. 1966. *Two Worlds of the Washo: An Indian Tribe of California and Nevada*. New York: Holt, Rinehart & Winston.

Downs, J. 1972. *The Navajo*. New York: Holt, Rinehart & Winston.

Ferguson, C., Heath, S. 1981. *Language in the U.S.A.* New York: Cambridge University Press.

Fujita, M. 1979. *A Review Essay on Community Studies in America*. Stanford Univ: Unpublished manuscript.

Gamst, F. 1980. *The Hoghead: An industrial Ethnology of the Locomotive Engineer*. New York: Holt, Rinehart & Winston.

Garbarino, M. C. 1972. *Big Cypress: A Changing Seminole Community*. New York: Holt, Rinehart & Winston.

Garretson, L. R. 1976. *American Culture: An Anthropological Perspective*. Dubuque, Iowa: Brown.

Gillin, J. 1955. National and regional cultural values in the United States. *Soc. Forces* 34:107–13.

Gilmore, P., Glatthom, A., eds. 1982. *Children in and out of School: Ethnography and Education*. Washington DC: Language & Ethnography Series.

Gorer, G. 1948. *The American People: A Study in American Character*. New York: Norton.

Grobsmith, E. 1981. *Lakota of the Rosebud: A Contemporary Ethnography*. New York: Holt, Rinehart & Winston.

Hallowell, A. I. 1957. The backwash of the frontier: the impact of the Indian on American culture. In *The Frontier in Perspective*, eds. W. Wyman, C. Kroeber, pp. 229–58. Madison: Univ. Wis. Press.

Harris, M. 1981. *America Now: The Anthropology of a Changing Culture*, p. 10. New York: Simon & Schuster.

Hatch, E. 1979. *Biography of a Small Town*. New York: Columbia Univ. Press.

Henry, J. 1963. *Culture Against Man*, pp. 283–322. New York: Random House.

Henry, J. 1966. A theory for an anthropological analyses of American culture. *Anthro. Q.* 39:Pp. 90–109.

Hicks, G. & L. 1976. *Appalachian Valley*. New York: Holt, Rinehart & Winston.

Hodge, W. 1975. Ethnicity as a factor in modern American Indian migration: A Winnebago case study with references to other Indian situations. In *Migration and Development*, ed. H. Safa, B. Dutoit. The Hague: Mouton.

Hodge, W. 1981. The first Americans in the larger contemporary society: the parts and the whole. In *The First Americans, Then and Now*, ed. W. Hodge, . New York: Holt, Rinehart & Winston.

Hoebel, E. A. 1977. *The Cheyenne: Indians of the Great Plains*. New York: Holt, Rinehart & Winston. 2nd ed.

Holmes, L. 1978. *The American Tribe*. Lexington, Mass: Xerox Publ. program.

Hostetler, J. A., Huntington, G. E. 1971. *Children in Amish Society: Socialization and Community Education*. New York: Holt, Rinehart & Winston.

Hostetler, J. A., Huntington, G. E. 1980. *The Hutterites in North America*. New York: Holt, Rinehart & Winston. Fieldwork ed. New edition 1996.

Hsu, F. 1953. *Americans and Chinese: Two Ways of Life*. New York: Schuman.

Hsu, F. 1972. American core values and national character. In *Psychological Anthropology*, ed. F. Hsu. Cambridge, Mass: Schenkman.

Hsu, F. 1973. *Rugged individualism reconsidered*. Colo. Q. 9:145–162.

Hsu, F. 1979. Roots of the American family from Noah to now. In *Kin and Communities: Families in America*, ed. A. Lichtman, J. Challinor. Washington DC: Smithsonian Inst. Press.

Hsu, F. 1981. *Americans and Chinese: Passage to Differences*. Honolulu: Univ. Hawaii Press.

Hymowitz, C., Weissman, M. 1978. *A History of Women in America*, p. 361. New York: Bantam Books.

Jacobs, J. 1974. *Fun City: An Ethnographic Study of a Retirement Community*. New York: Holt, Rinehart & Winston.

Jacobs, S. 1982. Women in development programs. *Am. Anthropol.* 84:366–371.

James H. 1976. The Plains gourd dance as a revitalization movement. *Am. Ethn.* 13:243–259.

Jefferson T. 1781. *The moral independence of the cultivators of the earth*. See Rapson, R. ed. 1971 pp. 18–19.

Jorgensen, J., Truzzi, M., eds. 1974. *Anthropology and American Life*. Englewood Cliffs, NJ: Prentice-Hall.

Kane, S. 1974. Ritual possession in a Southern Appalachian religious sect. *J. Am. Folklore* 87:293–302.

Keiser, R. L. 1979. *The Vice Lords: Warriors of the Streets*. New York: Holt, Rinehart & Winston. Fieldwork edition. Kennedy, E. L. 1979. A perspective of feminist studies. *Occas. Pap. Anthropol.* No. 1, pp. 189–193. Buffalo: State Univ. New York.

Kimball, S. 1955. Problem of studying American culture. *Am. Anthropol.* 57:1131–1141.

Kluckhohn, C. 1949. *Mirror for Man*. New York: McGraw-Hill.

Kluckhohn, C. 1951. Values and value-orientation. In *Toward a General Theory of Action*, ed. T. Parsons, E. Shils, pp. 388–433. Cambridge: Harvard Univ. Press.

Kluckhohn, F. 1950. *Dominant and substitute profiles of cultural orientation.* Social Forces 28:376–393.

Kohl, S. B. 1976. *Working Together: Woman and Family in Southwestern Saskatchewan.* Toronto: Holt, Rinehart & Winston.

Kottak, C., ed. 1982. *Researching American Culture: A Guide for Student Anthropologists.* Ann Arbor: Univ. Michigan Press.

Kunkel, P., Kennard, S. 1971. *Spout Spring: A Black Community in the Ozarks.* New York: Holt, Rinehart & Winston.

LaBarre, W. 1962. *They Shall Take Up Serpents.* Minneapolis: Univ. Minn. Press.

Labov, W. 1966. The Social Stratification of Non-standard English. Washington DC: Center of Applied Linguistics.

Labov, W. 1970. *The Study of Nonstandard English.* Champaign, IL: Nat. Counc. Teachers of English.

Lantis., M., ed. 1955. The U.S.A. as anthropologists see it. *Am. Anthropol.* 57:111–380. Special issue.

Leap, W. 1981. *American Indian languages.* See Ferguson, C., Heath S. 1981.

Lewis, H. 1978. European ethnicity in Wisconsin: an exploratory formulation. *Ethnicity* 8:174–188.

Light, L., Kleiber, N. 1981. *Interactive research in a feminist setting: The Vancouver women's health collective.* See Messerschmidt 1981 pp. 167–184.

Lynd, R., Lynd, H. 1929. *Middletown in Transition.* New York: Harcourt Brace.

Lynd, R., Lynd, H. 1937. *Middletown in Transition.* New York: Harcourt Brace.

Madsen, W., Guerrero, A. 1974. *Mexican-Americans of South Texas.* New York: Holt, Rinehart & Winston. 2nd ed.

Martin, M., Voorhies, B. 1975. *Female of the Species*, pp. 383–409. New York: Columbia Univ. Press.

Martineau, H. 1937. *Society in America, Vol. 3.* London: Saunders & Otley. See also Rapson R. 1076, pp. 19–24.

McDermott, R., Aron, J. 1978. Pirandello in the classroom: on the possibility of equal educational opportunity in American culture. In *Futures of Education for Exceptional Children: Emerging Structures*, ed. M. Reynolds. New York: Council for Exceptional Children, pp. 41–63.

McElroy, A., Matthiasson, C., eds. 1979. Sex roles in changing cultures. *Occas. Pap. Anthropol. No. 1*, Buffalo: State Univ. New York.

McFee, M. 1972. *Modern Blackfeet: Montanans on a Reservation.* New York: Holt, Rinehart & Winston.

Mead, M. 1943. *And Keep Your Powder Dry.* New York: Morrow.

Merelman, R. 1983. *Making Something of Ourselves.* Berkeley: Univ. Calif. Press.

Messerschmidt, D., ed. 1981. *Anthropologists at Home in North America: Methods and Issues in the Study of One's Own Society.* New York: Cambridge Univ. Press.

Meyerhoff, B. 1978. *Number Our Days.* New York: Simon & Schuster, Touchstone Books.

Mitchell-Kernan, C. 1972. Signifying and marking: two Afro-American speech acts. In *Directions in Sociolinguistics: The Ethnography of Communication*, ed. J. Gumperz, D. Hymes. New York: Holt, Rinehart & Winston.

Moen, E., Boulding, E., Lillydahl, J., Palmer, R. 1981. *Women and the Social Costs of Economic Development: Two Colorado Case Studies. Social Impact Assessment Set. No. 5.* Boulder: Westview.

Montague, S., Arens, W. 1981. *The American Dimension: Cultural Myths and Social Realities.* Sherman Oaks, CA: Alfred Publications.

Murphy, C. 1982. A survey of research. In *The Wilson Quarterly, special issue on "Men and Women,"* 6:63–80.

Nader, L. 1974. Up the Anthropologist: perspectives gained from studying up. In *Reinventing Anthropology,* ed. D. Hymes, pp. 284–311. New York: Random House, Vintage Books.

Nay, B. 1974. *American Values: An Anthropological Analysis.* Senior Honors project, Dept. Anthropol., Stanford University. Unpublished manuscript.

O'Barr, M. 1981. *The language of the law.* See Ref. 24, pp. 386–406.

Ogbu, J. 1978. *Minority Education and Caste: The American System in CrossCultural Perspective.* New York: Academic.

Partridge, W. L. 1972. *The Hippie Ghetto: The Natural History of a Subculture.* New York: Holt, Rinehart & Winston.

Perin, C. 1977. *Everything in its Place. Social Order and Land Use in America.* Princeton: Princeton Univ. Press.

Peshkin, A. 1978. *Growing Up American: Schooling and the Survival of Community.* Chicago: Univ. Chicago Press.

Peshkin, A. 1982. *The researcher and subjectivity: reflections on an ethnography of school and community.* See Spindler, G. 1982, pp. 48–67.

Philips, S. 1972. *Participant studies and communicative competence: Warm Springs children in community and classroom.* See Ref. 10, pp. 370–394.

Philips, S. 1972. *Acquisition of rules for appropriate speech usage.* See Ref. 10.

Philips, S. 1982. *The language socialization of lawyers: acquiring the "cant."* See Ref. 125, pp. 176–210.

Pilcher, W. W. 1972. *The Portland Longshoremen. A Dispersed Urban Community.* New York: Holt, Rinehart & Winston.

Potter, D. M. 1964. American women and the American character. In *American Character and Culture: Some Twentieth Century Perspectives,* ed. J. A. Hague, Ch. 8. Deland, Fla: Everett/Edwards.

Prince, H. 1974. *Cocoon work: an interpretation of the concern of contemporary youth with the mystical.* See Ref. 160, 255–274.

Quinn, N. 1977. Anthropological studies on women's status. *Ann. Rev. Anthropol.* 6:181–225.

Rapson, R., ed. 1967. *Individualism and Conformity in the American Character.* Boston: Heath.

Riesman, D. 1955. *Individualism Reconsidered.* Garden City, NY: Doubleday.

Riesman, D., Denny, R., Glazer, N. 1950. *The Lonely Crowd: A Study of the Changing American Character.* New Haven: Yale Univ. Press.

Rosaldo, M., Lamphere, L., eds. 1974. *Women, Culture and Society.* Stanford, Calif: Stanford Univ. Press.

Rosaldo, M., Lamphere, L. 1974. *Preface.* See Ref. 106, pp. v, vi.

Rosenfeld, G. 1971. "Shut Those Thick Lips": A study of Slum School Failure. New York: Holt, Rinehart & Winston.

Ruesch, J., Bateson, G. 1951. Communication: The Social Matrix of Psychiatry. New York: Norton.

Ruskin, G., Varenne, H. 1982. The production of kinds of ethnic discourse in the United States: American and Puerto Rican patterns. In The Sociogenesis of Language and Human Conduct: A Multidisciplinary Book of Readings, ed. B. Bain, pp. 132. New York: Plenum.

Safa, H. I. 1974. The Urban Poor of Puerto Rico: A Study in Development and Inequality. New York: Holt, Rinehart & Winston.

Scheffler, H. 1976. The meaning of kinship in American culture: another view. In Meaning in Anthropology, ed. K. Basso, H. Selby. Albuquerque: Univ. New Mexico Press.

Schneider, D. 1968. American Kinship: A Cultural Account. Englewood Cliffs, NJ: Prentice-Hall.

Schneider, D. 1969. Kinship, nationality and religion in American culture: toward a definition of kinship. In Forms of Symbolic Action, ed. V. Turner, pp. 73–81. Proc. Am. Ethnol. Assoc., pp. 116–125.

Schneider, D. 1977. Kinship, community, and locality in American culture. In Kin and Communities, ed. A. Lichtman, J. Challinor, pp. 155–174. Washington DC: Smithsonian Inst. Press.

Smith, J. F., Kvasnicka, R., eds. 1981. Indian–White Relations: A Persistent Paradox. Washington DC: Howard Univ. Press.

Smith, M. E. 1974. Portuguese enclaves: the invisible minority. In Social and Cultural Identity, ed. T. Fitzgerald. S.A.S. Proc. No. 8. Atlanta: Univ. Georgia Press.

Smith, M. E. 1976. Networks and migration resettlement: cherchez la femme. Anthropol. Q. 49:20–27.

Spindler, G. 1948. The military: A systematic analysis. Soc. Forces 29:305–310.

Spindler, G. 1948. American character as revealed by the military. Psychiatry: J. Oper. Statement Interpers. Relat. 11:V5–81.

Spindler, G. 1955. Education in a transforming American culture. Harvard Educ. Rev. 25:145–156.

Spindler, G. 1959. The Transmission of American Culture. Cambridge: Graduate School of Education, Harvard Univ.

Spindler, G. 1977. Change and continuity in American core cultural values: an anthropological perspective. In We the People: American Character and Social Change, ed. G. D. De Renzo, pp. 20–40. Westport: Greenwood.

Spindler, G., ed. 1982. Doing the Ethnography of Schooling: Educational Anthropology in Action. New York: Holt, Rinehart & Winston (Reprinted by Waveland Press, 1988).

Spindler, G., Spindler, L. 1971. Dreamers Without Power, the Menomini Indians. New York: Holt, Rinehart & Winston (Reprinted by Waveland Press, 1984).

Spindler, L., Spindler, G. 1958. Male and female adaptations in culture change. Am. Anthropol. 60:217–233.

Spindler, L., Spindler, G. 1979. Changing women in men's worlds. *Occas. Pap. Anthropol. No. 1*, pp. 35–48. Buffalo: Univ. New York.

Spiro, M. 1979. *Gender and Culture: Kibbutz Women Revisited*. Durham: Duke Univ. Press.

Spradley, J. P., McCurdy, D. 1972. *The Cultural Experience: Ethnography in Complex Society*. Chicago: Sci. Res. Assoc.

Spradley, J. P., Rynkiewich, M. 1975. *The Nacirema: Readings on American Culture*. Boston: Little, Brown.

Stack C. B. 1974. *All Our Kin: Strategies for Survival in a Black Community*. New York: Harper & Row.

Strickon, A. 1975. Ethnicity and entrepreneurship in rural Wisconsin. In *Entrepreneurs in Cultural Context*, ed. S. Greenfield, A. Strickon, R. Aubey, pp. 159–90. Albuquerque: Univ. New Mexico Press.

Strickon, A., Ibarra, R. (n.d.). *Norwegians and Tobacco in Wisconsin: The Changing Dynamics of Ethnicity*. Unpublished manuscript.

Sugarman, G. 1974. *Daytop Village: A Therapeutic Community*. New York: Holt, Rinehart & Winston.

Taylor, C. 1974. *In Horizontal Orbit*. New York: Holt, Rinehart & Winston.

Thumstrom, S. 1964. Poverty or Progress? Social Mobility in a Nineteenth Century City, p. 195. Cambridge: Harvard Univ. Press.

Toqueville, A. de. 1901. *Democracy in America*, transl. H. Reeve. New York: Appleton.

Townsend, J. 1979. *Cultural Conceptions and Mental Illness: A Comparison of Germany and America*. Chicago: Univ. Chicago Press.

Turner, F. J. 1921. *The Frontier in American History*. New York: Holt. See also Rapson, R. ed. 1967, pp. 25–27.

Varenne, H. 1977. *Americans Together: Structured Diversity in a Midwestern Town*. New York: Teachers Coll. Press

Varenne, H. 1978. Is Dedham American? The diagnosis of things American. *Anthropol. Q.* 51:231–245.

Varenne, H. 1982. *Jocks and freaks: the symbolic structure of the expression of social interaction among American senior high school students*.

Vidich, A., Bensman, J. 1958. *Small Town in Mass Society: Class, Power, and Religion in a Rural Community*. Princeton: Princeton Univ. Press.

Vogt, E. Z., Albert, E., eds. 1966. *People of Rimrock: A Study of Values in Five Cultures*. Cambridge: Harvard Univ.

von Hübner, G. 1874. *A Ramble Around the World*. London: Macmillan. 2 vols. See also Rapson, pp. 22–25.

Wallace, A. 1980. *Rockdale: The Growth of an American Village in the Early Industrial Revolution*. New York: Knopf.

Ward, M. 1971. *Them Children: A Study in Language Learning*. New York: Holt, Rinehart & Winston.

Warner, W. L. 1941. The Social Life of a Modern Community. *Yankee City Ser. I.* New Haven: Yale Univ. Press.

Warner, W. L., Meeker, M., Eels, K. 1949. *Social Class in America.* Chicago: Sci. Res. Assoc.

West, J. 1945. *Plainville, U.S.A.* New York: Columbia Univ. Press.

Whately, E. 1981. *Language among Black Americans.* See Ref. 24, pp. 92–110.

Whitehead, H. 1974. *Reasonably fantastic: Some perspectives on Scientology, science fiction, and occultism.* See Zarensky pp. 147–190.

Williams, M. D. 1981. *On the Street Where I Lived: A Black Anthropologist Examines Lifestyles and Ethos in an Urban Afro-American Neighborhood.* New York: Holt, Rinehart & Winston.

Wolcott, H. F. 1973. *The Man in Principal's Office: An Ethnography.* New York: Holt, Rinehart & Winston.

Wong, B. 1982. *Chinatown: Economic Adaptation and Ethnic Identity of the Chinese.* New York: Holt, Rinehart & Winston.

Yanagisako, S. 1977. Women-centered kin networks in urban bilateral kinship. *Am. Ethnol.* 4:207–226.

Yanagisako, S. 1978. Variations in American kinship: Implications for cultural analysis. *Am. Ethnol.* 5:15–29. Special section: American Kinship.

Yinger, J. M. 1982. *Countercultures: The Promise and the Peril of a World Turned Upside Down.* New York: Free Press.

Yinger, J. M., Simpson, G., eds. 1978. Special Issue: American Indians today. *Ann. Am. Acad. Polit. Soc. Sci.* 436:12–12.

Zaretsky, I., Leone, M., eds. 1974. *Religious Movements in Contemporary America.* Princeton: Princeton Univ. Press.

# Schooling in the American Cultural Dialogue
## (1990)

*George and Louise Spindler*

### Counseling for Success and Failure

The scene is the eighth grade room in Fairmount School in a coastal California community. There is a middle-aged woman standing in front of the room telling the children about their choices as they enter high school. There are thirty-five children in the room. About 50% appear to be Mexican American. Later I discover that the California mental maturity test, elementary form, indicates a range of 75 to 114. The mean is ninety-seven. This is what is described as a 'middle range' group.

The counselor says, 'You must be a good citizen, or they won't accept you. You can have two failures but not three. Now what do you need to get into junior college?' (Students raise their hands and repeat answers they have previously been given.) 'What do you need to get into San Jacinto State College?' (same response) 'Now what do you need to get into the University of California? Now you ask me questions, if there are any ... are there any? We've talked about this a lot here, but you haven't had a chance to ask many questions. Are there any?' (a three second pause, no questions) 'Now I want all of you to come and see me bring this slip. If you forget it, make another. You can remember what's on it. Now you may ask, when can we come to see you? Well, I'll be there at nine o'clock, ten o'clock, and later. You can get a pass from me. Or you can come after school, just any night you want to.'

The counselor continues with the task for that hour. She starts arranging some program choices for next year on the board. She writes down six numerals and puts 'P.E.' after number one, 'English' after number two and 'Social Studies' after number three and then turns to the class, 'Now you have to decide whether you want to take Algebra or not. You have to take Math all the way through high school, if you want to be an engineer. Now if you've gotten B's and C's all the way through eighth grade what are your chances of doing well in ninth grade algebra? (Children groan and mutter 'Not so good, that's right!'

The teacher continues, 'So what can you do?' (Someone says, 'Well, try to raise your grade.') 'Yes, that's one thing you can do.' (Someone else says 'work harder.') 'Yes, that's another thing you can do. But what else? (silence) Well do like I did, when I wanted to be an opera singer, but found I couldn't sing … what did I do?' (Children say various things but among them, 'you changed your plans.') 'That's right! I changed my plans!'

'How many here speak Spanish?' (Six of the seventeen who may speak Spanish raise their hand.) 'It will help you if you do. But you have to realize that there is some work to do. It is good if you speak Spanish if you want to go to college and need a language.'

'You can't take Spanish and general business. No they come on the same period. Now, one of the things is to be neat, and orderly. If you aren't good at that it might be hard for you until you've learned to do it better.'

'Now we come to mechanical drawing. This is exclusively a boys' class, but I don't know why some girls couldn't take it if they wanted to. But only boys take it.'

'Now let's look at agriculture as a possibility. This is also a boy's subject. You have to keep an animal of some kind. And you will be taken to a ranch.'

'Now about homemaking. This is just for girls.'

'Now when you come to see me, if I tell you to take general business instead of Spanish it should be understood that you don't have to take it. You can do just as you wish. But it means that I think you would do better in general business.'

'NOW about dramatics—you will learn to stand before a group, speak distinctly, and enunciate clearly. And once or twice a year you will get to put on a play.'

'Now you know there is something called girls' shop. There you learn to fix a wire if you're ironing and it breaks.'

'Now when you pass the typing class it looks interesting doesn't it? But do you know that there aren't any letters on those keyboards? You have to watch a chart at the front of the room, and if you look at the keyboard you fail!'

The bell rings and the children begin to get restless and prepare to go. The counselor says, 'Just a moment now. Are there any questions? No? Well, all right, then you may go.'

After the observation the counselor talked with the observer. 'This is a passive group. There's no spark in there. The better groups get quite excited about this. Of course most of the groups are college preparatory.' (The observer asks how many would be college preparatory in this group.) 'Only about three or four, maybe none of this group that you saw today will go on to college. Now I hope you understand that these are the scum of the middle group. They are not as good a group to observe as the one you were going to come to see on Thursday as originally planned. We thought of putting them in various classes but felt it was a shame to spoil the good groups.'

This counseling session took place in the early 1950s and one is inclined to say that it could not happen today. Our observations of schools in America, however, suggest that though the specific forms may have changed the spirit is often there. It is not that teachers or counselors intentionally disadvantage children or purposefully advantage children, as most are well-intentioned and of good heart. But the culture of the school, fitting the culture of our larger society and its dialogue, does separate out children for success and failure. These children were separated this way and they are now a parental generation. We are preoccupied with failure. As Ray McDermott has tellingly pointed out, failure is waiting for every child, but some children more than others, in every classroom and school in America. The failure or the learning disability is there before the child arrives. Given this structure, the counselor, or the teacher, has the task of finding children to fit the structure.

What this counseling session did was to open some gates for some children who, it was thought, were college bound, and closed gates for others. One would think there would be other gates opened if the college preparatory gate was closed but they were not. Some children were informed again and again that there really wasn't much hope for them, and most of those children were of Mexican descent. Even typing was too hard and too threatening as the counselor described it.

Now we will move on to a different kind of situation, a fifth grade classroom in another West coast school taught by a young man who is regarded within the school system as an individual of great promise.

## A FIFTH GRADE CLASSROOM AND TEACHER

Our purpose in this chapter is to analyze how the school may act as a cultural transmitter and the teacher as a cultural mediator. Another way of saying this is to ask how the school selects children to participate in the American dialogue in different ways. Some children will be incorporated in the mainstream dialogue. Others will be left out of the mainstream dialogue but will be encouraged to make a positive adaptation with it. Yet others will, in effect, be discarded, left so far outside of the center there is little hope for them to move into it.

How can this happen in one classroom of thirty-seven children and one teacher? The finishing touches are not put on the process until later in one's school career and after many other teachers and counselors have been encountered. Some children, perhaps as many as 25% in the nation's schools as a whole, drop out before the second year of high school. The proportion is much higher in some urban school districts. The combination of their experience in their home and community with the experience in the school has by then predestined them for marginality. But other children are promoted and encouraged in manifold ways.

Does this mean that the teacher is overtly prejudiced towards some children? Does it mean that the teacher is racist? In this case and in most of the classrooms that we have visited in America teachers are neither of those things. The teacher we studied in particular, a young man of twenty-five with three years of teaching experience, was determined to give every child in his classroom a fair chance. He believed that he was 'fair and just to all of the children', that he was 'fair in all decisions regarding children,' that he was 'easy for children to approach with their problems.' We know his self-perceptions because we asked him to rate himself in a number of behavior areas that we considered to be relevant to our analysis of his classroom interaction and his philosophy of teaching. The graph presenting his self-rating is presented in Figure 15. 1. If rank three is 'about like most other teachers' and rank five is 'definitely better than most teachers' you can see that he thinks well of himself as a teacher.

This teacher rates himself above this average rating on all counts excepting 'discipline of the class', 'assisting students in planning' and 'students free to work'. Actually his classroom was the most disciplined of those that we visited in his school and he is right in that students were not as free to work on their own projects as in some classes. He felt that the discipline in many other classrooms was not as strict as it should be and that his should be better.

He seemed to be a little too self-critical in his rating of assisting students in planning, but on most dimensions of the teaching role he rates himself as somewhat better than most teachers or definitely superior to most other

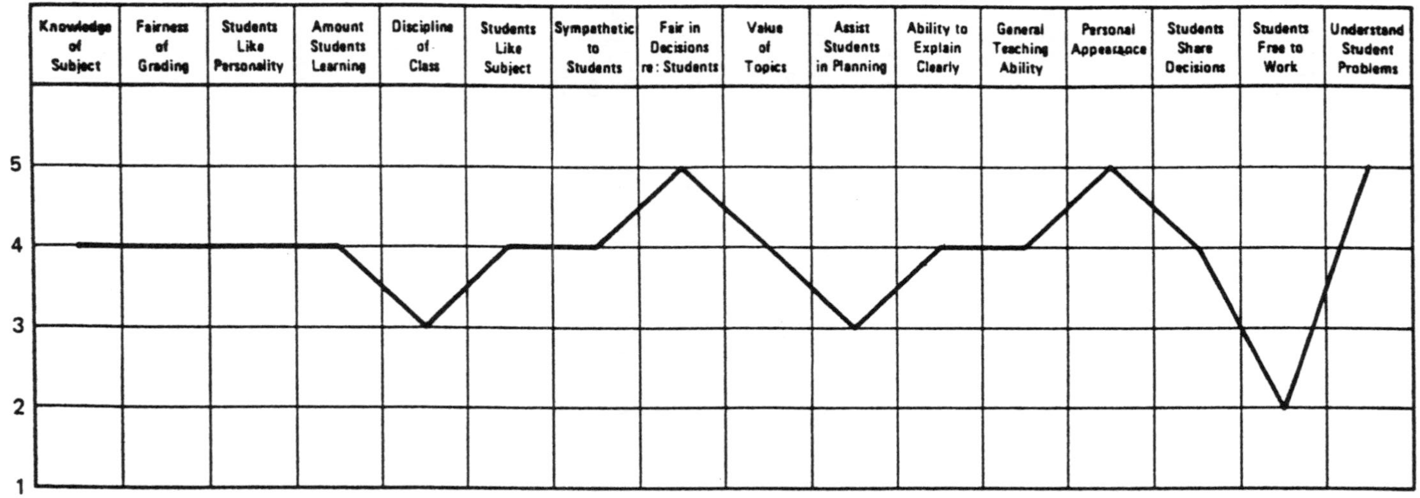

FIG. 15.1 Teacher's rating of self.

Source: G. and L. Spindler.

teachers. It is particularly notable that he rates himself as superior on 'fair in decisions concerning students' and 'understanding student problems.' He rates himself as 'somewhat' better than most teachers in fairness of grading, sympathy for students and students sharing decisions. These self-ratings are all directly relevant to the evaluation of equity in his classroom.

We asked all of the administrators and counselors who had any direct knowledge of his operation as a teacher to also rate him on the same scales. These included the principal and vice principal, all of the special services people who visited his classroom and all of the people in the superintendent's office, including the superintendent himself.

The administrators rate him higher than he rates himself (see Figure 15.2). There are no behavioral areas where he drops below the presumed average for other teachers.

We also asked him to evaluate himself on this scale but this time to rate himself as he thought the administrators would rate him. He rates himself a little higher, in this perspective, than he did when he was evaluating himself without regard for what the administrators would think of his work.

It is clear that this young teacher is very well thought of by the people who will judge him, promote him, and give him security within the profession and within the school system. It is also clear that he is confident of his effectiveness as a fairminded teacher and that he knows that others who evaluate him see him in this same perspective. The situation seems very positive.

These rating forms were administered very early in our contact with this teacher. We had an agreement with him that we would study his classroom for a period of several months and that we would share the results of our study with him as a contribution to his own professional self-improvement. He had volunteered for the study and seemed enthusiastic about it and the reinforcement he anticipated in the interaction with us as unprejudiced observers.

After this initial period of data collection we conducted what we have called the 'expressive autobiographic interview'. This interview procedure is quite different than collecting a chronological life history. It was developed by Louise Spindler in her early work with Menominee women adapting to rapid cultural change. We adopted it to many of our other research projects including the work with this fifth grade teacher. The expressive autobiographic interview allows the informant to start wherever he or she wishes but usually within a frame set by the interviewer. With teachers we were usually most interested in how they got into teaching and what formative experiences there had been that influenced them towards teaching. As the interview proceeds the interviewer is able to reinforce certain avenues of response and subtly discourage others. The autobiographical materials can therefore be clustered around the promontories of experience and reaction that seem most relevant to the purposes of the research.

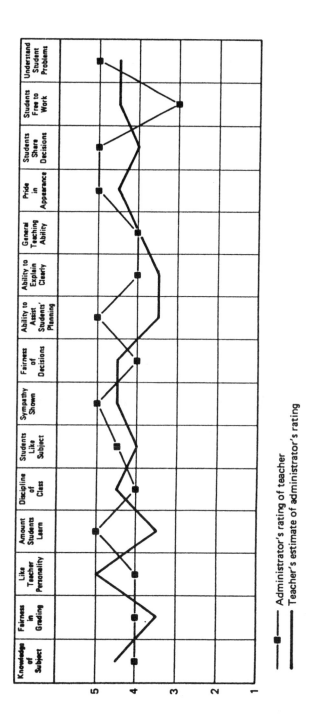

FIG. 15.2    Administrator rating of teacher and teacher's estimate of administrator rating.

We will not replicate any part of this teacher's expressive autobiographic interview in the interest of preserving anonymity. (We have already cloaked certain details to this same end.) We will paraphrase and comment on various aspects of the interview relevant to our presentation in this chapter. He seemed quite at ease during the interview and impressed the interviewer as 'uncomplicated' in the sense that he was pleasant, seemingly relaxed, but did not have a strong impact upon the observer. He seemed to accept himself, his role, the situation, and most parts of the transaction, without much attempt at manipulation.

The first question directed at him was 'I just want to get some understanding of your personal experience and background in relationship to teaching. We might start right there with teaching. How did you happen to go into teaching?' His answer was that he was really influenced by his mother who had been a music teacher and by his sister who also taught in grade school for a while. He had been in the army during the Korean War and wanted to develop a profession after he was discharged and felt that it was most definitely due to the influence of his mother and sister that he went back to school with the aim of becoming a teacher. He made it clear that he regarded teaching in the elementary school as a stepping stone to administration and was in fact working for his administrative credential at a West Coast university during summers and other released time. He expected to obtain the credential and the Master of Arts degree within two or three years and by that time have an administrative post, probably as principal of an elementary school. He thought of himself as ultimately destined for the superintendency.

Another question was 'Let's go back to before college. What was your family like?' He indicated that they had always gotten along very well in his family and then spoke of his mother and sister and how his sister had played at a number of recitals and that both his mother and sister were very talented on the piano. In the course of the interview he did not bring up his father spontaneously. He responded to a direct question about him that he was a manager for a large retail organization.

He went on to say that what they really enjoyed doing the most was driving up to their summer home in the mountains and that he would go with his mother and sister for a month or two every summer. His father would come up occasionally on weekends. The park where the summer home was located was maintained by the Masonic Lodge.

When asked more about his father he indicated that his father was very active in various civic organizations such as the American Legion, the Masonic Lodge, the Elks, and the Kiwanis. Both of his parents also went to the Methodist Church, attending frequently but not with absolute regularity. He himself attended church only infrequently.

Other questions had to do with the kind of neighborhood he was born into and any changes in residence that he had experienced with his parents. He indicated that there had been a more or less consistent progression towards bigger and better homes but that he has never lived in anything but a good neighborhood, as he put it.

When asked about his use of spare time he indicated that he read professional journals (*National Education Association Journal* and the *California Teachers' Association Journal*) but that he also liked to read the local community newspaper and the *Saturday Evening Post*. For recreation he liked going to the beach and spending the day relaxing best.

There are many details and events that this summary does not include, but it is apparent from his expressive autobiographic interview that he is mainstream and middle class. He probably qualifies as referent ethniclass because he is Anglo-Saxon Protestant. His father's status as a manager for a large scale retail organization would class the family economically and professionally in the upper-middle class. His own position as an aspiring-to-be school administrator does not by itself place him in this category, but it is clear that his socioeconomic status and cultural position are at least squarely within the middle class mainstream and that his origins are upper-middle class. He, himself, seems to be striving for this status and to match his father's success.

The question that we were interested in answering as we proceeded with the case study was in what ways his cultural background affected his interaction with the children in his classroom. The answer to this question required a great deal of observation and further interviewing. The mass of data is far beyond what we can even sample in this chapter. We will select out only a few highlights.

We observed his movements about the classroom and found that they took him to only certain parts of the room and near certain children on a regular basis. Furthermore, he eye-engaged, touched, and interacted only with certain children and rarely of not at all with others. He nodded, smiled, and appeared to approve as certain children performed before the class, as in 'sharing'—a period when children told about their weekends or other special experiences. He was never observed being mean or overtly hostile in behavior, facial expression or comment to any of the children.

We discovered that children seemed to be grouped by socioeconomic status and ethnicity. The explicit basis for the grouping, the teacher told us, was reading ability. About one-third of the class of thirty-seven were Mexican-American, Black, or Portuguese and these children were also of low socioeconomic status.

We interviewed each child for about twenty minutes and later administered a rating scale questionnaire to them concerning the teacher's behavior and the classroom in general. From the interviews plus school records and a house-by-house neighborhood and district evaluation we were able to determine socioeconomic status and ethnicity as well as family culture with a high degree of reliability.

When the children rated the teacher on some fifty points (Fig. 15.3) on the rating scale questionnaire we got a surprise. The children rated him below the average for other teachers they had had on five specific points. All five of the ratings had to do with his accessibility and what was perceived as selective interaction with some children. The lower socioeconomic status and non-mainstream children rated him as difficult to take their problems to, hard to get help from and not fair in his decisions concerning them. They also charged him with having favorites with whom he was always interacting.

These ratings by the children supported some of our observations of his classroom behavior. It appeared that a pattern of selective interaction was emerging quite clearly in our data. The question then became, what was the nature of this interaction?

Our sociometric data served us well at this point. We collected several forms of ratings from the children themselves concerning interaction in the classroom, particularly among peers, and checked them against our own observations. We also asked the teacher to estimate and describe each child's interaction with his or her peers and then matched his perceptions of these relationships with those that we collected from the children. We found that the teacher was biased in his perception of relationships. The bias was consistently in the direction of positive appraisals for upper status and mainstream children. He was as consistently *negative* in his appraisal of relationships for non-mainstream children as he was positive for the others.

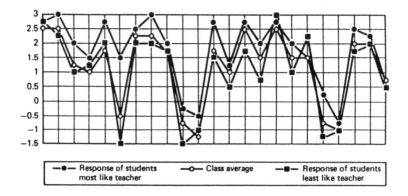

FIG. 15.3   Student's evaluation of teacher.

Some examples will clarify. If we take 'Mary' for example. He described Mary as 'my favorite pupil, a great sense of humor, everyone likes and respects her a great deal, she is a born leader!' The children leave her fairly isolated. On the sociogram (Fig. 15.4) constructed from a proximity rating by each child of his or her choices in the group, Mary is chosen by two children who are themselves entirely isolated, and her own first choices are not reciprocated.

Who is Mary? Her father is the owner of a string of retail clothing stores. The family income places them well into referent class position and they qualify in other respects—they are Anglo-Saxon, North European Protestant. Mary takes vacations with her family in Hawaii, Alaska, and Europe. The teacher enjoys her reports of these trips during the sharing period. Mary is a well dressed and attractive child. She speaks well and responds to the teacher's questions and participates in a lively manner in the discussions.

Another one of the teacher's favorites is a boy named 'Tom.' On the same sociogram that Mary appears on, Tom is not chosen by anyone and is rejected five times. He chooses Mary. He is designated as someone 'I would not like to sit next to' by five children.

The teacher describes Tom as 'a real go-getter, one of the most magnetic personalities of any young child I have ever known. He has a very warm personality and gets along well with anyone, anywhere. He is truthful, sincere, and has a wonderful sense of humor.'

During the sharing periods Tom gets up with a little black satchel filled with samples from one of his father's several retail drug stores. He goes into his sales pitch and, by the end of his time, has collected nickels and dimes from the children in exchange for the sample tubes of toothpaste, hair oil, perfume and powder, and various other odds and ends that he has brought to school to 'share.' The children appreciate the bargain but they do not appreciate Tom.

Tom's background is very much like that of Mary's. His family is well-to-do and his ethnic and cultural position, like hers, places him in the referent upper-middle class mainstream.

There are several other instances of this kind, but the point should be clear by now. This teacher quite unconsciously selected out children for approval and reinforcement that had backgrounds much like his and represented his aspirations towards success. He was not, as we have said, actively prejudicial in his relationships with children who did not fit into this category. He was essentially a kind and very well-meaning person. But it is clear that he gave further impetus toward achievement and success on mainstream terms to some children and unintentionally denied it to others. Of course some of the 'others' survived despite his inattention and when they showed strong interest in learning he would help them. The motivation had to come from them, however.

344

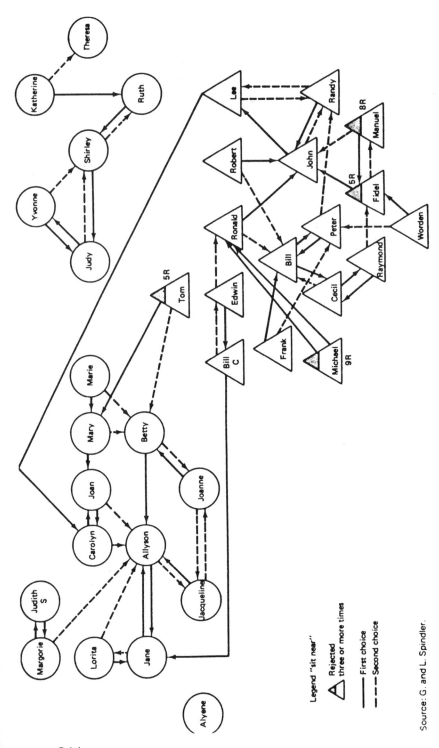

FIG. 15.4. Sociogram of the fifth grade.

Source: G. and L. Spindler.

This configuration is all the more remarkable when we remember that this teacher professed an ideology of fairness and equity. He had strong ideological commitments, but his selective and unintentionally prejudicial behavior in the classroom belied his professed ideology.

When we arrived at the point where our contractual relationship called for the sharing of our research findings, our relationship with the teacher suddenly became quite strained. When we showed him the results of our observations, the application of rating scales, our interviews, and sociometric data, and especially when we matched his perceptions against those of the children, he denied, at first, that it could be true. In fact, he became very angry and left the room, slamming the door. However, we were able to establish a working relationship and went through the body of data that we had collected and discussed their possible meaning. He gradually, if albeit reluctantly, came to accept most of the material. He kept saying 'I can't believe that I did that, I can't believe that I didn't see that happening.'

We pointed out to him his own cultural background and the way in which it appeared to have affected his perceptions of interaction with children in his classroom. This was hard for him to accept at first, but it was certainly much easier than if we had been concerned with a personality problem. We attempted to steer clear of psychological involvements as much as possible and focus almost entirely upon the cultural process.

We eventually came to call this relationship 'cultural therapy.' This may be in unfortunate term in that it implies that there was an illness that could be corrected by therapy. In a sense this was true, though this teacher and many others with whom we worked were not ill people; there was a cultural relationship that determined to what degree and in what ways children were caught up in the classroom interaction and ultimately, we believed, in the American cultural dialogue. This relationship was advantageous to some children and disadvantageous to others. Particularly when there was such an obvious mismatch between the teacher's beliefs in what he or she was doing, and what was actually transpiring, the term 'therapy' seemed appropriate.

It should be clear that we are not espousing a simple 'culture conflict' theory. We are saying that one's cultural background significantly influences what one will value, disvalue, and ignore. This teacher's problem was not so much disvaluing as ignoring. He simply did not interact in the same way or with the same intensity with children who did not match his own cultural experience and background. This process of selecting out certain children and certain behaviors for approval and reinforcement, and ignoring others, is potentially as damaging as the exercise of overt prejudice and hostility towards certain children. The cultural therapy in this teacher's case consisted of bringing him to realize that his own declared commitments were not being implemented in the classroom due to a cultural bias of which he was largely unaware. We feel that such sensitivity training should be incorporated in teacher training programs as well as in in-service work of the kind that we were doing. Each teacher is somewhat unique, but all teachers, as cultural transmitters, are subject to some of these same hazards.

## CONCLUSION

In the case of the eighth grade counselor there is blatant prejudice and both positive and negative selection. As a gatekeeper, this counselor had more power than she realized. She was sending some children on to glory with her blessing and condemning others to perdition with her curses. This statement is a little over-dramatic but it does fit the case. We did not find many other counselors so prejudiced and so damaging but we found elements of this kind among many, if not most, of the ones that we observed in action during five years of intermittent work in the schools.

When we did a careful study of academic achievement and California Mental Maturity (CMM) test scores for Mexican-American children in one West Coast school district, we found that the longer the children stayed in school, the more they dropped in academic performance in relation to expected performance at the appropriate grade level and that their CMM scores declined—not only in the verbal portion of the test scores but in the nonverbal portion. It is correct to say that the longer these children stayed in school, the lower their relative academic performance and the lower their intelligence quotient (as measured by this particular test). This is what alienation does: it dulls and destroys abilities and potentialities.

By the time this counselor had the power of channeling and gatekeeping over the children in the observed eighth grade group, they had already had enough experience to know where they belonged and where they were probably going to go. All she did was reinforce their expectations. The school is indeed a factory for both failure and success.

And who was this counselor? She was a woman in her sixties not far from retirement who had served in the school district faithfully for many years and was well regarded by the administration and by her peers. She was regarded as a 'little old fashioned' but certainly competent and sympathetic to children. She was the daughter of an Italian immigrant who had worked his life out as an intermittent day laborer. She had known poverty and had herself climbed the ladder to middle class status through her education and by becoming a teacher, then a counselor. One would think this kind of experience would lead her to a particularly effective relationship with non-mainstream children, as sometimes happens. Just as often however, it does not happen because the person is compensating for his or her past experience.

What this counselor wanted to do was to expurgate those qualities that led children, as she perceived them, to failure. In expurgating these qualities she also expurgated the children, but to her this seemed to be a necessary cost. When individual Mexican-American children showed special motivation or ability she would work with them. But she regarded the situation for most of them as hopeless.

The fifth grade teacher had much the same effect on children as the counselor but since he came from quite a different place culturally, he exercised his biases differently. He did not actively select children for failure, but he did actively select children for success. He selected those children for success who were already successful and like himself culturally. This positive pattern of interaction gave both him and the children that he was positive about a very good feeling. He left other children with a residue of disappointment and negativism. He was such a 'nice' teacher that this negativism did not show up in hostile behavior in the classroom. But the negativism was continuously reinforced by every positive move he made towards his favorites. By the time these children reach the eighth grade they will have been selected out for success and failure, and then they will meet another cultural agent who will put the finishing touches on their finishing.

American culture is a process. It is not only a process of opposition, accommodation, and resolution, but also of selection, reinforcement, and of success and failure. In an achievement-oriented culture where one of the salient and desired features of the mainstream culture is personal achievement and success, failure is all the more poignant. Children do not like to fail anymore than do adults. Children spend a great deal of their time avoiding failure—if not by achievement then by not engaging. Dropping-out begins early, but it is not a personal predisposition. It is a product of the interaction between people, institutions, and cultural patterns.

# Cultural Politics of the White Ethniclass in the Mid-90s
## (1998)

*George and Louise Spindler*

Our purpose in this essay is to explore the applicability of four concepts we have found useful in our recent analyses of dynamic processes in American culture, particularly recent radical rhetoric and action, as they affect education. The concepts are: the American Cultural Dialogue; types of adaptation to disruptive culture change; White ethniclass; and cultural therapy (G. and L. Spindler, 1989, 1990, 1992, 1994). *The American Cultural Dialogue* we will discuss shortly; Types of Adaptation refer to such processes as synthesis of opposing cultural elements, withdrawal, and reaffirmation, engaged in by populations experiencing radical culture change; White Ethniclass refers to the European-American majority and its ethnicity; and Cultural Therapy has to do with a process of reflection on one's own cultural biases. We will put recent ideological and political turmoil, particularly the attacks on established institutions issuing from sources ranging from fringe groups such as the Montana militia to respectable Republicans, into a broad but integrated sociocultural perspective using these concepts as the framework for analysis. We will conclude by discussing the implications of the turmoil for school programs utilizing cultural therapy. This is a biased paper written from a liberal point of view.

## THE AMERICAN CULTURAL DIALOGUE

We have used the term "American cultural dialogue" to stand for a process that has been, we believe, central to communication in America about virtually everything that matters for a long time (G. and L. Spindler, 1990). We

349

posit certain values such as honesty, hard work, individualism, freedom, sociability, success and achievement gained by hard work, equality, time, conformity, as pivotal in the dialogue, but as pivotal in the sense that they are centers of opposition as well as agreement. They constitute norms for one's own behavior and expectations for behavior from others, but they are subject to argument, criticism, debate. That is, they are when the dialogue is working. When the dialogue is working the oppositions as well as the agreements verify the active presence of the pivotal value. For example, arguments about the value of honesty acknowledge the virtue of honesty if it were practical, or possible, or if there were not so many dishonest people about. Or the individual is important but only as a member of the group or as a contributor to the welfare of the community. Or hard work is the way to become successful but a lot of people get ahead by luck, cheating, or "kissing ass."

There are certain of these pivotal values that are changing more rapidly than others. Our extensive sample of responses to an open-ended values projective technique, collected from Stanford students (and some others) since 1952, indicates that attitudes towards artists, intellectuals, nudity, concepts of personal success, sociability, have undergone substantial change. We are more tolerant of the kinds of deviance suggested by artists and intellectuals, we accept nudity as natural, if not always appropriate, we think that success is not merely material but a matter of personal balance and self-recognition, we balance sociability with listening to the inner self. (It is important to remember that a substantial minority has held on to the more traditional value orientations.) With the partial exception of the values of success, these values were never central, however, to the dialogue. Certain central values have undergone change as well. For example, the future is no longer seen with unguarded American optimism, but is more often seen as "bleak" or "uncertain." Success and achievement are perceived more guardedly, with reservations that were not heard, or rarely so, even ten years ago. We still think that equality is a basic ideal, but are more cynical about its attainment. There is more questioning of the right of the individual to act in his or her own behalf without regard for the welfare of others but individuals and their rights still stand supreme for the majority. In general, there is more dispersion of responses, so that the modalities are not quite so large.

For example, though from 40 to 60 percent of respondents complete the open-ended sentence "Honesty is ... the best policy" or words to that effect, now such responses as "useful sometimes," "not always best," "very rare" rob the majority response of its clear dominance. But note that these dispersive responses acknowledge the adage, "Honesty is the best policy," so the dialogue retains its integrity.

We hypothesize that the American cultural dialogue is in a tender state at present. We acknowledge that the Stanford sample is special. After all, Stanford students are selected from the "Top Three Percent" (though we do have samples from other institutions and even some high school students) but if the "cream of the crop" exhibits some deterioration of the stability of core values, the effect must be more pronounced among people who have suffered a decline in real wages for the past 10 years and whose employability may be in question. The core values are not as core as they were only a short time ago, though it is true that the 50s were challenged by the 60s and early 70s, that the 80s re-established the traditional profile (with some modifications), and that the 90s again challenge the temporary stability of the eighties. We will make something of this "tender state" later on. For now we want to turn to the second concept, typologies of adaptations to radical or disruptive culture change, that we are integrating into this essay.

## TYPES OF ADAPTATION TO DISRUPTIVE
## CULTURE CHANGE

In our field work with the Menominee Indians of NE Central Wisconsin we discovered that not all Menominee were the same (Spindler and Spindler 1984). There were the "native-oriented," peyotists, several kinds of transitionals, in-betweeners, laboring class acculturated, and elite acculturated. After several seasons of field work we came to regard these types of response as constructions, by the persons characterized in these ways, of adaptations to the disruptive, in fact transformative culture change the Menominee had experienced since the coming of Europeans to their area. Of course it was not merely culture change they experienced. It was sweeping changes in the economy by which they made their living, the political structures by which they were governed, and the very environment they inhabited. We can say that the result of all of these varieties of change was cultural, since we regard culture as the primary adaptation that humans make to changing conditions of survival. Be that as it may, there is no doubt that there were dramatic differences between these groups of Menominee. The elite acculturated appeared to be middle-class White in their culture, the "native-oriented" appeared (to us) to be quite traditional in their way of life. The peyotists appeared somewhat mixed, ranging from native-oriented to poor mainstream in culture but with a clear ideology and a workable synthesis of Christian and native religious belief. There were several kinds of transitionals—people who were culturally suspended, vegetating, vacillating between being White and being Indian; people who were trying hard to make sense of their lives, and experimenting with various kinds of cultural solutions; people who had withdrawn into alcohol and apathy; people who were marginal, some of them constructively and some destructively. And there were the two major types of acculturated; those who earned their living doing unskilled or semiskilled labor and those who were in managerial positions in the lumber mill or in the administration of the Menominee reservation. They were equally culturally American mainstream in its Wisconsin form. There were also a few individuals who were bicultural, apparently at home in both the Menominee and mainstream cultures. Of these various alternatives we will focus on the native-oriented for the purposes of our analysis.

We came to perceive the members of the native-oriented group as active, not passive, in their adaptation to disruptive change. We saw them as actively constructing and maintaining a way of life that asserted the old values and patterns of culture. They worked hard to carry on the rituals they understood as representing the "old way," such as the Dream Dance (Nemehetwen), Medicine Lodge (Mitawin), Chief's Dance (Oketshetaweshemon). They held "song services" several nights a week, using the "big drum" and singing songs from traditional repertoires. They buried their dead with spirit offerings and grave houses erected over the grave. They offered prayers and exhortations in the Menominee language. They lived well off the highway intersecting the reservation in shacks and quonset type huts they constructed themselves.

At first we thought this group consisted solely of survivors from the past. It was true that most of the old people who were truly Menominee in culture were members of this group. They monitored the rituals and were advisors for the traditional cultural content. But as we came to know the group better we discovered that all of the people under 50 had been out in the world, going to school or earning a living away from the reservation. They had tired of life in the mainstream and had come back to "get hold of the old ways." They were actively acquiring their own culture from the old people who knew it because they had never stopped living it. Eventually we described this group as "reaffirmative."

What we mean by "reaffirmative" is that the members of this native-oriented group were trying to reaffirm their traditional way of life as they understood it. Actually the religious organizations, such as the Dream Dance and the Medicine Lodge that they were reaffirming were not ancient ritual organizations. They had both been brought into and had been modified to fit the Menominee culture since contact with Europeans. In fact both of them were parts of revitalization, or "nativistic" movements that were set in motion by the impact of European invaders. But from the point of view of the members of the present-day native-oriented group they were traditional organizations and rituals. And it is true that they did express Menominee concepts and values. In any event, these organizations and their associated beliefs and practices were what the people wanted to reaffirm. To do this they had to attempt as "pure " a form of cultural practice as they could under modern circumstances and they had to exclude as much as they could of practices flowing from the outside world. Of course they were only partially successful on either count. Their practice was not pure, and their exclusion was far from perfect—they did use pickup trucks, transistor radios, western medicine and hospitals, and a myriad of other things and practices that were never a part of the traditional culture. But their reaffirmation was impressive.

When we were well back in the woods, crowded into a quonset type hut made of scrap lumber, bent saplings for a frame, covered by tar paper, with 6 to 10 men pounding a drum the size of a washtub and everyone singing in Indian style, the 20th century mainstream culture from which we came seemed to be in another dimension We lived as they did for months at a time, traveled with them, picked cherries with them, became quasi-members of their ceremonial organizations. To us, their reaffirmation seemed eminently successful.

What has this reaffirmative process to do with the intent of this essay, which is to attend to the cultural politics of the White ethniclass? We think that this ethniclass, or at least a significant portion of it, is engaged in a reaffirmative movement. What they are saying and doing, particularly those persons who are charged with speaking for the rest of us, in short, elected representatives, fit well the characteristic features of such movements. The resemblance to the Menominee situation seems quite clear.

## WHITE ETHNICLASS BEHAVIOR

Why do we say "White ethniclass"? We say it because the phenomena we believe denote reaffirmation appear to be almost exclusively engaged in by European Americans, "White" people. In fact, given the most visible actors on the current scene, one could say that much of the activity is engaged in by referent White ethniclass persons. This may be too subtle a distinction for our purposes. It is explained in some detail in the *American Cultural Dialogue and its Transmission* (Spindler and Spindler, with Trueba and Williams 1990). What this designation distinguishes is a "core" class of White ethnics, mostly upper middle class, who have historically had overwhelming influence on the manners and morals of American culture and by whom substantial power is wielded. There are some dangers in comparing White mainstream behaviors to those of the Menominee traditionalists. The differences in power are substantial, the Menominee engaged in reaffirmation were virtually powerless. The Gingriches, Doles, Bennetts, and Limbaughs and others spearheading current reaffirmation could be seen as essentially manipulating what they recognize as a swelling of sentiment among voters.

Though there are doubtless elements of this in the action, we think it is too cynical a view to be an accurate interpretation of the movement as a whole. So too is the "conspiracy" interpretation offered by most of our sociological or politically minded colleagues who have read this paper in draft. The vocalists in Washington, they say, are "looking out for their friends" by introducing and supporting legislation to loosen or eliminate controls on water and air pollution, or tobacco advertising, and eliminating agencies, such as the Department of Commerce, that get in the way of "free enterprise." This seems to us to be a "top-down" interpretation taking into account only the motivations of some of the elite. The internal consistency of reaffirmative statements and expression of sentiment by ordinary people as well as the leaders of the movement would be difficult to contrive, and even if contrived at some level, the mass of expressed sentiments taken together seems decidedly real.

By using the terms "White ethnics" or "White ethniclass" we are denoting our perception of all White Americans as having ethnicity, not just those of Italian, Polish, or Irish (among others) descent, so there is a cultural unity that is often overlooked in interpretations of White American behavior and attitudes that may or not reflect itself in political choices, but that is a decisive factor in supplying the energy for a reaffirmative movement.

There is ample evidence of reaffirmative behavior on the part of White Americans. A wide range of behaviors can be included in this category. When William Bennett visited Stanford in 1988, just as the faculty was engaged in a heated debate about proposed changes in the core curriculum for undergraduate study he publicly excoriated them, likening the responsible Stanford faculty to the agents of Vichy France, sellouts to a foreign power. The changes were mostly in the direction of including minorities and women authors on the required fist of readings, and inserting multiculturalism into the curriculum, with a corresponding diminution of the classics from the western heritage. His most recent book, The Book of Virtues, an 831-page volume extolling traditional values, confirms his reaffirmative position. His interview in Modern Maturity (1995) extends it. The enormous popularity of his book suggests that he is far from alone in his reaffirmation. Newt Gingrich has given us many examples of reaffirmative opinions, ranging over a wide variety of subjects, including health care, welfare, warfare, women, and the Clintons. Perhaps one of his most revealing remarks was directed at the President, whom he characterized as "countercultural." Various members of the Republican Party have recently made negative pronouncements on support for public broadcasting, the national geological survey, the Department of Commerce, the Department of Education, children's support and care programs, school lunches, welfare, health programs, controls on the tobacco industry, environmental regulation, aid to underfunded college aspirants, affirmative action, many of which seem to have a reaffirmative flavor, since in one way or another they seem to call for a return to the past, when government was simpler, and we, the mainstream, didn't have all those minorities to worry about, or at least though we might have had them, we didn't have to think about them and when poor people were somebody else's concern and besides, they were poor because they didn't work hard or weren't ambitious. Pete Wilson, governor of California and presidential aspirant (until his withdrawal) rides the reaffirmative bandwagon when he talks about affirmative action and immigration. The recent activism in the western states where all forms of governmental regulation of grazing on public land, timber cutting, and water rights are being contested, is more evidence of a reaffirmative movement under way. No interference with individual property rights. The least government is the best government. There are, of course other than reaffirmative elements imbedded in these actions and pronouncements.

There has recently been an outburst of extreme statements directed at the federal government and particularly at the attempts of its agents (the FBI and ATF) to control the stockpiling of assault weaponry. The invective is expressed not only by extreme fringe elements such as the Montana Militia, but by "respectable" organizations such as the NRA, and by elected representatives such as Helen Chenowith of Idaho. Though such sentiments have been smoldering in the United States for a tong time, the Randall Weaver and Waco incidents seem to have ignited the fire. Weaver's wife and 14-year-old son were killed during a siege by the FBI, and in the Waco incident 64 people died in a holocaust after a 51-day siege, including 24 children. To make matters worse, Weaver's wife was killed by an FBI sniper as she stood in the doorway of their ridge cabin holding her baby. (Her killing is held to be an accident by the FBI.) The penultimate expression of these sentiments took the form of the bombing of the federal building in Oklahoma City. Some interpreters of these events disavow any possible connection of the bombing to the invective, but the distance between word and deed is not untraversable.

The underlying tension seems to be fear and anger about changes that have taken place in our culture during the past few decades, and a desire to return to a simpler, clear-cut, mythically moral, past. In this and other ways the White ethniclass movement is like the "Native-oriented" Menominee. The Menominee reaffirmative movement rejected a whole way of life and celebrated the return to a version of traditional culture. The White ethniclass movement rejects mainstream developments of the period since the New Deal of FDR and celebrates a return to a version of traditional values. The central value appears to be a combination of individualism, success, and freedom—the individual person is not to be hampered in the pursuit of success by regulations, taxes, or concern for the common good, or the fate of the "down and out," single mothers, new immigrants, poor minorities, or anyone who isn't playing the mainstream games successfully. This is the core value configuration, as well, that all federal regulations are seen as eroding. It is a "White ethniclass" movement, there are virtually no minority persons making any such pronouncements or engaging in any such actions. There are, of course, some, but they are exceptions. Nor, with a few exceptions, are there women so engaged though many appear to give tacit support to the movement. The activists seem to be almost exclusively male and White. This is precisely where we would expect the energy for a movement of this kind to come from. White ethniclass males have the greatest stake in traditional values. Their values seem to be eroding (remember "tender state"?) and this population has been hit with corporate "downsizing," new technologies, and sudden obsolescence. One is not so sure that hard work and competence will pay off. Likewise, the eroding small towns of the middle and far west that are losing population, business, and life styles supply personnel for the militias now operating in at least 25 states (Klanwatch, Feb., p. l) and the energy for virulent anti-government rhetoric.

The ostensible purpose of the militias is to defend against enemies of the republic, and an enemy is anyone who represents an alien culture, especially immigrants, or anyone who might be a communist or even a "liberal", or anyone who might represent or be affiliated with the federal government. Paranoid statements provide the agenda for these organizations.

The ideas advanced by the extreme fringes as well as by the mainstream antagonists (such as the NRA) include the notions that Bill Clinton is an illegitimate President; liberals are the enemies of normal Americans; gun control is a conspiracy to tyrannize the populace; and a new world order is being put into place by foreign bankers (Adam Grobnik, p. 8). The radical extremists themselves go further: the U.S.A. is secretly building concentration camps to house resisters to the new world order; microchips are being implanted in the bodies of people to monitor their movements; road signs contain secret codes to direct foreign invaders, armed conflict with the federal government is inevitable (U.S. News and World Report, May 8).

Whether these expressed sentiments can legitimately be regarded as "reaffirmative" is moot. They go too far, one would think, to be included, if the reaffirmation is about the reaffirming of traditional values such as individual rights, and yet, they are a logical extension of such reaffirmations taken beyond the boundaries of sanity into what Michael Kelly describes as "fusion paranoia" (Kelly, 1995) melding the left and right extremes of opinion in America.

The life expectancy of reaffirmative movements may not be long, and American opinions and superficial value shifts tend to cycle through rather short time periods. The major phases of value shifts in our more than forty years of data collection at Stanford (supplemented by other sources as well) seem to have lasted about a decade each. The present situation is extreme, however, and such extremity does not, probably, last as long as a decade. It is true that reaffirmative movements eventually tend to assume conventional forms, they are institutionalized and lose much of their radical character. As of this writing, this is already beginning to happen at the political level as Congress and its Republican majority attempt to cope with swings in public opinion. The long term results, however, may last much longer than the movement itself.

It is our position that William Bennett, Newt Gingrich, the New Republicans, the N.R.A., the militias, the Oklahoma City bombing, the western activism, are all expressions of a reaffirmative movement, an attempt to revitalize a White America that has been increasingly threatened by massive political and social change (as seen by White America) and by an overwhelming increase in minorities that will eventually make White Americans a minority group. Many readers will resist putting all of these (and many more) groups and actions into a sweeping characterization as a reaffirmative movement. They will point out, for instance, that the new Republicans are not against government, they are just against the government the Democrats have constructed. This interpretation ignores the fact that the Republican attacks have been directed at almost every governmental agency from the Department of Education to the National Geographic Survey. They are aimed at dismantling government as it has operated since FDR's New Deal. The consequences are unclear. It remains to be seen whether dismantling antipollution regulations, for example, would not kill more Americans than the Oklahoma City bombing.

## Relevance to Education

What does this have to do with education? Education has been hit directly by reaffirmative trends. The antagonism to bilingual programs, second language programs and any other program that departs from the Eurocentric center of cultural transmission has been active for some time. All moves, such as English as the official language of America, can be considered reaffirmative, and are supported by the White ethniclass. The antagonism extends well beyond the language arena. Lately there have been attacks on multicultural education, efforts in the schools to raise the self esteem of minority children, any hint of an Afro-centric or Latino-centric curriculum, and in fact any addition of materials about the cultures of immigrants or minority children into the curriculum, or any "multicultural" emphasis. Teachers are embattled, subject to extra stress, for most of the younger ones at least, have been enculturated into a more or less liberal point of view concerning all of these matters in their professional education training. Coming at the same time as a general crunch on expenditures for education, and calls for elimination of the National Department of Education and many of the programs supported under its aegis, the situation of teachers must be considered rather desperate.

It remains for us to bring together with the elements of our argument one last segment, and that is cultural therapy. Cultural therapy has been one of our preoccupations for the last decade or so, though we did our first publication on it in the fifties.

## Cultural Therapy

What is cultural therapy? In its most straightforward form it is the process of getting to know one's cultural biases, particularly as they influence one's perceptions of others representing cultures different from one's own. Our most recent publication on it is *Pathways to Cultural Awareness; Cultural Therapy With Teachers and Students* (Spindlers 1994). Our favorite example of a successful cultural therapy is Roger Harker, a fifth grade teacher with whom George Spindler worked in the 1950s. The lessons learned in this extended case study have lasted for a career. Roger was a good teacher, well thought of by the administration of the school and school system where he taught. In fact he was one of the favorite young teachers. And, he was a good teacher by our standards as well. But he was a good teacher for only a minority of the students in his class—those who were culturally like him—upper-middle White ethniclass. This is understandable but intolerable in schools with diverse cultural elements.

George did a thorough ethnographic study of his classroom, focusing, after a sterile introductory period, on Roger's interaction with every student in his class. He collected ample evidence of Roger's selective bias in favor of those children culturally like himself. He was not mean or hostile to those unlike himself, but he knew little about them and didn't interact with them in the supportive manner that he did with those who were like him.

His cultural therapy consisted of a series of sessions devoted to holding up a mirror of his behavior. Together we went over the details of his interaction—both his statements about and to students, and his behaviors, such as frowns, winks, a friendly hand on the shoulder, facial expressions when he was listening to them give reports, etc. At first Roger was deeply resistant toward any data that displayed his cultural biases. In fact he bolted from the first interview in anger, but he returned for the next session and for many after that. He came to accept his biases as "natural" and to see that something could be done about it to make him a better professional. He could regard his "culture" as something from which he, himself, had a certain emotional distance. His cultural therapy did not change his personality but it changed his culture or at least his expression of it in the classroom. His therapy made his culture more open and gave him cultural knowledge about students from cultures other than his own that he found useful and that influenced his behavior toward them.

Roger's cultural therapy has served as a model for our work. It seems so clear-cut and so sensible. The model works and serves us well. There are, however complications. Teachers are not alone in their biases. Students bring to their classrooms profound cultural biases that directly affect their ability to succeed in school. Some regard education as the channel to success in life, and they are not all middle class White ethnic. Others regard school as anathema, and as irrelevant or in opposition to their projected way of life. We can do cultural therapy with the teacher but if the students remain untouched by this process it is much less effective than it can be.

Consequently we are moving into therapy of selected groups of students and teachers, sometimes mixing them, in whole classrooms, and even in whole schools. Our colleagues, as they report in *Pathways*, have taken cultural therapy in these modes further than we have. Our most successful effort to date has been the Schoenhausen/Roseville project (Spindlers 1989, 1992). This project did not start out as cultural therapy, but as our work progressed in the two schools, one in Germany and one in the U.S.A., it became evident that it was functioning as cultural therapy.

The essential feature of group, classroom, or school-wide cultural therapy is that a feasible means be employed to cause participants to reflect on issues about cultural relations with each other. This can be done, as we did in Schoenhausen/Roseville, by using video exposures of critical interactions and working through the interpretations of these with individuals and groups. It can also be done with discussion of relationships and issues without video exposure. Most of the workers reporting on their field experience in *Pathways* did it this way. We found that whatever method is used, a comparative analysis was critical in stimulating useful reflection. We termed our method a "comparative crosscultural, reflective interview." Comparison need not be between schools in different countries, as in our case, but may be made between schools in a single community, or even within schools, between classes.

Given the radical extremism and paranoid quality of much social and political action today it seems doubtful that cultural therapy could be applied successfully to the leaders of radical elements. In fact, trying to do it with them seems like a good way to get into a lot of trouble. But schools are not all battlegrounds, at least not yet, and it appears possible to carry on cultural therapy in some of them.

Paradoxically, just when cultural therapy seems most needed as a way to get culturally engendered issues out in the open, the forces of reaffirmation are most likely to avert or dampen, or wholly suppress, such efforts. Latent biases among teachers are reinforced. Open intercultural communication is blocked. Experimentation with multicultural programs becomes unpopular, even dangerous to professional survival. Teachers and students need help understanding the failures at communication that characterize schooling today, and help in dealing with mounting feelings of frustration and futility. They are unlikely to get either kind of help if the reaffirmative movement becomes the dominant reality.

If our analysis is even only partially correct, the very people who need cultural therapy the most are the ones most likely to resist, and with the support of reaffirmation, in fact, to scourge it, for themselves, and others. Cultural therapy itself will become regarded as subversive. We think that we are in for some hard times but in the long run the imperatives forced upon us by real, not mythical, conditions will prevail.

## REFERENCES

Bennett, William J. 1993. *The Book of Virtues*. New York: Simon and Schuster.

Bennett, William J. 1995. Interview by Peter Ross Range. *Modern Maturity*, March-April, pp. 26–30, 78, 80, 82.

Gropnik, Adam. 1995. "Violence as Style" *New Yorker*, May, pp. 60–70.

*Klanwatch*, Splc. Report, Dec. 1994, 24–55 pp. 1 and 5.

Kelly, Michael. 1995. "The Road to Paranoia" *New Yorker*, June 19, pp. 60–70.

Spindler, George and Louise Spindler. 1984. *Dreamers with Power: the Menominee Indians*. Prospect Hts, IL: Waveland Press. First published in 1971 as Dreamers Without Power. New York: Holt, Rinehart and Winston.

Spindler, George D. and Louise Spindler. 1989. Instrumental Competence, Self-Efficacy, Linguistic Minorities, Schooling and Cultural Therapy: A Preliminary Attempt at Integration. *Anthropology and Education Quarterly*, 20. pp. 36–50.

Spindler George and Louise Spindler with Henry Trueba and Melvin Williams. 1990. *The American Cultural Dialogue and its Transmission*. London and Bristol, PA.: Falmer Press.

Spindler, George D. and Louise Spindler. 1991. Crosscultural, Comparative, Reflective Interviewing in Schoenhausen and Roseville. In M. Schratz, ed. *Qualitative Voices in Educational Research*. London and Bristol, PA: Falmer Press.

Spindler George and Louise Spindler. 1994. Pathways to Cultural Awareness: Cultural Therapy with Teachers and Students. Thousand Oaks, CA: Corwin Press.

*U.S. News and World Report*, 1995, May 8, p. 38.

# Part V

# CULTURAL
# THERAPY

# Part
# V

# CULTURAL THERAPY

## Chapter 17

The processes of culture and person: Cultural therapy
and culturally diverse schools. (1993)
*George and Louise Spindler*

This part explains what cultural therapy is and how it may be applied to
teachers and students. Though the book edited by the Spindlers, *Pathways
to Cultural Awareness: Cultural Therapy with Teachers and Students*, 1994
(Corwin Press) presents more than 10 ways that one may apply cultural
therapy, this chapter focuses on the original conception and its complex dimensions. This is the original version of the paper written by George and
Louise and was published in Patricia Phelan and Ann Davidson, eds, *Renegotiating Cultural Diversity in American Schools*. New York: Teachers College
Press.

# The Processes of Culture and Person: Cultural Therapy and Culturally Diverse Schools

## (1993)

*George and Louise Spindler*

Our basic premise is that culture is not simply a factor, or an influence, or a dimension, but that it is in process, in everything that we do, say, or think in or out of school. As a teacher, a student, a delinquent, a superlatively good student, or a miserably inept student, or an antagonistic, alienated, or resistive student, we are caught up in cultural processes. With this in mind we designate the school as a mandated cultural process and the teacher as a cultural agent. Of course the school is also a political and a social institution and a lot more.

We regard education as a calculated interference with learning. This applies to all education but particularly to that which is the most massive interference in learning in Western society, and except for total institutions in Goffman's (1961) sense, such as prisons and monasteries, the most massive interference crossculturally—namely, the school. What we intend to convey is that schools teach selected materials, skills, and ideas. They also carefully exclude a great deal of cultural content that is being or could be learned by the students. Schools define what is not to be taught and what is not to be learned as well as taught and learned. A great deal goes on in schools other than calculated "intervention" (which we will now use rather than "interfer-

ence") in learning. The calculated interventions themselves have unanticipated consequences. The students learn a great deal from each other that
teachers don't control. Students also bring to school a lot of learning that
teachers would rather they hadn't acquired. A combination of what children
bring to school and what they learn from each other causes teachers trouble.
It is this "trouble" with which we are concerned in this chapter.

## INTRODUCTION

Our strategy here will be to describe and discuss certain models that we
have generated in our research over the years in our attempts to understand
how human beings adapt to changing circumstances in their lives. The
chapter has a certain egocentric quality because we are not directly concerned with the models our colleagues have generated, although they have
certainly been helpful.[1] We offer this chapter and the model of cultural therapy we promote as in process, exploratory, and in places, tentative. We intend it as a way of getting into a dynamic and significant area of
relationships and communication that is present in various forms in all
schools, in schooling, and in the act of teaching. We will doubtless modify
our thinking as we receive feedback and as we and our colleagues attempt
further applications of the model in school situations.

Much of what we have done as anthropologists of education, as teachers
of anthropology, as consultants in schools, and as authors of books and papers is intended as cultural therapy. We have, for example, long taught the
introductory course in cultural anthropology to Stanford students as a form
of cultural therapy—to widen their cultural horizons and their appreciation
of diverse lifeways. We teach education graduate students ethnographic
methods and self-examination as approaches to understanding cultural diversity. We work as consultants with individual teachers or with faculty
groups through simulations of cultural experience and interpretation designed to increase understanding of cultural diversity. We have rarely labeled what we do as such. When we do label anything we have done
"cultural therapy" people get quite excited and want to know very specifically what we mean by it. The answer that we just gave, that cultural therapy is virtually everything that we do as professional anthropologists, is
usually not very satisfying. One of our purposes in this chapter will be to
clarify what we mean by this phrase.

---

[1]We have drawn heavily in this chapter from our papers: "Instrumental Competence, Self-efficacy,
Linguistic Minorities and Cultural Therapy" (1989a); "Crosscultural Comparative, Reflective Interviewing in Schoenhausen and Roseville" (1993); and "The Enduring, Situated and Endangered Self in
Fieldwork: A Personal Account."(1993). "Three Kinds of Cultural Knowledge Useful in Cultural Therapy," George Spindler (1999) brings some new considerations into focus.

As a preliminary orientation we can state that cultural therapy is a process of bringing one's own culture, in its manifold forms—assumptions, goals, values, beliefs, and communicative modes—to a level of awareness that permits one to perceive it as a potential bias in social interaction and in the acquisition or transmission of skills and knowledge—what we later refer to as "instrumental competencies." At the same time one's own culture, brought to this level of awareness, is perceived in relation to other cultures, so that potential conflicts, misunderstandings, and blind spots in the perception and interpretation of behavior may be anticipated. One's culture as well as the other cultures, become a third presence, removed somewhat from the person, so that one's actions can be taken as caused by one's culture and not by one's personality. A certain comforting distance and objectification becomes possible, and relationships, such as those between teachers and students, can be explored without getting personal (or unduly upset) about it.

In our work with individual teachers we have found, excepting in cases where psychopathology is indicated, that the sociocultural position and experience of the individual is a better predictor of classroom behavior, particularly in respect to selective bias (on the part of the teacher) in perception of and interaction with students, than psychological factors as such, as indicated by psychological tests or interviews. In the case of our classic 5th-grade teacher, Roger Harker, for example, his troubled relationships and identity problems with his father, and his overidentification with his mother and sister did not have significant effects on his behavior as a teacher, but his narrow, upper-middle class, white Protestant cultural background did (Spindler & Spindler, with Trueba & Williams, 1990).

Doing cultural therapy, as we do it, has psychological concomitants, but they are not the focus. The focus is the culture of the teacher and the way it biases relationships with children in classrooms. For teachers, cultural therapy can be used to increase awareness of the cultural assumptions they bring to the classroom that affect their behavior and their interactions with students—particularly students of color (if they are white). For teachers, cultural therapy is an intervention that can be used as a first step to impact and change behaviors, attitudes, and assumptions that are biased (and often discriminatory) and thus detrimental to students whose cultural backgrounds are different from their own. Our use of cultural therapy has been directed at helping teachers and other adults to understand their own cultural positions and to reflect on and analyze the reasons why they might find the behavior of a culturally different person objectionable, shocking, or irritating.

For students, cultural therapy is essentially a means of consciousness raising—that is, to make explicit unequal power relationships in the classroom, the school, and the larger society. Further, cultural therapy can be used to help students clarify the steps necessary to obtain the instrumental competencies they need to gain access to opportunities within the school system (and hopefully the larger society). For example, many students of color do not have access to the "cultural capital" necessary to compete equally with the cultural majority for resources, knowledge, and experiences. The goal of cultural therapy for students (particularly minority students) is to empower rather than to blame them.

The experiences of our colleagues working with minority youth suggest that many students fault themselves for their inability to navigate the educational system. Almost none are aware of the implications of tracking; of the fact that they often receive inadequate help and assistance with respect to coursework, college application procedures, and so forth; or that attitudes, values, and beliefs, as well as pedagogical methods and school policies, frequently mitigate against their ability to succeed. Cultural therapy, as we conceptualize it, is intended as a method to increase students' understanding of the factors that work against them and to empower them to fight against the obstacles they encounter (rather than blaming themselves or engaging in behaviors that impede their access to skills and competencies necessary to ensure their access to power and opportunity).

With this preliminary understanding, we can turn to certain experiences and results from our field research as anthropologists in the manifold contexts of education.

## REFLECTIVE INTERVIEWING IN SCHOENHAUSEN
## AND ROSEVILLE

For some years we have been researching in Schoenhausen, a village of about 2,000 in a semirural but urbanizing area in *Land* Baden Württemburg, Southern Germany. Schoenhausen was known, and still is to a considerable degree, as an *ausgesprochner Weinort* (emphatically, a winemaking place). The native born are Swaebisch and Protestant. The Grundschule (elementary school) is charged with the responsibility of educating all of the children and preparing them for a changing Germany and world. Its 127 children are distributed in 4 grades staffed by six teachers, a Rektor (principal), and various other special services personnel.

The Roseville Elementary School, located in central Wisconsin, includes kindergarten through 8th grade and is somewhat larger than the Schoenhausen school, but is comparable in every other respect. The school district is rural but has many commuters who work in nearby towns, some of them as many as 40 or 50 miles distant. The majority of the children attending the school come from small dairy farms. The predominant ethnicity of the Roseville School District is German.

Over the years we have applied many different research techniques, some of which will appear in other parts of this chapter, but for our purpose at the moment we wish to emphasize some material that came out of an interview technique that we have most recently developed—the "crosscultural comparative reflective interview" (CCCRI). It was applied in Schoenhausen for the first time in 1985 and had been applied in Roseville in 1983 and subsequently.[2] The CCCRI is designed to stimulate dialogue about the pivotal concerns of natives in comparable cultural systems. Some form of audiovisual material representing two or more cultures is used to bracket the interview. That is, the interview is conducted as an inquiry into the perceptions, by the native, of his or her own situation and that of the "other," and the assumptions are revealed in reflections about those perceptions. We regard both the perceptions and the assumptions as cultural phenomena.

We had taken films in both the Schoenhausen and Roseville classrooms and our basic procedure was to show these films to our interviewees and thus elicit reflective discussion of their own situation and that of the others. We did this with teachers, administrators, and children in both research sites. A very rich body of material was generated by these interviews, from which we selected only a few instances from the interviews with two teachers, "Mrs. Schiller" in the Roseville school and "Frau Wanzer" in Schoenhausen.

## The Roseville School

GLS:                Now with respect to your underlying objectives as a teacher, that is Linda Schiller as a teacher, not necessarily what you get in the education courses, what would you say your basic purpose is?

Mrs. Schiller:    To teach them to be an individual, to be all they can, to the limits of their abilities and if I can get them to be a happy person as well as get them to do their best, then I think I've done

---

[2]We presented the first paper on the CCCRI at the American Anthropological Association meetings in November, 1986. The first publication demonstrating it was not by us, but by Mariko Fugita and Toshyuki Sano (1988) who had been instructed by us. The reflective interview technique was not inspired by recent work on reflective teaching or inquiry into teaching processes, though this work is not irrelevant to our purposes. It stems from anthropological concerns emerging particularly in the writings of postmodernists on reflective and reflexive ethnology and interpretation, anticipated by work of people such as Mead and Collier. The idea was inspired by Margaret Mead's chapter on evocative stimuli in fieldwork in *The Making of Psychological Anthropology* (1978); and by the work of John Collier., Jr. and Malcolm Collier in *Visual Anthropology* (1986). It has occurred to us that one way to encourage reflective, self-analytic, and self-aware teaching is to use culturally bracketed interview techniques such as the CCCRI. Our chapter in Schratz (1993), "Crosscultural, Comparative, Reflective Interviewing in Schoenhausen and Roseville" describes the technique, locates its origins, and demonstrates the results.

my job. [Further discussion of the individual, of activity, and of disruption in class.)

GLS:          Here in Roseville wouldn't you be able to walk out of the classroom, go down to the office, leave your class for 5 minutes or more?

Mrs. Schiller: Ah yes. I left the 1st graders up in front without any assignment just the other day, and Jeremy grabbed the pointer and started "A, B, C, D," etc., and the whole class repeated and then went on through the alphabet several times. I said, "That was so nice. You didn't waste any time!"

Mrs. Schiller went on to discuss how the children knew where the materials were and could get them when they wanted them or had time for them after they had finished their assigned task. She expected them to work quietly and either individually or with others. The children used charts, tape recorders, flash cards, and so forth. She says, "They're all little teachers, it's just built in." She claims that she doesn't really arrange the materials beforehand; they know where everything is and just go and get what they need.

Mrs. Schiller:  I have a lot of faith in kids. I think kids are neat! If you have high expectations, 98% of the time they will fulfill your expectations.

GLS:          What would you feel like if you went out in the hall or someone called you to the phone and you came back after 5 minutes and found things in considerabledisorder?

Mrs. Schiller: Well, I would tell them right off, "I am very disappointed! I had this important phone call and you couldn't sit still for 5 minutes while I answered it." I would let them know it hurt me personally. It's kind of a personal thing. Oh yes! You start building that up the first day of school. Then they feel "we can't hurt our teacher."

She went on to describe an instance where a little girl had to go to the dentist and she had to take her out to the car where her mother was waiting. She came back and found such a nice class and praised them for being so nice and quiet. "They just love praise!"

There was a great deal more in this interview about how she depended upon the personal trust between the children and herself and how she cultivated the feeling that they couldn't "hurt their teacher." She also discussed curriculum. She pointed out that the teachers in the Roseville school had direct input into the curriculum, in contrast to the situation in Schoenhausen where the curriculum plan (Lehrplan) comes down from the State Board of Education (its American equivalent).

## Schoenhausen Grundschule

For the first few minutes we talked to Frau Wanzer about what we wanted to do in her classroom and explained that we wanted her procedures and goals to be clear to the Roseville teachers when we showed the films taken of her (Frau Wanzer's) classroom. She had seen the Roseville films already.

Frau Wanzer: Ya, it was really difficult for me to see what was intended. Perhaps that was the ground for the feeling that many of us had, *Was lernen sie eigentlich?* [What are they learning really?].

GLS: We explained that the films shown were typical for this class and the *freiwillig* [free will] character of the classroom activity was indeed characteristic.

Frau Wanzer: I can scarcely understand how the teacher working at the table with some of the children would work on without looking to see what the other children were doing in the rest of the room. How do the children working alone know what they are supposed to do? With us there are difficulties and fighting. This was apparently not the case with the Roseville school!

GLS: Naturally, the children have specific lessons, but then when they are finished—they can do what they will.

Frau Wanzer: Sie können tuen was sie wollen! [They can do what they want!]

GLS: Well, they have various opportunities—such as tapes, computers, the library, flashcards, posters and so forth.

Frau Wanzer: There is naturally a great difference as compared to our school. In America they have so much more time and so when they are finished with their lessons they can do what they want, but with us there is no time.

GLS: To go back a little, so for every hour there is a specific goal you must reach?

Frau Wanzer: I have in my curriculum plan the goal that I must reach. Every hour has a part of goal. I must find out as the hour progresses if I'm going to have enough time to reach that goal. It depends on whether the hour goes well or badly, how much time I will spend.

Here she is speaking of the Lehrerplan [curriculum plan] from the Baden Württemburg [province] office of education.

GLS:                    Well, if you did have free time, how would you arrange it?
Frau Wanzer:  I would arrange materials beforehand that belonged to a specific theme. But in the framework of this theme, the children could do what they wanted. But I wouldn't just leave it up to them to choose from unorganized material. I would have the fear that they [would] choose things that were just play.

She goes on at some length to describe just how she would work this out and what kind of product she would expect, then ends with the comment: "This kind of procedure would work, but *volligfrei* [fully free]? *Dass macht nichts* [that makes nothing—that's of no use]!"
    We went on to discuss what would happen if she left the room and carne back and found chaos.

GLS:                    What would you do if you heard a disturbance in the room when you returned?
Frau Wanzer:  I would talk to the class. I would attempt to reach an understanding. Scolding does no good. Sometimes I have said that I am *traurig* [sad].
GLS:                    Would you say that you are *beleidigt* [hurt]?
Frau Wanzer:  No, never *beleidigt, nur traurig* (only sad).
GLS:                    Do you make the children feel guilty [*schuldig*]?
Frau Wanzer:  I feel that guilt is not understandable for children of this age. How can they understand who is guilty—the one who started the trouble or the one who responded to the trouble and who carried it on further?

We carried on discussions of this kind with Frau Wanzer several times and her interpretation of her own behavior in the classroom and that of the Roseville teachers she had seen on film was consistent. She saw the Roseville classrooms, as did the other teachers, as tending toward being directionless, without specific goals, and not organized for the attainment of whatever goals existed. She did find the quiet orderliness of the Roseville school impressive and as exhibiting good "teamwork."

Interpretation

Frau Wanzer and Mrs. Schiller are two experienced teachers of about the same age who teach the same grade, about many of the same things, in quite similar schools in parallel communities in Germany and in the U.S. Yet their handling of their classrooms and the assumptions that guide their behavior are significantly different at some critical points. And their perceptions of each other's classroom reflect these differences. Mrs. Schiller's classroom is relaxed, quiet, low-keyed, and diverse. Children carry out various activities on their own, in addition to those carried out by the teacher and the small group she is leading through a specific learning task. There is little or no disruptive behavior. These qualities were confirmed in many sessions of observation by us, are apparent in the films we showed to the Schoenhausen teachers, the principal, and the Schulamtdirektor (superintendent of schools) and his assistants.

Frau Wanzer perceives Mrs. Schiller's classroom as undirected, as almost without goals. At the same time, she acknowledges that there appears to be "teamwork," but that this method would be unlikely to work well in the Schoenhausen Grundschule.

These perceptions are apparent in the interview. Frau Wanzer's assumptions are clear: If children are undirected they, or at least a significant proportion of them, will do nothing at all, become disruptive, or choose to play rather than work. She also reports that when children have clear directions on an interesting topic they can become very enthusiastic about learning and will work hard at it. Frau Wanzer explains the differences observed in terms of time, which is short in Schoenhausen, and the fact that the curriculum plan there defines the goals to be reached quite precisely. She does not see these as cultural attributes, but as given, as practical, and as preconditions to what she does, and what the children do, in her classroom.

The differences run deep. Mrs. Schiller assumes that her goal is to help each individual develop to his or her fullest degree—to the limit of their individual capacities. Frau Wanzer assumes, as does the Schulamtdirektor, that her purpose is to help each child attain the standards set forth in the *Lehrplan*—that some will meet them fully and others only minimally. Frau Wanzer takes for granted the existence of a *Lehrplan*, which is furnished to the school by the state education office, and will directly guide her management of her instruction. Mrs. Schiller takes for granted the fact that teachers in her school district develop their own curriculum and that it is only an approximate guide. Frau Wanzer assumes that the children eventually learn to continue working when she leaves the classroom, but that one can't expect too much of the younger 1st and 2nd graders. Mrs. Schiller expects her 1st and 2nd graders to be responsible for keeping a quiet, on-task classroom when she is gone for a few minutes. Frau Wanzer would talk to her class if there were a disruption, but she would not act "hurt," only "sad," and she would not try to make her children feel "guilty." Mrs. Schiller would develop personal liking and trust with her children, would be "hurt" if they misbehaved, and would leave them all feeling guilty if they did. These two teachers have quite different conceptions of guilt. For Frau Wanzer guilt has to be established—there is a perpetrator, a reinforcer, and perhaps, a victim. For Mrs. Schiller there is a feeling state—guilt is internalized. The children feel guilty about their irresponsible behavior and about hurting their teacher.

These are the assumptions, as we see them, that lie behind both the be-haviors of the two teachers in their classrooms and their perception of each other's behaviors in situ. These are cultural differences, we believe, that are expressed in and derived from the German and American historical experi-ences. In our own terminology, they reflect the German and the American heritage cultures.[3]

The claim we made in the preceding paragraph always arouses criticism and rebuttal. We are properly abashed by the rashness of our interpretation. However, we do feel that the elicited dialogue represents something that we can call "German" culture and "American" culture. We have recently repre-sented the latter as a "cultural dialogue" (Spindler & Spindler, 1990), and we can understand certain of Mrs. Schiller's interpretations as expressions of (for instance) individualism, achievement, and internalization of author-ity and guilt, as a part of this dialogue. We can understand some of Frau Wanzer's discourse, and that of the Schulaimtdirektor (district director of education), as expressing certain aspects of a long-term German dialogue about authority, efficiency, collective effort, and the attainment of stan-dards. To claim that the little elementary schools in Roseville and Schoenhausen somehow express their respective national Zeitgeisten goes further than most of us want to go, and yet the implications are tantalizing and, we think, important. The action in these classrooms and the interpre-tations by the natives seem to be the tip of a cultural iceberg. The part of the iceberg that is under water is the enormous complexity of the national whole and its history. Just how to make the analytic connections remains obscure. Nevertheless, we feel that it is essential to take into consideration broad, pervasive aspects of cultural dialogue, such as those represented, when we talk about classrooms and confrontations in them. If the teacher goes into the classroom with undeclared, and possibly unverbalized (even to herself), culturally patterned assumptions of this kind and the students come with other kinds or assumptions, also undeclared, there will be serious difficulties in communication. "Cultural therapy" in this instance would be to make it possible for both the teacher and the students to verbalize these

---

[3]Our emphasis is on culture as a dynamic process (rather than a static historical experience) where the values and experiences of diverse groups of people play a significant role in an ongoing American cul-tural dialogue that is constantly being renegotiated. (We write about this topic extensively in The Ameri-can Cultural Dialogue and its Transmission [Spindler & Spindler with Trueba & Williams, 1990].)

basic assumptions. This is often done in "rap sessions," but the purpose of such discussion is unclear and there is usually little reinforcement of what is expressed or pursuit of any misunderstandings that may have occurred.

## THE ENDURING, SITUATED, AND ENDANGERED SELF

In 1987 we were invited to participate in a panel for the American Anthropological Association meeting on the fieldwork experience in anthropology. Rather than simply talk about our experiences in what is now some 28 field trips in five different cultures, we decided to talk about the "self" and we treated this ambiguous concept in three dimensions: the enduring, the situated, and the endangered self in fieldwork.

The *enduring self* is that sense of continuity one has with one's own past—a personal continuity of experience, meaning, and social identity (Hallowell, 1955). It provides the egosyntonic functions of the self and functions as an integrating principle of the personality phenotype (Levine, 1984). It seems to have, at least in our own experience and that of some of our informants, a romantic–ideal quality that may be quite lacking in the more pragmatic situated self.[4]

The *situated self* may be thought of as encompassing those aspects of the person required to cope with the everyday exigencies of life. This self is situated and contextualized. It is instrumental in the sense that we use the concept (Spindler & Spindler, 1989a, 1989b). This self is linked to the attainment of ends defined within the framework of a lifeway or social context. One's sense of self-efficacy—a concept used by learning psychologists—is a product, as we see it, of instrumental success or failure. Whereas the situated self is oriented to the present and the contexts (situations) one finds oneself in, the enduring self provides a sense of personal continuity with the past. This may imply that the enduring self is entirely conscious, and indeed much of it is—particularly the idealized features of identity, obscured by time and selected out of memory. But there are events and situations that occurred in the past, which contribute to contemporary feelings and self-evaluation, that are not readily conscious. For our purposes this is

---

[4]Our interest in the "self" is of long standing, as evidenced by Louise Spindler's memoir on *Menomini Women and Culture Change*. G. Spindler used self-other concepts in his early research in California schools (see G. Spindler, 1959). The notion of a "situated" self was stimulated by a symposium paper presented at Stanford University by Dorinne Kondo (1987). There are other possibilities such as the "constructed" self, made from the interaction of the enduring and situated selves, or the "saturated" self, which is overwhelmed by input from frenetic, divisive, fragmented social communication, or "multiple" selves, more diverse than the enduring self but more cohesive as reactive systems than situated selves. We find the "enduring" and "situated" selves as representing the poles of cohesion and diversification possible in the normal psychocultural constitution, and the "endangered" self as a consequence of severe conflict between the two.

not too important, but in individual cases it may be of great significance and would be brought out in extended counseling or therapy. For us, what is important is that any given student or teacher will have a sense of self that is relatively independent of the situation one finds oneself in. If this sense of self (the enduring self) is violated too often and too strongly by the requirements of the situated self that is constructed as an adaptive response to situational contexts, the enduring self will be damaged, or may even become the *endangered self*. This can occur in anthropological fieldwork and certainly occurs as children and youth of diverse cultural origins confront school cultures that are antagonistic to the premises and behavioral patterns of their own culture. This helps account, for instance, for the resistance of some minority youth to learning in school, where learning some aspects of what is being taught and accepting how it is taught may be regarded as a "sellout." We would regard this as evidence of a conflict between the enduring self and the situated self.

In 1970, in "Being an Anthropologist," we wrote that the ethnographer,

> if successful, is in truth friendly, in truth concerned with the welfare of his or her respondents, but in truth an observer. The job is to find out what the people think and feel as well as what they do. One must penetrate beyond the facade of rationalizations and diversions that all humans throw up around their activities and sentiments. But the ethnographer must not become one of the people being observed, though from the outside he or she may seem to become one. The ethnographer must keep his or her identity while he studies theirs. One may well observe oneself—this self-knowledge is necessary. But when the distance between oneself and one's respondents is lost and between oneself in the sense of personal identity and in the sense of the role as participant–observer, the ethnographer has lost his or her usefulness as a field-anthropologist. (p. 298)

Another point of view was expressed by Michel Leiris (1978) in "Das Augen des Ethnographen" in anticipation of an expedition to Africa:

> • … for me the trip has a prospect of fulfilling a certain childhood dream—the possibility of fighting against age and death—to go against the river of time—to lose my time-bound person in contact with humans very different than myself. I also wish that my artistic and literary friends could travel with me, not as tourists but as ethnographers, and therefore come into contact (with the "natives") in enough depth to forget their white, middle-class manners and to lose what they under their identity as intellectuals comprehend. (p. 34)

There are dimensions of the self embedded in these statements, and we will comment on them shortly in terms of our personal experience, but for the moment it is clear that the ethnographers, both ourselves and Michel Leiris, were doing what persons coming into a new cultural situation must do if they wish to get along and learn, and at the same time, to keep their identity. These are the problems, in our view, of the ethnic minority student or the lower class student in a middle-class school environment.

The problem, of course, is how to do this. The ethnographer has a role and in varying degrees is trained for it. The ethnographer is also highly motivated to perform adequately in an alien cultural setting. When we did our first in-depth field work with the Menominee Indians of Wisconsin, we risked our health and at times even our lives to get along and obtain our data.

We found the tradition-oriented group of Menominee most compatible. They were also culturally the most different (from us). They then (in the 1950s) lived in self-made shacks well back in the woods far away from the highway or amenities such as utilities, sewer systems, or electrification. These people carried on a way of life that was more than reminiscent of an aboriginal central woodlands culture. The ceremonial round, subsistence activities, language usage, burial customs, sorcery, and religious beliefs all exhibited specific traditional cultural features (Spindler & Spindler, 1984).

We were most interested in this group, spent the most time with them, wrote the most about them, and identified with them to a greater degree than with any of the four major groups of Menominee that we eventually described. We never thought we were Menominee Indians, but we felt that we were members of that group, and, indeed, were treated as such in many respects. None of this is too surprising. There was an obvious match between our romanticized, idealized, enduring selves and the place and people we found interesting.

What was not clear to us at the time and did not become so for some years was that the majority of the Menominee in that tradition-oriented group also bore enduring selves that were romanticized and idealized in the same direction.

All of the people in this group who were under 50 years old had extensive experience with the outside world—in schools and in the work force. Most had become disillusioned. They had come back to the "old people," as they put it, to learn and live their own life way again. All of them had traditional socialization experience, often with grandparents. All had experienced disruption and discontinuity. They came back, literally, to find themselves. The tradition-oriented group, we came to feel, was a kind of revitalization movement, guided by the surviving handful of knowledgeable elders. Of course, the individual life careers varied. We are speaking of over one-half of the total members of that group.

It is an oversimplification, but it is not wrong to say that both the tradition-oriented Menominee and we, the anthropologists, were engaged in the same quest—rediscovering and reasserting our enduring, romanticized selves. But they were more clear about that than we were.

We were less objective than we thought. We managed our situated selves effectively and maintained a working balance between objectivity and involvement. We would not do it differently if we had to do it over again but we understand better now our strong attraction toward this group. Other anthropologists who have worked with the Menominee were not similarly attracted. We think that such relationships are probably more common in fieldwork and are reflected more often in interpretation than is generally acknowledged.

We think that our experience, sketched above, suggests how complex self-other relationships may be. We were living and working in a social and cultural situation very different than the one to which we were accustomed. We were stimulated by this, as most anthropologists are in the field, and found it compelling in all sorts of ways. Our attraction was positive and we made a viable adjustment. But we did not fully understand what was happening—why we were so attracted to the traditional group of Menominee and also why we were not attracted by the acculturated portions of the Menominee population. To us, the latter seemed stuffy—too much like the people in small towns, or in big cities, for that matter, who we have tended to avoid in our personal lives. We might have seen the convergence in our romanticized-idealized-enduring selves if we had had those concepts worked out at the time, but we might not have seen the convergence between ourselves and those of the traditional Menominee.

A matching of selves, whether enduring or situated, is not simple. The fact that a kind of convergence could occur in our case may suggest that there are all sorts of ways in which convergences may occur between students and teachers and between students and school situations that are not apparent on the surface. There are, apparently, divergencies as well. These kinds of relationships require a deeper penetration than we can provide at this time but they are suggestive.

In this panel discussion at the AAA meeting we also dealt with dangers to the self, both enduring and situated, that might be inherent in the fieldwork process. We felt that there were some dangers. For example, we feel permanently marginalized in our society. Many of our colleagues must feel this too. Knowing our enduring self as we do and having found an alien identity with which to reinforce it, we feel we have left to us only our situated self to be played out in our own society. Our relationships to all of our everyday affairs and aspirations seem at times shallow. But we cannot go back. Our friends and informants in the tradition-oriented Menominee group are either dead or have themselves left behind much of their revitalized native identity. Even their rituals, some of which they still carry out, seem removed from the traditional context in which we first saw them. The echoes of the past are faint and only the sociopolitical realities of the day seem alive. But is this feeling anything more than simple nostalgia for our own youth and the reinforcement of the enduring self that we found there among the Menominee?

This is a situation peculiar to the field ethnographer, perhaps, and yet the feeling dogs us that the children from a minority group who attend a mainstream-dominated school must have many of the same kinds of feelings. They enter marginalized and their marginalization is reinforced. This is exactly parallel to what happened to us. We entered the field situation with the Menominee already somewhat alienated and disenchanted with much of mainstream society as we knew it. We found reinforcement for this marginalization and emerged from the 7 years of intermittent field experience permanently marginalized. We do not claim that our experience and marginalization are directly comparable to that of a minority child or youth. We are empowered by our position, our status, and our ethnicity. They may be disempowered. Nevertheless, our experience in the field where we made our adjustment to other's realities is suggestive and gives us, at least, some basis for empathy.

What may be most important here is that we learned how to make situational adaptations without destroying our enduring selves. Perhaps this is what many minority students with strong ethnic identities must do. They must keep their identity since this identity, in the sense of the enduring self, is essential to the maintenance of life itself. And yet they must get along in the world as it is. It is a world where instrumental competencies have to be acquired that are not required by the enduring self or one's ethnic identity. A sense of pervasive self-efficacy must be developed in order to cope with the exigencies of life as they happen in a complex technological society. Somehow minority youth as well as mainstream youth must be enabled to make this kind of adaptation, and they will be helped in doing this if the necessary instrumental competencies can be deemotionalized—removed from the value matrix of mainstream culture. Perhaps if we have clear concepts of enduring self and identities, and situational adaptations, and can verbalize them, make them explicit and applicable to everyday lives, we can help ourselves to make good working adjustments.

We end this section with another quote from our chapter from "Being an Anthropologist":

> We have never had a truly bad time in the field, though we have not, to be sure, endured some of the extreme exigencies that some of our colleagues have. But we have fallen ill, been cold, wet, and insect bitten, suffered from having to struggle along in someone else's language, been rejected by the very

people we wanted to know, harassed by children when we wanted to work with their elders, repulsed by offensive sights and odors (given our culturally conditioned sensibilities). Our lives have been threatened by people and by impersonal forces. But it was all the very essence of living. (1970, p. 300)

If somehow the struggle of the minority student could be converted to a struggle with some glory in it—as there was and still is for us—getting along in school would be perceived differently and reacted to with energy and determination rather than alienation. This may seem to be another kind of "blame the victim" concept but it need not be if cultural therapy could somehow incorporate some elements from this kind of orientation, the orientation of the ethnographer. Perhaps both teachers and students have to become ethnographers, studying each other and themselves.

## GETTING ALONG IN THE REMSTAL

One of our major research efforts in Germany has been to study the ways in which people perceive and make instrumental adaptations to the changing environment in which they live. The Remstal in Germany is an area of some 21 communities, ranging from very small villages to mid-size towns, but it is rapidly urbanizing and modernizing. One tool that we used, of our own invention and derived from field experience in Germany (and in all of the other places we worked as well) consists of some 30 line drawings of significant activities in which a person may engage or conceive of engaging in. These drawings are of occupations, houses, social situations, clothes, recreation, and places. They are clustered around two poles—the traditional way of life and a modern, increasingly urbanized way of life. The activities, the line drawings, and the conception of what is traditional and modern must be refit, of course, to each research site. The technique is emic in its evocative stimuli, but the underlying model or theory of relations, which is etic, remains constant. Respondents are asked to choose activities they would like to engage in, which means choosing certain line drawings, and to explain why they chose them. The drawings may be selected by the individual from the whole pile of drawings, as the Blood Indians (Kanai) insisted on doing, or presented one by one in any predetermined order. Alternately, the pictures may be presented in preselected pairs to groups of some size with two slide projectors, as we did in the Remstal with schoolchildren, their parents, and their teachers. The respondent makes choices, then defends the choices, either in writing or orally under conditions of individual ministration.

Though not initially designed for that purpose, the Instrumental Activities Inventories (IAI) elicits data that seem relevant to concepts of self and personhood. We can say that we become what we choose as instrumentalities. The advertising profession recognized this long ago, and we are bombarded with invitations to identify with the sophisticated by drinking Perrier and to become members of the "now generation" by drinking Diet Pepsi.

We cannot engage in a detailing of the results, which we found to be complex and revealing, but what became abundantly clear was that there are indications of the enduring self and the situated self in the responses of the Remstäler. The enduring self is clearly ideal–romantic. It is represented in choices of *Weingärtner* (vintner) profession, *Selbständiger* (the independent small shop owner), the *Kleinbauer* (small farmer), the *Grossbauer* (big farmer), the quiet evening at home, the traditional *Fachwerk* (open-beam structure) house, and the *Weinlese* (grape harvest). Images and values constituting an idealized lifestyle, now disappearing rapidly, were woven together in the defenses of these choices, the friendly village, kin, family, land and nature, fresh air and sunshine, history, beauty, independence, fresh natural food, freedom, and health. This cluster was represented in every IAI protocol, even when instrumental choices of a more pragmatic orientation were expressed. This cluster we regard as an expression of the romantic–idealized enduring self (Spindler & Spindler, 1989b).

The pragmatic lifestyle, represented in the choices expressing the situated self, centered around choices of the modern rowhouse, white collar work, factory jobs, the machinist and technical draftsman trades, the modern church, and the evening out in a festive pub. It is constructed of a cluster of quite different images and values: physical comfort, convenience, shopping, access to entertainment and medical care, regular income, paid vacations, less hardship, and clean work. This was the contemporary lifestyle actually available to most of the respondents. The ideal-romantic cluster represented in the enduring self was literally almost unavailable to the majority of the respondents.

We saw the cognitive management of these two opposing selves and supporting cultural clusters, the traditional vs. the urban–modern ways of life, as the primary task that the children learned in school and the teachers and parents taught. All teachers know that they themselves live, and that the children they are teaching will live, in the framework of the situated self (though they do not phrase it this way). And yet every teacher expressed the cluster of the ideal–romantic pole of the enduring self as desirable. Somehow the people of the Remstal seem to have been able to hold both the enduring–ideal–romanticized self, and the pragmatic-situated self, together without major breakdown. If they can do it, why do we have such difficulties with it in our schools?

We think that the answer is that the enduring self is related to the traditional Swaebish culture, which is of long standing in the Rems Valley.
It is the traditional culture. There is a literature in Swaebish, the royal
family of Baden Württemberg is Swaebish. The local Heimatmuseums
are about Swaebish home life, Swaebish artifacts, Swaebish quilts, and so
forth. People speak Swaebish at home. The teachers, although some of
them are not from the Remstal area, speak Swaebish when they have to.
The "newcomers," now third generation, from the outlying areas of Germany that had to be vacated after World War II, and from what was then
the "East Zone," understand Swaebish. Although there are jokes about
*die dumme Schwabe* (the dumb Swaebish) and their *unbeweglich*
(unmoving) character, they are not really prejudiced against, nor regarded as lower-quality, low-status, or undesirable people. The fact that
all children learn both Swaebish and *hoch Deutsch* is an indication of
this. Speaking Swaebish is not discouraged in school, but the teachers
teach in hoch Deutsch except when they have to explain something to a
very young child whose primary language is still Swaebish. In short, children are raised and teachers work in an environment where cultural differences and distinctions are taken for granted and not considered
invidiously. The problem in America and in American schools seems to
be that in order to establish some kind of identity, mainstream American
culture poses itself as dominant, supreme, moral, "right," to be observed,
and to be taught at all costs to everyone. In the not-too-distant past this
involved punishing children for speaking their native language, shaving
their heads and "delousing" them (in residential Indian schools, for example), and in general letting them know that if they weren't pretty
much Anglo-Saxon Protestant, or acting like they were, they were infe-
rior, on the back burner, and to be shaped up or shucked off. We are reap-
ing the harvest of our history, and although we are making efforts to
change it, such efforts are not fast enough, thorough enough, or deep
enough in our own psyches. There are very few consciously racist teachers but there are many teachers, perhaps even all teachers, who have
very strong biases that are quite unmovable because they are integrated
with their own sense of identity and self—in many cases the enduring
self. If we could just adopt a Remstal attitude, it would help. Cultural
therapy involves some self-examination along these lines on the part of
both students and teachers. We do not mean by this that there should be
a simple confession of sins by teachers, and in effect a kind of apology to
children (although sometimes this seems in order), but rather that there
be an analysis of the cultural persuasions involved on all sides. We are
currently doing this in an experimental course for people with Bachelor

of Arts degrees now returning to Sonoma State University to become teachers.

## THE SELF AND INSTRUMENTAL COMPETENCE

It is not difficult to conceive of a global relationship of self, and particularly self-esteem, to instrumental performance, for which schooling, in modern complex societies, is a major arena. Children with various sociocultural backgrounds attend schools predicated on mainstream, largely middle-class, and largely white, Anglo-Saxon, Northern-European, Protestant cultural assumptions. Such children acquire deficits in self-esteem when they fail to master essential instrumentalities in this context. This self-esteem is damaged not only by actual failure but by negative perceptions and low expectations of these children by teachers and other students. The processes for failure begin when a child enters school.

The equation is direct. When instrumental competence is acquired and displayed in school settings, positive self-esteem and good self-concept is often the result. In turn, this can lead to competent school performance. In contrast, lack of instrumental competence in the school setting leads to negative self-esteem and poor self-concept and in turn to incompetent school performance, and possibly alienation and dropping out. One condition feeds another, which in turn continues to feed the first.

But the problem is more complex than that. The assumption that the whole self-concept is dependent upon school performance may be quite incorrect. The concept of self-efficacy, a subset of self-esteem, seems useful here. We define self-efficacy as a prediction that one will be able to meet the demands of the situation effectively. A student with feelings of self-efficacy thinks that he or she can answer questions, pass exams, read adequately—get the work done as well or better than most others.

Self-efficacy varies across different behaviors in different situations (Bandura, Adams, & Howells, 1980). This concept, like "instrumental competence," is not passive, as in Cooley's "looking glass self" (Gecas & Schwalbe, 1983). It is constructed of self-determined perceptions and predictions of behavior that interact with those of others in situations such as classrooms that are not simply a reflection of those others. Instrumental competence and self-efficacy seem quite similar, although stemming from unrelated research projects and quite different disciplines. Instrumental competence requires that one understands what activities are linked to what goals and how to perform the activities. Self—efficacy in our terms is an expectation that one can exhibit instrumental competence in the appropriate context.

For example, minority children often fail to acquire instrumental competence in test taking. The importance of tests in Anglo-oriented schools is not appreciated. The skills and motivations necessary for students' getting control of the content they are to be tested on (and then letting it drop), the significance of time in testing, and the need for hurry and tensed, focused excitement (even anxiety) the whole pervasive complex of configurations of test taking in our schools—is not understood nor are the motivations for meritorious performance under the imposed and quite artificial conditions of test taking at present. The crucial linkage between goals, values, assignments, and priorities, and actual skills are not made. The child suffers failure, instrumental competence is not achieved, and self-efficacy is eroded.

Instrumental competence and self-efficacy are situational and may be considered to be expressions of the notion of situated self as employed in our interpretation of the Remstal case. We hypothesize that for minorities, as well as for Remstäler, there may be an enduring self that is sustained above and beyond the situated self or estimates of self-efficacy in school situations.

Children may fail in school because they do not perceive, understand, or master the instrumental relationships upon which schoolwork is predicated. They may develop low self-esteem and low estimates of self-efficacy in the school situation. But they may preserve an enduring self or identity that is comparatively intact and positive, formed and sustained in nonschool contexts.

Cultural therapy as relevant to these ideas would consist of trying to help children and teachers to acquire understanding of these instrumental competencies required in school. We are not thinking here of simply the competencies of test taking, or writing well, or doing math, but the broader context into which specific competencies are imbedded. The test-taking example is relevant here. There is not only the content of the test, the rightness or wrongness of answers, but also the test-taking cultural complex. We see this every day in our teaching at Stanford. Stanford students have been selected out for test-taking instrumental competence in its most complex and subtle sense. They are not always necessarily the best students. Much of school is ritualized, complicated, made difficult for those who are not raised in its shadow in ways that are irrelevant to ultimate instrumental competence. Part of our effort within the framework of cultural therapy would be to try to come to an understanding of what essential competence is as against ritualized, culturalized, competence—instrumental competence that has been imbedded within the framework of the majority culture but is not necessarily a part of minority cultures. Teachers need to understand this and children need to understand it, although we are not sure that teachers would find it entirely comfortable to have students understand too much.

## ADAPTATIONS

There is a further complication—if we read the possibilities correctly. Our researches have convinced us that under conditions of personally experienced culture conflict, especially where the conflict creates conditions for instrumental failure, people respond in certain predictable ways. These modes of response we can sum up as follows: reaffirmation, withdrawal, constructive marginality, biculturalism, and assimilation (Spindler & Spindler, 1984, 1989a). There are various subsets to each of these modes, "withdrawal," for example, can be vegetative or self-destructive. "Assimilated" can be adjusted or compensatory.

Among the Menominee, where our ideas about these modes of adaptation first emerged, the reaffirmative adaptation was represented by the native-oriented group. It was composed of a few older people who were essentially cultural survivors from the traditional past and a larger number of younger people who had met mainstream culture head-on in schools and in the work world and who were trying to recreate and sustain a recognizable Menominee way of life—and escape from the mainstream. They sought participation in the Dream Dance, Medicine Lodge, Chief's Dance, Ghost Feast, and tried to live Indian style. They were fully aware of their choice. It could be called a strategy of adaptation (Spindler, 1984).

Various forms of withdrawal were represented by others who were so torn by conflict that they could not identify with either the traditional or mainstream cultural symbols or groups. Many drank to oblivion and sometimes death. Others did nothing—they vegetated. "Constructive marginality" is represented by a number of Menominee who made a viable adaptation to culture conflict by avoiding strong identification with any group or any one set of symbols. They formed a personal culture that is instrumentally productive but is usually constituted of several different segments—some mainstream. They distanced themselves in greater and lesser degree from much of the conflict and maintained a wry view of it.

Among the assimilated Menominee there were some "150 percenters"—people who were more respectable than most respectable mainstream whites and who wondered how we could live and work with those "dirty Indians." They were compensators. There were others who were undifferentiated culturally from mainstream whites in the surrounding areas and who did not denigrate others who were more traditional. In fact they were interested in Menominee traditions, as described by Walter Hoffman, Alanson Buck Skinner, and Felix Keesing—anthropologists who had worked with the Menominee decades before we did, and who described the traditional culture in detail. There were also a few who appeared to be assimilated who had made a bicultural adaptation. They seemed equally at home in the traditional and mainstream context though the latter was socially dominant. This adaptation is extremely difficult to make because the distance between the two cultures is very great—we think greater than that for most minorities.

There's one other adaptation represented by the Peyote Cult, or Native American Church. Menominee Peyotism synthesized Christian religious belief and traditional Menominee belief and symbolism. The Peyote tepee, for example, has 13 poles, one for Christ and 12 for the disciples. There does not seem to be anything exactly like Peyotism in the current adaptation of minorities, though one could probably make a case for it.

The underlying principle is that conflict resolution is likely to take defensive forms, particularly when self-esteem is threatened. For example, the reaffirmative mode is characterized not merely by a return to a traditional or neotraditional pattern of behavior but also by the exclusion of perceived elements from the sociocultural context where one has suffered loss of self-esteem and has a low estimate of self-efficacy (contemporary resistance theory is an expression of this in a different theoretical framework). The assimilative mode may be characterized by a similar exclusion, but of perceived traditional cultural elements if these elements are perceived as a handicap or cause for instrumental failure. We hypothesize that something similar happens to many minority students. When instrumental competence is not attained in school and situational self-efficacy is damaged, the individual response may be to reaffirm, withdraw, or compensate. There can be an active rejection of the whole schooling context, and a reaffirmative celebration of street life, home life, or diffuse ethnic images and symbols, or a withdrawal characterized less by compensatory reaffirmation and exclusion of threatening elements than by self-destruction. There may be important differences in the adaptations between males and females that, to our knowledge, have not been explored in the existing literature (Spindler & Spindler, 1990; L. Spindler, 1989). We could go on exploring these possibilities, but we hope that our general intent is clear.

Cultural therapy with respect to this line of thought would consist of being able to bring out in free discussions the kinds of adaptations that students are making to the school, its culture, and its representatives. We are not inferring that the only adaptive strategies that are possible are included somewhere in the framework that we have delineated, but we do think that the framework orients us to some of the kinds of adaptation that are possible.

Knowing what one's adaptation is, one then can make a more cognitively based decision about whether or not this is the right strategy at the right time. It is very clear that some students are doing a kind of reaffirmative identification and in doing so withdraw from or become actively confrontive with school culture and purpose. Boundaries are created, and in fact boundaries are necessary for this kind of identity work. These boundaries may seem quite irrational and destructive to outside observers who are not "in the skin" of the adapter. The ultimate driving force is to maintain self-esteem, to at least not seriously damage the enduring self, and to make the situated self, in relation to the enduring self, tolerable.

## CONCLUSION

Cultural therapy is an orientation for remedial efforts directed (by us) primarily at teachers or teacher trainers, and by others at students—both mainstream and minority. The essential features of cultural therapy are: making explicit the nature of conflict in cultural terms, the involvement of the enduring and situated self in this conflict, and the requirements for instrumental competence in the school situation. Cultural awareness, both of one's own culture (familial, ethnicity, class, gang, and so on) and of the other (usually mainstream or minority) culture is crucial for both students and teachers. When the nature of the problem is seen in this objectified manner, self-determined choices may be made on a realistic and less self-damaging basis.

## ACKNOWLEDGMENTS

We wish to acknowledge the advice, reactions, and criticisms of colleagues and students at Stanford, The University of California at Davis, Sonoma State University, and the State University of California at Sacramento on the occasion of various presentations and colloquia on cultural therapy—and particularly to Patricia Phelan, Frank Logan, and Ann Locke Davidson at Stanford and Henry Trueba at the University of Wisconsin at Madison.

## REFERENCES

Bandura, A., Adams, N. E., & Howells, G. N. 1980. Tests of generality of self-efficacy theory. *Psychological Review, 84,* 191–215.

Collier, J., Jr., & Collier, M. 1986. *Visual anthropology.* Albuquerque: University of New Mexico Press.

Fugita, M., & Sano, T. S. 1988. Children in American and Japanese daycare centers: Ethnography and crosscultural interviewing. In H. Trueba & C. Delgado Gaitan (Eds.), *School and society: Learning content through culture* (pp. 125–163). New York: Praeger.

Gecas, V., & Schwalbe, M. 1983. Beyond the looking glass self: Social structure and efficacy-based self esteem. *Social Anthropology Quarterly, 46(2),* 77–88.

Goffman, I. 1961. *Asylums.* New York: Anchor.

Hallowell, A. I. 1955. *Culture and experience.* Philadelphia: University of Pennsylvania Press.

Kondo, D. 1987, February. *Company as family? Ideologies of selfhood in a Japanese family enterprise.* Paper presented at the Stanford University Colloquium, Stanford, CA.

Leiris, M. 1978. Das Augen des Ethnographen. *Ethnologische Schriften, 2,* 34–55. Frankfurt/M: Syndikat.

Levine, R. 1984. *Culture, behavior and personality.* New York: Aldine.

Mead, M. 1978. The evocation of psychologically relevant responses in ethnological field work. In G. Spindler (Ed.), *The making of psychological anthropology* (pp. 87–139). Berkeley: University of California Press.

Schratz, M. 1993. *Voices in Qualitative Research in Education.* London: Falmer Press.

Spindler, G. 1959. *The transmission of American culture.* The Third Burton Lecture. Cambridge, MA: Graduate School of Education, Harvard University.

Spindler, G. 1999. Three kinds of cultural knowledge useful in doing cultural therapy. *Anthropology and Education Quarterly.* December.

Spindler, L. 1962. *Menomini women and culture change* (Memoir No. 91). Menasha, WI: American Anthropological Association.

Spindler, L. 1989. A comment: Gender differences neglected. In H. Trueba, G. Spindler, & L. Spindler (Eds.), *What do anthropologists have to say about dropouts?* (pp. 135–136). London: Falmer Press.

Spindler, G., & Spindler, L. 1970. Fieldwork among the Menomini. In G. Spindler (Ed.), *Being an anthropologist: Fieldwork in eleven cultures* (pp. 267–301). New York: Holt, Rinehart, and Winston. (Reprinted 1984, Waveland Press.)

Spindler G., & Spindler, L. 1984. *Dreamers with power: The Menominee Indians.* Prospect Heights, IL: Waveland Press. (First published by Holt, Rinehart and Winston as *Dreamers without power: The Menomini Indians,* 1971.)

Spindler, G., & Spindler, L. 1989a. Instrumental competence, self-efficacy, linguistic minorities, and cultural therapy: A preliminary attempt at integration. *Anthropology and Education Quarterly, 10*(l), 36–50.

Spindler, G., & Spindler, L. 1989b. The self and the instrumental model in the study of culture change. *Proceedings of the Kroeber Anthropological Society* (pp. 109–117). Berkeley: University of California Press.

Spindler, G., & Spindler, L. 1990. Male and female in four changing cultures. In D. Jordan & M. Swartz (Eds.), *Personality and the cultural construction of society* (pp. 182–200). Tuscaloosa, Alabama: University of Alabama Press.

Spindler, G., & Spindler, L. 1992. The enduring, situated, and endangered self in fieldwork: A personal account. In B. Boyer (Ed.), *The psychoanalytic study of society* (pp. 23–28). Hillsdale, NJ: Analytic Press.

Spindler, G., & Spindler, L. 1993. Crosscultural, comparative, reflective interviewing in Schoenhausen and Roseville. In M. Schratz (Ed.), *Qualitative voices in education research* (pp. 53–93). London: Falmer Press.

Spindler, G., & L. Spindler, 1993. The processes of culture and person: cultural therapy and culturally diverse schools. In P. Phelan, A. Davidson and H. Cao. (Eds.) *Renegotiating Cultural Diversity in American Schools.* New York: Teachers College Press.

Spindler, G., & L. Spindler, 1994, *Pathways to cultural awareness: Cultural therapy with teachers and students.* Thousand Oaks, CA: Corwin Press.

Spindler, G., & Spindler, L., with Trueba, H., & Williams, M. 1990. *The American cultural dialogue and its transmission.* London: Falmer Press.

# Part VI

## ORIENTATION

# Part
# VI

# ORIENTATION

## Chapter 18

Making the Familiar Strange: The Anthropological Dialogue
of George and Louise Spindler (1998).
*Susan Parman*

The following article, by Susan Parman, provides an overview of the works
of George and Louise Spindler that spans their whole career. She observed
classes and seminars taught by them at the University of California at Santa
Barbara, and talked with them for hours over coffee, drinks, and under the
spell of the Pacific Ocean breezes. She wrote three essays based on this experience, one of which, "George and Louise Spindler and the Issue of Heterogeneity and Homogeneity in American Cultural Anthropology" is
published in Volume 17 of *The Psychoanalytic Study of Society* (1992). She
does not confine herself to their activity in "educational anthropology" but
samples the whole spectrum, thus providing useful context for this focused
volume. A reading of this piece will make the articles constituting the bulk
of the volume more understandable.

Susan Parman is Professor and Chair of Anthropology at California State
University, Fullerton. She has done research on Europe, Japan, Mexican-Americans, and the American South; on sociolinguistics, cartography,
ethnographic field methods, the neurophysiology and cultural interpretation
of dreams, the anthropology of islands, and the history of anthropology. Her

most recent books include *Europe in the Anthropological Imagination* (1998) and *Dream and Culture: An Anthropological Study of the Western Intellectual Tradition* (1991). She has done fieldwork in the Scottish Highlands since 1970, and began to work closely with the Spindlers when they edited her book *Scottish Crofters: A Historical Ethnography of a Celtic Village* (1990) in their Case Studies in Cultural Anthropology. She shares their interests in innovative teaching methods and ethnographic groundedness, and, like them, was trained in anthropology, sociology, and psychology. Above all, she shares the same enthusiasm for the sheer differentness of travel and intensive fieldwork in other cultures, and finds it just as difficult to return home.

Quotes from the Spindlers are from letters and interviews, from taped responses to questions posed by Henry Trueba many of which are in "The Lives of George and Louise Spindler" published in a special issue (vol. 17 of *The Psychoanalytic Study of Society* edited by Bryce and Ruth Boyer), and from their numerous writings.

# 18

# Making the Familiar Strange: The Anthropological Dialogue of George and Louise Spindler

(1998)

Susan Parman
California State University, Fullerton

*In the Spring of 1991, in a classroom at the University of California, Santa Barbara, in Education 270H ("Culture and Learning: Anthropological Approaches to the Understanding of Culture"), George and Louise Spindler are talking about the implicit cultural biases that teachers often bring to a classroom. The classroom is relaxed; questions, comments, and laughter come easily. GS is discussing the pseudonymous "Roger Harker" (G. and L. Spindler 1982b), an American teacher he met in 1951 while doing research in West coast elementary schools, who seemed to meet the ideal standards of effective leaching ("fair," "organized," "knows his subject," and so on)—except that he was totally insensitive to cultural diversity, and rewarded only those students similar to him in sociocultural background.*

*Sitting to his right, Louise Spindler says quietly, "You were Roger Harker." Both were school teachers before they became involved with anthropology.*

*They use the exchange to underscore the importance of becoming sensitized to one's own culture. Even so-called "objective" tests reflect cultural bias—a point GS illustrates by an episode from his adolescence, when after being skipped two grades he tested low on an IQ test, which brought forth a massive social response from the community that resulted in a more "appropriate" score a year later. "So you can see what happens with linguistic minorities that are denied access to self-efficacy. As a result of a culturally insensitive school environment, their scores of mental maturity actually decrease over time."*

*Moving from the American classroom to Germany, George and Louise Spindler take on the identity of "Hans" and "Greta," who are out in the fields pruning their grapevines and being interviewed by the ED 270H students whose task is to identify their pivotal areas of preoccupation and feeling—not just cultural knowledge, like how does a cocktail waitress 'serve drinks on the upper level' or how does a German peasant prune his vines, but cultural satisfaction and dissatisfaction, what turns them on. "Hans," the students discover through questioning, is dissatisfied with his son's lack of interest in the land and with the disappearance of small, private landholdings; life without the opportunity to work on the land is hollow.*

*"Why did you marry Hans, Greta?"*

*"My parents thought he was a good match. Underneath that feisty exterior, he's really quite kind. And of course, he had some land."*

For almost 50 years, George and Louise Spindler have carried on a dialogue with each other, mingling personal chemistry and experience with astute observation and theoretical inference in teaching, consultation, editing, and publication. Their numerous publications and presentations deal with a variety of issues: personal adaptation and culture change; the anthropology of education; Native American, German, and American culture; gender differences in psychocultural adaptation to change; and the development of multidisciplinary techniques used to reduce ethnocentrism, improve observation, and enhance teaching. They have been editors as well as writers. While editors of the American Anthropologist, 1963–1967, they proposed a number of innovative and influential developments, including the publication of special issues on Paleontology, Ethnography of Speaking, the New Guinea Highlands, and Ethnoscience; and as editors for Holt, Rinehart and Winston since 1960 (and now Harcourt) have developed several innovative series, including the highly successful Case Studies in Cultural Anthropology. But it is not only the diversity of technique, theoretical perspective, or fieldwork setting that distinguishes their work per se; it is also how they have used these different aspects to promote an underlying orientation toward human experience—an orientation that may be explored under the phrase "making the familiar strange."

In their article, "Roger Harker and Schoenhausen: From Familiar to Strange and Back Again" (1982b), George and Louise Spindler compare the experiences of doing ethnography in familiar and "exotic" settings. Each setting imposes its own anthropological dilemma: the first, how to observe situations so familiar that it is almost impossible to extract oneself from one's own cultural assumptions and be objective; the second, how to observe situations so different from what one is used to that one responds only to differentness, in effect "making the strange even stranger than it really is" (1982b:40).

The phrase "making the familiar strange" may be used to convey an orientation that includes not only methods of investigating different cultures but methods of teaching how to do ethnography in the classroom and methods of teaching that incorporate the findings of ethnographic investigation. The Spindlers are themselves patient, systematic fieldworkers; but they are also powerful educators who use the methods and results of their field experience to open minds and promote freshness and creativity in relationship to whatever subject matter or activity is involved. "Making the familiar strange" is the goal of every effective educator—that is, encouraging a state of mind in which one achieves a sense of distance and fresh perspective in relation to the situation or material under consideration—and it is also the ultimate goal of every anthropologist. After a lifetime spent examining the cultural "other," the anthropologist should also be able to bring distance and perspective—what some anthropologists call institutionalized alienation, or the sense of marginal strangeness—to the examination of the familiar. And just as Archimedes recognized that if he had a place to stand he could use a lever to move the world, anthropology provides both the place to stand and the lever by which one's own world can be treated as an object in the natural universe—to be moved, examined, and at the very least, to have its Roger Harker ghosts exorcised.

## BACKGROUND AND INFLUENCES

Both George Dearborn Spindler and Louise Schaubel Spindler grew up in households infused with a respect for and involvement with education. GS' father, Frank Nicholas Spindler, was a professor of philosophy, aesthetics, and educational psychology at what was then Central State Teacher's College in Stevens Point, Wisconsin. LS's mother, Cora Field, was an upperclass, independent woman from Racine, Wisconsin, who avoided the intense and restrictive social life of her female peers in favor of boat racing with her brothers, had no patience for stereotypes, and was always extremely supportive of advanced education. LS also identified strongly with her grandmother, a woman who read widely when this was not considered appropriate for young women, and who taught girls from Norway (where Louise's great-grandparent were from) how to read, write, and adjust to their new home in the United States. Before they ever began graduate studies in anthropology, both George and Louise Spindler were teaching; and it was while teaching high school in Park Falls, Wisconsin, that they met, and after a year of courtship spent largely hiking, fishing, and exploring in the north woods, were married in 1942.

Both were born to older parents—GS's father was 55 and his mother 42 when he was born in 1920; Louise's father was 63 when he married her mother, who was more than 20 years younger—and both felt a special bond with their parents, and deep regret when their fathers died when they were both young.

His father graduated from Oberlin and Harvard, had been a well-known football athlete in his 20s, read widely, knew Greek and Latin, and taught his son Latin and some knowledge and appreciation of Greek art and philosophy—as well as giving him, when he evinced some interest in the opposite sex, a beautifully illustrated copy of Boccaccio's Decameron ("I read it backwards and forwards and learned a great deal about sex but learned a great deal more about writing"). His mother, Winifred Hatch, "a woman of great resolve and dynamism," had been a court reporter, secretary, and then Registrar at Central State Teacher's College, and was very active in community politics.

LS was born in Oak Park, Illinois. Oak Park is now a suburb of Chicago but in 1854 it was farmland where her father, a self-trained lawyer actively involved in politics, was born to his parents, descended from German and French immigrants, who moved there from Pennsylvania. When LS was three years old her father moved the family to California to pursue a lifelong dream of emulating the early pioneers who had come to California during the gold rush. He bought an abandoned mine complete with tunnels, buckets, cars, and mining equipment, hired a crew to work it, and between the ages of 5 and 8, LS spent several weeks every summer helping her father enjoy his dream. When he died, her mother returned to the place of her birth, Racine, Wisconsin. And whereas Burbank, California, had been a place of cultural tolerance, educational experimentation and creativity for Louise, Wisconsin seemed socially and educationally rigid and intolerant. No longer identified with upper-class status, no longer identified with a particular niche in the rigidly structured hierarchy of Racine's class society, LS was snubbed by girls whose mothers had learned English with the help of her grandmother. It gave her a lesson in objectivity about what culture could do to people of a different class or ethnic group, as did her first teaching experience in a one-room school in rural Illinois where she encountered extreme prejudice against anyone who wore lipstick, liked to dance, and did not interpret the Bible literally.

LS received an Outstanding Woman Scholarship from the American Legion, and a scholarship from the American Association of University Women, to attend Carroll College at Waukesha, Wisconsin, near Milwaukee, and graduated Summa cum Laude in 1938. Her major interests were drama and literature, which she pursued during intermittent graduate work at the University of Wisconsin in 1940-42. She wrote, acted in, and organized plays at Carroll College. She worked on the school newspaper, edited the annual yearbook, and participated in a writer's club. At Central State Teachers College, GS was also editing his school newspaper and annual. Both shared a love of and skill in writing and editing, and an intense interest in experience from the individual's point of view.

GS received a B.S. from Central State Teachers College in 1940 and taught general science and biology courses at Park Falls High School, in 1941-42 incorporating anthropology after having taken a summer of graduate work under Morris Opler at the University of Wisconsin. The interest in social sciences remained with him through the war, which he entered in 1942 shortly after he and LS were married. During the war they traveled together to army camps around the United States—sometimes staying in dude ranches deserted because of gasoline rationing, sometimes in small shacks—where he trained neophytes on antiaircraft artillery and she worked at army posts and command centers (after the war she taught classes on aircraft engines and became so familiar with their sound that for years she would tell flight attendants on commercial flights if she suspected that an engine had problems). Their daughter, Sue Carol, was born in 1943. After two and a half years he was transferred to Italy where he served in the Air Force as a counterintelligence officer for enemy antiaircraft for the Mediterranean theater of operations, and then as member of a combat squadron along the Po Valley until the end of the war.

Returning to the midwest, they enrolled in graduate studies at the University of Wisconsin in anthropology, sociology, and psychology. The number of graduates was small. At that time it was possible to know most of the people working in the social sciences, and members of different disciplines collaborated with each other. They were influenced by systematic sociologists such as Howard Becker, C. Wright Mills, and Hans Gerth; by the physical anthropologist William Howells, for whom GS was a Teaching Assistant, by the British-trained Canadian C. W. M. Hart who had done fieldwork in Australia, and by psychological anthropologists associated with Harvard. The person with whom they worked most closely was H. Scudder McKeel, a psychological anthropologist who in 1936 had published *The Economy of a Modern Teton Dakota Community*, "one of the first anthropologists to use values as a conceptual tool in the analysis of culture change" (G. and L. Spindler 1963:517). His death in 1947 was devastating, but many of his ideas lived on, for example, in the Spindlers'development of techniques of assessing values, such as the "Values Projective Technique" that they have used to assess American values among Stanford students since 1953.

GS completed his M.A. in 1947 in the three fields of anthropology, sociology, and psychology (his M.A. thesis was titled Americans, Germans, and the Military), and his earliest publications reflect his multidisciplinary interests—an article called "American Character as Revealed by the Military" was published in Psychiatry (1948a), and two articles, "The Military—A Systematic Analysis" (1948b) and "The Doolittle Board and Cooptation in the Army" (1951), were published in Social Forces. All reflect a concern with psychological adjustments to sociocultural conditions and are remarkably eclectic in their use of theory. For example, GS (1948b) analyzes the military for its universal features—as a corporate structure that satisfies sociopsychological needs, as subculture, as band and bureaucracy, as having historical roots in feudalism, as spreading through cultural diffusion, as performing certain functions, and as shaping the personal adjustment of individual soldiers to make them conform to the "soldier ideal" of "virility and masculinity" (1948b:88).

The eclecticism has remained, as has the concern with the psychodynamics of individual adaptation, but over the years there has been a shift toward sociocultural analysis, especially with regard to the ethnography of education.

GS was working toward a Ph.D. at the University of Wisconsin, and LS toward her M.A., but problems with health dictated that they go to a warmer climate. A temporary move to UCLA, where GS received training in the adaptation of projective techniques to anthropological research under Bruno Klopfer and rigorous research design under Walter Goldschmidt ("he was rigorous, capable, and committed—I would say the same things about him today"), became permanent. At UCLA, their interdisciplinary training in anthropology, sociology, and psychology continued. G.S. and W. Goldschmidt published an article, "Experimental Design in the Study of Culture Change" (1952) which was described by one commentator on the period as a "gauntlet" thrown down as a challenge to anthropology to become more scientific (Sanjek, 1990:239).

"The feeling in the 50s was that everybody knew what anthropology was. Adamson Hoebel, Clyde Kluckhohn, others—they all agreed that what we were interested in was a crosscultural perspective, and that there was something real that was called culture. But now there is the implicit assumption that nothing is real; belief systems are not believed in but are constructed by anthropologists. So write whatever you like. This approach may be titillating, it may cause people to think a little differently, but it's not to be taken as any kind of data of the human condition."

Besides working with Walter Goldschmidt, GS was influenced by William Lessa in ethnography, as well as by others in anthropology such as Ralph Beals and Harry Hoijer. In sociology, Philip Selznick was a systematic sociologist who had studied the bureaucracy of the Tennessee Valley Authority. The biggest influence was Bruno Klopfer, whose projective technique seminar GS took for two years.

In psychological anthropology, the person who exerted the greatest influence on the Spindlers was neither at Wisconsin nor at UCLA. The writings of A. Irving Hallowell inspired their work on the Menominee, and in particular their use of projective techniques to study psychological adaptation (cf. 1978b; G. and L. Spindler 1991). But above all, "He was not narrow minded. He was interested in everything" from ceremonies to material culture to ecology to worldview. In effect, he provided for them the model of "the perfect anthropologist."

Questions about education, already emerging from family background and teaching experience, were incorporated in academic training when, after completing his M.A. in 1947, GS received a year-long fellowship from John Guy Fowlkes, Dean of the School of Education at the University of Wisconsin, to explore the relationship between education and anthropology. After moving to Stanford from UCLA, he was hired as a member of a research team under Robert Bush, Professor of Education, at Stanford University, to study and provide consultation in local schools, and held the title Research Associate in the School of Education and Department of Anthropology and in 1951 Assistant Professor at Stanford (and also served as President of the Peninsula School Board in Menlo Park from 1954 to 1956). His research methods were multidisciplinary—he did classroom observations and attitude surveys, made sociometric charts, collected autobiographies, conducted interpersonal ratings, assessed social class and ethnicity.

LS received her M.A. in Anthropology from Stanford in 1952. Titled The Autobiographical Approach to the Study of Culture Change: Menomini Indian Women, the thesis reflected research interests and techniques that were developed over the next 40 years in a variety of contexts: her interest in gender differences in psychocultural adaptation (cf. G. and L. Spindler 1990d), and an autobiographical interview technique called the "Expressive Autobiographic Interview," or E.A.I. (cf. L. Spindler 1978; G. and L. Spindler 1970, 1987g). In 1956 she was awarded the first Ph.D. in Anthropology from Stanford (Menomini Women and Culture Change: A Case Study of the Menomini Indians). After receiving his Ph.D. from UCLA in 1952, GS held joint appointments in Anthropology and Education at Stanford until his early retirement in 1978, when he received the

Lloyd W. Dinkelspiel Award for Outstanding Contributions to Undergraduate Education. Both GS and LS continue to lecture on ethnography of education, cultural transmission, psychological anthropology, and the anthropology of American culture at Stanford, the University of Wisconsin, the University of California, Santa Barbara, the University of California at Davis and currently at Harvard University.

Their current assessment of the most influential anthropologists of the 20th century is eclectic ("Evans Pritchard, Kroeber, Hallowell, Kluckhohn, Linton, Lowie, Mead, Boas, Levi-Strauss, Fortes, Edmund Leach, Max Gluckman, Needham;" Leslie White's writings on theory are "too abstracted from human process to be useful;" "Cliff Geertz isn't always saying more than others—just better"), their prognostications for the future of anthropology ambivalent.

> Most of our young anthropologists don't want to know anything about the history of American Anthropology and the influence of the American Indian on that history. They seem overweighted by theory and don't know much, or respect, ethnography. They skip the Germans and the Americans and go directly to France, worshiping Bordieu although what he has said has been said more directly by American educational anthropologists. A few ride the postmodernist bandwagon and believe ethnography is fiction, and many seem hag-ridden by the fear of being politically incorrect. We worry because anthropology seems to have lost its Vision as a broad, encompassing approach to human life in all its diversity, and specialized, isolated interests reign supreme. And yet, there are positive things happening. There is a flexibility, an openness about the influence of personal circumstances on perception, a reflectivity, that wasn't there in our youth. Anthropology changes as the world changes. Perhaps there will be a place for it in the future.

## THE SIGNIFICANCE OF ETHNOGRAPHY

GS begins the book *Doing the Ethnography of Schooling* (1982) with a quote from an anonymous official from the state department of education: "Anything anyone wants to do that has no clear problem, no methodology, and no theory is likely to be called 'ethnography' around here." When the Spindlers started their first ethnographic fieldwork among the Menomini in 1948, they had no training in ethnography and "it was thought that one could not be taught how to do ethnography. One could only learn through experience in the field" (1987e:15). In the folklore of the history of American anthropology, one of the relatively insignificant but often recalled contributions for which Alfred Kroeber is remembered is his famous instructions on how to do fieldwork: take a notebook and pencil.

They coined the term "anthroethnography" to refer to ethnography done by anthropologists—as opposed to socioethnography or psychoethnography (G. Spindler 1982-3; G. and L. Spindler 1983a). Unlike Kroeber, they set out to state explicitly the criteria of good ethnography: "A good ethnography is an orderly compilation of observations and native cultural knowledge" (G. Spindler 1982:22) in which observations are contextualized, generate hypotheses and questions, are prolonged and repetitive, emphasize the native view of reality, and so on (G. Spindler 1982:6-7; G. and L. Spindler 1992a). They argue that "Ethnography is the field arm of anthropology. An anthropologist without ethnographic field experience is like a surgeon without experience in surgery or a clinical psychologist without experience in clinics." (G. Spindler 1982:2)

The ultimate purpose of ethnographies is to broaden horizons and to break down barriers between groups (G. Spindler 1970a:vi). Gradually, the student of human behavior (whether the anthropologist, the student in an anthropology class, or an elementary school teacher struggling to understand a classroom full of children of diverse cultural backgrounds) learns to observe and develop inferences grounded in their observations rather than their own cultural preconceptions.

"We say to our students: you make no statement in your ethnography for which you do not have adequate grounding, and that means that you can supply a focus and specific body of data to support the statement. This makes a big difference in the way you write. Otherwise, you end up with a lot of interesting discursive stuff that isn't cumulative and can never be relied upon."

Although they are critical of many of the recent trends in anthropology, they recognize that the ethnographer is a crucial variable in the ethnography. They pioneered efforts to have anthropologists record their personal experiences in the field (G. and L. Spindler 1970), and in recent writings (e.g., G. and L. Spindler 1992 and 1993) they incorporate modernist and postmodernist arguments about positionality and giving voice to informants.

## The Ethnography of the Menomini, Kainai, Mistassini Cree

In the tradition of Boasian salvage anthropology that specified that the only legitimate research to be done by an anthropologist was among Native American cultures, to record traditions before they disappeared, and to study the changes in the culture by examining processes of acculturation, the Spindlers began their first fieldwork experience together among the Menominee in the summer of 1948 after an initial reconnaissance in 1947, continued every summer except one until 1955, and have continued to visit almost every year, sometimes intensively, and sometimes for brief visits. By the summer of 1958 they were camping along the Belly River in Canada and doing fieldwork among the Kainai or Blood Indians, and in 1966 they studied the Mistassini Cree in Quebec near James Bay.

Their initial research on the Menominee was concerned with how the Menominee adapted to mainstream North American culture (for overviews of the acculturative model and the use of projective tests to study personal adaptation and culture change, see G. and L. Spindler 1963; L. Spindler 1977 and 1978; G. and L. Spindler 1991). The frequently reprinted article, "Experimental Design in the Study of Culture Change" (G. Spindler and Goldschmidt 1952), and a more complete monograph called Sociocultural and Psychological Processes in Menomini Acculturation (G. Spindler 1955d), described five distinctive Menominee groups along a segmented continuum of acculturation. Individual Menominee were grouped after collecting information about them by using a sociocultural index schedule and then selecting variables that demonstrated statistical differentiation and association. An individual's psychological adaptation was measured by numerous methods, including the Expressive Autobiographic Interview (or E.A.I., a cross between a structured expressive interview and a chronological autobiography) developed by LS (L. Spindler 1962; G. and L. Spindler 1970; L. Spindler 1978), but primarily by the use of Rorschach tests. They then correlated psychological variables with positions along the acculturative continuum.

LS insisted that a matched sample of women be included in these studies, and her conclusions, stated in both her M.A. thesis and Ph.D. dissertation, were summarized in her monograph Menomini Women and Culture Change (L. Spindler 1962). "When I started working for my Master's and my Ph.D. I started using women as individuals; this was the first time that anyone had done it, and it was difficult to introduce." The Spindlers' article, "Male and Female Adaptations in Culture Change," published in the American Anthropologist in 1958, was considered by one reviewer to be the first clear statement of a complex set of relationships between gender differences and acculturation; in all their future research they continued to include matched samples of males and females (see L. and G. Spindler 1958, and G. and L. Spindler 1988, 1990d).

Ultimately becoming dissatisfied with the cultural ambiguity of the Rorschach test, they developed a more directive projective technique called the Instrumental Activities Inventory (G. and L. Spindler 1965a, 1965b, 1970; L. Spindler 1977) that they used not only among the Blood and Cree Indians but also among urbanizing Germans (G. Spindler 1974d, G. and L. Spindler 1989a).

The fieldwork they did among the Native American groups was inherently pleasurable, because they had always loved camping. The summers spent camping and entertaining their Menominee and Blood visitors not only freed them from reliance on certain cliques or families (an effective method of doing fieldwork) but also released them from the tension of graduate school, and later from the anxieties of 20th century American society. "It saved our lives, put us into an entirely different frame of mind." Throughout their lives, the differentness of fieldwork sharpened their sense of marginality (cf. G. and L. Spindler 1988) but also renewed, continuously, their interest in the complexity and variousness of the human experiment.

## The Ethnography of Germany

Their interest in German culture began during WWII, and they began working on the process of urbanization in 19591960 with Stanford undergraduates at Stanford's Study Center near Stuttgart, and did systematic studies on culture change and urbanization between 1960 and 1976, when the study center closed. In 1973 GS published *Burgbach: Urbanization and Identity* in a German Village, using his own research and that of more than 400 Stanford students. In 1968, GS began studying the small, urbanizing German village of Schoenhausen, including decision-making among elementary school children (cf. 1974d). In 1977, LS joined him in a restudy of the Schoenhausen elementary school, which seemed to be undergoing sweeping educational reform (cf. 1978d, 1982b). In interpreting the data, they distinguished between an "enduring" and a "situated" self (the former an ideal–romantic conception with historical depth, the latter a pragmatic conception associated with adaptation to the exigencies of modern life), and found a conservative shift toward the "enduring" self (G. and L. Spindler 1989a, 1990d). They continued their research even after the termination of the Stanford study center. Thus their field research in Germany has continued for over 25 years. In 1983 they began a comparison of the Schoenhausen school with an American school in the midwest (cf. 1987a, 1987d, 1987). One of the most important techniques they developed to help them understand the contrasts between German and American schools was the "reflective crosscultural interview technique" which asked teachers of both schools to reflect upon films taken of the school in the other culture as well as their own (G. and L. Spindler 1991, 1993a).

## The Ethnography of American Culture

Their initial work on American culture was GS' study of the military (1947, 1948a, 1948b, 195 1). From 1952 on, first GS and then both GS and LS collected data on American values, using the "Values Projective Technique," from students at Stanford—initially WASP, later minority groups including Blacks, Chicanos, Native Americans, and Asian Americans (cf. L. Spindler 1977:114–118; G. Spindler 1977; G. and L. Spindler 1990a). Students respond to 24 open-ended sentences designed to elicit responses concerning

American ideals (for example, "The individual is ... "). Responses to these sentences tend to consist of diametrically opposed sets (for example, "The individual is all-important" vs. "The individual is a member of a group"), suggesting that Americans engage in an ongoing cultural dialogue centered on certain historically enduring themes. They conclude several things: 1) The voices of the two sides of the dialogue wax and wane, resulting in cyclical trends of emphasis (for example, from individualistic, success-oriented responses in the 1950s to group-oriented, self-development concerns of the 60s and mid-70s with predictions that the 90s will replicate trends of the 60s); and 2) The complexity of class, gender, ethnicity, regionalism, and urban–rural differences in the United States is funneled through an assimilative process centered on this dialogue (see G. and L. Spindler 1990a).

The Spindlers' work on the anthropology of education has been rooted in the work that they continue to do in American culture. They are a living demonstration of the idea that theory must be rooted in practice. Whether their anthropology emphasizes economics, religion, or education, their major contribution has been to practice: how one teaches the anthropology of economics and religion is related to how one teaches anything, and how teaching itself works; so one must understand teaching, or processes of transmission (whether of culture in general or of particular subjects, including anthropology). To understand teaching, one must do fieldwork; and in the process of doing fieldwork, one learns more about fieldwork and culture, and becomes more effective at transmitting information.

An undeclared purpose of the consultation service conducted in American schools in the 50s was to provide "cultural therapy" by which teachers might become less ethnocentric, and in 1974 GS published an article on a technique called "transcultural sensitization" (1974e). GS' article "Education in a Transforming American Culture" (1955b) is frequently reprinted (also see G. Spindler 1956 and G. Spindler, Quillen, and Thomas 1956). In 1957 he was invited to give the Third Burton Lecture in Elementary Education at Harvard (published in 1959), and between 1977 and 1978 broadcast "Anthropological Perspectives on Research and Diversity in Education in the United States" through the Voice of America (1978a). He was concerned with the education of adolescents (1964c, 1970b), alcoholism (1964a), creativity (1964b), how minority groups are disadvantaged by schools (in 1974g), and dropouts (Trueba, G. Spindler, and L. Spindler 1989). He has taught an advanced education course on "Cultural Transmission" since 1953 at Stanford University, and occasionally at the University of Wisconsin, Madison, in the Department of Educational Policy Studies (1982) at the University of California at Santa Barbara and recently (1999) at Harvard University. He and LS edited Urban Anthropology in the United States: Four Cases (1978f), and together they wrote "Anthropologists View

American Culture" (G. and L. Spindler 1983b), and with Henry Trueba
and Melvin Williams wrote *The American Cultural Dialogue and its Transmission* (1990a).

"I think the American experiment is the single most noble experiment in
human relations and belief and ideology that humankind has ever created.
When you think of the problems that countries like Belgium have because
20% of their population is ethnically divergent from the original inhabit-
ants—but the United States is much more diverse, and we're gulping numerous people down by the millions. In all sorts of ways our experiment is
still working; we're speaking a common language. In the Hmong-owned
gasoline stations in San Francisco, in the Pakistani-owned hotels across the
country, the vernacular, actions, body movements, and air of
self-confidence are very American. Were having problems, but they're not
simply a matter of ethnic difference."

## The Ethnography of Schooling

GS is often credited with "being a father, or grandfather, of educational anthropology" (G. and L. Spindler 1982b:21). In 1954 he and LS organized a
conference on Education and Anthropology that was published by Stanford
University Press in 1955 under the same title, and this conference is often
cited as the beginning of the anthropology of education (see G. and L.
Spindler 1992a). In 1963 he edited *Education and Culture: Anthropological
Approaches*, composed of reprints from the 1955 book as well as new contributions (in which he said that "Probably the most substantial contribution
that anthropology could make to education would be the building of a body
of case materials based upon direct observation in a variety of educational
situations" [G. Spindler 1963c]), and in 1974 edited *Education and Cultural
Process: Toward an Anthropology of Education* (revised in 1987 and 1997),
and published an article on models for the study of cultural transmission
(1974f). In 1967 he and LS implemented a new series, Case Studies in Education and Culture, published by Holt, Rinehart, and Winston. In 1982 GS
edited, and both contributed, to the volume *Doing the Ethnography of
Schooling: Educational Anthropology in Action* (reprinted with a new Foreword in 1988); in 1983 GS wrote a review essay of case studies in education
and culture (1983) and in 1984 presented, from his perspective as a retiring
president of the Council for Anthropology and Education, his perspective
on the subfield; and both edited and contributed to the collection. Interpretive Ethnography of Education at Home and Abroad in 1987. GS was President and Louise "Adjunct" President of the Council for Anthropology and
Education (1982). In 1988 the Council for Anthropology and Education established the George and Louise Spindler Award for outstanding work in
the Anthropology of Education, since then awarded yearly.

Because of their wide-ranging field experiences and inductive methods, they often see relationships between diverse situations, such as linguistic minorities facing unfavorable classroom situations, acculturation of Indian groups, and urbanization of European peasants (for example, G. and L. Spindler 1989a, 1990e).

Their most recent work in educational anthropology has been on cultural therapy. Although G. Spindler first used the concept in his pioneering statement on "The Transmission of American Culture," published as the First Burton Lecture on Elementary Education in 1959, it did not appear as a significant and explicit part of their formulations until 1989 (G. and L. Spindler 1989). Subsequent work resulted in the publication, in 1994, of *Pathways to Cultural Awareness: Cultural Therapy with Teachers and Students*, in which a number of the Spindlers' former students joined them as they described how various aspects of their efforts could be thought of as cultural therapy. A previous formulation of the idea was published in a book resulting from a conference organized by Patricia Phelan at Stanford University (G. and L. Spindler 1993b). The essential feature of cultural therapy is to make teachers and students aware of their own cultural biases, and how these biases influence their perceptions and interpretations of others' behavior. The Spindlers use individual case studies of teachers and interpretation of videoed behavior as materials for raising cultural self-awareness.

## TEACHING ANTHROPOLOGY

### Case Studies

Besides writing their own ethnographic case studies (e.g., G. Spindler 1955d, 1973; L. Spindler 1962, G. and L. Spindler (1971), the Spindlers have edited the Case Studies in Cultural Anthropology (Holt, Rinehart and Winston), of which more than 200 now exist. Case studies have played a vitally important role in their teaching, which in turn has fed back into the development of their own research and writing. "Teaching is in some ways my life blood because I somehow get energy and ideas from the teaching process that to me don't come other ways."

" ... if you were in our lecture hall you would often hear more about cultures than about [culture theory]. Culture cases are our support system. Without culture cases we would not know how to teach. We would have little to say, and what we did say would lack reality and excitement, to us, as well as our students." (1990b:) Their goal is "to translate anthropology in such a way that whoever is taking the course can get a foothold and begin to build for themselves." They use what they call the "inductive case study approach" (G. and L. Spindler 1990c, 1996) that combines case studies, films, and other aids, by which "one moves from particulars to generalizations as one's expanding knowledge takes one." LS developed the use of "commentaries," or having students respond to information without being required to critically review it. "Doing fieldwork is not a mystic process. Almost anyone can become an ethnographer if given sufficient training."

They began working on the idea for a series while they were at the Center for Advanced Study in the Behavioral Sciences in 195657. At that time, no one talked about "ethnographies" with a capital E. They started the series because they were needed in teaching. The first six case studies were published by Holt, Rinehart and Winston in 1960 (*Being a Palauan* by Homer Barnett, *Bunyoro* by John Beattie, *The Tiwi* by Hart and Pilling, *The Cheyenne* by Adamson Hoebel, and *Tepotzlan* by Oscar Lewis). In 1990 they edited seven, and in 1995 seven more, with eight in-between. It is apparent that the case studies continue to be an important institution in the field of anthropology. They are now published by Harcourt.

The primary function of the case studies is to avoid professional jargon and achieve an immediacy in the students' experience of other cultures; "to make them citizens who will think differently about cultural differences, multiculturalism, ethnicity, imperialism and oppression than their still quite parochial origins would otherwise lead them toward." (1990b:5) Over the years they developed techniques in addition to the use of case studies that could be applied to other situations to break down cultural barriers. For example, from 1968 on they developed a technique called cultural sensitization to help Stanford students in Germany develop "a cognitive organization for observation and participation in a culture foreign to the student" (G. Spindler 1974e:450). Over 400 students provided the bulk of the fieldwork that eventually led to the collaborative case study, *Burgbach* (G. Spindler 1973). In cultural sensitization, students look at 10 slides and describe and interpret what they see; their responses are compared and discussed, and they learn to make more culturally appropriate interpretations. The cultural sensitization method was also applied to schools, to help students and especially teachers to avoid misinterpreting the behavior of people from other cultures (L. Spindler 1977).

They began ethnography training with educators in 1978, after GS took early retirement from Stanford, with a two-week seminar for the Milpitas school district near Stanford. They developed this training at the University of Wisconsin at Madison, at Stanford, at the Universities of California at Santa Barbara and Davis (cf. G. Spindler 1987e), and now at Harvard University. Their work with school systems has proved to be the most rewarding fieldwork they have ever done. "[The classroom is] one of the few areas where the materials and the people are accessible; it's multicultural and exciting.... It has all the problems necessary for doing good fieldwork."

## CONCLUSIONS

The work of George and Louise Spindler has constituted a complex dialogue. I use the term *dialogue* not only to convey the lifelong exchange between two intelligent, generous, and complex individuals, but to convey the complexity of ideas and methods with which they have tried to investigate and interpret human behavior: psychological vs. sociocultural variables, quantitative vs. qualitative methods, the traditional Native American Indian ethnographic setting vs. American and European settings, the field vs. the classroom, theoretical vs. applied, ethnology vs. ethnography. They have given passing respect to academic fads, adapting to the changing seasons of theory and disciplinary jargon, but kept their souls intact, rooted in the raw earth of ethnographic realism and classroom interaction.

There are many fields within the humanities and the social and physical sciences that convey a sense of *communitas*: biology has translated the complex biographies of all living things into a simple common alphabet; geology translates seashells on mountaintops and eroded lava into uniform processes; music and art are sometimes said to speak a universal language. Anthropology also has its message to convey about the underlying similarities in human cultures ("making the strange familiar"); but in this context I would like to emphasize the capacity of anthropology to make the familiar strange. The development of anthropology is, as Leslie White made the point in his article on the expansion of science (1947), a recent phenomenon in the history of science because it is difficult to achieve distance from something so close to us. The value of science is to increase our understanding of the world. To be curious, to nurture that curiosity—these may be goals of many teachers of anthropology, but few have managed to achieve it. The Spindlers have continued to generate curiosity and multiple modes of understanding the complexity of human behavior; their methods and their results are in their numerous writings and perhaps more important in the people they have known, in the classroom and out—students all, as they have themselves remained, in the classroom of human life.

*We were coming home by ship from Spain after a season of fieldwork in Germany. We came into the harbor at New York, past the Statue of Liberty. I happened to look over at Louise; tears were streaming down her face. I said something stupid like, "I had no idea you were so sentimental about the Statue of Liberty," or something like that. She said, "I'm not. I just don't want to go home."*

## BIBLIOGRAPHY

Beals, Alan, G. Spindler, and L. Spindler
1967. *Culture in Process* (revised ed. in 1973). New York: Holt, Rinehart, and Winston.

Sanjek, Roger
1990. *Fieldnotes*. New York: Cornell University Press.

Spindler, G.
1947. *Americans, Germans, and the Military*. Unpublished M.A. thesis, University of Wisconsin, Department of Sociology and Anthropology.

1948a. American Character as Revealed by the Military. *Psychiatry: Journal for the Operational Statement of Interpersonal Relations* 11(3):275–281.

1948b. The Military—A Systematic Analysis. *Social Forces* 27:84–88.

1951. The Doolittle Board and Cooptation in the Army. *Social Forces* 29:305–310.

1952. Personality and Peyotism in Menomini Indian Acculturation. *Psychiatry: Journal for the Study of Interpersonal Processes* 15(2):151–159.

1955a. Education and Anthropology. Stanford: Stanford University Press.

1955b. Education in a Transforming American Culture. *Harvard Educational Review*, Vol. XXV(3):145–156.

1955c. Projective Testing in Ethnography. *American Anthropologist*, 57(2):245–270.

1955d. Sociocultural and Psychological Processes in Menomini Acculturation. University of California *Publications in Culture and Society, Vol. 5*. Berkeley: University of California Press.

1956. *Educational Leadership*. Special issue on "related fields" (anthropology, sociology, psychology, philosophy, etc.). Guest editor, Vol. XIII.

1958a. *New Trends and Applications in Anthropology*. Chapter VII in the Twenty-Eighth Yearbook of 1958, National Council for the Social Studies.

1958b. Research Design and Ojibwa Personality Persistence. *American Anthropologist* 60(5):934–937.

1959. *The Transmission of American Culture. Third Burton Lecture in Elementary Education* (1957). Cambridge, Mass.: Harvard University.

1961. Review Essay on The Remaking of a Culture by T. Brameld. *Harvard Educational Review* 31(3):345–353.

1963a. Anthropology. *NEA Journal* (September), pp. 29–31.

1963b. (editor) Selected Papers in Method and Technique. *American Anthropologist* 63, 5 (a special issue).

1963c. (editor and contributor) *Education and Culture: Anthropological Approaches*. New York: Holt, Rinehart and Winston.

1964a. (special editor) Alcohol Symposium. *American Anthropologist* 66, 2.

1964b. *Our Changing Culture, Creativity, and the Schools*. The Edith P. Merritt Memorial Lecture Fund, Division of Education, San Francisco State College.

1964c. The Education of Adolescents: An Anthropological Perspective. *Proceedings of the 15th Annual Conference, California Association of School Psychologists and Psychometrists*, pp. 24–33.

1966a. Anthropotherapy—Toward Theory and Practice, by T. Brameld, a Comment. *Human Organization* 24(4):293–295.

1966b. *Primitive Education*. In New Catholic Encyclopedia.

1968. Psychocultural Adaptation. In *The Study of Personality: An Interdisciplinary Appraisal*. Edward Norbeck, Douglas Price-Williams, and William McCord, eds. New York: Holt, Rinehart and Winston.

1970a. (editor) *Being an Anthropologist: Fieldwork in Eleven Cultures*. New York: Holt, Rinehart and Winston.

1970b. The Education of Adolescents: An Anthropological Perspective. In *Adolescents: Readings in Behavior and Development*. E. Evans, ed. Hinsdale, IL: Dryden Press, pp. 152–161.

1970c. Studying Schooling in Schoenhausen. *Council on Anthropology and Education Newsletter* (CAE) 1(2):1–3.

1973. *Burgbach: Urbanization and Identity in a German Village*. New York: Holt, Rinehart and Winston.

1974a. Beth Anne—A Case Study of Culturally Defined Adjustment and Teacher Perceptions. In *Education and Cultural Process: Toward an Anthropology of Education*. New York: Holt, Rinehart and Winston, pp. 139–153.

1974b. (editor) *Education and Cultural Process: Toward an Anthropology of Education*. New York: Holt, Rinehart and Winston.

1974c. From Omnibus to Linkages: Models for the Study of Cultural Transmission. *Council on Anthropology and Education Quarterly* 1:2–6.

1974d. *Schooling in Schoenhausen: A Study of Cultural Transmission and Instrumental Adaptation in an Urbanizing German Village. Education and Cultural Process: Toward an Anthropology of Education*. New York: Holt, Rinehart and Winston, pp. 230–271.

1974e. Transcultural Sensitization. In *Education and Cultural Process: Toward an Anthropology of Education*. New York: Holt, Rinehart and Winston, pp. 449–462.

1974f. The Transmission of Culture. In *Education and Cultural Process: Toward an Anthropology of Education*. New York: Holt, Rinehart and Winston, pp. 279–310.

1974g. Why Have Minority Groups in North America Been Disadvantaged by their Schools? In *Education and Cultural Process: Toward an Anthropology of Education*. New York: Holt, Rinehart and Winston, pp. 69–81.

1976. Mittel und Mittelchen der Volksheilkunde. In *Beutelsbach die Wiege Wurttembergs*. Stuttgart: Walter-Verlagsinstitut, pp. 356–361.

1977. Change and Continuity in American Core Cultural Values: An Anthropological Perspective. In *Social Change and Social Character*. Gordon DiRenzo, ed. Westport, CT: Greenwood Press. (Results of a symposium held at the University of Delaware in 1975.)

1978a. *Anthropological Perspectives on Research and Diversity in Education in the United States.* Voice of America broadcast, November 1977 through January 1978. Published as part of a VOA Forum Collection, State Department, through the University of Wisconsin.

1978b. (editor). *The Making of Psychological Anthropology.* Berkeley: University of California Press.

1979. John Honigmann: The Man and His Work. *Journal of Psychological Anthropology* 11(3):441–451.

1982. (editor). *Doing the Ethnography of Schooling: Educational Anthropology in Action.* New York: Holt, Rinehart and Winston. (Waveland, 1988.)

1983. The Case Studies in Education and Culture from Cradle to Grave. A Review Essay. *Anthropology and Education Quarterly* 14(1):73–81.

1984. Roots Revisited: Three Decades of Perspective. Retiring President's Address, Council for Anthropology and Education. *Anthropology and Education Quarterly* 15(1):3–10.

1986. *Foreword for The Symbolization of America.* Herve Varenne, ed. University of Nebraska Press.

1987a. (editor). *Education and Cultural Process—Anthropological Approaches.* Revised edition. Prospect, IL: Waveland.

1987b. Joe Nepah, A "Schizophrenic" Menominee Peyotist. *The Journal of Psychoanalytic Anthropology* 10(1):1–16.

1987c. Joe Nepah, ein Schizophrener Peyote-Esser der Menomini. In *Die Wilde Seele: Zur Ethnopsychoanalyse von George Devereux.* H. P. Duerr, ed. Frankfurt am Main: Suhrkamp, pp. 294–315.

1987d. Teaching and Learning Anthropology: The Case Study Approach. In *Education and Cultural Process: Anthropological Approaches.* G. Spindler, ed. Revised edition. Prospect, IL: Waveland, pp. 496–504.

1987e. Thirty-three Years as a Marginal Native. In *Education and Cultural Process: Anthropological Approaches.* G. Spindler, ed. Revised edition. Prospect, IL: Waveland, pp. 78–88.

1988. (editor) Doing the Ethnography of Schooling. Reissue with new foreword. Prospect, IL: Waveland Press, Inc.

1997. (editor) *Education and Cultural Process: Anthropological Approaches* (Rev. ed.). Prospect Heights: Waveland Press.

Spindler, G. and Edward M. Bruner
1963. The Introductory Course in Cultural Anthropology. In *The Teaching of Anthropology.* David G. Mandelbaum, ed. Memoir 94, American Anthropological Association, pp. 141–152.

Spindler, G. and W. Goldschmidt
1952. Experimental Design in the Study of Culture Change. *Southwestern Journal of Anthropology* 8:68–83.

Spindler, G., I. J. Quillen, and L. Thomas
1956. *The Value Orientation of Teacher Education.* Ninth Yearbook, American Association of Colleges for Teacher Education, pp. 11–19.

Spindler, G. and L.

1957. American Indian Personality Types and their Sociocultural Roots. *The Annals of the American Academy of Political and Social Science* 311:147–157.

1959. Culture Change. In *Bienniel Review of Anthropology*. B. Siegel, ed. Stanford: Stanford University Press.

1961. A Modal Personality Technique in the Study of Menomini Acculturation. In *Studying Personality Cross-Culturally*. B. Kaplan, ed. Evanston: Row, Peterson and Co, pp. 479–492.

1963. Psychology in anthropology: Applications to culture change. In Sigmund Koch (Ed.), *Psychology: A study of a science* (Study II, Vol. 6, p.. 510–551). New York: McGraw-Hill.

1965a. The Instrumental Activities Inventory: A Technique for the Study of the Psychology of Acculturation. *Southwestern Journal of Anthropology* 21(1):1–23

1965b. Researching the Perception of Cultural Alternatives: The Instrumental Activities Inventory. In *Context and Meaning in Cultural Anthropology*. Melford E. Spiro, ed. In honor of A. I. Hallowell. NY: Free Press.

1970. Fieldwork with the Menomini. In *Being an Anthropologist: Fieldwork in Eleven Cultures*. G. Spindler, ed. New York: Holt, Rinehart and Winston, pp. 267–301.

1971. Dreamers Without Power: The Menomini Indians. NY: HRW. (Revised and published with new foreword in 1984 as Dreamers with Power, 1984, by Waveland Press.)

1975. A Man and a Book: A review essay on A. Irving Hallowell. *Reviews in Anthropology* 2(2): 144–156.

1976. Adaptations to the Study of Change. In Paths to the Symbolic Self. Essays in Honor of Walter Goldschmidt. J. Loucky and J. Jones, eds. *Anthropology, UCLA* 8: 85–97.

1977a. The Menominee. In *Native North American Cultures: Four Cases*. G. and L. Spindler, eds. New York: Holt, Rinehart and Winston, pp. 361–499.

1977b. (editors) *Native North American Cultures: Four Cases*. New York: Holt, Rinehart and Winston.

1977. (editors). *Cultures Around the World*. New York: Holt, Rinehart and Winston.

1978a. Changing Women in Men's Worlds. In *Sex Roles in Changing Cultures*. SUNYAB Occasional Papers. Ann McElroy and Carolyn Mathiesson, eds. Vol. I, pp. 35–49.

1978b. *Die Vermittlung von Kulturellen Werlen und Spezifischen Anpassungsmechanismus in einen Dorf mitzunehmend städtischen Gepräge*. In *Rheinisches Jahrbuch für Volkskunde*. Universitat Bonn, ed. by Max Matter, 22 Jahrgang, 2. Halbband, pp. 85–96.

1978c. Identity, Militancy, and Cultural Congruence: The Menominee and Kainai. *The Annals of the American Academy of Political and Social Science* 436:73–85.

1978d. A Restudy of Cultural Transmission and Instrumental Adaptation in an Urbanizing German Village. *Anthropology and Education Quarterly* IX(3):235–236.

1978e. *Schooling in Schoenhausen Revisited: A Restudy of Cultural Transmission and Instrumental Adaptation in an Urbanizing German Village.* Preliminary report of research spring and summer 1977. (Versions published in 1978b and 1978d.)

1978f. (editors) *Urban Anthropology in the United States: Four Cases.* New York: Holt, Rinehart and Winston.

1982a. Do Anthropologists Need Learning Theory? *Anthropology and Education Quarterly* XIII(2):109–124.

1982b. Roger Harker and Schoenhausen: From Familiar to Strange and Back Again. In *Doing the Ethnography of Schooling: Educational Anthropology in Action.* G. Spindler, ed. New York: Holt, Rinehart and Winston, pp. 20–46.

1983a. Anthroethnography. In Teaching Fieldwork to Educational Researchers. *Anthropology and Education Quarterly* 14(3):191–194.

1983b. Anthropologists View American Culture. *Annual Reviews in Anthropology* 12:49–78.

1984. Oppositions. *Anthropology and Education Quarterly* 15(4):330–333.

1986. Ethnography: An Anthropological View. *Educational Horizon* 63(4):154–157.

1987a. Cultural Dialogue and Schooling in Schoenhausen and Roseville: A comparative Analysis. *Anthropology and Education Quarterly* 18:3–16.

1987b. Do Anthropologists Need Learning Theory? In *Education and Cultural Process: Anthropological Approaches.* Revised edition. G. Spindler, ed. Prospect, IL: Waveland.

1987c. Ethnography: An Anthropological View. In *Education and Cultural Process: Anthropological Approaches.* Revised edition. G. Spindler, ed. Prospect, IL: Waveland.

1987d. In Prospect for a Controlled Crosscultural Comparison of Schooling: Schoenhausen and Roseville. In *Education and Cultural Process: Anthropological Approaches.* Revised edition. G. Spindler, ed. Prospect, IL: Waveland, pp. 389–400.

1987e. (eds.) *Interpretive Ethnography of Education at Home and Abroad.* New Jersey: Lawrence Erlbaum Associates.

1987f. Schoenhausen Revisited and the Rediscovery of Culture. In Interpretive Ethnography of Education at Home and Abroad. G. and L. Spindler, eds. NJ: Lawrence Erlbaum Associates, pp. 143–171.

1987g. Teaching and Learning How to do the Ethnography of Education. In Interpretive Ethnography of Education at Home and Abroad. G. and L. Spindler, eds. NJ: Lawrence Erlbaum Associates, pp. 17–37.

1988. A Life with Ethnography: A Conversation with George and Louise Spindler. *Qualitative Studies in Education* 1:167–178.

1989a. Instrumental Competence, Self-Efficacy, Linguistic Minorities, and Cultural Therapy: A Preliminary Attempt at Integration. *Anthropology and Education Quarterly* 20:36–49.

1989b. The Self and the Instrumental Model in the Study of Cultural Change and Modernization. *Kroeber Anthropological Society Papers*, Nos. 69–70:108–116.

1990a. (with H. Trueba and M. Williams) *The American Cultural Dialogue and its Transmission*. Bristol, PA: Falmer Press.

1990b. *Anthropology 001, Case Studies, and Post-Modernism*. Paper presented at the American Anthropological Association, New Orleans, November 28-December 3.

1990c. The Inductive Case Study Approach to Teaching Anthropology. *Anthropology and Education Quarterly* 21(2):106–112.

1990d. Male and Female in Four Changing Cultures. In *Personality and the Cultural Construction of Society: Papers in Honor of Melford E. Spiro*. David Jordan and Marc Swartz, eds. Tuscaloosa: University of Alabama Press, pp. 182–200.

1990e. There are no Dropouts Among the Arunta and Hutterites. In *What do Anthropologists have to say about Dropouts?* Trueba, H., G. Spindler, and L. Spindler, eds. Bristol, PA: Falmer Press, pp. 7–15.

1991. Rorschaching in North America in the Shadow of Hallowell. In *The Psychoanalytic Study of Society, Vol. 16 Essays in Honor of A. Irving Hallowell*. Bryce and Ruth Boyer, eds. Hillsdale, NJ: Analytic Press, pp. 155–181.

1992a. Cultural Process and Ethnography: An Anthropological Perspective. In Handbook for Qualitative Research in Education. Judith Preissle and Margaret LeCompte, eds. San Diego: Academic Press, pp. 53–92.

1992b. The Lives of George and Louise Spindler. In *The Psychoanalytic Study of Society, Vol. 17, Special Issue honoring George and Louise Spindler*. Bryce and Ruth Boyer, and Stephen Sonnenberg, eds.

1993a. Crosscultural, Comparative, Reflective Interviewing in Schoenhausen and Roseville. *In Qualitative Voices in Educational Research*. M. Schratz, ed. Bristol, PA: Falmer Press.

1993b. *The Processes of Culture and Person: Cultural Therapy and Culturally Diverse Schools. In Renegotiating Cultural Diversity in American Schools*. Patricia Phelan and Ann Locke Davidson, eds. New York: Teachers College Press, pp. 27–51.

1994. (Editors) *Pathways to Cultural Awareness: Cultural Therapy with Teachers and Students*. Thousand Oaks, CA: Corwin Press.

1997. *Education and Cultural Process*, 3rd edition. Prospect Heights, IL: Waveland Press.

1996. Teaching Culture Using Case Studies. In *The Teaching of Anthropology: Problems, Issues, and Decisions*. C. Kottak, Jane White, R. Furlow and P. Rice, eds. Menlo Park, CA: Mayfield Publishing.

Spindler, G., L. Spindler, and Anthony D. Fisher

1963. *The Blood Indians of Alberta: A Report to the Economic Development Division, Indian Affairs Branch*. Ottawa, Canada. Dittographed, 102 pp.

Spindler, L.

1952a. *The Autobiographical Approach to the Study of Culture Change: Menomini Indian Women*. M.A. Thesis, Stanford University.

1952b. Witchcraft in Menomini Acculturation. *American Anthropologist* 54:593–602.

1956. *Menomini Women and Culture Change: A Case Study of the Menomini Indians.* Ph.D. Dissertation. Stanford University.

1957. 61 Rorschachs and 15 Expressive Autobiographic Interviews of Menomini Indian Women. *Microcard Publications of Primary Records in Culture and Personality.* B. Kaplan, ed. Vol. 2, No. 10. Madison: University of Wisconsin Press.

1962. Menomini Women and Culture Change. *American Anthropological Association,* Memoir 91.

1963. Psychology in Anthropology: Applications to Culture Change. In Psychology: A Study of a Science. Sigmund Koch, ed. New York: McGraw-Hill, pp. 510–551.

1970. Menomini Witchcraft. In Systems of North American Witchcraft and Sorcery. Deward Walker, ed. Anthropological Monographs, University of Idaho, #1.

1975. Researching the Psychology of Culture Change. In *Psychological Anthropology,* Vol. I. T. R. Williams, ed. Mouton.

1976. The Menominee. In *Handbook of North American Indians, Vol. 15.* The Northeast. Bruce Trigger, ed. Smithsonian Inst.

1977. *Culture Change and Modernization: Minimodels and Case Studies.* New York: Holt, Rinehart and Winston. (Revised and Reissued in 1984 by Waveland Press.)

1978. Researching the Psychology of Culture Change and Modernization. In *The Making of Psychological Anthropology.* G. Spindler, ed. Berkeley: University of California Press, pp. 174–200.

1979. Review: Sex Roles: Biological, Psychological, and Social Foundations, by Shirley Weitz. *Journal of Psychological Anthropology* 2:252–254.

1983. Review: Indian–White Relations: A Persistent Paradox, by Jane Smith and Robert Krasnicka (1981). *Journal of Psychoanalytic Anthropology* 6(3):316–319.

1984. *Culture Change and Modernization: Mini Models and Case Studies.* Waveland Press.

Spindler, L. and G. Spindler
1958. Male and Female Adaptations in Culture Change. *American Anthropologist* 60(2):217–233.

Trueba, H., G. Spindler, and L. Spindler, eds.
1989. *What do Anthropologists have to say about Dropouts?* Bristol, PA: Falmer Press.

White, Leslie
1947. The Expansion of the Scope of Science. *Journal of the Washington Academy of Sciences* 37:181–210.

# MEMOIR

Memoir Written for the Memorial for Louise Spindler
on March 4, 1997

I'll never forget the first afternoon when I encountered George and Louise Spindler, as their teaching assistant. Of course, their reputation preceded them, and I was eager to meet them but not sure what to expect.

The Spindlers seated themselves in front of twenty or so graduate students in a manner which made us feel we were in their living room. They began to tell the kinds of stories that made the would-be graduate students drool—tales of Indian life and peyote ceremonies, of interactions with Margaret Mead and Gregory Bateson. At first it seemed as if George would narrate and Louise would correct him, gently saying things like, "it wasn't quite like that, George." We were amused, as if we had become audience to their married life. I soon began to realize, however, that what they were doing was a subtle technique which added dimension and dialogue to their subject. By playing point counter-point, their stories became triangulated, and therefore, more real. It was Louise, with her dry humor and sweetly critical remarks, who brought the drama to life. I feel very lucky to have witnessed it, and to have known her.

Lorie Hammond
Former Teaching Assistant, University of California, Davis

417

# CONCLUSION

Books written as this one is written can have no conclusion. Work goes on, although one of us is not here; her spirit lives on, and conversations with her are still possible in my mind and heart. She will be in the next book, and the next one after that.

*George Spindler*
*Editor*

# SOURCES

Chapter 4. Beth Anne: A Case Study of Culturally Defined Adjustment and Teacher Perceptions. From *Education and Cultural Process.* 1974. New York: Holt, Rinehart and Winston. Reprinted by permission of Waveland Press, Inc. From G. Spindler *Education and Cultural Process.* 3rd edition. 1997. Prospect Hts., IL.

Chapter 5. Why Have Minority Groups in North American Been Disadvantaged by Their Schools? G. Spindler, 1974. *Education and Cultural Process.* New York: Holt, Rinehart and Winston. Reprinted by permission of Waveland Press, Inc. From G. Spindler, *Education and Cultural Process.* 1997. Prospect Hts., IL

Chapter 6. The Transmission of Culture. Reprinted with minor revisions from *Culture in Process,* A. R. Beals, G. Spindler, L. Spindler. Copyright © 1967, 1978, Holt, Rinehart and Winston, New York. Reprinted by permission of Holt, Rinehart and Winston.

Chapter 7. There Are No Droputs Among the Arunta and Hutterites. From *What Do Anthropologists Know About Dropouts?* H. Trueba, G. and L. Spindler, eds., 1989. London and Bristol, PA: Falmer Press.

Chapter 8. Das Remstal, From Male and Female in Four Changing Cultures. G. and L. Spindler, 1990. From *Personality and the Cultural Construction of Society.* M. Jordan and T. Swartz, eds., Tuscaloosa, AL: Copyright Alabama University Press. pp. 192-200.

Chapter 9. Roger Harker and Schoenhausen: From Familiar to Strange and Back Again. From *Doing the Ethnography of Schooling: Educational Anthropology in Action.* G. Spindler, ed., 1982. Reprinted by permission of Waveland Press: Prospect Hts., IL. (reissued 1988). All rights reserved.

Chapter 10. Cultural Dialogue and Schooling in Schoenhausen and Roseville: A Comparative Analysis. 1987. From *Anthropology and Education Quarterly*, pp. 3-14, vol. 18, no. 1. Copyright American Anthropological Association, 1987.

Chapter 11. Teaching and Learning How to Do the Ethnography of Education. G. and L. Spindler. From *Interpretive Ethnography of Education at Home and Abroad*. G. and L. Spindler, eds., 1988, Mahwah, NJ: Lawrence Erlbaum Associates, pp. 17-32.

Chapter 12.. Transcultural Sensitization. G. Spindler. From *Education and Cultural Process*. G. Spindler, ed., 1997. Reprinted by permission of Waveland Press, Inc., Prospect Hts.: IL.

Chapter 13. Crosscultural, Comparative, Reflective Interviewing in Schoenhausen and Roseville. G. and L. Spindler, 1993. From *Qualitative Voices in Educational Research*. Michael Schratz, ed., pp. 150-175. London and Bristol, PA: Falmer Press.

Chapter 14. Consensus and Continuity in American Culture. G. and L. Spindler. With permission from the *Annual Review of Anthropology, Volume 12*. Copyright © 1983 http.www. Annual Reviews, Org.

Chapter 15. Schooling in the American Cultural Dialogue. From *The American Cultural Dialogue and Its Transmission*. G. and L. Spindler with H. Trueba and M. Williams. 1990. pp. 56-90. London and Bristol, PA: Falmer Press.

Chapter 16. Cultural Politics and the White Ethni-class in the Mid-Nineties. G. and L. Spindler. Reprinted from *Ethnic Identity and Power: Cultural Contexts of Political Action in Schools and Society* (pp. 27-47). By Yali Zou and Enrique T. Trueba (Eds.) by permission of the State University of New York Press. ©1998, State University of New York. All Rights Reserved.

Chapter 17. The Processes of Culture and Person. Cultural Therapy and Culturally Diverse Schools. From *Renegotiating Cultural Diversity in Schools*. P. Phelan and Ann Davidson, eds., 1993, pp. 27-51. New York: Teachers College Press.

Chapter 18. *Making the Familiar Strange: The Anthropological Dialogue of George and Louise Spindler*. Susan Parman, 1998 (written especially for this book).

# Author Index

# Subject Index

## A

Accommodation, 315–318
Acculturation, 81–85, 402
Achievement orientation, 101, 309
Adaptations, 43–44, 351–353, 384–386
Adapted teacher, 107, *see also* Teachers
Adjusted type, 84
Adjustment, culturally defined and teacher
  perceptions
  classroom and Beth Anne's place in it,
    112–113
  evidence, 113–122
  interpretation, 123–125
  teacher response to evidence, 122–123
Administrators
  cultural awareness importance in education,
    61
  disadvantaged minority groups, 135
  traditional/emergent value systems, 103, 104,
    105
  teacher rating and American cultural
    dialogue, 338, 339
Adult life, cultural transmission
  Eskimos, 158
  Hano, 151–152
  Palau, 142–145
  Ulithi, 147, 148–150
Aggression, intergroup, 77
Alienation, 131
Ambaquerka stage, 183, *see also* Arunta
Ambiguity, 270, 271, 274
Ambivalent teacher, 106–107, *see also* Teachers

American culture
  consensus and continuity
    background, 309–312
    collections and case studies, 323–324
    diversity, conflict, and accommodation,
      315–318
    individualism and conformity: key
      opposition, 312–315
    languages, 322–323
    problem of women, 319–322
  diversity and definition, 229
  education in a transforming, 101–108
  ethnography, 403–405
  independent/dependent behavior, 148
  transmission
    acculturation of the school teacher,
      81–85
    analysis, 40–42
    case study, 85–89
    conflicts, 76–81
    cross-cultural perspective, 89–91
    cultural therapy, 91–94
    focus versus goals, 27
    unresolved dilemmas, 94–95
American English, 322
American school, 36–37, *see also* Education;
  Schooling
Amish community, 30, 136–138
Analytic procedures, 260
Anthroethnography, 400–401
Anthropology, –education
  anthropologist roles in educational context,
    68–70
  complexity, 9

427